Histoires de Kanatha

Vues et Contées

Histories of Kanatha

Seen and Told

Histoires de Kanatha

Vues et Contées

Essais et discours, 1991–2008

Histories of Kanatha

Seen and Told

Essays and discourses, 1991–2008

Georges E. P. Sioui

Sélection et présentation
Dalie Giroux

Les Presses de l'Université d'Ottawa
University of Ottawa Press

© Presses de l'Université d'Ottawa, 2008. Tous droits réservés

© University of Ottawa Press, 2008. All rights reserved.

Les Presses de l'Université d'Ottawa reconnaissent avec gratitude l'appui accordé à son programme d'édition par le ministère du Patrimoine canadien en vertu de son Programme d'aide au développement de l'industrie de l'édition, le Conseil des arts du Canada, la Fédération canadienne des sciences humaines en vertu de son Programme d'aide à l'édition savante, le Conseil de recherches en sciences humaines du Canada et l'Université d'Ottawa.

Les Presses reconnaissent aussi l'appui financier dont a bénéficié cette publication provenant de Faculté des arts de l'Université d'Ottawa.

The University of Ottawa Press acknowledges with gratitude the support extended to its publishing list by Heritage Canada through its Book Publishing Industry Development Program, by the Canada Council for the Arts, by the Canadian Federation for the Humanities and Social Sciences through its Aid to Scholarly Publications Program, by the Social Sciences and Humanities Research Council, and by the University of Ottawa.

We also gratefully acknowledge The Faculty of Arts at the University of Ottawa whose financial support has contributed to the publication of this book.

CATALOGAGE AVANT PUBLICATION DE BIBLIOTHÈQUE ET ARCHIVES CANADA

Sioui, Georges E., 1948-

    Histoires de Kanatha vues et contées - Histories of Kanatha seen and told : essais, contributions, discours et oraisons, 1991-2007 / Georges Emery Sioui ; sélection et présentation, Dalie Giroux.

Texte en français et en anglais.

Comprend des références bibliographiques.

ISBN 978-2-7603-3035-1 (relié).–ISBN 978-2-7603-0682-0 (br.)

    1. Indiens d'Amérique–Canada. 2. Philosophie indienne d'Amérique–Canada. I. Giroux, Dalie, 1974- II. Titre. II. Titre: Histories of Kanatha seen and told.

E77.S46 2008   305.897'071   C2008-906691-XF

Au souvenir sacré de ma mère, Éléonore Sioui Tecumseh, et pour tous les Gardiens de la foi de tous les Premiers Peuples, qui vivent pour la défense de la verité de notre histoire car sans Verité il n'y a pas de Beauté et sans Beauté, personne ni rien ne vit.

To the sacred memory of my mother, Éléonore Sioui Tecumseh, and for all the Faithkeepers of all the First Peoples, who live in defence of the truth of our history, for without Truth, there is no Beauty, and without Beauty, no one nor nothing lives.

À la mémoire de Bruce Graham Trigger, un parent canadien-wendat dans notre clan de la Grande Tortue et que nous n'oublierons jamais.

To the memory of Bruce Graham Trigger, a forever dear Canadian-Wendat relative in our Big Turtle Clan.

À nous, les Wendat! To us, the Wyandot!

Avant-propos

« Awendio Etchesense » « Ô Maître de l'Univers, Aide-nous à guérir le monde ! » Telle fut la prière de ma mère, et de sa mère, et de mes ancêtres.

De tous temps, les Hurons-Wendat Tséawi ont été des porte-parole, des hommes et des femmes-médecine, des « chefs des guerriers », des éclaireurs. Ils ont été les Donnacona, les Deganawidah, les Kondiaronk et les Sastaretsi. Ils ont été les défenseurs de la première heure, les « hérétiques », les mauvais Indiens, ceux à faire disparaître.

Les Tséawi, « ceux du Soleil Levant », ont voulu et veulent faire du monde leur Nation. « Fais-toi Huron, a dit le grand Kondiaronk au baron de La Hontan en 1700, ou sinon, tu n'iras jamais dans le bon pays des âmes ». Même au temps où ils marchèrent sur une Terre presque morte de la douleur d'avoir perdu la quasi-totalité de ses enfants, au lendemain de leur holocauste, les Wendat Tséawi n'ont jamais perdu le sens du combat qu'ils devaient mener.

Déjà, en 1534, ils avaient initié la mondialisation des peuples de leur continent, lorsqu'ils consentirent à laisser Jacques Cartier emmener en France deux de leurs jeunes hommes capturés par celui-ci. En 1701, le même grand Kondiaronk Séawi termina l'œuvre de sa vie en réalisant le Traité de la Grande Paix de Montréal, qui mit fin à 92 ans de guerre importées d'Europe. En 1825, ils furent reçus par le roi britannique George IV et obtinrent le retour de territoires injustement pris aux premiers peuples par les gouvernements coloniaux. En 1950, ils plaidèrent devant le Conseil de sécurité des Nations Unies le droit au statut de nations pour les autochtones, ainsi qu'à leur place au sein des autres peuples et nations du monde. En 1990, le clan Tséawi remporta au nom de sa nation huronne-wendat une victoire historique en Cour suprême du Canada dans un litige impliquant leurs droits spirituels et territoriaux autochtones.

La présente collection de textes est une expression de cette antique tradition des Hurons-Wendat Tséawi et de tous les premiers peuples de l'Amérique dans l'esprit de la reconnaissance du grand Cercle de la vie, l'intégrité, la respectabilité et la toute-importance de la pensée des peuples de l'Amérique pour le mieux-être futur de la grande famille humaine.

TABLE DES MATIÈRES

PRÉFACE	XII
REMERCIEMENTS	XIV
LA SAGESSE DU CONTINENT. UNE INTRODUCTION À LA LECTURE DES HISTOIRES DE KANATHA. PAR DALIE GIROUX	XVI

LIVING HISTORY

LA FLAMME DE VIE DU CANADA	1
RELECTURE AUTOCHTONE DE L'ÉVÉNEMENT DES 500 ANS	3
LETTRE AU PREMIER MINISTRE DE L'INDE	13
1992: THE DISCOVERY OF AMERICITY	19
LA SIGNIFICATION INTERCULTURELLE DE L'AMÉRICITÉ	33
POINT DE VUE WENDAT SUR LES TRANSFERTS CULTURELS EUROPE-AMÉRIQUE, 992-1992	39
THE CULTURAL PROPERTY OF INDIGENOUS PEOPLES	51
PERSONAL REACTIONS OF INDIGENOUS PEOPLE TO EUROPEAN IDEAS AND BEHAVIOUR	55

PARDONNEZ MA PRÉSENCE

LES WENDAT : UN PEUPLE PLURIMILLÉNAIRE	73

OUR RESPONSIBILITY AS INDIGENOUS PEOPLES: SUGGESTIONS TO ANTHROPOLOGY	81
FOLLOWING A WENDAT FEELING ABOUT HISTORY: THE SIOUI CASE	91
CANADA'S PAST, PRESENT AND FUTURE FROM A NATIVE CANADIAN PERSPECTIVE	99
CANADIAN AMERINDIAN NATIONS OF THE 21ST CENTURY	109
REBUILDING FIRST NATIONS: IDEOLOGICAL IMPLICATIONS FOR CANADA	117

INDIEN SANS TERRE MAIS AVEC PLUME

WHY WE SHOULD HAVE INCLUSIVENESS AND WHY WE CANNOT HAVE IT	131
WHY CANADA SHOULD LOOK FOR, FIND, RECOGNIZE AND EMBRACE ITS TRUE, ABORIGINAL ROOTS. THE TIME OF THE TOAD	145
CANADA AND THE FIRST NATIONS: THE NEED FOR TWO FEET TO STAND ON	157
FAVORISER L'INTÉGRATION. POINT DE VUE MATRICENTRISTE	167
L'AMÉRINDIEN PHILOSOPHE	177
THE SPIRITUAL REVOLUTION: LOOKING AFTER THE EARTH FROM AN INDIGENOUS (MATRICENTRIST) PERSPECTIVE	193

FOR AN AMERINDIAN AUTHOHISTORY: THE FOUNDATIONS OF A
PROPERLY AMERICAN SOCIAL ETHICS   203

AMERICA, MY HOME

QUATRE AMÉRIQUES, UNE SEULE GRANDE ÎLE
SUR LE DOS DE LA TORTUE   211
KONDIARONK SEAWIAGA SASTARETSI ET LA
GRANDE PAIX DE MONTRÉAL DE 1701   223
L'AUTOHISTOIRE AMÉRINDIENNE :
L'HISTOIRE MISE EN PRÉSENCE DE LA NATURE   229
QUÉBÉCOIS ET CANADIENS DANS L'ORDRE HISTORIQUE AMÉRINDIEN   241
LE RACISME EST NOUVEAU EN AMÉRIQUE   251
CHINA'S NORTHERN ETHNIC MINORITIES AND CANADA'S
ABORIGINAL PEOPLES: HOW BOTH COUNTRIES
CAN INSPIRE AND HELP EACH OTHER   265
FAIS-TOI HURON (BECOME A HURON): AMERICIZING AMERICA   277

BRIDGES

CANADA: ITS CRADLE, ITS NAME, ITS SPIRIT   289

LES ALGONQUINS EN 1857	303
THE METAPHOR OF THE ACCIDENT: A NEW HISTORICAL PARADIGM FOR THE INCLUSION OF CANADA'S FIRST PEOPLES	309
ÉDUCATION ET GOUVERNANCE AUTOCHTONE	315
THE SOUL OF EEYOU/EENOU GOVERNANCE	329
A REFLECTION ON EEYOU/EENOU EDUCATION	339
OTTAWA : UNE CAPITALE IMMÉMORIALE	349
LES PREMIÈRES CIVILISATIONS DES AMÉRIQUES : RETOUR SUR L'HISTOIRE DANS L'ANTHROPOLOGIE	353
BIBLIOGRAPHY	367

Preface

Since the 1980s, Georges Sioui has been a central figure in a profound metaphysical and epistemological movement that goes to the heart of what it means to be human, to be Canadian, to be a citizen of the world. This movement challenges the dominant images of the past by offering hope and inspiration drawn from ignored, or forgotten or marginalized realities.

Once upon a time—though not too long ago—the history of Canada was presented as the story of a French colony that became a British colony before developing as a new country within the British Commonwealth. Then the story was changed to emphasize Canada's distinctiveness in North America and its special location between Europe and the United States.

Along the way, Canadians began recognizing the importance of 'knowing ourselves', as Tom Symons insisted, rather than importing assumptions, theories and practices to inform everyday life. One result was that the study of Canada became a central feature of schools and universities in all provinces during the

Preface

later 20th century. During this period, a Eurocentric narrative of two 'founding peoples' gave way to a more appropriate emphasis on Canada's Aboriginal peoples. But, as is clear from Georges Sioui's compelling writings, we are still only beginning to appreciate how Canada's diverse and complex past can help us make a better future. We are still learning to know ourselves—who we are, and where we might go.

This collection of writings exudes an optimism, a deep belief in human potential, a courage to insist that we are all 'from the Circle'. Let us hope that future generations look back on our era as a time when we embraced the possibility of a world united by respect, tolerance and understanding. Georges Sioui will certainly be remembered then for his efforts to create such a world.

Chad Gaffield
February 10, 2008

Remerciements

Aucun merci ne sera jamais digne de l'amour ni de la profondeur d'âme d'une mère, ni d'un père, ni de mon fils, ni de mon épouse. *Attouguet* (merci) à mon amie et collègue la professeure Dalie Giroux, qui, avec les yeux de son cœur de guerrière de l'esprit, a vu un fil quintessentiel qui a permis de tisser la trame de ce livre. *Kitche Migwetch* (grand merci, en algonquin) au grand ami des miens, le sage et chef William Commanda et à ma sœur spirituelle, sa petite-fille Claudette Commanda. *Attouguet* à Caroline Andrew, une grande « mère de clan » dans notre université et dans le monde ; ce fut Caroline qui « vit » le lien intellectuel et spirituel qui existe entre Dalie Giroux et moi. *Attouguet* à Darren O'Toole, étudiant au doctorat, autre guerrier de l'esprit métis et compagnon de vie de Dalie. Darren passa de nombreuses et solitaires heures de fins de semaine à numériser les textes à l'aide d'appareils assez rudimentaires. *Attouguet* à Shelley Nixon, étudiante finissante au doctorat dans notre Département d'études classiques et de sciences des religions, qui aida généreusement à éditer des textes. *Attouguet* à mon amie et ancienne étudiante Amy Shenstone, qui fut toujours disponible, même à distance, pour aider à la mise en page. *Attouguet* à Marie-Claude Bois, qui fut mon assistante au programme d'études autochtones et me libéra souvent au-delà de ses heures normales de travail afin que je puisse travailler sur ce livre. *Attouguet* à mon frère quechua-aymara Marcelo Saavedra-Vargas, mon Second et conseiller au Programme d'études autochtones et à sa fille Iana qui nous prête main forte. *Attouguet* à mon doyen George Lang, toujours sensible et attentif aux besoins du programme d'études autochtones et à mon propre besoin de vivre intellectuellement par l'écriture en dépit de mon existence d'administrateur. *Attouguet* aussi à mon université pour le respect qu'elle montre en tout temps à mon endroit et à l'endroit de la communauté autochtone: merci à Lori Burns, à Leslie Strutt, à Geneviève Mareschal et à toute l'équipe de la direction de la Faculté des arts. *Attouguet* à mes collègues des départements d'Histoire et d'Études classiques et de Science des religions ! *Attouguet* à Pierre Anctil, mon ami et collègue de l'Institut d'études canadiennes et à son nouveau directeur, David Staines.

Un autre grand merci à mon ami Gilles Paquet, directeur des Presses de l'Université d'Ottawa, ainsi qu' à son excellente équipe, Eric Nelson, Marie Clausén et Jessica Clark. Merci pour le cœur mis à produire « notre » livre !

Finalement, merci spécial à plusieurs collègues professeurs pour leur encouragement et leur inspiration : Marie-Françoise Guédon, Michel Gardaz, Pierluigi Piovanelli, Shelley Rabinovitch, Lucie Dufresne et un très grand *Attouguet* à mes nombreux et très chers étudiants et étudiantes. Nous sommes vraiment toutes et tous une famille ! We truly are all one family !

I am fortunate enough to have a circle of Elders and teachers who enrich the life of many, including my own: Herb Nabigon (Ojibway), Leo Yerxa (Ojibway), Bertha Blondin (Dènè), Annie Smith-Saint Georges (Algonquin), Steven Angustine (Mi'kmaq), Rarihokwats (Mohawk), Dominique Rankin (Algonquin), Guy Bénard (Métis), Derek Rasmussen (Sotch – Danish), Tommy Akulukjuk (Inuit), James Bobbish (James Bay Cree), Michele Penny (Saulteaux), Peter Decontie (Algonquin), and four others who have gone on back to the Land of the Souls, Peter Ochiese (Saulteaux), Eddie Bellerose (Plains Cree), Abraham Burnstick (Stoney – Cree) and Roy Thomas (Ojibway) and many others, all very dear to me.

La sagesse du continent. Une introduction à la lecture des histoires de Kanatha.

Par Dalie Giroux

Voici réunis pour la première fois les essais, contributions, discours et oraisons de Georges E. Sioui, fier Wendat originaire de la réserve du Village-des-Hurons (Wendaké) au Québec.

L'auteur présente dans cette collection de textes, fruit de 17 années de réflexion, d'action politique et d'engagement spirituel, le visage d'un chasseur de paix, d'un voyageur symbolique et d'un chantre des territoires de l'Amérique. Il vient à la rencontre du lecteur comme un ambassadeur d'une parole que l'on a crue égarée, celle des peuples qui détiennent la sagesse du continent, la sagesse de la Grande Île portée par notre grand-mère la tortue.

Georges Emery Sioui, fils d'Éléonore Sioui, poétesse, guérisseuse et docteure en philosophie, est issu de deux lignées de chefs traditionnels. Premier Amérindien à obtenir un doctorat en histoire au Canada (1987-1991), Georges Sioui, avant d'amorcer une riche carrière universitaire, a été dans les années 1970 éditeur et rédacteur en chef de la revue *Kanatha* (fondée par Éléonore

Sioui à Wendaké en 1972), et plus tard, au ministère des Affaires indiennes et du Nord, rédacteur en chef de la revue culturelle *Tawow*.

Depuis, il a publié deux ouvrages importants, traduits en anglais, en espagnol, en allemand, en japonais et en mandarin, largement diffusés dans le domaine des études autochtones. Le premier, *Pour une autohistoire amérindienne* (1999[1989]), est issu de son travail de maîtrise (1983-1987). Préfacé par Claude Lévi-Strauss, l'ouvrage rénove l'historiographie des Indiens d'Amérique et du Nouveau monde en élaborant les fondements d'une démarche spirituelle de redécouverte de l'histoire orale qui puisse s'inscrire dans le travail historique occidental sur les sources. Le second ouvrage, issu de la thèse de doctorat de l'auteur, sera publié sous le titre *Les Hurons-Wendats : une civilisation méconnue* (1994[1999]). Cette monographie, dans laquelle on trouve une application de la méthode de l'autohistoire, s'inscrit avec force dans le champ de l'histoire des autochtones en proposant notamment une interprétation radicalement nouvelle des relations entre Hurons (Wendats) et Iroquois (Hodenosaunee).

Le penseur amérindien a aussi œuvré, au début de sa carrière universitaire et après des études postdoctorales à la Newberry Library à Chicago (1991), comme administrateur universitaire, notamment en tant que doyen au Saskatchewan Indian Federated College (1992-1997), premier collège universitaire géré par des autochtones, devenu depuis la First Nations University of Canada (qui est maintenant la première université gérée par des autochtone au Canada), et comme président à l'Institute of Indigenous Government à Vancouver (1999-2001). Entièrement dédié au rayonnement et à la floraison de la sagesse amérindienne en Amérique, l'auteur est aujourd'hui attaché à l'Université d'Ottawa et a créé un programme d'études autochtones à la hauteur de ceux qu'on trouve désormais dans l'ouest du Canada et dans le sud-ouest des États-Unis.

Polyglotte, conférencier très prisé, Georges Sioui a donné des centaines d'allocutions dans sa carrière. Dans la tradition ancestrale telle qu'elle lui a été transmise, et en accord avec sa discipline historique telle qu'il a contribué à la transformer, le polyvalent auteur et orateur raconte à ses auditoires sans frontières disciplinaires ou culturelles la découverte de l'Amérique ou l'histoire du Contact. Parlant depuis le point de vue amérindien, il préfère appeler cette histoire celle de l'« Accident ».

Je me suggère, dans cette introduction, d'établir pour le lecteur des ponts entre l'action de l'auteur et ses écrits, entre son geste et sa parole, à la fois dans son parcours de vie, dans son action culturelle et politique ainsi que dans son écriture. Je propose ici une brève exploration des thèmes de son travail de pensée, ainsi que quelques indications relatives au choix des essais, contributions, discours et oraisons offerts au lecteur dans cet ouvrage.

Je reste bien conscient, par-delà cette tentative, d'illustrer la vie et l'œuvre de l'auteur, que la seule véritable rencontre avec l'héritage que transmet et revitalise Georges Sioui est le fruit d'une longue démarche, d'un engagement qui commence par l'ouverture à l'autre, et qui se réalise dans la saisie de l'importance et de la beauté de la sagesse de la pensée circulaire. Cet engagement est une décision très intime.

Penser l'américité

En plus d'être un chasseur, un poète, un dramaturge, un musicien et un professeur adoré de ses étudiants, en plus d'être un frère, un père, un mari et un oncle, Georges Sioui est un activiste, un critique et un sage. C'est surtout par cela que j'aimerais présenter au lecteur les thèmes de la pensée du Wendat.

L'activiste

Les cercles de guérison, mouvement initié dans les communautés autochtones de l'Ouest canadien dans les années 1960 et 1970 et qui se sont développés et multipliés jusqu'à nos jours, sont le phare d'un travail culturel de revitalisation du savoir traditionnel et de la prise en charge spirituelle et politique des peuples blessés et décimés par le processus de colonisation – qui demande encore d'être combattu. Ils se sont développés selon différentes formes, en dehors des institutions dominantes, auprès de toutes sortes de personnes avec toute sortes de difficultés. Les cercles de guérison ont en commun d'être le fait d'initiatives nées dans les communautés, souvent sous l'impulsion de la mobilisation de groupes de femmes et d'aînés, et engageant à l'aide des ressources de la tradition amérindienne un processus thérapeutique axé notamment sur les effets de la colonisation, faisant par là de la guérison un référent politique. Au Canada, depuis une vingtaine d'années, on vient de partout sur le continent à la rencontre des aînés de l'Ouest dans le but d'acquérir ce savoir thérapeutique qui exige de faire un usage spirituel du territoire – un savoir qui s'est effrité dans les zones de colonisation précoce.

Au tournant des années 1980, auprès des aînés Peter Ochees, Eddy Bellerose et Abraham Burnstick, essaimant librement leur territoire au nord d'Edmonton, Georges Sioui et quelques camarades participent à un cercle de guérison, pendant lequel ils sont initiés aux rituels de purification, aux jeûnes et aux usages spirituels de la nature. Cette rencontre de guérison est le moment, pour Georges Sioui, de ce qu'il a appelé son retour aux sources, d'une renaissance spirituelle. À partir de ce passage, le sens de sa lutte et de son engagement envers la culture amérindienne, qui ont toujours – depuis l'enfance auprès de sa grand-mère – été siens, s'inscrit dans une tâche très précise de rénovation des bases spirituelles qui appartiennent en propre au continent américain. Après cette expérience, Sioui se donne pour mission de participer au transfert culturel de ce savoir des aînés de l'Ouest vers l'Est du Canada. Le geste est, à contre-courant du mouvement de colonisation, pareil à une reconquête, une remise « à l'endroit » du pays, d'ouest en est.

> Vous savez, explique Sioui en 1991, que pour les Amérindiens, ainsi que pour tous les peuples du Cercle, la vie, l'existence, est une chaîne de relations, ainsi qu'une reconnaissance de parenté avec les autres êtres de la Création ; une reconnaissance d'un caractère spirituel contenu dans toutes les manifestations de la Vie, non seulement dans les êtres humains ou, bien souvent, dans certaines classes d'êtres humains, mais aussi dans les êtres, ou « peuples » non humains, si on peut parler de « peuples » d'animaux, peuples de poissons, peuples de pierres, de montagnes, d'esprits, etc. Les peuples autochtones, pour parler de ceux de l'Amérique en particulier, se rejoignent très facilement au niveau de la pensée du cercle. Ils reconnaissent facilement qu'ils sont dépendants de la Nature pour vivre.

INTRODUCTION

L'Amérique est un lieu sacré, dit en substance Georges Sioui, et il faut en réapprendre de nos aînés l'usage respectueux et bénéfique. La tradition des anciens habitants du continent, parce qu'ils ont développé un lien harmonieux avec la terre d'Amérique, est porteuse d'une éthique sociale particulièrement précieuse.

La (re)découverte et la (ré)invention des spiritualités traditionnelles, dans un mouvement de rénovation du pouvoir culturel et moral, mènent de manière nécessaire à la redécouverte du lien entre les peuples et le territoire comme source de vie. Cette (re)découverte est que la terre est source de vérité immanente, condition de toute existence, et que la spiritualité est ainsi une topographie morale du continent. Cette topographie morale est le savoir très ancien que les habitants les plus anciens du Nouveau monde possèdent et ont conservé jusqu'à ce jour, mais qui est en grand danger de se perdre. La conservation et le rayonnement de ce savoir demandent en effet d'avoir accès au territoire sacré, celui qui énonce la vérité du continent. Le travail que se donne alors Georges Sioui est de faire la culture éthique de cette terre, et d'en enseigner les rudiments, pour que tous puissent jouir de ses fruits. La spiritualité et l'activité politique se lient alors dans l'action de Georges Sioui en un nœud très solide, un nœud que les juges de la Cour suprême du Canada devront plus tard trancher. Cette histoire est commune aux luttes politiques autochtones partout sur le continent.

En effet, c'est dans ce contexte épistémologique et spirituel de protection du savoir des usages moraux du territoire qu'il faut comprendre les processus politiques et légaux de réappropriation des lieux sacrés, partout en Amérique. De l'Arizona à la Colombie-Britannique, en passant par le Montana et jusqu'au Québec, dans un esprit de partage et de recherche d'équilibre, des traditionalistes ont entrepris de demander de voir reconnu leur droit de faire un usage spirituel de la terre, comme leurs ancêtres avant eux l'ont toujours fait. Georges Sioui, sa mère, Éléonore, et ses frères, Konrad, Hugues, Régent et Vincent font partie de ces traditionalistes. En 1982, ils occupent pendant quelques jours, le temps d'un jeûne rituel en famille, un espace du Parc de conservation de la rivière Jacques-Cartier sous le contrôle du gouvernement québécois, territoire traditionnel wendat. Arrêtés puis poursuivis, ils défendent, jusqu'en Cour suprême, la légitimité de leur droit d'usage spirituel du territoire. Sioui dira : « Notre Église, c'est la terre ».

L'arrêt Sioui, prononcé en 1990, leur donnera raison, non pas sur la base de la reconnaissance du droit inhérent d'usage spirituel de la terre, non pas dans le langage traditionnel autochtone, mais parce qu'un document rédigé par le second du lieutenant gouverneur de l'époque de la colonie française peut être tenu pour un traité (dans le langage colonial de la Cour). Victoire néanmoins dont le principal instigateur, comme en témoignent certains des textes présentés dans ce livre, portera le récit aux quatre coins du monde. À ce propos, Sioui dira devant une sous-commission de l'ONU : « *We won basically because we were able to make the Euro-American courts and governments understand their deep and vital interest in protecting our profoundly spiritual vision of the world which, in the end, is their best – indeed, perhaps their only – chance of being able to understand and give direction to their existence on our American continent* ». Le cas Sioui a été discuté abondamment – et critiqué durement – chez les historiens et légistes québécois et d'ailleurs.

Le critique

Dans la droite ligne de ce retour à la sagesse du continent, parallèlement à la lutte politique et légale qu'il a mené pendant la décennie 1980, Georges Sioui devient historien et entreprend l'élaboration d'une critique aussi radicale que sereine de l'Amérique des Européens, celle qui est la nôtre aujourd'hui. Le cœur de cette pratique de la résistance culturelle, constitué d'une multitude de luttes qu'il mènera cette fois non pas à la barre des accusés mais devant l'académie canadienne et québécoise, est le développement d'un point de vue amérindien sur l'histoire du Nouveau monde.

Pour initier cette résistance avec des outils intellectuels, Georges Sioui, inspiré en cela par l'anthropologue Bruce Trigger, a développé une historiographie nouvelle de l'histoire amérindienne, qui inclut dans la preuve historique les sources écrites, orales, pictographiques, esthétiques et mnémoniques qui forment le point de vue amérindien, dont on trouve notamment de nombreuses traces dans les sources documentaires habituelles (preuves ethnographiques et archivistiques). Le postulat derrière le développement de cette méthode est que la philosophie amérindienne se trouve encodée dans les écrits des premiers Européens : il s'agit dès lors de faire de « l'archéologie spirituelle et intellectuelle », en plus de se fonder sur le témoignage des Sages, vivants et disparus. Cela s'appelle l'autohistoire.

Cette sensibilité nouvelle nous aura donné, dans le travail de Sioui l'historien, plusieurs éléments d'un nouveau portrait de l'histoire du Contact. Sioui propose entre autres une nouvelle lecture de la guerre entre Hurons et Iroquois, selon laquelle les Hodenosaunee n'ont pas détruit la Huronie mais ont plutôt adopté et assimilé les survivants wendats dans le but de les préserver de la destruction inévitable. Sous sa plume, nous redécouvrons également des vignettes oubliées de la rencontre entre Jacques Cartier et les Stadaconas, alliés et parents ethniques des Wendats : l'explorateur aurait marié en 1535 la nièce matrilinéaire (sa « fille ») du grand chef Donnacona qui lui aurait été offerte en signe d'alliance, sur les rives du Saint-Laurent. Ailleurs, dans un morceau plus littéraire, Kondiaronk Soiaga Sastaretsi, grand chef Wendat, nous apparaît, grâce à la magie de l'autohistoire, vivant, acteur et témoin de la Grande Paix de Montréal en 1701.

Puis, entre les lignes du texte de 1703 du Baron de Lahontan, dans lequel ce dernier discute avec Adario, le bon sauvage huron, Sioui retrouve la sagesse de ses ancêtres, celle qui répond à sa propre mémoire, à son propre héritage. Il y voit non pas une projection européenne sur une Amérique idéalisée, comme on a voulu le lire du point de vue européen jusqu'à présent, mais bien une fiction authentique qui met en scène les valeurs traditionnelles de l'Amérique – au premier chef celle de la liberté. Il y voit le désir réel des nouveaux arrivants, selon la belle expression de Georges Sioui, de s'« ensauvager » : « Volonté réelle des Français en arrivant en Amérique de découvrir une nouvelle façon de vivre et une pratique à laquelle les autorités cléricales tentaient de s'opposer ».

L'autohistoire, regard à la fois savant et amérindien sur l'histoire des Amérindiens et du Nouveau monde, présente la découverte de l'Amérique non pas comme l'apparition à la conscience européenne d'un nouveau pays, un pays vierge aux possibilités infinies, mais plutôt un Accident. L'Accident, vécu par les peuples habitant le continent dont la culture était celle de la liberté et du respect, de l'interdépendance et de la circularité. Accident qu'a été l'arrivée d'explorateurs, de marchands et des robes noires envoyés par des monarchies absolues pratiquant le mercantilisme. Accident qu'a été l'arrivée de nouvelles pratiques de la guerre, de nouvelles pratiques du commerce, de nouvelles maladies et d'une manière fort étrange de comprendre le rapport à la terre. Accident qu'a été l'imposition d'un régime foncier, religieux et éducationnel complètement étranger à la culture et aux modes de vie en place, hérités selon le récit de temps immémoriaux. Accident spirituel :

> La maladie s'est mise à gagner sur la santé. L'Europe, au moment d'arriver accidentellement en Amérique, n'était qu'un grand foyer d'épidémies, tellement la Ligne avait intégralement remplacé le Cercle. On pourrait même dire que l'Europe, chroniquement et mortellement malade, a frénétiquement cherché un remède et son salut à la fin du 15e siècle. Ainsi, le seul sens acceptable d'une célébration de l'arrivée des Européens ici en 1492 serait le salut physique d'une Europe condamnée à mort, puis son retour graduel à la santé physique, mentale et spirituelle, dans l'air sain et salutaire de la Grande Île amérindienne. Cette guérison, toujours très incomplète, est une tâche à laquelle les Amérindiens continuent de vouloir contribuer. Voilà ce à quoi nous réfléchissons, nous dont le cœur bat au rythme de celui de cette Amérique, terre de vie pour tous, pendant que d'autres cœurs célèbrent encore un vieux monde que l'on a fui parce qu'il ne promettait que la mort.

Georges Sioui, avec beaucoup de douceur, oppose une fin de non-recevoir à ce monde de souffrance, ignorant de la sagesse de la terre d'ici.

Le sage

L'activisme politique et le travail d'historien de Georges Sioui, activités essentielles pratiquées en parallèle dans sa vie quotidienne, témoignent d'un engagement dans le monde dont l'assise est quelque chose de la sagesse. Qu'est-ce que la sagesse par rapport à la connaissance ? Elle est chez Sioui la certitude du geste, cette certitude que l'on tire de l'accord de l'action avec les principes qui nous habitent et qui procèdent d'une vérité du monde, telle qu'elle se déploie dans la présence à l'autre, humain et nature. Elle est vision vécue d'une vérité qui donne à la vie sa profonde douceur, riche des possibles les plus élevés. La sagesse de Sioui est contenue dans ce qu'il appelle « la pensée circulaire ».

INTRODUCTION

Chez les Wendats, m'a déjà expliqué Georges Sioui, l'échelle de la supériorité civilisationnelle est en quelque sorte à l'inverse de l'échelle européenne. Alors que mesurée à cette dernière, la civilisation la plus avancée est une civilisation technique, une civilisation du confort et de la gestion du risque ; pour les Wendats, la supériorité est affaire de spiritualité, d'accès par la nature au monde surnaturel. Aussi, historiquement, les nations algonquiennes, faites de ces chasseurs-cueilleurs qui vivaient de la forêt boréale au nord des territoires traditionnels wendats dans la baie georgienne, étaient considérées, avec leurs connaissances de la chasse, de l'esprit de la forêt et des rituels entourant la fréquentation de ces esprits et l'usage du territoire, comme supérieures aux Wendats eux-mêmes ou à leurs voisins agriculteurs du Sud, les Hodenosaunee, les gens de la maison longue. Cette déférence pour les peuples les plus proches de la nature et ainsi plus puissants est également rapportée comme ayant également existé pendant la période de la traite de fourrure chez les Cris de la baie James et les Inuit.

Dans cette échelle où l'intimité du contact avec la nature détermine le niveau d'ajustement, la civilisation européenne qui arrive au moment de l'Accident est une civilisation très pauvre. Elle l'est toujours, maintient Sioui, qui dit : « Nous sommes toujours riches, ils sont toujours pauvres » :

New epidemic diseases defy conventional medicine ; economic oppression of the poor, whose ranks are inexorably growing, is an apparently insoluble problem ; the natural world is threatened with extinction because of aggressive political and financial interests of leading elites ; justice systems are subject to the dictatorship of organized crime : there are many negative points of similarity between white America and ancient Europe.

Le constat de Sioui est que les nouveaux arrivants n'ont non seulement pas encore accédé à la sagesse du territoire qu'ils appellent Amérique, mais ils s'en éloignent plutôt. Une cure spirituelle, croit le fils de guérisseuse, est nécessaire. Les anciens habitants, qui ont préservé le savoir de la topographie morale de la Grande Île, supérieurs spirituellement, ont dès lors pour mission de procéder à l'éducation spirituelle de l'Amérique des Européens. « *The basic thought that always comes to us, when we reflect on the meaning of all this history, this pain, this massive process of destruction of our land, our air, our water, our food sources, our people, is : how can they truthfully believe that we will accept their ways as superior to ours »* ?

Le fardeau du sauvage, pourrait-on dire, est de porter l'américité, le savoir moral de la terre, comme le projet d'une révolution morale et culturelle de toutes les Amériques. Le rôle des Amérindiens, tel que Georges Sioui l'entrevoit dans le Canada du futur, est d'être, comme ils savent le faire depuis des temps immémoriaux, les interprètes, les cultivateurs spirituels et les passeurs de la sagesse de cette terre, celle de la pensée circulaire. Sioui estime donc important de contribuer à fonder des institutions de savoir dont la mission est de conserver, de développer et de diffuser la pensée du cercle, d'y intégrer les porteurs du savoir traditionnel, et de contribuer à la formation de penseurs amérindiens ou américisés, de porteurs de l'américité, dans le but de faire rayonner cette pensée partout en Amérique. Cette éducation, du point de vue du cercle, est une éducation non coercitive, et elle commence au sein même des communautés autochtones qui, selon Sioui, ne sont pas prêtes à l'autodétermination si elles ne sont pas enracinées dans leurs traditions : les intellectuels amérindiens ont pour rôle d'amener les chefs actuels et futurs aux valeurs traditionnelles.

La question de l'identité (multiculturalisme) et de la démocratie canadiennes devrait, selon Sioui, après ces efforts, pouvoir être posée dans les termes de la sagesse amérindienne. Pour le sage qui s'adresse à tous ses frères et à toutes ses sœurs, la phase de l'innocence est terminée dans l'histoire canadienne. Nous sommes au point où la Terre-mère nous ordonne d'être matures et de trouver le sens profond de notre existence collective. Il faut passer de l'existence matérielle à l'existence spirituelle. La mise en partage des fondements circulaires de la culture amérindienne pour l'ensemble des Canadiens est aujourd'hui un impératif vers le progrès moral hors de la société coloniale :

> *Where a true democracy, in the circular sense of the word, will come to exist and be a model for the rest of humanity. A circular, or holistic democracy will be one where all beings, human and non-human, will have their place and their rights in a universal relation of respect and interdependence. That, to me, and to many of my people, is the profound sense and vocation of Canada. At this moment, the Canadian Multiculturalism cannot have its full meaning,*

INTRODUCTION

because Canadian thinking is still profoundly linear and the concept of multiculturalism does not agree with linear thinking.

Les premiers à être appelés Canadiens (« Canadois »), rappelle Sioui, sont les Montagnais et les Algonquins, que les Français ont rencontrés dans la vallée du Saint-Laurent, après le départ des Nadoueks. Chez les Amérindiens, on trouve une forte résistance au modèle européen d'État-nation. L'échéancier traditionnel relève d'une tâche spirituelle, il s'agit d'abord d'un état de l'âme et de l'esprit. Si le Canada a été créé, c'est parce que le vieux monde avait besoin d'un endroit comme ici. Ce sont les Amérindiens et les penseurs du cercle qui transportent l'esprit du territoire. La guérison de l'Europe malade, sa réconciliation avec la sagesse du sol qui l'a accueillie il y a 500 ans, se fera sous le signe de la rencontre avec la pensée du cercle, rencontre avec l'Amérindien et sa tradition, et procédera d'un désir de l'Européen de se faire adopter par cette sagesse, par cette terre – d'accepter, pour s'émanciper du malheur civilisationnel dans lequel il se trouve, de se faire amérindien. « *But First nations people have to get busy with the task of assimilating. Indianizing the non-Indian society and thereby, avoid what's coming our way if we keep on with this linear thinking, this path of destruction* ».

La sagesse de Georges Sioui, qui baigne toute son action, est enseignement de l'être-là de l'Amérique, sens éthique de cette terre. Le sage de la pensée du cercle est le nomothète du cœur américain, héraut, comme Vine Deloria Jr. aux États-Unis, d'une transvaluation culturelle à venir de cette « ère aveugle » qui est la nôtre, dans laquelle la conversion de la terre en argent sera renversée, et l'Amérique matérielle, réappropriée.

Sur les essais, contributions, discours et oraisons

Les essais, contributions, discours et oraisons que Georges Sioui offre en partage représentent plus de quinze années de travail en plusieurs langues dont nous n'avons retenu ici pour les lecteurs canadiens que les écrits en langue française ou anglaise. On y trouve des conférences présentées lors de colloques savants partout au Canada, en France, aux États-Unis, en Allemagne, dans les pays d'Amérique latine ou en Mongolie, des contributions littéraires et scientifiques sous forme d'articles dans différentes publications nationales et internationales, des discours tenus lors de réunions politiques dans les communautés autochtones, dans les institutions d'enseignement et devant différentes instances de l'ONU, une oraison pour la commémoration de la Grande Paix de Montréal et un retour ironique sur le cinquième centenaire de la découverte de l'Amérique, le tout parsemé de partages spirituels, de légendes, d'entrevues et d'autres réflexions personnelles.

À la lecture des textes présentés dans cet ouvrage, la diversité de formes et la répétition des thèmes peuvent au premier abord surprendre, voire inquiéter. Elles ont pourtant leur sens et leurs forces. Il est impossible d'aborder ces textes à l'occidentale, en y cherchant thèse et arguments, réfutations et linéarité. Cela serait même, je le crois, contraire à l'esprit de leur création. Ils sont des textes de circonstance, ne se présentant pas comme les pierres qui permettent de construire l'édifice de la science, mais plutôt comme des voyages circulaires, au cœur du cœur amérindien, au cœur de la sagesse de l'Amérique. À ce titre, chacun des textes est un enseignement. Chacun des textes transporte et transmet les motifs et les figures du projet de transvaluation culturelle de Sioui. Chacun des textes est, tel un aphorisme, condensation de toute une pensée, qui est naturellement et stylistiquement circulaire. C'est de cette manière qu'il faut les lire, toujours enracinés dans la terre spirituelle, fruit de la moisson d'une vie entière dédiée à l'américité, parsemant le parcours réel de l'auteur, marqué par l'histoire contemporaine, par les situations diverses qui réclament sa parole, par les gens qui demandent de l'entendre.

Ainsi, les textes proposés permettent au lecteur de sillonner le cercle symbolique qu'habite Sioui depuis la victoire qu'est l'arrêt Sioui jusqu'à aujourd'hui. Telles qu'elles nous sont offertes, dans leur variété nécessaire, ces *Histoires de Kanatha* s'inscrivent dans la vie immémoriale de leur auteur et ne peuvent être comprises qu'en se laissant adopter par lui, en assimilant le point de vue amérindien de l'histoire. Car c'est bien ce que Georges Sioui nous propose, lorsqu'il annonce qu'il va nous « manger » :

> *And I think that we're in the process of reclaiming our people that say that they are part-Indian, part-Cree, part-Cherokee, part-anything. They are going to come back and be the First Nations people. And the door is also open to non-First Nations people : we were always able to transform non-Indians*

into Indian people, because we all come from the Circle […]. Slowly, they will have to adopt our worldview, because it's a circular worldview. So, we are going to eventually adopt and assimilate them, or as we said in our old Wendat language, « eat » them. The English word « assimilate » carries the same meaning : to eat someone up, culturally.

Voyageant d'ouest en est, à rebours de l'Accident, ces essais, contributions, discours et oraisons contribuent à la diffusion et à la valorisation de la culture spirituelle des anciens habitants du continent, et ils offrent une initiation à la topographie morale conservée jusqu'à aujourd'hui et depuis les temps immémoriaux par les aînés.

Aborder les écrits de Georges Sioui signifie découvrir l'exceptionnel parcours personnel, social et culturel de cet auteur. Les textes permettent d'accéder à une parole forte, radicale autant que généreuse, d'une bonté exigeante, et d'inscrire cette offrande symbolique dans la grande entreprise spirituelle et révolutionnaire qui lui donne son sens.

C'est un très grand honneur que Georges Sioui m'a fait en me permettant de participer au rayonnement de cette pensée ; et c'est procédant d'une très grande générosité de la part de leur auteur que ces textes en forme de visions sont offerts aux lecteurs.

LIVING HISTORY

Living History

Those who live on the edge
Of survival
Are the very heart
Of history
I am a Wendat
I am the living History

La Flamme de Vie du Canada*

Ce qui distingue le Canada du reste du monde est son esprit libre et ouvert et son être physique pur, vaste et abondant. Le Canada est la chère, bonne, vieille Terre, excellemment maintenue dans sa beauté par un fils d'un amour et d'un respect uniques, l'Indien d'Amérique. La vision de la vie, ou la culture de l'Amérindien, est le souffle qui créa l'originalité gagnante du caractère du Canada.

Le Feu Originel du Canada se découvre aux premiers feux qui ont réchauffé et éclairé les corps, les esprits et les âmes des nouveaux venants, dans les anciens wigwams et les anciennes maisons longues des riches peuples de ce plus vieux des continents.

Par conséquent, si nous voulons protéger la précieuse Flamme de Vie du Canada, nous n'exposerons pas de raisons humanitaires ; encore moins

---

* Ce texte est paru dans le magazine culturel *Tawow*, publié par le ministère des Affaires indiennes et du Nord (Ottawa) de 1973 à 1980 ; vol. 6, no 2 (1978), p. 2-3.

n'énoncerons-nous la politique et les finances : c'est par souci moral que nous allons défendre la belle culture primitive (ou spirituelle) du Canada.

Car la nostalgie qui habite l'esprit de l'Amérindien ne vient pas du traitement qu'il a reçu ou de l'indifférence trop souvent évidente montrée pour son existence. La nostalgie du premier Canadien n'est ni passive, ni apitoyée sur elle-même ; elle est positive, active et très riche en forces à donner parce qu'elle provient de la conscience simple d'une force morale supérieure, une force morale qui a permis la survivance et la vie améliorée de millions d'hommes, de femmes et d'enfants.

La Flamme de Vie du Canada est vivante, mais très faible, parce que l'habitation originelle du Canada a été envahie et détruite, et les premiers enfants du Canada n'ont cessé de périr dans la noirceur, le vent, la pluie et le froid, comme la Flamme.

La maison a besoin d'être reconstruite au-dessus de la Flamme, et les enfants ont besoin de pouvoir réintégrer cette demeure à eux ; les nouveaux enfants du Canada ont besoin d'être accueillis dans cette maison et de sentir leurs craintes s'évanouir près du feu original de leur pays afin de pouvoir découvrir un passé d'ordre, de beauté, de courage et de dignité et espérer tranquillement un bon avenir, au lieu d'être précipités dans un présent et vers un avenir apeurants et esseulés d'un passé qu'on méconnaît et qu'on a appris à cacher.

Les nouveaux enfants du Canada ont besoin d'entendre leurs frères et leurs sœurs nouvellement trouvés raconter l'histoire de leur pays à leur propre manière, par des sons, des récits, des objets, des images, des danses et des cérémonies inspirés par cette Terre. Ils ont besoin de pouvoir regarder dans l'idée et de sentir l'esprit des grands hommes, des héros et des héroïnes qui ont continuellement préservé ce beau pays où hommes et femmes peuvent et doivent réapprendre la bonne vie entre humains, sur terre.

Relecture autochtone de l'événement des 500 ans[*]

Salutations et remerciements aux deux présentateurs (Lucie et Guy), ainsi qu'à l'organisme international qui m'a invité, Entraide missionnaire. Salutations à l'assistance.

La tradition amérindienne me dicte de m'incliner d'abord devant le poids de l'âge et de la sagesse représenté dans cette salle. Ce sera donc en toute humilité que je proposerai les idées qui suivront. Je remercie, en dernier lieu, les gens qui nous accueillent dans leurs maisons.

J'ai apporté quelque chose que connaissent les gens familiers de la campagne et de la forêt. Il s'agit d'un foin appelé ici *foin d'odeur*, un foin qui a la propriété de parfumer l'air lorsqu'on le fait brûler, tel que je le fais en compagnie de ma famille, chaque matin. C'est un lien avec la Nature, même lorsqu'on est parmi le béton, le plastique ou le métal. Ainsi, on ne se sent jamais complètement isolé de la Nature, d'où l'on vient, comme être humain.

---

[*] Conférence prononcée à Montréal en septembre 1991, lors du Congrès d'Entraide missionnaire, Actes du Congrès, p. 9-15.

Je commencerai ma présentation par un rappel du principe fondamental de toutes les cultures autochtones ou amérindiennes. Je sais que certains d'entre vous ont œuvré parmi les cultures du Sud, mais nous parlons d'un principe reconnu par toutes les nations, ou peuples amérindiens, ainsi que par tous les peuples qui ont conservé une capacité d'harmonie avec l'environnement, ou encore la Nature ou la Création. Je les appelle les sociétés du Cercle.

Une première constatation serait la dichotomie, ou la différence, entre la pensée linéaire et la pensée circulaire, donc entre le Cercle et la Ligne. Vous savez que, pour les Amérindiens, ainsi que pour tous les peuples du Cercle, la vie, l'existence, est une chaîne de relations, ainsi qu'une reconnaissance de parenté avec les autres êtres de la Création ; une reconnaissance d'un caractère spirituel contenu dans toutes les manifestations de la Vie, non seulement dans les êtres humains ou, bien souvent, dans certaines classes d'êtres humains, mais aussi dans les êtres, ou « peuples », non humains, si on peut parler de peuples d'animaux, peuples de poissons, peuples de pierres, de montagnes, d'esprits, etc. Les peuples autochtones, pour parler de ceux de l'Amérique en particulier, se rejoignent très facilement en ce qui concerne la pensée du Cercle. Ils reconnaissent facilement qu'ils sont dépendants de la Nature pour vivre. C'est là un trait culturel qui peut découler surtout de l'éducation reçue, mais aussi d'un long contact avec les forces de la Nature. Il est ainsi facile de reconnaître que l'on ne peut impunément maltraiter la Nature, ou les êtres non humains, de façon régulière et indéfiniment. Tous ceux qui ont vécu au contact de la Nature et au contact de communautés paysannes ou des forêts, spécialement en tant que missionnaires, savent que ces gens rejoignent facilement la Nature, c'est-à-dire qu'ils peuvent parler et communiquer avec des plantes ou des animaux et, donc, reconnaître spontanément leur parenté avec les autres êtres de la Création. Voilà ce dont on parle lorsqu'on dit le Cercle. Le Cercle est une réalité sécurisante, non seulement pour les autochtones, mais pour quiconque en a connaissance. Les sociétés qui suivent la Ligne, ou les sociétés évolutionnistes, ne connaissent pas la sécurité du Cercle, puisqu'elles suivent un certain progrès dont personne ne peut connaître l'aboutissement ; une majorité de gens, aujourd'hui, ont plutôt la certitude que ce progrès ne réserve rien d'harmonieux pour le genre humain, ainsi que pour le reste de la Création. Lorsque l'humain reconnaît sa place dans le Cercle, par contre, tout est circulaire : on ne va nulle part en particulier ; on ne fait que respecter l'ordre établi depuis toujours pour l'homme et les autres créatures par Dieu, par le Créateur, ou peu importe le nom par lequel on le/la désigne dans les langues du monde. On ne ressent donc pas le besoin d'« évoluer » vers de plus en plus de progrès, de confort, parce que ces choses-là isolent l'être humain par rapport à la Vie elle-même, à ce qui donne et entretient la Vie elle-même. Et spécialement quand on est Amérindien, on fait périodiquement un retour délibéré vers le Cercle, de façon à se rajuster par rapport à celui-ci. Par exemple, dans plusieurs cultures nord-amérindiennes, mais aussi chez certains peuples sud-américains (et, de toute façon, tous les peuples ont leurs propres moyens de la faire), nous pratiquons la « quête de la vision ». C'est-à-dire que les hommes (au sens masculin du terme) ont une tendance naturelle à en arriver à se croire supérieurs au reste de la Création. Aussi, périodiquement, de préférence au printemps, à l'époque où toute la Nature se renouvelle, il est coutumier que les jeunes hommes (les jeunes filles peuvent aussi le faire) s'isolent et se privent de nourriture, d'eau, de compagnie humaine, de façon à se rendre compte de notre dépendance envers les autres êtres. Après un, deux, trois ou même quatre jours sans eau, nourriture et société, on perd son sentiment d'être important ou grand et on redevient humain et ajusté au Cercle. Voilà une des voies par lesquelles les Amérindiens peuvent enseigner quelque chose d'important au reste du monde.

De la même façon que les Amérindiens ont accueilli les autres ordres de vie, les ont inclus dans leur Cercle et ont reconnu leur existence, ils ont accueilli les Européens qui sont venus ici, il y a presque 500 ans, en pensant que les Européens allaient aussi les accueillir. Dans leurs différences. Mais ils se sont vite rendu compte que si les sociétés circulaires étaient capables d'accueillir les sociétés linéaires, l'inverse n'était pas vrai. Les gens qui suivent la Ligne, qui croient au progrès, qui croient en la suprématie de certaines cultures, surtout des cultures européennes, ne sont pas capables, ne sont pas disposées culturellement à reconnaître leur parenté avec les autres cultures, leur égalité vis-à-vis celles-ci. Je viens d'une nation (la nation des Wendats, ou des Hurons) qui a, de façon particulièrement dure, subi l'effet de l'incapacité des Européens à rejoindre l'esprit du Cercle. Mes ancêtres étaient un peuple nombreux qui avait développé une civilisation remarquable, bien que méconnue. J'ai fait moi-même le suivi archéologique de mes ancêtres wendats. Il est visible que ce peuple a adopté l'agriculture vers les années 900 ou 1000 de notre ère et qu'à partir de ce point, il s'est constitué une place centrale auprès de ce qui devint une grande famille de nations amérindiennes du Nord-Est. Vers les années 1200 à 1300, les Wendats étaient actifs au cœur de grands réseaux de commerce et d'échanges, non seulement matériels : on s'échangeait aussi des pratiques religieuses, des croyances, des gens, etc. Une harmonie remarquable habitait déjà toute cette grande nation bien avant l'arrivée des Français et d'autres Européens parmi eux.

L'arrivée des Européens en Amérique du Nord-Est, au début du XIVe siècle, apporta assurément un grand bouleversement, surtout en raison des épidémies d'origine européenne. Cependant, les Wendats, comme tous les Amérindiens en général, eurent le réflexe culturel d'accueillir les nouveaux venus, d'échanger avec eux, et reconnurent que cette arrivée devait être dans l'ordre des choses, ou dans le plan d'une Volonté bien supérieure à la nôtre, la Volonté d'un Grand Esprit, et qu'il fallait commercer et étendre les réseaux d'échanges existants à ces gens. Bien sûr, les épidémies firent leur œuvre de façon très rapide et radicale. Après quelques générations, les gens ne furent plus capables de maintenir leurs cultures et leurs sociétés, leur grande société, leur ordre culturel, économique et politique. La société wendate commença à se désintégrer. Cette désintégration s'accentua à partir du moment où les religieux, surtout les Jésuites, à partir de 1634, régularisèrent et imposèrent une présence forte de leur ordre parmi les Wendats. En l'espace d'une quinzaine d'années, tout ce qui avait constitué le cœur de cette grande société de nations amérindiennes a été détruit.

Il est bien sûr impensable que ces gens soient venus dans le but de détruire toute cette civilisation. Néanmoins, l'intention de ces missionnaires, à l'époque dont on parle, était, fondamentalement, de recréer les conditions nécessaires à la naissance d'une Église, d'une Église chrétienne. On reconnaissait que l'église chrétienne avait pris naissance dans des conditions d'une dureté absolue, c'est-à-dire la maladie, la guerre, la destruction et toutes ces choses. Ils n'ont donc pas pu compatir au sort des Wendats et des autres Amérindiens. Dans leurs écrits, on remarque facilement, et de façon constante, l'indifférence de ces religieux vis-à-vis du sort des Amérindiens, vis-à-vis de la disparition de grandes quantités de gens. Ils imputèrent de façon facile cette disparition aux guerres, surtout celles entre les Hurons et les Iroquois, qui avaient été fortement intensifiées par la présence même des missionnaires. On n'a pas intégré, dans l'interprétation de l'Histoire, le fait que ces gens avaient, c'est sûr, leurs guerres, leurs divisions, leurs querelles, mais qu'ils s'équilibraient, c'est-à-dire qu'un ordre existait. Personne ne voulait détruire ou exterminer personne. Le dossier archéologique est clair à ce sujet : les gens ne se faisaient pas grand tort par leurs guerres ; il s'agissait plutôt d'exercices de jeunes gens, de vengeances, de raccords, d'échanges de captifs, tel que cela se fait encore aujourd'hui, en ce moment même, dans certaines parties intactes de l'Amérique, comme au centre du Brésil. Je sais, par exemple, qu'en 1988, et probablement au moment où je vous parle, il y a des gens qui vivent encore de cette façon-là et qui ont connu la même séquence de malheurs que les Wendats d'il y a 350 ans.

Cette indifférence que l'on remarque dans les relations des Jésuites, en particulier, et dans les relations de tous les religieux vis-à-vis du sort des Wendats et du sort de tous les Amérindiens, est quelque chose qui a laissé des marques profondes dans la conscience et dans l'inconscient des nations amérindiennes. On a voulu leur bien, on a voulu les convertir, mais était-ce toujours vraiment pour des motifs humanitaires ou spirituels ? On peut s'interroger là-dessus. On a dit tout à l'heure que les Amérindiens accueillaient les nouvelles idées religieuses de façon naturelle, puisque tout a sa place autour du Cercle. Cependant, les Amérindiens ont vite et souvent remarqué que, dans bien des cas, c'étaient des motifs matériels qui inspiraient les convertisseurs. Tout comme aujourd'hui, comme on a pu le voir dans le film qui nous a été présenté hier, *La Terre de nos enfants*, on est encore en train de convertir les Cris parce que ce qu'on veut convertir, au fond, c'est le territoire. On veut convertir le territoire en argent. Là est la vraie conversion. Conséquemment, les Amérindiens sont profondément marqués par l'idée d'être convertis, parce qu'on arrive au terme de la conversion du continent américain. On a enlevé les populations amérindiennes : ce qui est arrivé aux Cris nous est arrivé aussi et de façon encore plus radicale et à l'insu de la majorité du monde, mais c'est le même processus qui se perpétue. Ce qui arrive aux Kayapos au centre du Brésil, au moment où l'on se parle, est encore la même chose : c'est le désir de « convertir » ces gens-là, pour les neutraliser, les réduire et prendre tout ce qu'on pourra prendre de cette Amérique matérielle.

Je pense qu'à l'occasion du 500ᵉ anniversaire de l'arrivée des Européens en Amérique, les Amérindiens en général tournent leur regard vers les traditions de leurs ancêtres. Simultanément, ils retrouvent l'idéologie originelle des gens qui s'occupent encore à les convertir ; et je ne parle pas seulement des religieux, mais aussi des développeurs de toutes sortes qui, trop souvent, mais pas toujours, ne sont pas suffisamment dénoncés par les Églises. Cependant, ils se rendent compte que pour que, tous, nous puissions survivre collectivement, ils ont, eux aussi, une mission ; une mission de convertir. Lorsque l'on parle de convertir la pensée et le cœur des humains, des personnes, on se tourne premièrement vers leurs chefs spirituels. Les chefs spirituels, ce sont, évidemment, les gens des Églises, les gens les plus portés à vouloir comprendre les intérêts profonds et réels de l'humanité, des sociétés. Et je suis sûr de véhiculer l'idée d'un grand nombre d'Amérindiens traditionalistes en faisant appel aux représentants des Églises chrétiennes, et des autres, en disant que nous avons besoin des chefs spirituels des Églises autour du Cercle. Notre mission est de « circulariser » les Églises chrétiennes et les autres.

Dans un ouvrage produit il y a deux ans et qui était ma thèse de maîtrise, intitulé *Pour une autohistoire amérindienne*, je parle de l'*américisation* du monde. La plupart des traditionalistes amérindiens ont reçu l'enseignement, de la bouche de leurs Anciens, que cette façon de traiter l'humanité et le milieu naturel ne pourra pas durer toujours et, même, qu'il ne durera pas très longtemps. Cinq siècles, à l'échelle du temps et de la vie, sont très peu de temps. Les Anciens ont dit qu'un jour, assez tôt, nous parviendrions à prendre conscience qu'il faut changer l'idée et la conception spirituelles du monde et se rendre compte de la valeur de l'idéologie fondamentale des Amérindiens, et que cette idée doit représenter le vrai salut, non seulement physique, mais aussi et surtout spirituel de l'humanité. Il s'agit d'un processus initié lors de l'arrivée des Européens en Amérique. Au début, ces gens arrivèrent avec la ferme conviction qu'ils venaient porter la lumière à un continent qui en était privé, un continent où le diable régnait en maître. Seulement 500 ans plus tard, les Amérindiens voient leur conviction confirmée que ces premiers arrivants étaient ceux qui avaient besoin de venir ici pour ajuster la conception spirituelle de leur société en fonction de la réalité naturelle. Encore une fois, je crois interpréter fidèlement le sentiment de mon peuple en faisant un appel aux Églises de venir s'asseoir avec nous autour du Cercle et de délaisser l'idée qu'elles ont de vouloir nous faire rejoindre la Ligne. Nous ne voulons pas rejoindre la Ligne parce que le monde est fait pour être circulaire.

Les Euro-Américains ont traditionnellement invoqué bien des raisons pour déprécier les sociétés autochtones. Parmi celles-ci. Il y a eu l'absence d'une tradition écrite chez beaucoup de ces peuples, et la différence de leur conception du temps. Encore une fois, le temps des sociétés euro-américaines est un temps linéaire, un temps qui se découpe en un passé, un présent et un futur. Tout ce qui est passé est inférieur à ce qui va venir, puisqu'il faut progresser. Mais personne ne sait réellement vers où cet ordre linéaire nous emmène. En revanche, pour les sociétés autochtones, le passé n'existe pas réellement, ni le futur ; il n'y a qu'un présent, un présent continu, dans lequel l'ordre de la vie doit être maintenu. On n'a pas de respect fondamental et immobile pour les hauts faits de grands personnages. On n'a pas le désir d'enregistrer les événements, ni de goût pour les chronologies, ni pour ce type d'histoire. L'histoire, son écriture, ou plutôt sa réécriture, doit être une réflexion morale, une réflexion spirituelle, parce que le temps n'existe pas aussi absolument que chez d'autres sociétés. L'homme n'a le devoir que de reconnaître un ordre parfait et éternel ainsi que d'aider à le maintenir, et tout effort d'enregistrer ou de reconnaître le passé, ou un besoin d'évoluer vers quelque chose d'autre, est un sacrilège pour les Amérindiens. C'est la négation de l'œuvre de Dieu lui-même.

Les Amérindiens ont été intéressés et attirés vers l'Église chrétienne d'une façon spontanée. C'est vrai et ils le sont toujours, parce que l'Église, les Églises, prêchent l'amour. Mais je crois que, jusqu'à présent, les Églises n'ont intégré d'autres intérêts que ceux de la société de laquelle elles viennent. Je suis cependant convaincu que nous sommes à la conjoncture historique où les Églises doivent aussi reconnaître, en leur cœur et leur esprit, le besoin qu'a l'humanité entière de revenir plus près de la Vie, et cesser de seulement prêcher le Cercle, pour enfin le reconnaître et le pratiquer. Il leur faut dorénavant inclure dans leur discours les droits et l'existence des autres êtres, des autres peuples de la Création car, si on est incapable de reconnaître ces autres peuples de la Création, on est privé du réflexe de les protéger ou, en tout cas, on reste indifférent à leur destruction. Beaucoup de peuples amérindiens, peut-être dirais-je la totalité des peuples amérindiens, attendent le moment où les Églises vont avouer leur responsabilité dans leur démantèlement et leur spoliation matérielle. Je pense qu'à partir du moment où il y aura une reconnaissance d'une conduite qui jadis fut dommageable à tous ces peuples et à l'humanité, et qui fut donc cause d'une perte profonde d'un capital spirituel de l'humanité, nous pourrons commencer à parler d'une rencontre entre les autochtones et les allochtones.

On parle actuellement beaucoup de rencontre à l'occasion de ces dates, 1492-1992, sans se rendre suffisamment à l'évidence que l'on a introduit quelqu'un de force sur le terrain de l'autre, qu'on a converti cet autre par tous les moyens possibles, qu'on lui a fait ainsi admettre qu'il était inférieur ; on voudrait maintenant que cette personne, cette collectivité, parle de la même façon que soi de rencontre, ou admette qu'il s'est agi d'une rencontre. En réalité, la rencontre n'a pas encore eu lieu. Je pense bien que 1992 sera le moment et l'occasion d'une vraie rencontre. L'exercice que nous sommes collectivement en train de faire, ici, ce matin, me donne encore davantage la conviction que les gens sont maintenant prêts à faire cette rencontre. Car si les Églises viennent à la rencontre des Amérindiens, tel que je sens qu'elles le font ce matin, je suis assuré que la société elle-même va suivre ses chefs spirituels et venir à la rencontre des peuples amérindiens, et non plus simplement arriver ici et nier ce qui existe. Il s'agit de rencontrer avec le cœur et l'esprit ce qui existe déjà ici. Comme le disait hier une dame du Mexique : « L'Esprit de ce continent a fonctionné très longtemps avant que les Européens n'arrivent ici ».

Revenant à notre propos de conversion, j'ai parlé d'une mission que l'Amérindien conçoit pour lui-même auprès des autres peuples. Il faut cependant parler ici d'un trait de la philosophie amérindienne distinctif entre tous. Il s'agit du respect sacré et inviolable du point de vue de toute personne ainsi que de la liberté de chacun d'agir en accord avec celui-ci. Ce respect de la liberté individuelle, élément essentiel de la démocratie elle-même, avait existé en Europe, mais à l'état d'utopie. Chez les Grecs, réputés avoir inventé la démocratie, le respect de la liberté individuelle était fonction de l'existence de classes d'esclaves. Ici, en Amérique, la liberté individuelle n'était pas une utopie. Les premiers observateurs européens ont invariablement remarqué l'absence de classes parmi la vaste majorité des sociétés autochtones. Chaque individu était vu naturellement comme la volonté d'un Grand Esprit et d'un monde spirituel insondable pour l'humain. Les gens étaient laissés libres dans leur individualité et intègres dans leur humanité. Beaucoup de gens sont donc venus ici à cause de leur soif de respect pour leur propre personne, de même que pour leur famille et leur collectivité. Ils sont venus se transplanter en Amérique parce qu'existait ce respect de façon réelle et effective, et non seulement à l'état d'utopie ou dans des livres. Ces Européens virent des gens pratiquer ce respect entre eux. Je parle de la presque totalité des peuples autochtones. Il y eut, bien sûr, des sociétés hiérarchiques, mais celles-ci étaient, à un degré considérable, des sociétés également circulaires. Je parle évidemment des Incas, des Mayas, des Aztèques et d'autres qui, un jour, que j'espère prochain, écriront leur propre histoire.

Je pense qu'on peut dire que ce pouvoir convertisseur qu'a l'Amérique, est un pouvoir qui prend origine dans la reconnaissance du droit à la liberté de chaque individu, de chaque être. Lorsqu'on parle de ce type de respect, on parle en même temps d'amour et, si on parle d'amour, on se comprend tous, parce que les messages des Églises sont des messages d'amour. Et si nous nous rejoignons autour de l'idée que nous voulons tous et recherchons tous la même chose et si nous sommes arrivés, après 500 ans, au point de nous écouter mutuellement dire ce que cette chose représente dans nos esprits respectifs, je pense que nous ne sommes pas loin de nous comprendre d'une façon très profonde.

Nous allons, en terminant, faire référence au film visionné hier, *La Terre de nos enfants*, qui fut une bonne illustration de ce que nous ressentons tous. Nous y avons vu des gens à l'œuvre pour convertir la baie James en argent et en pouvoir, non pas pour nous, mais pour certains individus, ou certaines classes d'individus. Et il faut résister, il faut résister à cela, parce que l'homme est très petit pour avoir la prétention de changer, de convertir à ce point son environnement, de le détruire ; nous sommes en train de détruire notre lieu naturel, notre habitat. L'Église doit aussi inclure dans son discours, et dans son rapport d'amour avec la vie, l'amour pour la Création. Car on sait qu'à la base, les sociétés amérindiennes célèbrent la vie, célèbrent la joie, célèbrent la beauté de la vie.

Ce que l'on voit aujourd'hui dans les sociétés industrielles c'est le mépris, le mépris pour la vie, pour la beauté de la vie. Et qu'en enseignant ainsi à mépriser la vie, à mépriser la foi, pour ensuite attendre dans un autre monde pour avoir accès à une foi ou à des beautés, nous avons contribué à mépriser et à détruire l'environnement. Il faut apprendre à aimer profondément la maison, la Mère que le Grand Esprit nous a donnée, qui est la Terre. À partir du jour où on l'aimera et célébrera sa beauté, nous aurons réellement changé d'esprit et pourrons réellement constituer un Cercle tous ensemble.

Merci de m'avoir écouté.

Lettre au premier ministre de l'Inde[*]

Wendake, Canada, 12 octobre 1992[1]

Très cher et honoré Président,

Permettez-moi d'abord de vous saluer au nom de la nation la plus récemment reconnue de la terre (bien que possiblement l'une des plus anciennes), la nation indienne d'Amérique, dont je suis le premier Chef Suprême.

---

[*] Conférence prononcée à Montréal en septembre 1991, lors du Congrès d'Entraide missionnaire, Actes du Congrès, p. 9-15.

[1] Texte écrit par Georges E. Sioui en avril 1979, en prévision du cinquième centenaire de l'arrivée européenne en Amérique. Texte paru dans la revue littéraire *Liberté*, vol. 33, n°s 4-5, octobre 1991, p. 158-162 (Montréal, Québec). Ce texte a aussi paru en anglais dans le livre *Dear Christopher. Letters to Christopher by Contemporary Native Americans*, sous la direction de Darryl Wilson et Barry Joyce, Native American Studies, University of California (Riverside), 1992. Fait intéressant, ce texte arriva éventuellement dans les mains du premier ministre de l'Inde par l'entremise d'amis indiens en contact avec le premier ministre de leur pays d'origine. L'intérêt littéraire du texte fut remarqué dans l'entourage du premier ministre. Archives de l'auteur.

L'an dernier, avant la déclaration officielle de l'Assemblée mondiale des Nations reconnaissant notre nation, j'avais proposé à notre Conseil national, dont j'étais le vice-président, que notre première démarche diplomatique officielle vous soit adressée. Le Conseil national avait alors accueilli avec empressement ma proposition.

Le Conseil et moi-même savons pertinemment que cette démarche diplomatique paraîtra étrange à votre Excellence, mais je dirai dès à présent qu'elle n'est en aucune façon plus étrange que le sort fait à notre nation, lequel sort est d'ailleurs à l'origine de notre requête.

Il y a 500 ans aujourd'hui, un accident est survenu qui presque aussitôt changea le cours de l'histoire ainsi que la représentation du monde dans son ensemble : un marin européen, Christophe Colomb, se trouva perdu sur les côtes de notre continent.

Cet accident, ainsi que le voulut le Créateur et le Maître de toutes choses, fut une bénédiction pour les autres peuples du monde, mais signifia la ruine et le désastre complet pour nos nations ancestrales.

Je ne pense pas devoir vous instruire, bien cher Président, de l'état naturel et social harmonieux dans lequel vivaient les premiers peuples d'Amérique. Je ne dirai sur ce point que ce que Christophe Colomb lui-même a dit : il était arrivé au Paradis terrestre… qu'il confondit avec les Indes. Étrangement, l'idée ne lui est jamais venue, pas plus qu'à aucun de ses innombrables successeurs, que le pays qu'il cherchait, aussi plein de richesses qu'il pût être imaginé, était pauvre en réalité si on le comparait avec la terre qu'il venait de « découvrir ».

Pour en venir au sujet de la présente adresse, je dirai que les Espagnols et les autres Européens, qui entreprirent de s'approprier notre continent et de sauver nos âmes au nom de « nous savons quoi » et avec des effets que nous subissons toujours, nommèrent notre terre « les Indes » et, pour le reste du monde, ses habitants s'appelèrent « Indiens ».

C'est avec le respect le plus sincère que nous utilisons ce nom, que nous partageons avec votre peuple, en sachant bien que votre pays a mis du temps à connaître l'histoire et à se rendre compte de l'affliction de nos peuples, bien qu'il n'en fût jamais la cause. De plus, nous espérons et nous croyons fermement que notre nation n'a jamais outragé la dignité, le sens de la beauté et la volonté de paix que le nom des Indiens orientaux est venu à symboliser ; pour ces vertus et ces qualités, l'admiration de notre peuple vous est acquise pour toujours.

Permettez-moi encore, cher Président, quelques remarques et explications avant de vous dévoiler la nature de notre requête, que votre peuple voudra peut-être regarder favorablement.

Notre nation, pendant 500 années, a vécu et vit toujours un dilemme profondément démoralisateur qui l'affaiblit : celui d'exister sans avoir un nom. Pour illustrer la gravité de ce fait, disons seulement qu'en affublant notre nation d'un nom historiquement incorrect, les envahisseurs suggéraient que, physiquement ou culturellement, où que ce soit sur le continent, nous n'avions pas le droit d'exister. Nous étions des Indiens ; par conséquent, nous étions sans droits, nulle part chez nous.

Bien que nous nous réjouissons du fait que l'Assemblée mondiale des Nations ait adopté certaines mesures pour assurer notre protection, nous sommes toujours, cher frère Président, après cinq siècles d'exposition à toutes sortes d'agressions, un peuple sans nom. Il faut de la compassion pour comprendre le malheur d'un peuple entièrement uni par son histoire, ses valeurs et ses aspirations, mais ne possédant pas un nom pour se définir et se désigner. On peut être sûr qu'au cours de l'histoire, chaque Indien a ressenti ce vide et a tenté d'imaginer un nom, un meilleur nom mais aucun de nous n'a pu inventer ou découvrir un nom capable vraiment de signifier notre nation.

Cher frère, le seul nom qui, après tout ce temps, soit devenu naturel à nos esprits et à nos oreilles, c'est le nom *Indien*, et c'est pourquoi ce mot, mis à part les noms de nos proches et de nos tribus, est pour nous le son le plus doux qui soit. Il est probable que jamais un mot n'a mieux défini un peuple que celui-là. Il n'est pas un seul de nos contemporains qui, entendant le mot « Indien », ne pense d'abord à notre peuple et à quelques-uns des nombreux préjugés que ce nom évoque (en exceptant, bien sûr, vos respectés compatriotes qui sont venus habiter notre pays).

Frère, nous affirmons très respectueusement qu'avec le temps, ici en Amérique, le nom « Indien » est désormais plus généralement associé à notre peuple qu'il ne l'est au vôtre. La preuve en est que, pour désigner vos gens, on doit adjoindre au mot « Indien » l'épithète « oriental », ou encore préciser « qui vient des Indes ». De plus, nous sommes certains qu'à l'intérieur du vaste continent asiatique, il serait plus juste de désigner votre peuple par un nom appartenant à l'une des principales langues de votre pays et par lequel vous devriez, en toute logique, être mondialement connus.

Cher frère Président, l'essentiel de notre demande est que votre pays fasse le don officiel du nom « Indien » à notre nation récemment reconnue mais encore dépourvue de nom. Grâce à votre cadeau, ce nom, que nous aimons et désirons, serait nôtre en souvenir du dur destin qu'a connu notre peuple durant cinq siècles ; il rappellerait aussi les valeurs morales essentielles au nom desquelles nous avons inconditionnellement résisté à l'assimilation. Cette reconnaissance, venant tout particulièrement de votre pays, laisserait une marque qui serait de très bon augure pour la jeune nation indienne d'Amérique ; de plus, elle scellerait de manière officielle une alliance morale tacite déjà ancienne entre nos deux nations.

Si cette alliance très spéciale se concrétisait, nous voudrions, à notre tour, vous obliger de la façon suivante : la nation indienne d'Amérique établira des relations économiques et politiques privilégiées avec votre pays en vous offrant un libre accès au marché américain, ce qui vous a été refusé jusqu'ici. L'Inde et ses partenaires commerciaux du tiers-monde seraient les premiers clients des biens que nous commercialiserons ; vous seriez libres d'établir des quartiers diplomatiques dans nos villes et nos territoires ; la nation indienne d'Amérique s'opposera à toute manifestation raciste ou injuste que rapporteraient à leur attention les membres de votre Alliance ; la nation indienne d'Amérique assurera en toutes circonstances le soutien matériel et moral aux membres de votre Alliance, à condition qu'ils ne soient pas engagés dans des actions militaires offensives.

Tel que je l'ai suggéré au début de la présente lettre, notre démarche, tout étrange qu'elle puisse paraître, s'inscrit dans un processus de réparation d'un geste (la spoliation des droits autochtones) qui, dans son contexte d'origine, apparaît infiniment plus étrange que celui que nous proposons. Cela dit, frère Président, dois-je ajouter que notre Conseil, notre Sénat et moi-même sommes anxieux de connaître votre réponse ?

Enfin, je vous prie, cher Président, de transmettre nos salutations fraternelles aux membres de votre gouvernement et aux peuples de l'Inde quand vous leur soumettrez la présente demande. Quelle que soit leur décision, dites-leur, s'il vous plaît, que nous attendons l'occasion d'aller visiter les gens de ce pays que nous avons voulu voir depuis longtemps et que nous verrons bientôt.

Puisse le Grand Pouvoir de l'Univers vous bénir ainsi que votre peuple.

Le Chef Suprême de la nation indienne d'Amérique, en ce 12 octobre 1992.

1992: THE DISCOVERY OF AMERICITY*

Rewriting Amerindian History

Late Pueblo historian Dr. Alfonso Ortiz thus summarizes Amerindian opinion about conventional non-Native history of Amerindians:

> ... historical documents enshrine the worst images ever visited on Indian peoples. In this sense, our written history has been the handmaiden of conquest and assimilation. Conventional history is so at odds with the facts that Indians often simply ignore it. Ironically, many tribes regard history as more acceptable to them than ethnography because they believe history has nothing to do with what they consider important to their identity as Indians. That is to say, they do not fear or worry about

---

* Written for the book *Indigena: Contemporary Native Perspectives*, edited by Gerald McMaster and Lee-Ann Martin and published separately in French and English by the Canadian Museum of Civilization on the occasion of the quincentennial year of the arrival of Europeans in America.

historians because history does not usually deal with what they really value about their native cultures: their languages, religions, oral traditions, arts and kin networks. History is so distorted it is irrelevant.[1]

The best example of bad conventional historiography about Amerindians I can think of is that of the Wendat (Huron) and the Hodenosaunee (Iroquois). Due to the centrality of this whole episode in the development of a new world geopolitical scenario based in northeastern North America, the destruction of this important Amerindian civilization by Europeans has strong ramifications even on a hemispheric scale. The dispersal of the 'good Huron' by the 'bad Iroquois' and the crowning by martyrdom of the French Black Robes' heroically generous efforts to impart their true faith to hordes of brutish, vengeful savages (among whom the Iroquois stand as champions), provided the basic discursive elements that Canada's first historians (essentially French and Catholic) used to produce Canada's history. The effects that the work of these otherwise well-intentioned fathers of Canadian social thought had on the minds of numerous generations, are still only too easily felt and witnessed throughout the land.

While the indifference of Native people to conventional history seems wholly justified, the task of questioning and reinterpreting accredited colonial documentary sources from a Native viewpoint will always stand to be addressed, for such 'sources' continue to exist as the ultimate fortress of Euro-American discourse on Amerindians. However, the bastion is not as impregnable as it is thought to be. Anyone familiar with the practice of historiography knows that new trends in sociological and ecological thinking, along with new developments in anthropology (such as the ethnohistoric method) and new attitudes and methods in archaeology, allow the student to use conventional non-Native historical sources in such ways as to often reverse the sense of formerly unquestioned, quintessential 'evidence'.

My experience in dealing with the stereotypes of conventional Wendat-Hodenosaunee[2] historiography has resulted in the elaboration of a new

---

1 Dr. Alfonso Ortiz, in the introduction to *Indians in American History*, edited by Frederick E. Hoxie (Chicago : Harlan Davidson, 1988).

2 The Wendat (People of the Island) and the Hodenosaunee (People of the Longhouse) were close ethnic kin.

methodology which I have called *Amerindian autohistory*.³ Its aim is to demonstrate, by showing convergence with non-Native documents, the 'scientific' validity of Native historical sources (written, oral, pictographic, mnemonic, aesthetic, etc.) as testimonies of Native perceptions of themselves and their world. Practically, the method extracts from the conventional documents undisputed testimonies of early non-Native observers about Native people's philosophy, self-vision and typical behaviour. It establishes intrinsic, enduring similarities with the subsequent and current self-perception of Native people, as evinced in the whole range of their conceptual, philosophical, artistic and sacred expressions. Besides conferring 'scientificity' to oral and other Native traditions, the method of *Amerindian autohistory* (which, incidentally, is not thought impracticable by non-Natives) tends to give substance to the often misunderstood notion of the universality of Native American essential values, as it is an exercise in distinguishing what are and what are not essential, persisting ideological traits of the original Native American thought system.

The very premise of the existence of such a thing as a universal Native American philosophical system breaks the image of the Amerindian that puts in doubt his very mental and spiritual adequacy as a human, and replaces it with one of a thus far unconsidered, wealthy contributor to the solving of a worldwide, ideological bankruptcy. The 'Indian' can thus cease to exist as a problem and begin being known as an important part of a solution.

Coming now to what is customarily termed the cornerstone of non-Native Canadian historiography, that is, the 'destruction of the Hurons by the Iroquois', descriptions by early Europeans (essentially French Jesuits) show the people of these two confederacies living by exactly the same social and spiritual ideals. They acknowledged the perfection of an all-powerful Creation, the interdependence of all beings, the inherent vulnerability of man and his essential duty to share with others whatever wealth he is fortunate enough to obtain. Historical records are eloquent about the astonishing capacity of

---

3 Georges E. Sioui, *Pour une autohistoire amérindienne* (Presses de l'Université Laval, 1989). (English translation published at McGill-Queen's University Press in 1992 : *For an Amerindian Autohistory.*)

these two peoples to create peace between themselves in spite of constant, systematic and sometimes concerted efforts of theoretically rival European powers. Archaeology shows no conclusive proofs of the existence of seriously destructive or prolonged prehistoric conflicts between them. In fact, the early historical record, as well as oral tradition and archaeology itself, all amply indicate that the so-called wars that many Wendat-Iroquoian (or *Nadowek*[4] as they were called by their Algonkian neighbours) people waged on one another were mere 'mourning wars'. These were normally organized—or countered—by Councils of Ancients Councils of Clanmothers to effect the capture of a few enemies destined either to replace some male or female member of the family, clan, nation or confederacy lost through war or some other cause, or to die by torture and fire, if the offence suffered by the people concerned demanded such satisfaction. It should be noted that such executions were performed in a communal way[5] with astonishing restraint, rationality and even humanity, as a necessary act, and that the captives lived out their ordeal until death with the most exemplary calmness and fortitude. Such 'wars' carried no notion of a need to exterminate other human entities for profit and consequently should not be put (as they commonly are) on a cultural par with what Europeans, Euro-Americans and others meant and still mean by war.

A central fact in the social ethics of Western civilization is that war is almost the only way to win something. This cultural trait is necessarily and universally projected upon the 'conquered' peoples, thus justifying the global war process on which that civilization thrives. This same logic was applied to the historiography of the Hodenosaunee. However, historical documents and the Iroquois oral traditions, as well as the memory stored and kept in wampums, masks, condolence canes and other sacred word-enshrining objects, all speak profusely and eloquently about the Hodenosaunee's social and spiritual vision. Written

---

4 Nadowek is the collective name by which many nations of Wendat and Iroquoian stock were designated by their Algonkian neighbours. The word 'Nadowek' is proposed as a substitute for the term 'Iroquoian' in Georges Sioui's PhD dissertation, *La civilisation wendate* (now the book *Huron-Wendat : The Heritage of the Circle*, UBC Press, 1999).

5 Compare this with the European practice of torturing and executing people of one's own community or nation, with the aim of terrorizing and subduing the dominated classes.

and oral sources, especially the Hodenosaunee's own, show that this Aboriginal confederacy had done an imposing amount of practical thinking on how peace could be possessed and extended to the rest of the universe.

During the first decade after contact, the destruction by epidemic diseases of the great majority of the original human population of the American hemisphere, though so thoroughly documented in the primary sources, was hardly mentioned by the first historiographers who took on the task of producing the histories of the newly formed New World states. Instead, it was deemed quite convenient to place the blame for the human destruction on certain Native nations or groups of nations. The Iroquois were granted the privilege of that role. From being a group of Aboriginal nations that, as archaeology has begun to verify, had, by the time the first Europeans landed in America, achieved a high degree of political stability inside and around their own world, the Hodenosaunee passed to being, in the accounts of the invaders, an essentially irrational set of human beings, intent on destroying anyone they came near, an utter mistake of the Creator that could only be amended through extirpation. During almost the whole seventeenth century, France conceived a central part of its moral and political duty in New France to be precisely this: the extermination of the Iroquois.

What were the original Hodenosaunee in the geopolitical reality? In the Amerindian world in the northeast, their geopolitical situation was marginal. At the moment of contact, the Five Iroquois Nations appeared to be dissenting from the general trading system in use among the vast majority of Native nations with which they were in contact. That system—at the centre of which were the Wendat, whose language was universally used in trade and diplomacy—included virtually all the other Algonkian and Nadowek nations of the vast region of the northeast, actually surrounding the Hodenosaunee on all sides.

Why did the Iroquois appear dissenting at that moment? My conjecture is that some political stress, probably related to the appearance of the deadly Old World diseases, came at a very early moment after contact (Henry F. Dobyns has surmised around 1524), and upset the existing balance of forces. At any rate, no explanation given so far has proven satisfactory in terms of all the existing evidence. Although old racist and deterministic theories have now been discredited, none of the newer ones has been able to offset the stereotype of the 'imperial Iroquois'. Francis Jennings, in his landmark book *The Ambiguous Iroquois Empire*, while efficiently denouncing the myth of an Iroquois empire in the 17th and 18th centuries, does not basically alter the negative image affecting the Iroquois. They are still easily imagined as hailing the arrival of the white man on the political scene of the northeast as a means of procuring the wherewithal to bring down their enemies and establish themselves at the centre of a thus-emptied Amerindian world and of a new colonial political game where they would wield lots of power.

The pathetic reality is that because they were not in the Wendat country—or Wendake—the Hodenosaunee, though also very severely affected by the European epidemics, did not have to face the white enemy directly. This meant that the Hodenosaunee was not compelled to abide by all the conditions of trade imposed on the Wendat-Algonkian alliance, the direst of which was the religious condition, which imposed the presence of several missionaries in each of the principal Wendat towns. Obviously, the Black Robes, besides being prime spiritual and social destabilizers, were real though unwitting biological warmongers. Under the cataclysmic circumstances that, according to the Jesuit Relations, then prevailed throughout the Amerindian country, the Hodenosaunee acted out the role that they knew was theirs—they gathered, *manu militari*, the remnants of rapidly disappearing Native nations around them. According to Wendat-Hodenosaunee social practice, defeated peoples were formally adopted and made room for as equals and, indeed, relatives. The Iroquois are, in fact, descendants of an amalgam of refugees and adoptees from several dozens of Native nations. Their heritage even includes white adoptees who, as a rule, elected to remain Iroquois when offered the opportunity to return to their own people, a fact that demonstrates the more humane nature of Amerindian concepts of race and identity compared to Euro-American ones.

By combining the Hodenosaunee's perception of their own particular social ethics with the widest possible range of historical evidence, the autohistorical method makes the Hodenosaunee appear not as a race of senseless butchers lusting after European trade goods and power, but rather as people desperately trying to find an alternative to the French, Dutch and English 'Indian policies' that were reducing and engulfing the Amerindians. This is no slight conceptual turnabout. It presents the possibility of untangling one of the most masterful historiographical manipulations effected by the original historians of the invading Europeans.

This rereading of Wendat-Hodenosaunee history of contact offers hope for a cure for the old 'Iroquois-destroyed-Huron' paradigm, which has been an important part of the moral and spiritual burden felt and carried by all Amerindians in relation to their history. Once again, Alfonso Ortiz gives his perception of this as an Amerindian and a professional historian:

> To be concrete: in the many histories written of Indian-White relations in the Eastern Woodlands, I have rarely read about Indians who are believable as Indians or even, sometimes, as human beings. They are not presented as fully sentient and multidimensional beings.[6] By contrast, their white counterparts are usually fully fleshed out, and one can understand their values, their motivations and their self-interests. I mention the Eastern Woodlands because they represent the arena of longest encounters between Indians and whites in the English-speaking 'New World'. Hence, if we cannot present plausible Indian actors there, where can we?[7]

The Missing Dimension of History about Amerindians: Morality

The writing of Amerindian history is too inseparable from the process of invasion and destruction to be denied a fundamental moral dimension. History, in the case of Amerindians, has a responsibility to go beyond its normal exercise of recreating and interpreting the past. 'Good' (apologetic) Amerindian history, as it is now fashionable to write, too seldom enriches our understanding of the

---

6 Bruce G. Trigger has keenly perceived this and has done much, in his works on the Wendat and their Eastern Woodlands neighbours, to correct the mutual and self-perceptions of peoples of both cultures.

7 Ortiz, 10.

profound spiritual vision of America conveyed by its Native thought systems. In reality, the America we live in draws an irresistible spiritual strength from this source.

But this white America, still little more than an old Europe, was cured, through its contact with red America, of its social, biological, spiritual and other infections. The cure was supposed to preserve the European philosophical heritage and launch it on a genial, glorious adventure that was to last at least five millennia or so. How is it, then, that only five centuries later the glorious age of 'Americanism' seems to be near its end? Five centuries instead of five millennia. What has happened?

Once theories of white superiority were consolidated, the vastness and wealth of the continent allowed the believers in that civilization to forget about the socio-ecological consequences of a new Euro-American way of life. In five centuries, the limit of America's material strength, thought without possible limits not so long ago, has been reached. America itself is now sick from diseases shamefully similar to the ones that the first Euro-Americans had fled by coming here. New epidemic diseases defy conventional medicine; economic oppression of the poor whose ranks are inexorably growing is an apparently insoluble problem; the natural world is threatened with extinction because of the aggressive political and financial interests of leading elites; justice systems are subject to the dictatorship of organized crime: there are many negative points of similarity between Euroamerica and ancient, 'pre-American' Europe.

If, however, the pain is felt at the physical level, the remedy has to be searched for at the spiritual level. While material America may well have been sacked, plundered, robbed and in every way abused, the America of the spirit remains very little known and explored. As our world stands on the eve of this second half-millennium of the post-Columbian era, I firmly believe that it is on the verge of making the real Discovery of America. The next five centuries will see the resurrection of red America and the consequent enactment of the integral spiritual universalization of our world.

In order to find its cure, America needs to deeply rethink its vision of its history. The most difficult problem now is to determine exactly what the world has lost through the invasion and the destruction of America. Society must salvage and resuscitate what it can of the essential nature and the spiritual meaning of this 'new world'.

New trends and developments in the historical discipline surely have the merit of helping living Amerindian peoples recover a sense of their worth and the reason for their existence. However, history still rarely carries the moral dimension on which we are reflecting, and which is necessary to create the state of consciousness and the sense of responsibility that history must breed in the individual. In fact, 'good' Amerindian history does not necessarily de-marginalize the Native nations that exist today, in the sense of doing away with the stereotypes that present them as picturesque, vanishing peoples (thereby underlining the greatness of white America). A moral dimension allows one to go a few steps further: beyond attempting to prove that Amerindians were not, at first, any more bloodthirsty, cruel or socially repugnant than other peoples, such a complementary dimension authorizes one to argue that the Aboriginal Amerindian society inspired and produced the metamorphosis of a decadent, feudal European society into a so-called 'American' society, infinitely more humane and alive, from which the rest of humanity has drawn physical, intellectual and spiritual sustenance, as from a nurturing mother. Further, the moral dimension urges one to pay attention to the philosophical and spiritual contents of documents that deal with Aboriginal peoples' history, as well as to devise techniques of ethnographic investigation that will define and identify remedies to apply to the spiritual ills of the so-called dominant society, thereby regenerating the latter's capacity for producing conscious and responsible individuals and for better fulfilling its nurturing, harmonizing role in relation to the rest of humanity.

1992: The Discovery of Americity

> As we consider the Columbus voyages of 500 years ago, we have a challenge and an opportunity in the decades ahead to explore, gather and bring forth real Indian history, some views from the other side of the white man's frontier.... If we do not do more to tell the Indian people's

stories as they would tell them, the task will remain—and grow more difficult—for future generations. In addition, we need to assess the impact the New World has had on the Old over 500 years of continuous contact. We need to go beyond books like Alfred Crosby's *The Columbian Exchange* and focus our attention instead on the many ways America has affected Europe and the rest of the world. That exploration should examine in particular the nonmaterial realms of exchange, as they are not well known.[8]

It is very well known, nowadays, that Europeans landed in the Indies, on October 12, 1492, but it is not yet known what was discovered. There is a need to give a name, an explanation, a universal mental locus to the signification of America since 1492—I mean *the ideological unification of the world*—or else this very important phenomenon is relegated to the realm of chance. Europeans, at first, called it their discovery of a new world; in the nineteenth century the people of the United States called it Manifest Destiny; I suggest we could realistically call it The Americization of the World.

On October 12, 1992, it was 500 years since the 'New World' had its decisive and definitive contact with the Old. Rather than admitting that they had found, by pure chance, a continent fully explored and occupied by other peoples who had elaborated remarkable civilizations in the north as well as in the south, the first European immigrants chose to convince themselves that they had discovered a new world, justifying in this way the singularly aggressive and destructive invasion to which they proceeded from the very first moments of their presence on this Amerindian soil.

Today, the word 'meeting' is used to refer to this event. In order to talk about a 'meeting', there would have had to be mutual recognition and respect. However, it is a fact of universal notoriety that such has not been the case with the Europeans' accidental coming to America: as a rule, what are commonly termed cultural exchanges and borrowings between Euro-Americans and

---

8 Ortiz, 16.

Amerindians have been but the product of chance and, in a general way, of brutal force. One crucial and obvious fact remains: five centuries after contact, the 'meeting' has yet to take place.

My approach does not seek to point out the responsibility of particular actors for the way history has unfolded. On the contrary, I maintain that history is the course that life dictates to itself, and that people universally come under the empire of its forces. I am simply saying three things: first, that an authentic meeting between the heirs of the two worlds whose destinies were united long ago on American soil still has not occurred; secondly, that this absence of mutual acknowledgement is the reason that numerous American peoples suffocate—some even die out every passing year—under the weight and through the effect of blind, insensible systems maintained against them; and finally, that 1992, the year that introduced the second half of the first millennium of universalized America, manifestly appears as the moment when those who have the conscience and the power to do it must cause that meeting to take place, at last.

Americity

Like every other continent, America has ways of being and seeing that make it ideologically autonomous and unique. Because of its isolated geographical situation, America can even pretend to possess a world view surpassing in originality that of all other continents. As to the value represented by this properly American philosophy for the rest of mankind, no ampler proof of it is necessary than the irresistible appeal, indeed the fascination, that the American continent has had for countless people of all regions of the world since 1492. The myth of the Noble Redman (*le bon sauvage*), despite the continuous misadventures of this imaginary character, has existed from the very moment Europeans set eyes on the 'New World' and observed its aboriginal inhabitants. For all of mankind, America has always evoked beauty, abundance, happiness, freedom and peace.

What social ethics underlie this unique character of America? The notion of men's freedom to arbitrarily divide the land into 'fatherlands' was absent in Aboriginal America. 'Religions', likewise, were absent. Rather, all peoples acknowledged the physical and spiritual reality of the Earth, Mother of all and therefore indivisible. The sacred was omnipresent and sovereign: one could say that America was but one great theocracy where all categories of beings possessed and exercised certain forms of rights. The Amerindians felt and lived an integral democracy, including not only human beings (or certain categories of them), but all beings of all orders. Unfortunately, today the American peoples deprived of the material and spiritual benefits of their fundamental ideology are the ones having the strongest biological and psychological ties with this continent—that is to say, the numerically important Métis populations of North and South America (Euro-Amerindian, Afro-Amerindian, Asian Amerindian, and their hybrids), the Inuit and the Amerindians. Drawing with unrestrained freedom from the incredible material wealth of this new continent, the countries that have formed in it, mostly the United States to the north, very rapidly came to symbolize for the rest of the world the ultimate model of successful ideology and of material well-being. Standing on their belief in the inexhaustibility of Nature's wealth and thus in their own greatness, these so-called developed states have had little difficulty in imposing, on a world scale, the political and social way of Americanism. This offers an illusion of material progress, benefiting certain select groups of their society while at the same time concealing the social destitution of the majorities. It cannot be dissociated from the misery of the other orders of life more commonly called 'the environment'.

Americanism is the materialistic, shallow philosophy that the Euro-American, deprived of access to an intimate, spiritual comprehension of his or her continent of adoption, has invented and with which he has upheld an image of prestige, protective power, indeed of magnanimous generosity. From this viewpoint, Americanism appears as the false ideology that has, until now, usurped the true spiritual visage of America, that is, Americity.

Americity, then, implies and defines the character of spirituality and thus a social idea that is America's own. It is the consciousness of a power as well as a duty belonging to this continent—to define and to offer to the rest of the human and cosmic family a vision of life and the universe that can transform our human world into a truly unified, universalized society. Essentially,

Americity signifies the formulation, for the benefit of the beings of all orders, of the reasons for and, especially, the ways of adopting the circular vision so characteristic of America. This circular vision has allowed America to be a haven of tolerance and hope for many human beings.

While it is true that the lessons of the past must eternally live in our hearts, minds and spirits (for, as many have said, a people without a past is a people without a future), we have had to approach 1992 facing the times ahead. We have to truly understand the spirit of this land and its original peoples. America is not a place for racial or ideological purity. Rather, America is forever destined to be the place of fusion of all superficial, imaginary differences, where the true beauty of a common human nature is revealed and where, therefore, respect, the first condition for attaining peace, can cease to be a subject for discourse and become reality for each and every living being. Let us have hope that the next century will bring winds of change that will see America's first peoples begin to enact in earnest with their arts, their words and their teachings, the vision of balance and beauty that they have preserved against all odds and expectations for half a millennium for this time when it is truly needed and searched for. Long live our America, long live its Peoples and long live our Earth!

La signification interculturelle de l'américité[*]

Je remercie le Congrès de l'ACFAS pour me donner cette chance d'exposer et de partager les idées incluses dans le titre de mon exposé d'aujourd'hui. Je remercie tout spécialement madame Nadia Khouri, qui non seulement a désiré et permis que je sois ici, avec mon épouse Barbara et mon fils Miguel, mais nous a fraternellement fait profiter de son extrême cordialité.

Les idées dont je viens vous parler, bien que familières à ceux qui connaissent la tradition de mon peuple, me paraissent presque trop étranges pour être exposées dans le cadre d'un colloque si officiellement scientifique. Pourtant, mon sens d'une responsabilité que nous avons tous d'apporter ce que nous pouvons, individuellement, pour tâcher d'augmenter nos chances collectives de bonheur et de paix grâce à une meilleure communication, fait que je désire tout mettre

---

[*] Témoignage prononcé dans le cadre du Congrès de l'ACFAS, 21-22 mai 1991 ; 1992, ACFAS, p. 209-213.

en œuvre en moi-même pour vous révéler dans leur simplicité ces principes essentiels de la pensée amérindienne.

Les Anciens de nos sociétés amérindiennes ont enseigné que la vie est un grand Cercle de Relations entre les êtres de toutes les espèces, matérielles et immatérielles, un Cercle éternel mû par la volonté d'un Grand Pouvoir, infiniment sage et bon, puisque la Vie triomphe toujours.

Le grand Cercle comprend toujours quatre éléments : quatre directions, quatre saisons, quatre âges de la vie, quatre familles de peuples, les Blancs, les Noirs, les Jaunes et les Rouges, mais tous unis dans le Cercle et censés ne faire qu'une grande Famille humaine.

Nos ancêtres amérindiens nous ont aussi enseigné que l'être humain, pour comprendre et réussir sa vie, devait être amené à « voir », de façon individuelle et sacrée, la réalité du Cercle. Voilà pourquoi le jeune homme et, si elle le veut, la jeune fille, doit s'isoler, jeûner, se mettre à l'épreuve de quelque façon, afin de recevoir une vision, c'est-à-dire tâcher de comprendre le sens profond et sacré de sa vie personnelle à l'intérieur de la Vie, de la Création. Une telle vision est censée faire accéder la jeune personne à un nouvel ordre de conscience en lui révélant l'Unité de la Vie et, donc, la Parenté de tous les êtres qui la constituent.

Cette philosophie amérindienne vient essentiellement de la notion que le Pouvoir de la Création s'exprime de façon unique et irreproductible dans chaque être, humain ou non humain. Jamais il n'y eut et jamais il n'y aura deux êtres avec la même vision de la Vie et de la réalité. Et, pourtant, toutes les visions sont des découvertes de l'unité de la Vie et de la parenté qui unit toutes les formes de vie. De ceci vient l'idée, si propre aux Amérindiens, du caractère unique de l'individu, qui le consacre dans une essentielle et inviolable liberté. Voilà le trait idéologique le plus essentiel à l'Amérique : *le respect de la vision de l'autre*, qui est, au-delà de son existence physique et charnelle, l'expression de la volonté d'un monde supérieur « habité » de forces surnaturelles, ou d'« esprits ». L'*américité* est cette vision acquise au contact des peuples aborigènes de l'Amérique, du grand Cercle sacré des Relations de Parenté reliant *tous* les êtres. L'américité est l'enseignement de nos ancêtres amérindiens, intégré peu à peu par les nouveaux enfants de l'Amérique. L'américité est plus qu'une religion rappelant momentanément l'existence du Cercle et le comportement humain qui devrait s'y rattacher : elle est un autre type de conscience, une vision de tous les instants, une religion circulaire plutôt que linéaire.

Typiquement, les Amérindiens de tradition n'ont pas de difficulté à se représenter un monde exempt des concepts de nation et de religion. Plus encore, ces deux créations de la pensée linéaire lui paraissent être les deux principaux obstacles à l'élaboration d'un monde vraiment fait pour l'humain, où l'existence et la survie des êtres non humains, et donc celle de l'homme, ne seraient pas si absurdement compromises comme elles le sont dans le présent règne de la pensée linéaire.

Plutôt qu'en nations, le penseur circulaire vit en sociétés, à la fois indépendantes et complémentaires les unes des autres. Dans un monde circulaire, l'homme n'est pas seul à avoir des droits : la « démocratie » s'étend aux autres peuples non humains. Les arbres, les plantes, les animaux, les pierres, la terre, l'eau, les esprits ont aussi des droits, puisqu'ils, elles, contribuent au maintien de la Vie dans son ensemble.

Le Temps lui-même est de nature circulaire. Rien n'est réellement passé ou futur ; tout appartient plutôt à un présent éternel, ou continu. Les êtres, y compris les humains, naissent, vivent, meurent, puis reviennent. Un grand homme, une grande femme quitte la société : on les « relève » en de nouveaux individus et le monde, la société, sont ainsi rétablis dans leur intégrité, dans leur immortalité. On comprend ainsi le peu d'intérêt pour les généalogies et pour l'histoire dans les sociétés du Cercle, où l'on n'admet pas la toute-importance du « temps qui passe ».

Les guerres qu'ont connu les sociétés du Cercle ne visaient pas à conquérir, exproprier, anéantir ou « convertir » ; elles étaient relativement de faible conséquence, consistant en des expéditions de vengeance ou de capture d'individus, qui étaient soit exécutés rituellement, de façon à assouvir le besoin de vengeance de certaines familles, ou encore adoptés pour remplacer, physiquement et socialement, quelqu'un de disparu dans le groupe. L'adoption, non seulement sous cette forme, mais sous une infinité d'autres, est une pratique sociale extrêmement courante chez toutes les sociétés amérindiennes traditionnelles. La provenance ethnique ou raciale des gens à adopter n'importe pas, puisqu'il y a une unité idéologique dans la reconnaissance partagée du Cercle. Il n'y a donc pas de notion de pureté ethnique ; l'humanité doit logiquement et nécessairement devenir une, puisque la pensée humaine est circulaire.

Les sources écrites de l'histoire blanche des Amérindiens parlent abondamment de la spontanéité des sociétés amérindiennes à reconnaître non seulement leurs congénères, mais aussi les Blancs, en dépit de toute leur apparente différence, comme des parents dans le grand Cercle. Ces premiers Euro-Américains furent toujours étonnés, voire édifiés par l'hospitalité et la générosité de leurs hôtes amérindiens. L'idée de familles de peuples (ou de nations, pour employer un terme moderne) réunis autour d'idéaux d'échanges et de paix était déjà implantée en Amérique depuis des siècles, même des millénaires, au moment où arrivèrent ici les Blancs, habitués quant à eux depuis aussi longtemps à l'intolérance, à l'exploitation de l'homme par l'homme et, donc, à la misère sociale de majorités.

L'archéologie est aujourd'hui assez avancée pour permettre aux spécialistes de reconstituer, souvent en détails, la vie et les idées sociales des anciens Amérindiens. Un exemple pourrait être celui des Wendats, mieux connus sous le nom dérogatoire de Hurons. On sait présentement, grâce à une science archéologique appuyée sur une rare somme de témoignages ethnographiques, que ce peuple fut formé dès le début des années 1400 par l'union en confédération d'un important nombre de petites sociétés. Cette confédération de peuples agricoles et matricentristes colonisa alors un pays – le Wendaké, ou la Huronie ontarienne – situé à la limite des terres des chasseurs du Nord, qui devint le centre commercial, économique et politique d'une vaste région du nord-est de l'Amérique du Nord, habitée par une grande quantité de peuples dont, nous disent les sources, une cinquantaine utilisait la langue wendate comme langue du commerce et de la diplomatie à l'époque du contact de cette région avec les Blancs, vers l'an 1610. Les Français reconnurent le génie commercial et politique des Wendats, ainsi que de leurs partenaires, et furent forcés de s'intégrer aux coutumes et aux usages établis et intégrés par tous ces peuples depuis déjà de nombreux siècles et basés sur une universelle et intégrale pensée circulaire.

On peut avec intérêt citer le cas d'un explorateur français qui, un siècle plus tôt, pensa pouvoir mépriser impunément l'ordre établi par les Wendat-Iroquois du Saint-Laurent, et posa des actions que lui dicta sa cosmovision linéaire. Lui-même et son pays durent en payer le prix. Jacques Cartier arriva en 1535 à Stadaconé, site de l'actuelle ville de Québec, avec l'idée, inspirée de Pizarro, Cortez et tant d'autres, de se servir des autochtones pour se faire montrer la route des Indes et des richesses et, en même temps, renverser et détruire l'ordre existant dans le pays qu'il venait de « découvrir ».

Ses observateurs, les gens de Stadaconé, voyant bien que ces gens arrivaient de loin sans femmes ni enfants mais avec la seule idée de dominer ce qu'ils voyaient et de s'en accaparer, pensèrent qu'un premier geste envers eux devait être d'offrir au capitaine Cartier une de leurs jeunes femmes, une femme de statut très spécial vu leur mode social matricentriste.

Cartier, un chrétien, ne pouvait se rendre à l'idée de gens païens. Pour la forme, il accepta la jeune femme lors d'une cérémonie de mariage amérindienne mais, ensuite, la refila à ses hommes qui, nous dit le récit de Cartier, la « battirent », puis la renvoyèrent à ses gens. Cartier, tout au long de ce voyage, continua à bafouer les Stadaconiens en se comportant en maître du pays et en faisant fi des conseils et des avertissements des autochtones. Lorsqu'il repartit en mai 1536, après avoir perdu 25 hommes qui périrent de froid et de maladie à cause de l'ambition de leur capitaine (Cartier nous informe comment les Amérindiens sauvèrent les autres), Cartier enleva traîtreusement le premier chef et plusieurs autres principaux de Stadaconé. Les sources historiques françaises rapportent que de dix Stadaconiens enlevés par Cartier, une seule jeune femme survécut plus de deux ans en France, mais ne revit plus jamais son cher pays, que Cartier avait, pour les temps à venir, nommé le Canada.

Ces gestes de Cartier, typiques d'une vision du monde linéaire, eurent comme résultat l'obstruction subséquente faite par les Stadaconiens à tout plan d'établissement français sur leur territoire et, donc, l'annulation probable des meilleures chances d'une implantation vraiment forte de la France en Amérique du Nord.

Nous voyons donc par cet exemple, et par une infinité d'autres qu'on pourrait donner, que le partage, l'égalité et l'acceptation des différences, naturels aux sociétés à pensée circulaire, ne sont pas compatibles avec la pensée linéaire.

Les Iroquois (les Gens de la Longue Maison) sont une autre société de peuples que l'histoire s'est appliquée à dépeindre de façon péjorative et négative, mais dont toute la carrière historique a été marquée par l'effort de communiquer aux immigrants européens leur conception d'une grande confédération de tous les peuples réunis sous le Grand Arbre de la Paix, dont les racines couvrent les quatre directions ; les Iroquois étaient unis par leur foi en la capacité commune à tous les humains de raisonner universellement pour évoluer vers des pensées et des actes produisant la sécurité, le respect de tous les êtres et, donc, la Paix.

En conclusion de mon exposé, je dirai, à ma façon, ce que peu de gens n'ont pas senti, dit, pensé, écrit ou exprimé artistiquement : que l'humanité n'a pas d'autre choix que celui de revenir au Cercle. Car, soit que l'on reconnaisse individuellement et socialement la dignité de toute forme de vie et le droit de toute société, de toute culture à la vie, soit qu'on se propose, consciemment ou non, de supprimer toute vie, y compris la sienne. Je veux, quant à moi, améciciser l'individu moderne.

Point de vue wendat sur les transferts culturels Europe-Amérique, 992-1992[*]

Nous sommes au printemps 992, le 2 mai, probablement dans un village situé à une demi-journée du Beau Lac, le Gontario, à l'est, vers la Grande Rivière qui va vers l'Eau Salée. Le village est habité par le peuple tshastetshi, ancêtres des Wendats. Il contient dix-sept grandes maisons (*ganonchias*) et environ 400 personnes. C'est un grand village, un *Kanatha*.

Les grains pour les semences du maïs ont été mis à germer il y a quelques jours, selon l'avis des Femmes Principales des maisons. Dans le village, il est beaucoup question d'ensemencement et de travaux des champs. Les *arendiouane* (personnes-médecine) et leurs sociétés de savoir préparent une grande fête en l'honneur de la Terre et de tous les esprits féminins : en l'honneur aussi du maïs (*onneha*), la plante sacrée surgie du cerveau de l'aïeule de tous les Tshastetshi, la

---

[*] Présentation à la Conférence internationale « Transferts culturels Europe-Amérique 1492–1992 », tenue au Musée de la civilisation, Québec, 30 avril- 2 mai 1992. Publié dans mon livre *Les Hurons-Wendats. Une civilisation méconnue* (Presses de l'Université Laval, 1999).

fille d'Aataentsic, la fondatrice de ce continent, la Grande Île sur le Dos de la Tortue. Aussi, on invoque et on remercie Inon et ses aides, Esprits du Tonnerre et de la Pluie, Esprits de vie par excellence et Ennemis implacables de tous les ennemis tant surnaturels que matériels du Peuple.

Les Anciens commémorent le temps de leurs lointains ancêtres, lorsque les Tshastetshi ne vivaient pas dans des villages permanents, comme aujourd'hui, mais chassaient et voyageaient presque toute l'année, comme les Akwanake (ou Akwanaki : prononciation wendate du mot Abénaqui, qui devint « Algonquin » en français – explication personnelle), et comprenaient parfaitement le langage de tous les animaux. Mais les temps avaient changé. Les Akwanake avaient occupé cette partie nord de la Grande Île avant ceux qu'ils nommaient les Nadouek (« ceux d'une autre origine »), dont les Tshastetshi étaient un peuple parmi de nombreux autres. Les Akwanake étaient nombreux et puissants. Ils vinrent, avec le temps, à occuper presque tout le territoire. Ce fut alors que l'Esprit bienveillant, Yoscaha, petit-fils d'Aataentsic, apporta aux Tshastetshi ces graines miraculeuses sorties du cerveau même de sa mère après qu'elle décéda.

Commença ainsi une nouvelle vie pour le Peuple, et aussi pour les Akwanake. Les Anciens nous ont dit que tout changea très vite dans tout le pays. Dès que l'on fut en possession de la plante magique, le peuple arrêta de bouger. Les femmes enseignèrent au Peuple une nouvelle façon de vivre. Elles firent construire par les hommes de grands villages et elles leur firent déboiser beaucoup d'espaces pour planter et cultiver la plante magique, et d'autres plantes, données aussi par notre Père Yoscaha.

Ce fut le début d'une vie réellement différente, et intense, et riche. Nous connûmes une grande abondance de tout, et les gens commencèrent à former de grandes alliances entre familles, entre groupes de familles, entre villages. De nouveaux alliés, des Animaux Esprits (animaux claniques), devinrent les symboles de nos alliances et de notre parenté, qui devint universelle. Nous commençâmes à instituer de nombreuses fêtes, destinées à maintenir et à agrandir les réseaux de nos liens. Notre amitié de toujours avec les Akwanake et nos autres voisins se renforça. Nous eûmes tellement plus de choses qu'auparavant à nous échanger. Nous reçûmes des objets, des connaissances de très loin ; plusieurs de ces choses comportaient un grand pouvoir. Grâce à la plante sacrée que nous cultivions, nous devînmes le peuple très riche et très puissant que nous sommes aujourd'hui.

Maintenant, nous chassons beaucoup moins ; nous sommes surtout un peuple de voyageurs et de commerçants. Nos amis akwanake, eux, n'ont pas cessé de chasser. En plus de leurs viandes séchées et de leurs fourrures, ils continuent de nous apporter la connaissance et le lien intime avec le monde des Animaux Esprits, lien que nous avons choisi de perdre, peu à peu. L'hiver, ils viennent nous visiter durant des lunes entières et nous entendons, en leurs voix, les paroles de nos puissants Ancêtres. Souvent, ils nous laissent de leurs jeunes gens, qui apprennent notre langue et se marient parfois avec les jeunes de nos nations. Ainsi, nous devenons uns avec eux et nous enterrons ensemble, lors de nos Grandes-Fêtes-des-Âmes, les corps de nos parents partis de ce monde.

Mais nous n'avons pas que des amis. Nos jeunes hommes, souvent, se lassent de la vie et des travaux des villages et offrent d'aller exposer leur vie pour venger la perte de ceux qui nous sont enlevés ou sont tués par des peuples ennemis. Leur offre, bien sûr, est souvent acceptée par les Femmes Principales de nos Clans, dont le désir le plus pressant est toujours de remplacer ceux et celles qu'elles ont perdus, en adoptant des gens capturés ou bien encore en les « jetant au feu », lorsqu'une perte a été trop douloureuse et est irréparable autrement. Curieusement, nos ennemis ont presque toujours été des gens de même origine que nous, dont nous comprenons les langages, des gens appelés, comme nous, « Nadouek » par les Akwanake.

Wendake, 2 mai 1492

Cinq autres siècles ont passé, sur cette Terre éternelle. Il y a plus de 200 ans, nos Ancêtres sont venus habiter cette merveilleuse Île du Wendake (prononcé Wendaké), située aux confins sud des terres akwanake du Nord et à la limite nordique des terres des agriculteurs nadouek. Nos villages sont disséminés sur tout le pays du Wendake. Nous sommes les Wendats, descendants des Tshastetshi, le premier peuple créé sur la Grande Île sur le dos de notre très ancienne Grand-Mère, la Tortue. Nous sommes composés de deux grandes Nations, les Attignaouantans et les Attignenongnahacs, elles-mêmes des confédérations de plusieurs peuples venus, anciennement et récemment, habiter le Wendake. Le Wendake est le territoire du centre du monde. Par lui passent tous les grands chemins du commerce, et tous les peuples de notre grande société comprennent et utilisent notre langue pour traiter entre eux. Nos sages Ancêtres avaient bien vu. Nous sommes devenus un Peuple très nombreux et très puissant. Sur nos chemins de traite circulent les choses les plus rares et précieuses qui soient. Notre pays est le cœur d'un vaste monde d'échanges et de relations. Notre capacité de production et de commerce est inimaginablement grande. Presque tous les Peuples de toutes les provenances sont nos parents et traitent avec nous.

Nous avons aussi des ennemis en lesquels nos jeunes gens trouvent des adversaires de taille et extrêmement valeureux, même si nous n'avons aucun motif de les craindre. Ce sont nos voisins, au sud du lac Gontario, les gens de la Longue Maison, qui, comme nous, forment une Ligue, beaucoup moins puissante que la nôtre, laquelle inclut tant de Peuples de ce monde. Nous sommes les Wendats, descendants des Tshastetshi, le premier Peuple de l'Île sur le Dos de la Grande Tortue. Nous sommes les premiers et les Maîtres. Notre histoire et notre destin sont de succès et de puissance.

Wendake. 2 mai 1642

Nous sommes un Peuple presque mort. Les Wendats, descendants des Tshastetshi, le premier peuple créé sur cette Île merveilleuse, très bientôt ne seront plus. Nous sommes un géant frappé à mort, qui agonise dans une misère sans nom. Nous qui jamais n'avions connu la crainte ou la défaite et qui présidions depuis le commencement des temps sur un empire de paix et d'abondance ; nous qui avons vécu forts, heureux et si prospères, avons été abattus sans même pouvoir nous défendre par d'étranges et faibles ennemis venus de l'Est, au-delà de la Grande Eau Salée ; si faibles, en apparence, mais possédant un pouvoir si dangereux que tout ce qu'ils font nous fait mourir. L'air même qui sort de leur bouche empoisonne l'air de tout le pays et fait rapidement mourir même les gens de ce pays qui ne les ont jamais vus. Nos Pères les ont accueillis il y a plus de 100 hivers sur la rive nord de la Grande Rivière, où nos gens avaient alors de nombreux villages. Nos Mères les ont même soignés, et sauvés d'une mort certaine, à une lune de nos villes, qui se nommait Stadacona. Nous savions que leurs venues, depuis plus de 40 hivers, faisaient mourir beaucoup de gens à l'Est, mais nos Peuples pensèrent qu'en traitant avec eux et en devenant leurs Parents, ces étrangers cesseraient d'utiliser leur mauvais pouvoir contre nous. Il n'en fut absolument pas ainsi : ces étranges humains commencèrent bientôt à nous maltraiter et à se comporter comme si notre pays était à eux. Ils se mirent même à capturer nos Principaux, à nous tuer et à nous empoisonner, alors même qu'ils nous assuraient être nos Frères.

Très tôt, nos Sages nous avertirent de ne pas traiter avec cet étrange et fatal Peuple, mais il fut, bien sûr, impossible d'empêcher tous nos gens de prendre le risque de se procurer les objets merveilleux que souvent nous leur trafiquions sans heurt ni danger. D'autant plus que ces objets, surtout ceux de fer et d'autres nouveaux métaux, devinrent vite indispensables à la survie de nos Familles et de nos Nations, ainsi que pour nous protéger de nos ennemis, qui connaissaient le même malheureux sort que nous.

Au fil des années, les étrangers s'approchèrent de notre pays du Wendake, le centre et le rempart de toutes les Nations. Ils y arrivèrent enfin, il y a 27 hivers. J'étais encore un garçon et je me souviens que nos Anciennes pleuraient et prédisaient que notre grand Peuple et notre grande Société seraient bientôt détruits et que les survivants connaîtraient une misère indicible. Regardez maintenant tout autour de nous. Dites-moi si vous voyez autre chose que mort, malheur et désolation. Entrez dans nos Conseils et voyez si on y parle d'autre chose que de la mort déjà presque accomplie de notre grand et beau Pays. Les Robes Noires, qui professent nous vouer le plus grand amour possible, déchirent à loisir les lambeaux qui restent de nos Peuples. Ils ont même changé notre nom et ceux de tous les lieux de notre Pays, qu'il disent d'ores et déjà être le leur. En seulement huit années, une dizaine de ces Mauvais Okis a converti le Pays le plus beau et le plus prospère qui ait existé au monde en un lieu de la plus grande misère qui se puisse imaginer. Tous les gens originaires de ce sol de la Grande Île sont en train d'être détruits par l'invincible pouvoir des étrangers, qui bientôt auront réussi à s'approprier tout ce qui fut à nous, qui n'eûmes pourtant de désir que de le partager avec eux. Ils se réjouissent en ce moment de nous voir mourir, et ce qui nous arrive présentement arrivera à tous les Peuples de notre Grande Île.

Ô Ciel ! Ô Grand Esprit ! Ô Intelligence Infinie de l'Univers ! Fais que nous survivions et que nous vivions à nouveau !

Point de vue amérindien lors du cinquième centenaire de l'arrivée européenne sur notre continent

Comme certainement plusieurs autres Amérindiens cette année, je me retrouve assez fréquemment dans la position d'avoir à donner à une assemblée composée surtout de non-Amérindiens un point de vue amérindien sur les 500 années de présence européenne sur notre sol d'Amérique. Même si, en cette année centenaire, l'atmosphère festive est remarquablement plus tempérée qu'il y a 100 ans, si l'on s'en rapporte aux journaux et périodiques du temps, le camp (euro-américain) de la célébration est nettement plus nombreux que celui du deuil et de la réflexion (Amérindiens et sympathisants).

Pourquoi célébrer l'arrivée des Européens et leur invasion de l'Amérique ? Les réponses à cette question sont amplement claires dans le discours de la célébration : l'Europe nous a apporté ses lumières sociales et religieuses, ses langues, son bagage génétique, ses arts de vivre ; les Indiens sont une race améliorée par la présence blanche et vivent aujourd'hui infiniment mieux qu'il y a 500 ans. De toute façon, pourquoi se sentir coupable de la victoire d'un système, ou d'une « structure » contre une autre et, d'ailleurs, comment et pourquoi nier l'éblouissant triomphe de la civilisation américaine eurogène, à l'échelle mondiale ?

Simultanément, dans l'autre camp (n'est-il pas même étonnant qu'il en existe un ?), l'ambiance est au deuil et à la réflexion. Notre deuil est pour les quelque dix dizaines de millions de nos gens dont l'arrivée de colons signifia la mort atroce par maladie épidémique ou par agression violente, surtout durant les 100 premières années de l'invasion européenne. De ce plus grand holocauste de l'histoire humaine, le dixième peut-être mourut par la voie directe d'armes contre lesquelles on n'eut pas de défense, ni morale ni matérielle : fusils, canons, épées, chiens tueurs des Espagnols, etc., mais, surtout, l'esprit de convoitise, de traîtrise, de misanthropie, du goût pour le carnage, le vol, le viol et l'annihilation. Je ne parle pas ici particulièrement des Espagnols : la science historique est parfaitement bien informée que ce comportement extrêmement violent fut celui, toutes les fois que les conditions du contact le permirent, des sept nations européennes qui prirent une part active dans l'invasion. La réflexion des Amérindiens porte surtout sur le pourquoi de cette agressivité infinie qui fut et est encore la marque principale de la civilisation eurogène en Amérique.

« *Mens sana in corpore sano* », disons-nous tous. Le fait le plus évident qui se dégage de toute comparaison, au plan sociobiologique, entre les civilisations européenne et amérindienne, au temps du contact, est celui de l'extrême développement d'un complexe microbien en Europe, par opposition à une étonnante santé physique des Amérindiens. Et l'insensibilité morbide des découvreurs et de leurs suites vis-à-vis de l'existence, de la disparition et du droit des Peuples originaires, ainsi que vis-à-vis de toute forme de vie en général, ne doit apparaître que comme le corollaire d'un état physique également morbide d'une grande quantité d'Européens de ces siècles. Car qu'indiquent l'agressivité insensible, le mépris de la vie, la soif insatiable et aveugle de possessions matérielles, le goût de l'anéantissement et toutes les autres pathologies mentales antisociales, sinon une biologie souffrante, exaspérée ? Personnellement, je vois dans la compréhension de ce simple fait le début de la possibilité d'une meilleure coexistence entre toutes nos cultures.

Et quelle était la nature de la civilisation, ici, en Amérique ? Tous nos peuples (amérindiens) se conçoivent comme issus du sol même de cette Grande Île qu'est l'Amérique. Très nombreux sommes-nous, à l'échelle de l'hémisphère, à dire que cette Grande Île a d'abord été formée sur le Dos de la Grande Tortue et qu'un Conseil d'Animaux et d'Esprits Créateurs a présidé à l'arrangement de ce grand Pays en vue de son occupation par les Êtres de nature humaine. Et lorsque le monde terrestre fut prêt pour nous, nous y fûmes conduits, à partir d'un monde souterrain. Ce que nos premiers et lointains ancêtres virent à ce moment-là était un monde de beauté, d'abondance et d'équilibre, qu'il leur incombait de contempler avec les yeux de l'âme pour le comprendre. Vision d'un Grand Esprit, ou d'une Intelligence Infinie, cette Terre était, comme tous les Êtres créés, un Être doué d'intelligence, de pensée, de vision. Toutes les créatures composant ce monde étaient vues comme pourvues elles aussi d'un sens, d'une âme, faites d'une même essence spirituelle, et indispensables à l'ordre de l'ensemble. Ce monde était une chaîne infinie de relations, organiquement solidaires et interdépendantes, fonctionnant selon des cycles immuables, le Tout se présentant à l'entendement humain comme un grand Cercle Sacré de Relations, ou de la Vie. La loi fondamentale du Cercle est une double reconnaissance : celle de la parenté entre tous les êtres et celle de l'individualité insondable et inviolable de chaque être.

Les peuples évoluent de façons presque toujours fort différentes. Certains, à cause de contraintes physiques ambiantes, surtout climatiques et géographiques, épuisent ou voient s'épuiser de façon critique les ressources de leurs territoires. Ils n'ont alors que le choix de s'engager sur la voie d'une perception linéaire. Cela signifie que certains de leurs membres entreprennent d'organiser ces sociétés en fonction de la conquête économique d'autres sociétés. Les individus de ces sociétés cessent donc alors de chercher à reconnaître la nature intime et unique de chaque être, humain et non humain. Plutôt, les êtres sont alors vus et évalués selon leur potentiel d'exploitabilité qui se traduit concrètement en valeur monétaire.

La chaîne des relations sacrées entre tous les êtres est ainsi rompue, les êtres sont désolidarisés. Le pouvoir monétaire ainsi produit est canalisé dans les mains de certaines élites, dont le but doit nécessairement devenir la concentration la plus rapide et la plus forte possible du plus grand pouvoir possible, de façon à gérer toutes les mauvaises velléités d'un peuple désormais opprimé. La femme elle-même, dès qu'est apparue la marchandabilité universelle, donc la propriété privée, marque du règne patriarcal, est passée de penseure et maîtresse au centre de sa société dans une civilisation de la parenté, à servante-objet, dominée, possédée, également exploitée par l'homme propriétaire et héritier. La sensibilité et l'attention contemplative aux autres êtres, conditions *sine qua non* de l'existence de sociétés humaines, sont disparues à mesure que les êtres, humains et non humains, ont perdu leurs lieux naturels d'existence, donc leur existence même. Cette nature sapée, fondue lentement mais résolument au creuset du pouvoir des élites (civiles et religieuses), a signifié un étouffement simultané de la force vitale des individus. La maladie s'est mise à gagner sur la santé. De grandes parties de l'Europe, au moment où ce continent arriva accidentellement en Amérique, n'étaient qu'un grand foyer d'épidémies, tellement la Ligne avait intégralement remplacé le Cercle. On pourrait même dire que l'Europe, chroniquement et mortellement malade, a frénétiquement cherché un remède et son salut à la fin du XVe siècle. Ainsi, le seul sens acceptable d'une célébration de l'arrivée des Européens ici en 1492 serait le salut physique d'une Europe condamnée à mort, puis son retour graduel à la santé physique, mentale et spirituelle, dans l'air sain et salutaire de la Grande Île amérindienne. Cette guérison, toujours très incomplète, est une tâche à laquelle les Amérindiens continuent de vouloir contribuer. Voilà ce à quoi nous réfléchissons, nous dont le cœur bat au rythme de celui de cette Amérique, terre de vie pour tous, pendant que d'autres cœurs célèbrent encore un vieux monde que l'on a fui parce qu'il ne promettait que la mort.

Mais notre propre survie à nous n'est-elle pas quelque chose, la seule chose, même, que nous pourrions et devrions célébrer, en cette cinq centième année depuis le début de l'invasion ? Même s'il apparaît certain que nous aurions dû disparaître, si certain même qu'une grande majorité d'Euro-Américains croit que c'est chose faite ou virtuellement accomplie, très rares sommes-nous, Amérindiens, à penser que notre survie est quelque sorte de miracle, ou d'accident. Plutôt, nous croyons que, comme le Cercle de la Vie elle-même, notre existence et notre pensée (circulaire) sont indestructibles. Peu importe la violence d'un choc dirigé contre eux, la Vie et son Cercle se recomposent toujours. Notre vision circulaire a permis que nos peuples, tous décimés et autrement voués à l'anéantissement, se rejoignent, se regroupent, oubliant souvent les inimitiés traditionnelles les ayant opposés. De l'extrême misère venue avec les colons naquit ainsi une conscience limpide de la supériorité morale d'une vision panamérindienne circulaire, ainsi que du mensonge de la vision apportée d'Europe et de l'impossibilité du succès de sa transplantation en cette terre d'Amérique, terre sacrée du Cercle par excellence. Et pour celui ou celle qui veut voir, tous les signes de morbidité de cette vieille vision linéaire, destructrice, ne sont-ils pas maintenant présents ? Je citerai à cet effet, et pour terminer, les propos récents de deux penseurs étas-uniens, l'un euro-américain, l'autre amérindien. Le premier, le célèbre auteur, professeur et écologiste new-yorkais Kirkpatrick Sale, dit dans son dernier livre, *The Conquest of Paradise* : « Nous pouvons donc garder l'espoir. Il n'y a qu'une seule façon de vivre en Amérique et c'est celle des

Américains, je veux dire des Américains indigènes, car c'est cela que demande la terre d'Amérique. Depuis cinq siècles, nous avons tenté de résister à cette simple vérité. Nous continuons d'y résister seulement au risque de notre propre perdition, et même pire, de la destruction de la terre ».

Le second, le célèbre auteur et professeur Dakota Vine Deloria Jr., écrivit dans l'épilogue du livre *America in 1492* : « Les anciennes prophéties indiennes disent qu'entre tous ceux qui sont venus sur ces continents occidentaux, l'Homme blanc [cela voulant dire la philosophie euro-américaine linéaire] aura séjourné le moins longtemps. D'un point de vue amérindien, continue Deloria, le thème général selon lequel nous devons comprendre l'histoire de l'hémisphère serait le degré auquel les Blancs ont répondu aux rythmes de la terre, le degré auquel ils sont devenus indigènes. De ce point de vue, notre jugement au sujet des Européens doit être sévère ».

2092 : A Personal Projection*

The year 1892 was the year white America proclaimed to the world its definitive victory against 'primitivism'. The Sioux, the last 'wild' Indians of North America, had been massacred and crushed two years before, at Wounded Knee. With the forces of stagnation finally destroyed, white America could show the triumphant face and the lordly air of magnanimity, which would henceforth be its own. The fourth centennial year of the discovery of the New World by Christopher Columbus was celebrated in a way which would be worthy of much more sumptuous and ample celebrations of centennial years yet to come. Regardless of what any surviving pagan prophet might secretly think or say, the last chapter of American 'prehistory' had been written, the book closed and hastily put away.

In this year of 1992, the celebration is intense and boisterous, in many countries around the world. However, the celebrators' camp is annoyed by the existence of a rather strong and vocal camp of people of many countries who say that this quincentennial year should be spent in mourning the original destruction, by invading Europeans, of very important treasures of human knowledge accumulated over tens of millennia of life and civilization-building on this continent. Certainly almost all the descendants and survivors of the invaded Americans, as well as their countless sympathizers and friends believe that this fifth centennial year has to be thought of as a moment when a true encounter between Aboriginal Americans and all other peoples of the world must take place in order to reflect on how to halt the ever-accelerating spoliation of our home, the Earth, and therefore, the destruction of our own human species.

Some things, however, do deserve to be celebrated this year. A first one is certainly the manifest survival of the Aboriginal American people and therefore of the spiritual essence of the true American civilization, for all of us to discover. A second one, for the Euro-Americans, is their own survival by coming here, fleeing their own homelands which, in 1492, offered them only economic and

---

* A personal projection to the year 2092 from an Amerindian/Indigenous perspective.

religious repression and wholesale death by epidemics. A third one, the most important, is that, for better or for worse, and in spite of all past hardships and injustices, we all are now forced to realize that any future we have as a species lies in our capacity to recognize each other, with the weaknesses, but mostly with the strengths, which all peoples individually possess. We now have to look forward to an ever more unified world society in which superficial differences between us will more and more be looked at with admiration for Life's Infinite Beauty, Diversity and Intelligence.

It looks rather certain that most humans in 2092 will have abandoned any idea of celebrating the beginning of the destruction of aboriginal America. Rather, a lot of people will be convinced of the need of actualizing what will then be seen as the primordial Amerindian vision, that is, a vision of a spiritually unified world, human and non-human. Inheritors of a very impoverished Earth, our descendants of 2092 will be a highly spiritual people, markedly more racially mixed than we are, who will perform unthinkable wonders in their mission of bringing back as much as possible of the beauty and order that were lost to the Earth during the Colonial, or Blind Era.

The Cultural Property of Indigenous Peoples[*]

Madam Chairperson, members of the Working Group, dear brothers and sisters of our indigenous nations united in the same feeling of respect for our Mother the Earth, and for the Great Spirit of Life, whom we usually call the Creators. Dear brothers and sisters of the non-indigenous world who live in Switzerland and Europe and who understand our spiritual language, it is a great joy and honour for me to address you as a Huron—or Wendat, our name in our own tongue—and also as a professor of Amerindian history and philosophy in the Saskatchewan Indian Federated College at the University of Regina, Saskatchewan, the ancestral lands of the Amerindians of the Canadian and American prairies.

I am always deeply moved and saddened when I hear the Native peoples of each country where we still exist express their grief at being ill-treated,

---

[*] This paper is my oral presentation of July 30, 1993, to the Eleventh Session of the Working Group on Indigenous Populations, Sub-commission on the Prevention of Discrimination and the Protection of Minorities, Human Rights Commission, United Nations, Geneva, Switzerland, from July 19 to July 30, 1993.

decimated, reduced to a state of destitution and dependence, facing extinction, and when I listen to their desperate cries for help. I too belong to an indigenous nation decimated in the past by the arrival of the French and other Europeans. The great nation of my ancestors reached the brink of extinction, its cries of despair unheeded by the authorities of New France who were even often self-avowedly well pleased at our fate. However, by a miracle, we survived, although in a condition of weakness and dependence.

In order to show how absolutely essential it is for us to protect and preserve our cultural, intellectual and spiritual heritage, a treasure that could never be replaced, I should like to tell you today, Madam Chairperson, dear brothers and sisters, how in 1990 we were given a breath of life when we recovered a large part of our ancestral hunting grounds from which in times past we had been quite simply and summarily expelled. I should like to tell you that we drew the strength that enabled us to overcome the Province of Quebec and the Queen in the Supreme Court of Canada after eight years of struggles, not simply at the level of the legal, political or physical confrontation, but rather from the power of the spirituality that we possess in common with all the world's indigenous peoples or, as we often say, the peoples of circular thought. We won basically because we were able to make the Euro-American courts and governments understand their deep and vital interest in protecting our profoundly spiritual vision of the world which, in the end, is their best—indeed, perhaps their only—chance of being able to understand and give direction to their existence on our American continent.

In this connection, I would appeal to all my brothers and sisters, whether they be Native or non-Native, engaged in the struggle towards liberation and reconciliation, to let their path be illuminated by the wisdom provided by the spirituality of the Circle, which teaches that all the creatures that make up Creation are equal in dignity and importance, and are dependent on one another.

At this point, I should like to express the sorrow and, to a certain extent, the fear felt by many brothers and sisters of all nations and traditions when they notice the lack of seriousness that occasionally characterizes the statements and responses made by the observers and officials from certain countries. In a spirit of brotherhood, I should like to give some advice to these observers:

before setting out to undermine and diminish the spirit and the essence of the Declaration of the Working Group, they would do well to follow the lead of the Supreme Court of Canada in the case to which I have referred, and consider the fact that the wisdom of the Native peoples of the world universally and consistently expresses the apprehension and the fear that the linear, non-indigenous world view is leading the inhabitants of our planet, both human and non-human, down a path of deterioration and impoverishment, indeed even to the speedy destruction of our planet and Mother Earth.

I would ask them as well to consider that the Aboriginal peoples of the world see themselves universally as possessing the true spiritual and philosophical basis of human civilization and, consequently, as the guardians and the natural and essential guides of their brothers and sisters of the linear world.

I should like to speak to you now, dear brothers and sisters, about the surest, long-term solution to the problems caused by the dire condition to which our peoples and nations have been reduced. I mean by this that we must ourselves take charge of our own education; we must reaffirm its values, protect and develop it. This was the course that the Amerindian nations of Saskatchewan, among others in Canada, opted for in 1976 when they created the Saskatchewan Indian Federated College.

At present, our college is one of the oldest Amerindian post-secondary institutions in North America and it is certainly the one that has experienced the most growth. Our Amerindian university college was born of the dreams, the prayers and the will of the spiritual leaders and the Amerindian people of Saskatchewan and of the Canadian and American prairies. Our college is a place where Amerindian philosophy and spirituality are a sacred guiding principle. Our thirteen hundred students, two-thirds of whom are indigenous people, benefit from the constant presence and wisdom of the Elders of our nations, who guide our thoughts and actions with their advice, their ceremonies and their prayers.

Since its inception, our college has also drawn its strength and its success as an institution from the constant, unconditional support of the more than seventy chiefs of the Saskatchewan First Nations who together constitute the Federation of Saskatchewan Indian Nations, which, in 1976, set Canadian

Amerindians on a new and important political path: Indian control of Indian education. Having worked for a year in the Saskatchewan Indian Federated College, I can say that this is truly the most fundamental principle underlying the thought and spirit of those in positions of authority at our college and in our nations. As a professor, I can experience directly the pride of students, of Elders and of my Amerindian brothers in seeing their knowledge and spirituality treated with respect, protected and promoted by an institution that is as much theirs as it is ours.

Our college receives students from every province in Canada and it is proud to be chosen and attended by an ever-increasing number of non-Native students from a wide variety of backgrounds. Of special note is the fact that our college has had a very active section of international indigenous studies since 1986. To date, thirty-nine Amerindian students from South and Central America as well as from the Caribbean have been with us for periods of eight months and have, in their turn, greatly enriched us with their own special intellectual and spiritual strength. Our program of international indigenous studies is growing rapidly and invites all our indigenous brothers and sisters to contribute to and take part in it. We firmly believe that our educational, intellectual, social and spiritual togetherness provides the surest basis for the collective strengthening and restructuring of our peoples and nations. North and South alike will be assured of a good future only if they act collectively and in solidarity like the brothers and sisters that we really are. In the Saskatchewan Indian Federated College, education based on the circular Amerindian vision of the world is the response that we have been developing for the last seventeen years, not only to the extremely difficult social and economic conditions that all our indigenous people are experiencing but also to the social, spiritual and intellectual impasse in which even the so-called advanced countries find themselves.

Brothers and sisters, Attouguet! Etsagon! (Thank you! Keep cheerful!)

Personal Reactions of Indigenous People to European Ideas and Behaviour*

Helen Hornbeck Tanner Speaks

Speaking today on behalf of my colleague, Georges Sioui, as well as myself, I would like to bring you some views that have come from my own historical research, and as a conclusion, present the contemporary viewpoint of Dr. Sioui.

The people indigenous to the North American continent are by now well accustomed to being called 'Indians', so I will use that convenient term. Indians were not accustomed to expressing their thoughts using the kind of abstract vocabulary that delights the intellectual world of Western European tradition. Indian orators eloquently conveyed their ideas by the use of colourful images, vivid figures of speech and stories that clarified a point of view or moral

---

* Co-presented with US historian Helen Hornbeck Tanner at the Conference "Culture and Colonization in North America : Canada, United States, Mexico" held in August 1992 at the University of Groningen, Netherlands. Published at Septentrion (1994) under the direction of Jaap Lintvelt, Réal Ovellet and Hub. Hermans.

lesson. In the spirit of traditional Indian discourse, my contribution to this presentation will begin by recounting a few actual experiences of Indian people in dealing with European ideas and behaviour. These narratives, reconstructed from historical documents and literary sources, deal with matters of basic importance in Indian life: achieving justice when killing has occurred; the central role of giving and sharing with kinfolk and allies; concepts of time; methods of education and child-rearing; and religious beliefs and the power of the spirit world. The vignettes and examples are intended to help to clarify the Indian reaction to the ideas and behaviour of European newcomers, which they often found to be puzzling, sometimes frightening, but also occasionally humorous. All of these events take place in the upper Great Lakes region of Canada.

The first narrative describes the repercussions following the death of two Frenchmen near Keweenaw Bay on the south shore of Lake Superior on April 12, 1683.[1] More than three hundred kilometres away, the human drama resulting from the two deaths unfolded at Michilimackinac (the present St. Ignace) and the Ojibwa village of Bawating (the present Sault Ste. Marie), two communities on the eastern end of the Upper Peninsula of the present state of Michigan. Reports of the two Frenchmen, spread throughout the country by the 'moccasin telegraph', laid the responsibility on a Menominee from Green Bay, on the west side of Lake Michigan, and the sons of the important Keweenaw Bay leader, Achiganaga, who had all subsequently gone on a long expedition west of Lake Superior to fight their traditional enemies, the Sioux.[2]

Late in October, however, news came to Michilimackinac, French headquarters in the 'Upper Country', that the Menominee had come back to Sault Ste. Marie along with a large party of local Ojibwas, but Achiganaga and his family were encamped about thirty-two kilometres away in their home territory. The officer in charge at Michilimackinac, Daniel Greysolon, Sieur de Dulhut, determined to apprehend the Indians responsible for the deaths of his

---

1 In Dulhut, 1902, pp. 114–125. « Indian Murders Punished by Dulhut », in Reuben G. Thwaites (dir.). *The French Regime in Wisconsin, 1634-1727*. Collections of the State of Wisconsin.

2 For locations of the 17th-century Indian towns, French posts and missions, see Tanner 1987, Map 6, pp. 32-33 ; and Map 8, p. 36. *Atlas of the Great Lakes Indian History*, Norman, University of Oklahoma Press.

countrymen, and punish them in accordance with French law.[3] This decision set in motion a sequence of events that well illustrates Indian views of European justice and the problem of devising a solution that would conform to different value systems.

Dulhut immediately sent out the most experienced and influential coureur de bois in the region, Jean Peré, to bring Achiganaga to Sault Ste. Marie for questioning.[4] Dulhut himself set off by canoe for Sault Ste. Marie, taking along six trusted French companions. About a mile downriver from destination, he disembarked and went through woods to the settlement, arrested the Menominee and locked him up. The local Ojibwa community, consisting of about a hundred households, vastly outnumbered the local French trading community at Sault Ste. Marie.

Meanwhile, Jean Peré located the Keweenaw Bay Indians, made them take him to the place where the Frenchmen had been killed, and recovered their much-damaged property from about fifteen places where it had been concealed under the roots of trees. Achiganaga attempted to 'dance the calumet', employing a pipe ceremony that would be the first step to making peace, but Jean Peré refused to listen. Achinaga then offered to give captives to compensate for the loss of life. Jean Peré also refused this alternate strategy for conflict resolution and demanded that they all report to Dulhut.

The third week in November, Jean Peré, with Achiganaga and his four sons, reached Sault Ste. Marie. They expected that after explanations and a council, they would be free to return to their home country for winter hunting. On the other hand, Dulhut expected that once the perpetrators were identified, the Ojibwas themselves would recognize that a crime had been committed and take the responsibility for carrying out a death verdict against the guilty parties. But the Bawating Ojibwas did not want any blood spilled on their ground.

At the first council, held on November 24, Dulhut tried to proceed in the

---

3 Dulhut was credited with establishing a tenuous peace between the Sioux and the Ojibwas in a council at the western end of Lake Superior in 1679. In 1683, he returned to Lake Superior. Cf. *Dictionary of Canadian Biography II*, pp. 261–264.

4 Jean Peré left the Lake Superior region after this event. He was arrested by the Hudson's Bay Company later in 1684. *Dictionary of Canadian Biography I*, pp. 536–537.

manner of a trial, with formal questioning and recording of testimony. Two of Achiganaga's sons readily admitted that they, along with the Menominee, had killed the Frenchmen and barely covered the bodies with branches, then left the broken canoe at a distance to create the appearance of an accident. Although Dulhut tried to implicate Achiganaga, all others agreed that the father himself had no part in the incident. When Dulhut announced at the end of the council that the three guilty men should be executed, the assembled Indians refused to approve the verdict. For the next three days, the Indians took counsel among themselves.

To the Indian people gathered at Sault Ste. Marie, the punitive methods of European law seemed wrong: two murders are not settled by committing three more. In their view, the initial injury to society—to all the people—should be healed and not compounded; the rip in the social fabric should be mended and not enlarged. To restore balance to society, Indian people in northeastern North America have two basic strategies: first, to provide gifts and services to compensate for the loss, and, second, to turn over actual human beings to the person who has suffered the loss: that is, to give lives to take the place of the lives lost. In Indian figures of speech, action is taken, either to 'cover the dead' with gifts as a form of restitution, or 'raise up the dead' by replacing a life lost with another human life.[5] Everyone has a stake in restoring harmony, in making the social order whole again. Dulhut had refused to cooperate in the accepted Indian methods of conflict resolution.

As the discussions became more involved, primary responsibility rested with the relatives of the accused. The Menominee from Green Bay had relatives among the Ottawas, and four divisions of Ottawa were represented at the inter-tribal councils in progress at Sault Ste. Marie. Among the participants were Ottawas and refugee Hurons (Wyandots) from villages near the mission at St. Ignace at Michilimackinac. The Ojibwas at Sault Ste. Marie, as relations of the Keweenaw Bay band, could not join in the councils, so they brought in the Amikwas from the north shore of Lake Huron to speak for them. The Ottawas declared that Dulhut should secure from the French governor a grant

---

5 Cf. Jaenen 1976, p. 97. *Friend and Foe: Aspects of French-Amerindian Cultural Contact in the Sixteenth and Seventeenth Centuries.* Toronto : McClelland and Stewart.

of freedom for the accused. Since the Ottawas had recently granted freedom to an Iroquois prisoner at the governor's request, the act would balance out. Dulhut tried to explain that killing in war is different from killing off the battlefield. The Indians, in turn, noted that the Iroquois was an enemy, while the Ojibwa people were allies of the French. Why would the governor save the life of an enemy and demand the death of allies? Such behaviour by French officials was inappropriate in the minds of the Indians in the Great Lakes country.

Dulhut also received pleas for clemency from eighteen Frenchmen spending the winter at Keweenaw Bay. They urged Dulhut to conciliate the Indians because they feared for their own lives if antipathy increased towards the French in the Upper Country. Dulhut did make a concession during his appearance at the council held on November 29 in the cabin of an Ottawa leader, Le Brochet. He pointed out that the Indians themselves on occasion demanded a life for a life, and he would spare the life of the younger of Achiganaga's two guilty sons. But the older son and the Menominee should die as the two Frenchmen had died, by gunfire. In handing down this verdict, he placed the blame on the elders who should have instructed their young so that they would not kill Frenchmen. The Amikwa elder, speaking for the Ojibwas, praised this decision to spare a life and said that the lives of the others were in the hands of the French. An hour later, allowing time for the condemned men to be baptized, the Menominee and the eldest of Achiginaga's four sons were shot close to the fort, in the presence of four hundred Indians and forty-two Frenchmen.

The double execution marked the beginning rather than the end of concerted efforts to achieve justice and restore harmony among all the people involved. So far as the Indians were concerned, two more murders had taken place. Two days later, three Ottawa groups held a council to "cover the bodies of the dead, and to efface the blood that had been shed, so that the earth would be clean in the future". To carry this message they gave away six beaded collars, two each for the French, the relations of the Menominee, and Achiganaga's family.

Dulhut himself, although he was acquainted with Indian customs, learned he had violated strict laws of hospitality in speaking about the deaths of the two Indians while he was in the cabin of Le Brochet without first asking his host's permission. To balance that misdeed, he held a great feast the next day at Le Brochet's cabin, providing gifts of wheat and tobacco. At separate ceremonies, the Huron (Wyandot) presented three collars to Dulhut and three to the Menominee and the Ojibwas. The Huron were widely respected, despite their decline due to disease and warfare, and still served as the final arbiters in inter-tribal affairs. These collars represented messages of peace and restored equilibrium.

Achiganaga and his family did not start on their return trip to Keweenaw Bay until well into January. Before they left, Dulhut gave them blankets, heavy shirts, leather leggings, guns, powder, lead, axes, knives, twine for nets and two sacks of grain for food until they should have success in hunting. Dulhut described all these items as supplies necessary for travel in midwinter, but the Indians clearly recognized these gifts as 'covering the dead', Dulhut's atonement to the family for a son and brother. Just before departure, the local Ojibwas gave Achiganaga's party special collars so there would be no trouble over the deaths in their family, and to restrain them from carrying out evil designs after they returned to Keweenaw Bay. Unfortunately, Achiganaga died two days after setting out; Indians blamed his death on the French. Dulhut's explanation was a severe sore throat.

Dulhut gave his official account of his handling of the punishment for the deaths of two Frenchmen, the only existing report, in a letter dated April 1684, probably written just as the ice was breaking up and the first canoes were leaving for Montreal.[6] One important factor, never satisfactorily explained, was the motivation for the original murders. Dulhut writes of "robbery", but the property of the Frenchmen was all left, concealed to be sure, in the vicinity of the site where the encounter took place. During the two-year period which encompassed the Achiganaga affair, thirty-seven Frenchmen were killed by Indians in the 'Upper Country'. Indian people abhor thievery, except from enemies, and usually do not take a life without provocation. More likely the motivation was resentment of French in the Upper Country. Dulhut tried to enforce a peace between the Ojibwa and the Sioux in order to promote trade into the Sioux country of the Mississippi River. Ojibwas were angered to learn

---

6 Cf. White 1991, pp. 76–82. *The Middle Ground : Indians, Empires and Republics in the Great Lakes Region, 1650–1850.* Cambridge, New York, Melbourne, Sydney.

that the French were shipping goods and guns to their traditional enemies by way of Green Bay, bypassing the route from the head of Lake Superior.

Traders were the largest class of people from whom Indians derived their impressions of Europeans. In the interior of Canada, away from the port towns on the Saint Lawrence River, the other class of significant individuals in contact with Indian culture was missionaries. The next story indicates the reaction of the Ojibwas to Jesuit missionaries in Ontario in the mid-19th century. The labours of the Jesuits among the Huron in the 17th century are well known; they also made converts among the Ottawa allied with the Huron. But the Jesuits had little success among the large population of various Ojibwa bands living in the Upper Country, and resistance remained strong almost two centuries later.

The Jesuit order returned to Canada in the 1840s, sending twenty-eight priests to stations as distant as the Pigeon River at the western end of Lake Superior during the period from 1843 to 1852. They chose as a particular challenge the Ojibwa and Potawatomi community of about seven hundred people living on Walpole Island. This reserved area is located on the northeast side of Lake St. Clair along the waterway from Lake Huron to the Detroit River and Lake Erie. The next story focuses on the reaction of the Ojibwa leaders to the uninvited appearance of the Jesuits, or the Black Robes, on their island in 1844.

The background information for the story indicates that the Jesuits had secured permission from the Canadian government to establish a mission and school on Walpole Island, but no one had consulted the Indians. In late April of 1844, two French members of the order managed to land their small boat on the edge of the island, and set up a tent where they had a view of the busy waterway with canoes, wooden boats, schooners and occasionally at night, a brightly lit steamboat on an excursion from Detroit with a band playing martial music. Father Dominique du Ranquet and Brother Joseph Jennesseaux received a rather cool reception.[7] Animosity grew after the two men cut down century-old oak trees near their campsite to begin building a chapel. A final confrontation took place on July 31, after a delegation of Ojibwa elders came

---

7 Point 1973, pp. 165–167. "3e lettre, 10 mai 1844", in Laurent Cadieux (dir.), 1973. *Lettres des nouvelles missions du Canada, 1843-1852*, Toronto, Les Éditions Bellarim : Paris, Maisonneuve et Larose, pp. 159-167.

to explain why the missionaries should cease work on the chapel and leave Walpole Island. The Ojibwas' point of view was expressed eloquently by their great orator and war hero, Oshawano, who had fought beside Tecumseh at the Battle of the Thames in 1813, when Tecumseh was killed. His statements were reinforced by the leading chief, Petokechig, while the opposing arguments were set forth by Father du Ranquet and Father Pierre Chazelle.

In the first place, Oshawano pointed out that the Black Robes had not asked for permission to set up camp. (It is usual for a visitor, if not previously invited, to ask for "a little space to lay my bed". Hospitality is a highly admired trait among Indian people, and only unusual circumstances would dictate withholding a hospitable reception for strangers.) The campsite was also beside a burial mound of great antiquity, and practically on top of an area of newer gravesites with their wooden markers. These two Jesuit culture-bearers from across the ocean had settled on a place sacred to the Ojibwa people. Cutting the oak trees was an unpardonable desecration.

Oshawano, a man of great status because of his age and experience, expressed his amazement that a young man like Father du Ranquet would dare to propose a change in the religion practised by the Ojibwa people. His missionary efforts showed no respect for elders. Oshawano addressed Father du Ranquet as a brother in his formal oratory, but more often referred to him as the "man with a hat", while he himself was a "man of the forest". Oshawano forcefully explained that his people had received their blessings and their knowledge of medicines from their elders, and would pass on the same blessings and knowledge to their children. To be sure, for the "man with a hat" knowledge came from books, but for the Ojibwas, knowledge came from the heart.

The Ojibwa leader explained to the young "man with a hat" from the other side of the great sea that he should realize that the Great Spirit had created people differently in different places. There were people with white skin, people with black skin and people with red skin. Though their own lands had suffered encroachment, the Ojibwas on Walpole Island were living on land that the Spirit created for the 'redskins' to carry on the blessings and beliefs of their ancestors. (In terms of current 20th-century ideas, Oshawano made a strong case for multiculturalism.) He insisted that the ideas and behaviour of people from overseas should not be imported and imposed on the 'redskins', particularly not on the people of Walpole Island. He further pointed out the diversity created by the Great Spirit, a diversity evident everywhere in the natural world. People were as different as the leaves on the trees. Indian people had observed the different ways that birds fly in the air, and the different ways that fish swim in the water, and understood that there were different ways to reach the Great Spirit. The 'redskins' had their way, for they inherited the blessings and wisdom of their elders. They had no reason to adopt the way of 'The Prayer' advocated by the Black Robes.

Oshawano's speeches indicated the Ojibwas' view of Christianity. They found common ground with the Jesuits in their belief in a Great Spirit who had created everything in the sky and on the Earth. The Ojibwas observed that the Black Robes had pictures and small statues in heir dwelling, and recognized that these images helped them to contact the Great Spirit. Oshawano pointed out that the Ojibwas as well had their images and sacred objects to help them contact the Great Spirit. He acknowledged that the Indians did not have paper and ink, but they made their drawings on birch bark.

Clearly, these Ojibwa elders had thought over the differences and similarities between their own beliefs and those of the Jesuits. They were well acquainted with the different forms of exposition and persuasion by the Jesuit order to gain Indian converts. They were not at all swayed by Father Chazelle's sincere declaration that the Great Spirit had sent his Son to earth with a message to save all people, including those on Walpole Island. Oshawano explained to the "man with a hat" that the people on the other side of the great sea had obviously been bad people so that the Great Spirit felt obliged to send his Son with a message. But the Great Spirit did not need to send his Son to the 'redskins'. Furthermore, those people on the other side of the great sea had killed the Son sent to them by the Great Spirit, and Ojibwas would not follow the way of 'The Prayer' associated with such a wicked deed.

Reiterating his sincere faith in his own religion, Father Chazelle made an emotional plea, declaring that he would be overjoyed to die for his belief. The assembled Ojibwa elders reacted with shocked silence. They understood facing inevitable death with bravery, but to joyously seek destruction was irrational and utterly foolhardy behaviour. Ojibwas had no particular respect for people who stood firmly against all opposition; rather they admired the talent for flexibility, adjustment and compromise. They saw nothing praiseworthy in martyrdom. The lengthy exchange that took place on July 31, 1844, ended with the admonition from Oshawano to the "man with a hat" advising him to stop building the chapel and go someplace else.[8]

Despite this warning, the two Jesuits felt bound by their vows to continue their difficult missionary efforts on Walpole Island. A few Indians did eventually come and camp near their crude chapel. A report in 1846 indicates that after more than two years of intense missionary work there were sixty Roman Catholics at Walpole Island. Protestant religions also came to the island, the greatest success going to those whose ministers could preach in Ojibwa. In 1858, the religious affiliation of the band was reported as follows: Church of England, 230; Methodists, 53; Roman Catholics, 19; and 522 'Pagans' who were still practising their centuries-old religion. Late on the night of March 22, when both the Jesuits were off the island, their chapel inexplicably burned to the ground.[9]

Turning to another concept, let us consider the matter of *time*, very different in the minds of Europeans and the Native people of North America. For North American Indians, and indeed for indigenous people all over the world, time is part of the natural order of life. Indian time is environmental time, based on close observation of the sun, moon, stars and the changing seasons. Indians took note, when weather permitted, of the occurrence of the winter and summer solstice and the vernal and autumnal equinox. Years were counted as a certain number of 'winters'; divisions of the year followed the lunar cycle; and days were actually 'sleeps'. Time of day was noted as the angle of the sun. When precision was needed to coordinate war expeditions, leaders distributed packets of small sticks, one stick to be broken each day. Action began at the end of the 'broken days'.

---

8 Chazelle 1973, pp. 252–275. "13ᵉ Lettre, 24 janvier 1845", in Laurent Cadieux (dir.), *Lettres des nouvelles missions du Canada, 1843-1852*, Toronto, Les Éditions Bellarim : Paris, Maisonneuve et Larose.

9 Nin Da Waab Jig 1987, p. 41. *Walpole Island : The Soul of Indian Territory*, Windsor, Commercial Assoclates/Ross Roy Ltd.

The European need to measure everything, including time, puzzled many Indian people. And of course, Europeans expressed considerable scorn for 'Indian time', which still means something imprecise, but probably two hours later than announced. Indian people learned that Europeans treated time as a commodity; they could 'spend' time, 'save' time, 'lose' time, and do something very bad which was 'waste' time. Europeans put a high value on watches and clocks, which should be 'on' time. An Indian philosopher and humorist from Manitoulin Island at the north end of Lake Huron has explained his own difficult experience trying to comprehend European time when he first attended school.[10] He learned about hours, minutes and seconds, but these ideas had no tangible reality. He tried in vain to find a way to grasp and hold a 'minute', or grab a 'second' out of the air. He was not convinced by explanations of the uniformity of accurately measured time. He knew from his own experience that all time was not alike. When he was happily engaged, time passed swiftly. Furthermore, everyone recognized the 'waiting' time was longer than any other kind of time. But he did ultimately learn the true function of clocks. He figured out that the teacher and the principal were not actually in charge of the school; the clock, an instrument of great power, really ran the school.[11] The dependence of the modern working world on clocks has been a subject of Indian humour. As one Indian commented with a smile, "The white man has to look at his watch to find out if he is hungry."

In the field of education, Indian people of Canada—as in other parts of America—have had some of their most direct confrontations with European ideas. Since education and training are not separated from daily life and child-rearing, the school, like the church, was an unfamiliar institution. In the Indian way, grandparents usually took over the primary responsibility for child-rearing, since parents were younger and lacked the experience and knowledge of the elders. Children were taught good behaviour by having their attention called to exemplary actions, as they were taught the consequences of unacceptable behaviour. They acquired the ability to hunt, fish, plant gardens, and master other vital skills by direct participation. Everyday life was a series of 'on-the-job'

---

10 Pelletier 1972, pp. 44–53. "Time", in Ralph Osborne (dir.), *Who is the Chairman of this Meeting?* Toronto, Neewin Publishing Co.

11 Ibid., p. 42.

training experiences. No special science laboratory was required to learn to dissect a fish or a frog.

Indian people were universally opposed to the corporal punishment inflicted in schools with European teachers. With some acquired wisdom in the field of child psychology, they contended that the child who is beaten will grow up to beat other people, promoting violence in the community. Nevertheless, in the Indian schools of Canada, and elsewhere, punishment was considered a necessary part of the program for assimilating young people into the dominant society. It was one of the agents of 'civilization'.

While many Indian children endured considerable suffering as part of the educational system, others, less easily repressed, found considerable humour in the schooling process. In his sensitive and revealing account of his own school days, Basil Johnston recounts the efforts of teachers at Garnier Residential School in Spanish, Ontario, to bring the boys into the mainstream of Canadian life. Little use was made of the instruction, yet the Jesuit fathers taught tailoring, shoemaking and farming, along with more intellectual instruction. But the curriculum advanced to a new level of assimilation goals when the schoolmaster decided that the boys had to learn proper behaviour in a formal tea, and how to conduct themselves on the dance floor, though they had to practise the waltz and foxtrot with only other boys as partners.[12]

Today, the differences between indigenous people and people of European heritage are not as visually apparent as they were two or three centuries ago. On city streets or in large groups, everyone generally follows fairly standardized styles of dress and general deportment. It is impossible to identify a person of Indian heritage simply by appearance. Forcing Indian children to cut their hair and wear uniforms did not reclothe their minds. The ideas and values handed down by the elders for many centuries continue to dominate the minds and hearts of sincere people of Indian heritage. A man can wear a tweed jacket and a tie, and still carry a small pouch of tobacco or sage to be used for spiritual purposes. Ideas and concepts formerly dismissed as merely 'primitive' or 'pagan' are increasingly brought to the attention of members of the dominant European culture. Television provides a powerful medium for exchange of ideas.

---

12 Johnston 1988, pp. 228–229. *Indian School Days*, Toronto, Key Porter Books.

One of the prominent Canadian speakers on behalf of the ideas and values of Amerindians is George E. Sioui, who has created the term 'Americity' to define his concept of the spiritual aspect of all Amerindian societies, the moral order symbolized by the Sacred Circle embracing all forms of life.[13]

Dr. Sioui contrasts 'Americity', which comes out of indigenous culture, with 'Americanism', which is a transplanting of European values and goals that has been destructive to Native society. Americanism is a linear, historical line of thought, characterizing the remote past as primitive and tracing a line of progress and technological development leading to further progress in the future. Dr. Sioui has elaborated on the significance of the opposing symbols, the line and the circle, in other writings. Now he is emphasizing the added symbolism of the 'four directions', each direction also signifying a special colour. The circle and the four directions are embodied in ritual throughout North and South America. He has composed the following paragraphs, which form the conclusion to our joint presentation.

George Sioui Speaks

I am from the part of North America now called Quebec, a vast province of the immense territory now called Canada, a word meaning 'Great Village' in the language of my direct ancestors, the Wyandots, nicknamed 'Hurons' by the French in the beginning of the 17th century. I, however, like the majority of my fellow Amerindians, look at myself as an Aboriginal person of the continent now commonly known as America. Why don't I take any special pride in being counted as a Canadian or a Québécois? It is because these Euro-American territorial entities are constituted as the private property of the people who legally and politically form them. And what is so wrong with calling a country one's own?

According to our point of view, it is simply because from the moment you start believing that the Land, the sacred Earth, belongs to you, at that very moment you begin to lose awareness of the fact that actually you too belong the

---

13 Sioui 1992 "1992 : This Discovery of Americity" in Gerald McMaster and Lee-Ann Martin (dir.), *Indigena : Contemporary Native Perspectives*, Vancouver/Toronto, Douglass & McIntyre : Hull, Canadian Museum of Civilization, pp. 59-70. And Sioui 1999. *Pour une histoire amérindienne de l'Amérique*. Québec, Les Presses de l'Université Laval.

Earth, that you are the Earth. And thus, you begin to see and treat our common sacred home and mother, the Earth, as a piece of material property. Therefore, instead of looking at countries and nation-states as lands of specific peoples, we look at them as causing and promoting the deterioration of our universal home and mother, the Earth, and of all that sustains our very life as humans and non-humans.

Our most ancient and sacred traditions tell us that the Earth-Home that our first ancestors found when they were being led out of their primordial subterranean worlds was a place of utmost beauty, order and abundance. It was the work of the infinite intelligence of a council of supernatural Creators. It. was a world in which man was to live gratefully, admiringly, harmoniously. The idea that humankind's purpose is to dominate the rest of the creatures, and rearrange the world to satisfy human interests and needs, simply was not conceivable.

Our ancient traditions also inform us that Life is conceived as one Great Circle of Relations uniting all beings, and that this Great Circle of Life is divided into four equal parts. Four is thus for us a sacred number. There are four directions, four parts to the year, to the day, to the lunar month; four ages of human life, four parts to our most important ceremonies. There are also four families of peoples, each possessing a special power to share with the others. Around the Great Circle of all humans, there is a place, corresponding to each of the four directions, for each one of the four families of peoples.

There are also four sacred colours. The south is the position of the Yellow Family of Peoples possessing the gift of understanding; they are the guardians of light and sky. The west is the position of the Black Family of Peoples, gifted with a special power of reason; they are the guardians of water. The North is the position of the White Family of Peoples, gifted with the power of movement; they have in trust the element of air. Fourthly, in the East position is the Red, or Amerindian Family of Peoples. Their special power is vision. They are the guardians of the Earth.

The vision of the First Peoples of America stems from their unalterable belief in the complementary and equal dignity of all beings forming the Great Circle of Life. The Amerindian peoples know that their own genius is in the process of bringing into reality a spiritually unified human and non-human family, and that this is the only real 'discovery' of America. The First Peoples of America know that they have a very special and unique sensitivity for, and knowledge of, our Earth-Mother. They also know that some human peoples, because of various kinds of constraints, and not because of lesser moral capacity, have abandoned the circular thought and become linear in their social and ideological orientations. More and more people in the world acknowledge that linear thought can no longer be trusted to produce viable social and ideological models for human behaviour on a small or on a global scale, and more people are taking genuine interest in the health of the Earth and the various orders of its inhabitants. But the high-level discussions about the saving of the Earth involve only three Families of Peoples. Around the table of nations, where are those who look at themselves as the guardians of the Earth and possessors of a vision of a true, healthy and secure world order of the future?

And how is the Fourth Family of Peoples faring in its home continent? Just like their home and motherland, the Amerindians this year are mourning five hundred years of a most aggressive and unjustified war against them. The linear peoples that have invaded them during all this time have spared no effort or resource of the human imagination to wipe out all traces of Native American existence. In order to help their own cause, the Euro-Americans have even affirmed all along that America's 'wild peoples' would very soon no longer be in existence, or already had disappeared, as they ought to. And any surviving group or individual still professing to be Indian was—and still is—officially 'not truly Indian', and persecuted accordingly.

But the Amerindians, in almost every region of their continent, have survived. And one of the main reasons for this apparently inexplicable survival is probably the extreme violence displayed by their invaders. Indeed, how could anyone have ever believed in any intrinsic moral superiority claimed by the colonizers of America? Through the extremely harsh history of its contact with the Euro-American Line, the Amerindian Circle have learned that the Line can only produce violence, aggressiveness, a taste for destruction, and a mad and insatiable craving for material wealth. Therefore, it can also only produce disease, both physical and psychological.

Long ago, our Amerindian ancestors knew that our peoples would go through a long period of death and intense suffering because of the arrival of Europeans on their soil, but our oral histories are steeped in the feeling that this type of 'civilization' would be relatively short-lived on our continent. During this time, we have often found spiritual comfort and assurance in the knowledge that the time would come relatively soon for us to assume our role as guardians and caretakers not only of our own continent, but of the Earth herself.

To us, 1992 marks the 500th anniversary of the beginning of the destruction of our Motherland, America, by Europeans. The message underlying our thoroughly unified denouncing of the Euro-American celebration of this anniversary is that the Peoples of the Fourth Family universally feel and believe that the time has indeed come for us to fulfill our role as peoples at the east of the Circle, and so give new vision and hope to the rest of our common human family.

The genius of America consists of seeing, creating, extending and maintaining relationships with beings, human and non-human, so the Great Circle or family of beings may be sustained and strengthened. And our consciousness of our need to participate in world interaction as Amerindians is much reinforced by the wide and ever-increasing support we receive from our non-Amerindian brothers and sisters. We are therefore beginning this other half-millennium of coexistence with the rest of the world with an irrepressible sense of our duty to exercise the most important right that has been denied to us during the age of destruction that we have survived: *the right to participate* in the world as its Fourth Family of Nations. I, in the name of our peoples, wish to thank my dear, beloved sister Dr. Helen Tanner for conveying my words to this beautiful, important gathering, and all of you, dear brothers and sisters, for listening to what I had to say. I also wish to give thanks to the organizers of this conference for creating the possibility of expressing our collective thoughts at such an important moment. May our Great Circle of Life be ever stronger!

Ho! Ho! Ho! Attouguet! (Many heartfelt thanks!)

Pardonnez ma présence

Pardonnez ma présence

Pardonnez ma présence,
J'ai passé trop de temps
Au pays des âmes,
Mes gens sont presque tous morts,
La fin du monde est tombée sur nous,
Regardez mon pauvre canot
Hier si puissant, si magnifique,
Il a reçu tant de coups,
Sa peau d'écorce de Bouleau
Est toute déchirée,
Il m'a porté, moi et mes frères combattants,
Sur tant de lacs houleux,
Dans tant de rapides périlleux.
J'ai tant de blessures sur mon corps,
Mon âme saigne et souffre,
Tant de fois frappé à mort,
Je sens l'incendie, l'effroi, la peste,
L'angoisse que mon beau peuple ne soit plus,
Pardonnez ma présence
Dans votre monde si parfait,
Je ne veux pas retourner à hier
Où je suis mort cent fois
Je suis avec vous ici
Mais mon âme ne veut pas
Me suivre.
Pardonnez ma présence.

Les Wendat : un peuple plurimillénaire

Conversation avec Georges Sioui

Interviewer : Carlos Graña Sarmiento, correspondant pour la revue indigène péruvienne Chirapaq.

Georges Sioui nous reçoit dans sa demeure. Une peinture indigène d'une grande beauté est la toile de fond de notre dialogue. Il exprime avec fierté qu'il est un Amérindien de la nation Wendat, que les Français ont naguère appelés « Hurons ». Il parle de sa jeunesse, il raconte qu'il a été un guide dans les forêts de son territoire. Nous parlons des canots de cèdre que son peuple fabrique, un bois qu'ont aussi utilisé les Phéniciens et les Grecs dans le monde antique pour fabriquer leurs embarcations. Georges nous montre un canot qu'il a apporté de Québec, fabriqué par sa nation. Le canot était un important moyen de navigation dans les zones de lacs et des rivières. Son poids léger facilitait son transport. Les autochtones le transportaient sur leur dos quand ils devaient faire un portage.

Georges parle plusieurs langues dont le français, l'anglais et l'espagnol qu'il a appris de sa femme Barbara, née en Colombie. Miguel Paul Sastaretsi, son fils de six ans, est aussi avec nous. Polyglotte comme son père, il parle déjà trois langues. Georges a obtenu son doctorat en histoire à l'Université Laval, considérée comme une des meilleures universités du Canada. Son premier livre, *Pour une autohistoire amérindienne*, publié dans sa version originale par les Presses de l'Université Laval, a paru en version anglaise aux presses de l'Université McGill-Queen's et a reçu l'éloge du fameux anthropologue français, Claude Lévi-Strauss.

En 1492, quels peuples vivaient au Canada en 1492 ?

Le peuple autochtone n'était pas très dense au Canada, comme c'était le cas en Amérique Centrale et en Amérique du Sud. Le territoire était habité par des peuples chasseurs et agriculteurs, comme les Wendat et les Iroquois. Dans l'ouest, certaines populations pratiquaient aussi l'agriculture en 1492. Peu à peu, ces peuples se sont transformés en chasseurs après l'arrivée des Européens puisque cette présence d'étrangers chez eux signifia qu'ils durent quitter leurs territoires et fuir les maladies que les Européens emmenaient avec eux. Ceci entraîna des dérangements très profonds pour toutes ces populations. Dans l'est il y avait des peuples maritimes. Dans les provinces de l'est et dans les territoires des Grands Lacs il y avait des peuples semi agriculteurs et nomades, tels que les ancêtres des Sioux et des Ojibway. Plus à l'ouest il y avait des peuples qui habitaient les Prairies. Leurs populations n'étaient pas très denses. De l'autre côté des Montagnes Rocheuses, il y avait une zone plus peuplée où existait une variété de peuples et de cultures parce que l'on suppose que plusieurs de ces peuples arrivèrent d'Asie par la côte du Pacifique. Le nord était peuplé de chasseurs. Les Amérindiens cultivaient dans leurs territoires et chassaient les animaux. Ils vivaient selon les cycles de la nature. Ils protégeaient les espèces animales pour qu'elles ne s'éteignent ni ne se sur peuplent.

Comment communiquaient entre eux les peuples indigènes si leurs langues étaient toutes différentes ?

Il y avait la communication par signes. Il existait aussi des langues connues et utilisées par de nombreux peuples. La langue des mes ancêtres Wendat, par exemple, était utilisée par plus de 50 nations différentes, tout comme nous utilisons l'anglais aujourd'hui. Ils avaient leur langue wendat et toutes les nations environnantes connaissaient cette langue. L'échange de biens et de produits se faisait dans cette langue.

La plupart des nations indigènes parlent du cercle. Qu'est-ce que cela signifie ?

Le Cercle est ce qui distingue essentiellement la pensée des Amérindiens et des autres peuples naturels par opposition à la pensée linéaire qui est venue d'Europe. Le Cercle veut simplement dire que l'homme qui possède cette façon de voir est capable de reconnaître la parenté qui existe entre toutes les formes de vie, non seulement entre les êtres humains. Il est capable de voir que sa propre existence dépend du bien-être des autres êtres. Les penseurs linéaires, pour leur part, ont perdu cette capacité de concevoir la relation et la parenté qui nous unit à tous les autres êtres.

Nous avons trouvé des exemples de ceci dans la façon dont l'explorateur Jacques Cartier a agi avec la population indigène du Canada et dans la façon dont Hernan Cortez a agi au Mexique contre Moctezuma, aussi bien que dans la façon dont Francisco Pizarro a agi contre le peuple d'Atahualpa au Pérou.

Qu'arriva-t-il avec Donnacona, le chef des gens de Stadacona, où était située la ville actuelle de Québec ? Parlez-nous un peu des agissements de Cartier envers les populations indigènes de cet endroit.

Cette similitude entre l'agir de ces différents conquérants n'a pas été étudiée ni établie, mais elle est réelle. Il est possible que Jacques Cartier, qui arriva un jour de juillet de 1534, ait eu connaissance de ce qui était arrivé au sud du continent.

Pour cette raison, il voulut conquérir le nord d'une façon similaire. Il arriva où il y avait des populations et un ordre territorial respecté par tous les peuples et il s'enquit de qui était au centre de cet ordre territorial. Il se rendit compte que le peuple de Stadacona était le peuple principal de cette région. Après que les autochtones eurent aidé ces Français à survivre et après qu'ils eurent guéri leur équipage du scorbut, Cartier se décida à rompre l'équilibre et l'ordre que ces peuples avaient établi. Il réussit à capturer Donnacona le 3 mai 1536. Donnacona avait été le chef principal de toute la région entourant l'actuelle ville de Québec et que Cartier nomma « Canada », mot qui dans la langue des gens de Stadacona voulait dire : « notre grand village », ou « notre village principal ».

Jacques Cartier invita dix personnes dans son bateau, disant qu'il voulait leur donner des cadeaux. Dans ce groupe il y avait six adultes et quatre jeunes personnes. Donnacona était accompagné de ses deux fils, Domagaya et Taignoagny, que Cartier avait enlevés lors de son premier voyage, en 1534, pour montrer ces deux « Sauvages » au roi François I. Cette fois-ci, Cartier captura le chef principal des Stadacona. Il promit à cette nation qu'il reviendrait avec leur chef l'année suivante, mais son bateau ne réapparut que six ans après, sans aucun des Amérindiens à son bord.

Cartier mentit à ces gens. Il leur dit que ceux qu'il avait enlevés avaient voulu rester en France, où ils étaient maintenant de riches seigneurs. Or, les sources historiographiques françaises révèlent que tous ces gens, excepté une jeune fille, étaient morts en moins de deux ans. Les Amérindiens ne crurent pas les paroles de Cartier et commencèrent à poser des obstacles à la venue des Européens sur leur territoire. Une guerre froide s'ensuivit, un conflit qui dura plusieurs décennies dans cette région.

Cela est à dire que les Français agirent de la même manière que les Espagnols, les Portugais et les Anglais. Tous agissent selon la pensée linéaire qui ne permet pas de voir que d'autres cultures ont la même dignité et ont le même droit égal de vivre. Ils verront toujours, ils penseront toujours que ceux qui ne sont pas de leur culture, de leur civilisation, doivent abandonner leurs lieux et qu'ils doivent disparaître et donner la place aux gens qui sont supposément plus évolués. Cette forme de penser n'existe pas parmi les cultures à pensée circulaire, il n'existe qu'un sentiment d'égalité.

Quel est votre concept de la création et de l'origine de l'homme d'Amérique ?

L'indigène n'a pas de notion d'avoir vécu ailleurs. Il n'est donc pas juste de dire que l'Amérindien est arrivé d'autres parties du monde. Il n'y a pas de tel concept dans la pensée indigène. L'indigène pense qu'il est né de la terre même de l'Amérique. Les scientifiques proposent diverses théories et la plus populaire est celle du Détroit de Bering.

Cette théorie est contestée par les peuples indigènes même si elle peut être fondée. Il n'y a pas de tel souvenir dans la conscience indigène. Les autochtones se voient comme des gens qui ont été créés sur ce continent même. Leur première impression au sujet de leur monde américain en fut une d'admiration devant un ordre infini, un monde de pure beauté et voilà la raison pour laquelle l'indigène n'a pas l'ambition d'altérer ou de changer son environnement. Pour lui, la nature est fondamentale. Même si les temps changent, il a toujours la même attitude face à la nature. La création du Grand Esprit de Dieu, peu importe le nom que nous donnons au Grand Mystère de la Vie, est quelque chose que l'on ne peut pas changer, puisque cette création, cet ordre, sont parfaits.

Plusieurs peuples indigènes possèdent le concept que le monde est établi sur le dos d'une grande tortue. Ce fut une femme, un esprit féminin, qui vint du monde céleste avec le but de donner forme et origine à la vie humaine. Quand cette femme descendit, il n'y avait que de l'eau sur la terre. Alors, les animaux demandèrent à leur chef, qui était la grande tortue, ce qu'ils devaient faire pour recevoir cette femme. La grande tortue instruisit les animaux marins d'aller au fond de la mer chercher un peu de boue. Le crapaud, qui était le plus humble d'entre eux, fut celui qui put se rendre au fond de la mer et en ramener un peu de terre qu'il déposa sur la carapace de la tortue. D'abord, une île se forma qui s'étendit et créa le continent américain. En-suite, la femme donna naissance à une fille qui grandit et, à son tour, eut deux garçons. L'un d'eux était disposé à créer des obstacles dans la vie des hommes et l'autre à rendre facile la vie des ces mêmes êtres. Les deux avaient la mission de préparer le monde pour la venue des humains. Les deux frères avaient chacun une manière opposée de voir la vie. La grand-mère des deux garçons se chargea d'établir l'équilibre entre les caractères de ses deux ancêtres des humains. Pour cette raison, la femme, chez les Amérindiens, a le rôle d'équilibrer la volonté des êtres masculins qui tendent à s'opposer, à lutter entre eux. La femme est vue comme un être qui vient équilibrer les volontés et les ambitions des hommes.

Les historiens euro-américains ont « distorsionné » l'histoire. Ils affirment que ce furent les Iroquois qui exterminèrent les Hurons. Qu'est-ce que vous en pensez ?

Oui, vous avez bien choisi le mot : « distorsionné ». Je pense que c'est là la pierre angulaire de l'historiographie euro-américaine au sujet des peuples du Canada, généralement du nord-est de l'Amérique du Nord. Il s'agit d'un mensonge historique, il s'agit d'une façon fausse qui vise à responsabiliser les victimes. Nous savons tous que ces peuples, les Hurons et les Iroquois, ne se faisaient pas grand tort. Même s'ils étaient parfois en guerre, ils étaient parfois des alliés. Quand les Français arrivèrent, ils se rendirent compte que les Hurons étaient alliés à presque tous les autres peuples amérindiens, ils étaient au centre des réseaux de commerce qui existaient dans cette région. Pour cette raison, afin de fonder leur empire en Amérique du nord, ils s'allièrent aux Wendat. Cette nation autochtone était tout à fait centrale et très prospère. Les Iroquois ne faisaient pas partie de ces grandes alliances. Les Hollandais, quand ils virent que les Iroquois étaient en dehors de cet ordre économique, s'en firent des alliés. Ils leur fournirent librement des armes à feu et les Français essayèrent de faire les choses de façon similaire. De cette façon, la grande famille des nations amérindiennes du nord-est fut sacrifiée aux priorités économiques et religieuses des Européens. Les Anglais, qui remplacèrent les Hollandais en 1664, profitèrent de la situation et utilisèrent les Iroquois pour détruire la France et ses alliés indiens. Le résultat fut que deux pouvoirs s'établirent et grandirent et que les nations amérindiennes furent vouées à la quasi-destruction. Plusieurs nations amérindiennes furent rasées par les nations européennes. Ces mensonges concernant la destruction des Hurons par les Iroquois existent toujours. Ils sont présents dans la majorité des livres d'histoire. L'histoire euro-américaine est basée sur des mensonges.

J'aimerais que vous me parliez des wampum. Je pense qu'il y a une similitude avec les kipu des anciens Péruviens.

J'apprécie que vous nous fassiez remarquer la similitude entre le kipu des Incas et les wampum de nos nations. En réalité, tous les peuples de la côte atlantique utilisaient le wampum. Il était fait de morceaux de conque taillés et était de deux couleurs, le mauve et le blanc. Les Amérindiens avec grande habileté travaillaient ces conques et en faisaient des perles de deux couleurs. Ces grandes coquilles venaient des états présents de la Nouvelle-Angleterre et on en faisait des ceintures de perles qui contenaient des motifs, des dessins, qui représentaient une histoire, un traité, un événement important. Ils étaient les archives de nos peuples. Dans chaque nation il y avait des gardiens de ces archives de wampum et il existait aussi des historiens qui apprenaient à interpréter les wampum et qui conservaient le souvenir de tous ces faits.

Parlez-nous de votre peuple, les Wendat.

Nous qui sommes communément appelés Hurons avons un nom propre pour nous désigner. C'est le nom de Wendat, ce qui signifie « ceux qui habitent une île ». Ceci peut avoir une relation avec le concept de la création dans la pensée indigène, c'est-à-dire, de la femme qui vint d'un monde céleste et qui forma une île. Les Wendat furent appelés Hurons par les Français. Le mot était péjoratif et voulait dire « ceux qui sont sans manières, sans civilisation ». Les Wendat étaient une confédération de nations très importantes qui s'était positionnée, dans les années 1200-1300, dans les terres agricoles qui avoisinaient les territoires de chasse des nations algonquiennes, situées plus au nord. Ceci veut dire qu'ils se localisèrent à l'endroit où leurs produits agricoles pouvaient être échangés avec les produits venant des peuples du nord, de l'est et de l'ouest. Ils s'étaient taillé une vocation de commerçants et d'agriculteurs et ils adoptèrent le mode de vie matrilocal et matrilinéaire. Ce peuple devint important. Les Wendat développèrent un grand pouvoir de défense et un grand pouvoir commercial. Ils étaient de grands commerçants et parcouraient toute cette partie du continent du nord-est pour échanger leurs produits et pour créer de nouvelles alliances. On trouvait dans leurs territoires des articles de troc venant de toutes les nations. Ils étaient au centre de l'économie. Leur pays était le cœur de toute cette partie du contient et ceci fut reconnu par les Français qui, pour cette raison, s'établirent dans le pays des Wendat.

Très rapidement s'effectua la destruction de cette civilisation et de la confédération des Wendat, qui avait été formée par une alliance de cinq nations. Elle avait été la première confédération de nations dans le nord-est de l'Amérique du Nord. Il existe actuellement un peu plus de 1 000 descendants des Wendat, qui habitent principalement la réserve du Village-des-Hurons (aussi nommée Wendaké), près de la ville de Québec. La langue quasi-disparue, mais survit encore dans quelques communautés agnié (mohawk) de la région de Montréal, l'une d'elles étant Kanesatake, ou Oka, où il y eut un conflit avec la police québécoise et l'armée canadienne en 1990. Malgré tous les changements, nous conservons notre identité. Nous conservons un sens très vivant de notre histoire et surtout une conscience de la manipulation de celle-ci et des fausses notions qui se créèrent à notre endroit. Nous conservons encore une place importante parmi les nations de l'est. Nous avons toujours des gens qui occupent des positions centrales dans les champs politique, culturel, éducatif, artistique. Malgré que notre population soit réduite, nous comptons plusieurs artistes, écrivains et professeurs. Nous essayons de compenser la perte de nos gens avec l'éducation. Nous ne perdons jamais de vue notre origine, notre histoire.

Je pense que les Wendat peuvent servir d'exemple parce qu'en dépit de nous être mélangés avec les Anglais, les Français et d'autres afin de survivre comme nation, nous conservons très bien notre identité. Je vois que plusieurs Amérindiens de l'ouest ont peur de perdre leur identité parce qu'ils sont en train de perdre leur langue ou parce qu'ils ne vivent plus comme avant. Je puis assurer plusieurs de nos gens, tel que je le fais dans ma condition de professeur avec mes étudiants, que le mode de vie peut changer mais que les valeurs se conservent. Ce sont les valeurs qui distinguent un peuple, beaucoup plus que la couleur de la peau.

OUR RESPONSIBILITY AS INDIGENOUS PEOPLES: SUGGESTIONS TO ANTHROPOLOGY*

Greetings, brothers and sisters!

I wish to thank the University of Costa Rica and the organizing committee for welcoming me to this congress. I feel honoured since this is the first time I have participated in a Central or South American congress. The theme of this conference is closely related to the importance for Aboriginal peoples of global recognition of the values of our civilization.

My name is Georges Tseawi (Rising Sun). I am of the Wendat Nation and of the Turtle Clan. My personal name in Wendat is Wendayeteh, which means 'the one who carries an island on his back'. Our story of creation of what we call 'the Great Island' (the continent of America) is based on the belief that the world was founded by the First Woman upon the back of the big turtle, and that

---

* Presentation by George E. Sioui at the First Central American Congress of Anthropology, University of Costa Rica, October 5, 1994.

this woman began to form the earth from a little bit of mud that was brought from the bottom of the sea by the humble toad—which is why we look at Toad as one of our ancestors. The First Woman's name is Aataentsic, which means 'our old, wise and powerful grandmother'. Aataentsic came from a heavenly world and she was already pregnant. She had a daughter who had died some time after giving birth to two sons, who were therefore raised by Aataentsic. These two grandsons were given the task of preparing the Great Island for the human species to live on. Our linguistic family is the Huron-Iroquois. The French gave us the pejorative name 'Huron', which means uncivilized. Our own name is Wendat, and it means 'dwellers of the island'. Our historical tradition, as well as the science of linguistics, indicates to us that our people originated from Mexico. Likewise, our relatives, the Sioux and the Caddos, originate from Mexico. They now live in Texas and other southwestern states and also in the Canadian provinces of Manitoba and Saskatchewan.

Two Civilizations

At the time of the arrival of the Europeans, our society had, besides a very rich culture, a very prosperous economy based on agriculture, fishing and active trading with the non-agricultural peoples of northeastern North America. Our territories were mainly situated in the vast, rich regions of the Great Lakes in the present-day province of Ontario and along the shores of the St. Lawrence River in the southern part of the present-day province of Quebec. At that time, our populations were among the densest in North America.

As in all parts of the continent now called North America, the coming of the Europeans, with the devastating sicknesses that they brought, spelled a rapid and drastic depopulation of all our peoples, principally the sedentary and agricultural populations. Many of the European invaders brought not only physical diseases, but also spiritual disorders which, for more than five hundred years on our Great Island, have never ceased to produce impoverishment and misery for all human and non-human inhabitants of these lands—where, although perfection did not exist, there was an equilibrium between all the beings in the original universe. This spiritual and mental affliction is called by many Aboriginals and non-Aboriginal thinkers 'linear thought', which means in practical terms the incapacity to see and feel the sacred relation that exists between all beings in the universe. As well, the European newcomers saw the spiritual and social order in this land as an invitation to universal and anarchic competition to convert every created thing into power and material wealth. Obviously, this kind of thinking can only result in violence, racism, anthropocentrism, sexism—in other words, the denial and the destruction of life, which is the most precious treasure that we possess.

As I have said in the past, the typical behaviour of Euro-Americans and the Euro-Americanized on our sacred island must not be attributed to an inherently evil character, but to the linear thinking that made many of the European immigrants abandon their own continent in the first place, and afterwards continue here with the same destructive result.

This said, I wish to give my opinion on the anthropological discourse, occurring throughout the entire continent, about the indigenous peoples. I disagree with social sciences as a whole about the theory they have developed. According to this theory, social and economic liberation of the oppressed majorities must be based on the unification and solidarity of all the marginalized elements of these dispossessed majorities. I disagree for two reasons.

First, my response to this theory is that history teaches that in this way we can only succeed in exchanging our common oppressors for other, new ones. As many of our elders and sages believe, along with a growing number of non-indigenous scholars, what we do not need is this discourse about marginalization, which has always brought about continuing oppression and suppression of the indigenous nations, whose civilization and circular "cosmovision" are fundamentally incompatible with the linear vision that we all know will never produce harmony and order. What is needed is the recognition, by the social sciences in general and anthropology in particular, of the existence of a properly American civilization—which Guillermo Bonfil Batalla and I and others have called 'the deeper America'. The thought of this civilization is circular; that is, its principal and fundamental characteristic is to give the human being the capacity to see, to feel and to respect in its social practice the complementarity and dignity of all components of our society. This society we Indians name the sacred Circle of Life. This regenerating social vision, and not the obsolete destructive vision imported from Europe today, denounced by the continent itself, constitutes the key to the liberation of all the human and non-human beings marginalized and mistreated, on this continent and others.

The second reason for my disagreement with the conventional anthropological discourse resides in the universal ideological and social values of the indigenous peoples. If the oppressed majority marginalizes all the oppressed minorities, it will deprive itself of the important, strategic capital for change that it possesses. (We have said that the indigenous nations are the possessors of the true civilization of this continent and that therefore they cannot be relegated to the status of sub-class of the societies that oppress them.)

The vocation of anthropology is laudable if it recognizes that *indigeneity* by itself constitutes a unique potential for real change. Without such change we will see an increase in times to come of the misery of our own species and of the other orders of beings that share our Earth. Nothing but the recognition of the true civilization of this continent, our Great Island (now called Abyayala by many Aboriginal peoples), can realistically bring about change in our collective world. Life is not a linear process directed by a few individuals unaware of the misery and the violence that they are inflicting on the rest of creation: life is a sacred circle of relations uniting all beings. Life is a circle; we are all a family. Some of us have forgotten what life is; others of us can remind us once again about this. At this time in our common history, it is vital that we, indigenous members of the human family, carry out our responsibility to the rest of the human family. This is what I have desired to help us all understand in this brief presentation.

"To Be Indian Is to Know That We Are All One Family"

In this second part of my presentation, I wish to speak about a concrete case of religious and territorial rights in which the reaffirming of the essential Amerindian philosophy led to a legal victory for my nation in the Supreme Court of Canada. In the spring of 1980, I, along with two friends of the Anishinabe (Ojibway) Nation of Ontario, met in Ottawa (where all three of us were living at the time), two Amerindian Elders from the region of Edmonton, a city close to the Rocky Mountains, in the province of Alberta. At that time, many traditionally oriented indigenous persons were beginning to have a new faith in the survival of their culture and a belief that this survival had to be based on the teachings of the Elders, whom we commonly call holy men or holy women, or medicine people.

In that summer of 1980, my friends and I went to the Rocky Mountains to do a spiritual fast (four days without water or food) under the care and the guidance of the Elders. During the eight days that we were receiving teachings, we learned about some ceremonies and we talked in depth about the way of looking at life that all Amerindians and other "circular thinkers" share. Those moments passed in the company of our western relatives were quite determining. I only need say that my two friends and I were, without knowing it at the time, liberated for good from a habit that is very harmful, and so common among all the oppressed: the addiction to alcohol.

From the moment we had this very beneficial experience—beneficial not only at the personal level but also at the family and community level—each one of us (and others who were inspired by our example) conceived it to be his duty to help reinstate this spiritual strength for our peoples, through other similar exchanges and experiences. We began to recognize at that time that the western Canadian nations, because they have been in contact with non-Aboriginal people for less time than we in the east have, were able to preserve their original world view, the authentic Amerindian spirituality, in a more intact form. We also learned that our brothers and sisters of the west see in us eastern nations, a strength acquired from a longer period of contact with the non-indigenous—a superior capacity, as they say—and therefore a stronger determination to resist the assimilation that the dominant society always intends for the indigenous people.

The next year, in 1981, we did our annual spiritual fast in Ontario in the territory of the Anishinabe, the nation of my two friends. Then, in 1982, I proposed to them that we go to the territory of my nation, the Wendat, in the province of Quebec. One of my friends was not able to come, and therefore there were two of us going on the fast. A few kilometres from where we were fasting (a piece of ground traditionally circumscribed by an offering of tobacco), three of my own brothers and their families were camping. Both had small children, and because they were so close to us in the mountains we hoped to teach their children some elements of fishing and gathering natural herbal medicine in the context of spiritual communion with nature.

These territories of ours were appropriated by the provincial government at the beginning of the 20th century and made into a provincial park. In spite of eight decades of dispossession and governmental intimidation, at times violent in decades past, some "rebellious" families had continued to frequent these territories in the capacity of guides for rich Canadian and American tourists, and also as illegal hunters and trappers during the winter months. Of course, my own family was among the non-conformist ones.

Many times during the preceding fifteen years we had been arrested by the government agents of the Ministry of Tourism, Fishing and Hunting, and every time we refused to respect their authority over us as Indians, and over lands that we said were still ours. They always let us go, we never paid their fines, we never bought their permits—although, as some of those officers rightly said, many members of our nation bought their licences to fish and hunt, and also paid their fines when they were caught breaking some law. They let us go in peace, saying that as long as things had not been clarified between our respective societies, they were under orders to "tolerate" the non-conformists.

In 1976, the Parti Québécois was brought to power in Quebec. In its vision of a sovereign Quebec, separated from Canada, this government declared that its territory was integral and began to put an end to the policy of tolerance of any group of "Québécois" Indians. After having frequently escaped the grip of the law using the arguments already mentioned, we were now arrested. The "agents of conservation" entered with their weapons into our ceremonial grounds (where metal objects must not enter) and told us to leave, and said if they found us still there the next day they would take us out by force. Because of the physical and spiritual state in which I and my fasting companion found ourselves, we did not offer any resistance. We (along with my mother, who arrived from my brother's campsite) only explained to them that we were in the process of bringing our territories back to the ancestral ways of honouring nature in order to once more find our place in the reality of things as human beings and members of an Aboriginal nation.

To the argument of these officers that this territory was a newly created conservation park, we answered that, seeing so many square kilometres of destroyed forests in the name of so-called 'forest development', we were not able to believe in the capacity of their society to conserve nature, and that, at any rate, these lands were ours and we had always been able to use them. As well, we explained to them that our uninterrupted efforts to cultivate and protect our own things was not for us alone: it also aimed at helping the immigrant society, which has no valid solution to the terrible social and ecological problem it has created for lack of a social and environmental vision.

"We are going to defend ourselves from any accusation," we told them, "and we will win a victory for the good of all and the good of nature, and we are going to come back here someday, and we are going to rebuild the fire of our ceremony and finish it. We are going to affirm our right legally; we need to do this for ourselves and for you also." This principle that our struggle was not self-centred, but aimed at liberating humans and non-humans—that is, recognizing that life is a sacred circle that unites all beings—took our cause out of the frame of simple legal politics, with its confrontational processes. This same principle elevated our legal case to the spiritual level, which, as our traditional leaders tell us, is the highest form of politics. This meant that after eight years of legal proceedings, we would obtain a unanimous decision in our favour in the Supreme Court of Canada.

At the first level, in the Cour des sessions de la paix du Québec, in 1983, we based our defence on our ancestral rights. The court decreed that only Indians protected by a treaty are exempt from obeying the provincial laws in many legal areas, among which are the laws concerning hunting, fishing and trapping, and that at any rate the Wendat did not have ancestral rights in the province of Quebec because they are descendants of immigrants from Ontario who survived the Iroquois wars of the 1640s. (I refuted this old historical argument in a book that I published in French in 1989 and in English in 1992.)

At the second level, in the Cour supérieure du Québec, in 1984, we decided to bring out of our national archives, in order to have it recognized as a treaty, a brief document signed by our chiefs and by the British military commanders in 1760, the year in which this European nation vanquished the French in North America and ended their regime. This document, obtained from the British by our chiefs three days before the capitulation of their French allies, reads as follows:

> This is to confirm that the chief of the Huron and their warriors have laid down their arms before me and have made peace with the British crown. They will be maintained in the free exercise of their customs, their religion and their trade with the British. We order our soldiers in our garrisons to treat them humanely upon their return to their settlements. Signed by me in Longueuil (close to Montreal) this 5th day of September of 1760: General James Murray.

The decision of the preceding court was maintained. However, our case, already then famous under the name of the 'Sioui Case', began to attract the attention of other Aboriginal nations of Canada and of other countries. Two of my brothers, who were political leaders at many levels, including local, provincial, national and international, succeeded in convincing other leaders of our own nation to hire good lawyers and to pay for them. Also, we obtained the strong support of the Assembly of First Nations, the national First Nations organization of Canada, which also put its best lawyers to work on our case. The principal reason for this significant help was that Aboriginal nations were seeing that the Sioui Case was going to reinforce and amplify the interpretive substance of all the other Indian treaties, especially the numbered treaties in western Canada. The lawyers who worked at those different levels of jurisdiction during the eight years the case was in Canadian courts based their argumentation on the testimony that I gave in the primary phase of the legal proceeding. I did not use the services of a lawyer because I judged that no legal advisor (we did not have Wendat lawyers at that time) would be able to understand and therefore defend our cause successfully, because it was about our spiritual culture.[1]

Our nation, by then supported by very many people, both indigenous and non-indigenous in Canada and abroad, appealed the decision to the Court of Appeal of Quebec. A new feeling of strength and a new determination came

---

[1] Since our victory in the Supreme Court, we have discovered that it is possible for non-Aboriginal legal practitioners to comprehend and successfully defend cases involving traditional beliefs and practices. Also, significantly, there has been a marked increase in the number of Aboriginal lawyers and in their ability to advance our cause through the judicial system.

into being among our Wendat people. A new preoccupation also began to grow among the Quebec population, mostly among the elite of the sovereignist majority, historically conditioned to believe that the culture of the Aboriginal people in Quebec was already disappearing.

For two more years our team of investigators, researchers, lawyers, traditionalists and supporters continued to reinforce the defence and refute the arguments of Quebec. In the fall of 1987, the Court of Appeal of Quebec gave us a favourable verdict: two judges out of three affirmed that our document was, indeed, a treaty, which exempted us from provincial laws. Alarmed by this worrisome decision, the Province of Quebec appealed to the Supreme Court of Canada. Three more years of very systematic work allowed us to refute each one of the historical and legal arguments of the Quebec authorities. On May 30, 1990, exactly eight years after our arrest, the Supreme Court of Canada gave us a unanimous verdict supporting the decision of the previous court: the nine judges of the Supreme Court established our treaty, many times denied by the legal court of Quebec over a period of 230 years.

A few days later, we went to the place where our ceremony had been interrupted in 1982, we removed the moss that had grown over the stones where our fire had been, and we relit our fire with the same coals from the same wood. Then we finished our ceremony. The prayers of our parents and of our Elders had been answered. Now we have our right. And the forest conservation officers, when they drive by, try not to make too much noise and give us their greetings. They too have learned something: the Indian culture is important and, thanks to God, is now beginning to live again. Like the stones underneath the moss, the Indian culture was only sleeping, waiting for another time. We are all family. What I have forgotten, my brother will help me to remember. What my other brother lost, very willingly I will help him recover. We are all brothers and sisters. To be Indian is to be human. To be Indian is to know that each and every one of us is part of the same family.

Brothers and sisters, thank you for listening to me. Etsagon!

Following a Wendat Feeling about History:
The Sioui Case*

First, I would like to greet and thank our Elders; secondly, Stan and Peggy Wilson, who have organized this conference for us. It's a monumental undertaking which is also having monumental success. I would also like to thank the students, and all who have collaborated in making this possible.

My clan name is a name of the Turtle Clan of my nation, the Wendat, the real name of the Huron People. My name, Wendaye: te, means 'The one who carries an Island on his back'. I am pretty sure that Elder Tom Porter can understand the meaning of that word.[1] My original language, which my nation no longer speaks, is, I would say, the same as Elder Porter's, or very close to it. I speak many other languages but none of them is my native language. When

---

* Allocution by Dr. Georges E. Sioui, March 17, 1995, at the conference "Autochtonous Scholars : Toward an Indigenous Research Model", education conference held at the University of Alberta, Edmonton, Canada, March 15–18, 1995.

1 Tom Porter is an Elder of the Mohawk, or Kanienkha: ka nation.

I hear Elder Porter speak, I hear my native language, and even though I don't understand it, I'm sure my ancestors within me understand it. And when I hear the Cree and the Saulteaux and the Blackfoot and all the other Amerindian languages, I'm sure my ancestors understand those languages.

I will just say a few words about the experience of Amerindian nations in the East, as compared to the West. What makes our feeling about history very distinct in the East from that of tribes in the West is that *we were there* when the first visitors arrived from Europe. We were there. We were not impressed, because they were weak, and they were sick and they were poor. They asked us for a little place to live. This very much conditioned our feeling about history. When they arrived here, when the invaders arrived here, in the West, they could show much more power, because they had taken so much from the land, they had removed so many of our peoples. So people here in the West had a reason to be more impressed. In the East, we—the Wendat, the Iroquois, the Mohawk, the Abenaki, the Mi'kmaq and all the eastern peoples—have this sense of our history: we refuse to be controlled, we refuse to be impressed by the value system of others who had to leave their land in the first place. We never had to leave and so we consistently refuse to be controlled and to be impressed, as I said, because we know the harm that was done to our people. We had great nations, we had great confederations of nations. Today, the Iroquois Confederacy represents what remains of large confederacies of Wendat, Neutral, Erie, Tobacco, Susquehanna peoples and an infinity of Algonkian nations with whom we traded before the Europeans came. The Iroquois were able to save the remnants of all of these destroyed nations and confederacies. The Iroquois are very representative of what we are today as Native peoples. I very much believe that we all suffered an unimaginable shock, an awesome destruction, and that today (I think that our ancestors and our Elders know that) we are giving one another the remaining strength that we still have, and I believe that together we will recompose a great Indian nation, which will not be Wendat, which will not be Cree, or Huron, or Iroquois entirely. It will be a great Indian Nation. It's coming together right now.

So just the thought of going through the exercise of tackling the dominant society's educational models and coming out still alive, still able to speak from the heart and speak as First Nations people, not destroyed in our spirits and our souls, is a very welcome one. It's a sign that the times are changing. They're not only changing: they have changed. There is a new trend that exists right here in the air of our land, here; nobody can do anything against this change: it is here already. We have suffered a very severe shock these past 503 years, but we are taking our place again as the leaders and the protectors of our Land.

Our nation, the Wendat, like the Iroquois, had a very keen gift for adopting people, assimilating them into our society. Yesterday, Elder Porter made us (the audience) repeat one Mohawk phrase. Then he said that we were all Mohawk. That's very Mohawk, it's very Iroquois and it's beautiful because that's what it's all about: adopting one another. Our Wendat ancestors were able to survive because they went on war expeditions supposedly to help the French fight the English, but their real agenda was to go and capture English children, English people, bring them back to their villages and raise them as Wendat people. The Iroquois did the same against their French enemies, and many Amerindian peoples did the same, but we Wendat did this very systematically. And today there is not this notion among our people that you are 'part-Indian'; that does not exist. I'm not part-Indian, even if I have this French accent; you all have an English accent or a Spanish accent; it does not mean anything. I'm a Wendat. And I think that we're all in the process of reclaiming our people who say that they are part-Indian, part-Cree, part-Cherokee, part-anything. They are going to come back and be First Nations people. And the door is also open to non–First Nations people; we were always able to transform non-Indians into Indian people, because we all come from the Circle. There is no such thing as distinct races and civilizations; there is only one civilization that is adapted to the human being and to the natural world: it's the civilization of the Circle. And the peoples who have chosen to become linear, who had to leave Europe because they had adopted this linear world view, are not able to sustain their civilization much longer here in our land because it's not adapted to our land. Slowly, they will have to adopt our world view, because it's a circular world view. So we are going to eventually adopt and assimilate them or, as we said in our old Wendat language, 'eat' them. The English word 'assimilate' carries the same meaning: to eat someone up, culturally. Even though we had very small numbers, we Wendat, as well as many tribes in the East, were always able to 'eat up' the dominant society. We never lost our distinct identity. We're not part-Indian. We're Wendat. We would never think of Elder Porter as 'part-Mohawk', would we? He's got his people's spirit and vision intact.

To talk a little bit about my academic experience—I went to school twenty-nine years. I went to high school and formed the dream of rewriting Amerindian history. Those who have read my first book will know that when I was six years old, my father told me that one day I would have to write other history books. So I did that. I first tried to go and study history at Laval University in Quebec. That university was then still controlled by clerical people and ideas to a large extent. So I dropped out of there and told them that I would be back sometime when they had finished their time and I started studying languages. I think I studied about ten languages—Russian, German, Spanish, Portuguese, Inuktitut, Cree, Montagnais, English, Latin, Ancient Greek—and amused myself learning and studying languages, while my dream of becoming a historian and rewriting (or unwriting?) Indian history was always present in me. I eventually went back to university to do this.

I went back after meeting someone [I point with my outstretched hand at Elder Eddie Bellerose, sitting in the first chair at my left in the audience. There is a five-second pause, during which I struggle to hold back tears]. It makes me emotional to talk about this person, my Elder here, Eddie Bellerose.[2] It's just coincidental that this conference occurs in the city of Edmonton and that in two days it will be fifteen years ago that I met my uncle Eddie Bellerose and other Elders—Blackfoot, Dènè, Saulteaux and Assiniboine—and my two Mushums, Abe Burnstick[3] and Peter Ochiese.[4] These Elders, my grandfathers, were able to liberate me and my friends from alcohol. My family, like most of our First Nations families, has suffered a lot from alcohol. We still do. But

---

2 Eddie Bellerose, one of the greatest teachers I have known, and my close spirit-relative. We lost Elder Bellerose in 2000.

3 Abraham Burnstick, a truly great spiritual person, a leader. I am very thankful he was my Mushum, my dear "grandfather".

4 Peter Ochiese, one of the most remarkable men I have known : a truly holy person, the greatest medicine-person of our time. He went on the spirit-road last February 2006, at 114 years, still active, working to help the people.

we were relieved and liberated through the teachings of our Elders. So I very deeply respect Eddie Bellerose. Meeting Eddie Bellerose and Elders that you have here in the West meant that ten years later I and my brothers would beat the Province of Quebec in the Supreme Court of Canada over a case of religious and territorial rights, now come to be known as the *Sioui* case,[5] because we learned with Eddie and the Elders. Eventually, we had wanted to take this learning back to our own home territories in Ontario and Quebec. When we did take it back to Quebec, we fasted, in 1982, in Quebec, on some of our traditional hunting land. My stubborn family (as the Siouis have always been known in Quebec) had always kept up the custom of going to those territories to hunt and fish and collect plants. That time, we were not doing any of that, we were fasting, and that's why we won, eventually. It took eight years; we went to court four times and we eventually won in the Supreme Court.[6] The *Sioui* case started with this person [I indicate Elder Bellerose], and it meant a very great upheaval in Quebec politics, and Canadian politics and world politics as regards indigenous peoples. And it started here in Alberta, on the Kootenay Plains, with your Elders!

We were arrested for, they said, "mutilating the forest".[7] We had made some fasting lodges, using willow saplings, and thus had "mutilated the forest", while the rest of thousands of square kilometres of forest was clear-cut. The bush was all destroyed but that is 'forest exploitation' for linear-thinking people. We had mutilated the forest and so were prosecuted by Quebec. We finally pulled out from our archives an old document that we had. It was signed by the hand of the British Brigadier-General James Murray on September 5, 1760, at the

---

5 *R. v. Sioui*, [1990] 1 S.C.R. 1025.

6 In 1982, the Cour des sessions de la paix J.E. 83-722 found the Sioui brothers guilty of having cut saplings, camped and made a fire in a non-designated location in the Parc de la Jacques-Cartier, in contravention to Articles 9 and 37 of provincial rules relating to the Parc de la Jacques-Cartier (decree 3108-81 of 11 November 1981, 113 G.O. 11 4815), passed in accordance with the Law Concering Parks, L.R.Q., ch. P-9. The Cour supérieure, J.E. 85-947 has confirmed that decision. The Cour d'appel du Québec, [1987] R.J.Q. 1722, [1987] C.N.L.R. 118, has infirmed the verdict of the Cour supérieure, which decision was unanimously maintained by the Supreme Court of Canada in May 1990.

7 Article 9 of the Law states that "In this park, users must refrain from cutting, mutilating, taking or introducing any plant species or part thereof."

behest of our leaders, and it said that under the new English regime, our tribe would be "left in the free exercise of our customs and our religion and our trade with the English". So we looked at this as a treaty because it talked about our customs, our religion and our trade. The authorities of Lower Canada, later to be called Quebec, had historically considered this document to be only a safe-conduct to allow our combatants to go back to our settlements without being attacked by the British troops. So we fought, and through the vision, through the tradition that the Elders gave us back, this understanding of our deeper identity, we were able to infuse a new meaning into that document, which was only a scrap of paper, 230 years old. We were able to put new life into this dead piece of paper. And we eventually we had it recognized by the Supreme Court of Canada that it was indeed a treaty. This had grave implications for Quebec.

By explaining this case, I meant to stress the importance of Elders, the importance of spirituality, of relating ourselves to our own experience. We already had our pride and our consciousness as Indian individuals belonging to this eastern, very battered tribe, the Wendat, so-called Huron, but we lacked this deeper understanding of our spirituality, of our Indianness, a deeper sense of our being as Indian People, and the Elders, your Elders here, gave that back to us. That accorded with what our parents always told us about our Indian people: that we are all one family. "Wherever you go, South, North, East or West," they told us, "approach your Indian people as your relatives, and treat them as relatives, and you'll be treated as relatives." The Elders gave us back what we had lost, the same way that today, as Indians, we have to give back to the non-Indians what they have lost. They have had to become linear, for some reason. It's none of their fault. That linear thinking can only produce disrespect, thus destruction; there is only one word for what's been happening and what's still happening to our land and to us: destruction. We have to give them back the Circle, their original circular vision, where we all come from as human beings.

I would have liked to use a little bit more humour, because our brother, Dale Auger, gave us such a strong medicine at the opening banquet. He has that gift of that strong medicine which is humour, and I said to myself: maybe I should not be so serious all the time [there is laughter in the audience]. I guess that medicine will be working in me, so that next time we'll see each other, I'll be a little bit more humorous.

With this, I would like to stress that I thoroughly enjoyed the presentations that were given to us by the various participants. All of them, as I said, come from different nations, different parts of our land, and all of these are efforts to share, give what we still have. As a Wendat, I don't have very much left, but I have something very important left, which is my sense of history. And I receive all the time, continuously; I receive from everyone, and I really believe that together, we are forming a very powerful people, a very powerful nation. I very firmly believe that we are going to come back to a position of command in this land of ours. When I say "our land"—I want to stress that when we say "our land"—we mean that we *come from* the land, just as when I say my mother, my father, I come from them. I don't say my mother is *mine*, she *belongs to me*; I belong to her. The linear-thinking people say: *my* land; it *belongs to me*. That's what we have to change all around. If we are able to give to them that feeling, that they belong to this land, instead of this land belongs to them, we'll be okay. If we fail in meeting that challenge as First Nations, and Aboriginal and Inuit people, what awaits all of us is that great hunger in times ahead, which our Elder talked to us about this morning. I still think that we can hope, if we stand all together. But First Nations people have to get busy with the task of assimilating, that is, Indianizing the non-Indian society, and thereby avoid what's coming our way if we keep on with this linear thinking, this path of destruction. We all know that if we bring society back to seeing Life as a sacred Circle of Relations, we are going to achieve our goal and responsibility as First Nations people, in relation to our White and Black and Yellow brothers and sisters, the great human family of which we are a part.

Ho! Ho! Ho! Attouguet!
Niawen Kowa!
Kitche Meegwetch!
Thank you very much!
Merci beaucoup !

Canada's Past, Present and Future from a Native Canadian Perspective*

First, following the custom of our people of the Canadian and other First Nations around the world, I wish to greet the Korean people and the Korean land. May the Great Spirit, our Maker, and all the all-powerful Spirits of Life preserve the Korean people and make them ever stronger and more prosperous, and may we always thrive on our friendship and brotherhood. *Niaweh Kowa! Kitche Meegwetch!* Thank you from the heart for having me with you! It truly is for me and my people a great honour.

Then I would like to greet and thank Professor Sang Ran Lee, whom I first met in Ottawa this past June, at the 1995 International Council for Canadian Studies Conference. Professor Lee, myself, and several other participants had had quite interesting discussions on topics relating to Canadian multiculturalism, including the topics of the history of Canadian First Nations and of their participation in Canadian and international life.

---

* Presentation at the Conference "Multicultural Policy and Development in Canada" organized by the Korean Association for Canadian Studies, Seoul, Korea, October 6–7, 1995.

Finally, personally and in the name of my institution, the Saskatchewan Indian Federated College, I would like to thank the Korean Association for Canadian Studies and the Sookmyung Women's University for their dedication and professionalism in realizing this very exciting conference which, I am sure, will bring success to all involved. This said, I wish to briefly present myself. My name is Georges Paul Emery Sioui. My family name, Tseawi (now Sioui), in our language means People of the Rising Sun. My personal Wendat clan name is Wendaye: te. It means He-carries-an-Island-on-his-carapace. I am of the Big Turtle Clan. I am, by my mother and my father, a member and a Customary Chief of the Tseawi Clan and a citizen of the Huron-Wendat Nation. My nation, through the extreme social and demographic upheaval that followed the arrival of the Europeans in our continent, has come to inhabit reserves in the North American territories now called the province of Quebec, in Canada and in the state of Oklahoma, in the USA. Even though very drastically depopulated at first by new diseases and warfare highly intensified through the presence of Europeans, many of our nations were saved from total extinction thanks to our own Aboriginal social systems, which we still preserve. One of the most remarkable features of our governments was, and still is today, their matricentrism, which allowed our peoples to see others as their equal and not have too rigid a sense of nationhood. Thus, remnants of survivors spontaneously joined together to form new nations. Also, our peoples' remarkable, even mysterious survival can be explained by the widespread custom of adopting strangers, often going to war with the primary intent of capturing people, especially women and children, and this usually came in the form of a plea addressed to prominent *Garihoua Doutagheta* (defence captains) by the Clanmothers. These new members came from enemy European settlements and enemy nations; they were eventually sacrificed or, more customarily, formally adopted and made full-fledged members of our nations. Patricentric peoples do not have this capacity of looking beyond race and nation, and therefore have less power to survive. Thanks to our ancestral forms of government, my nation, and others, though mixed with Europeans through capture, adoption and intermarriage, have survived and kept a very strong sense of identity. And so I am extremely proud to be first a Wendat before being a Canadian or Québécois. I am a member of a First Nation in Canada, a nation that has never given or sold any of its territory to any European nation, and has never reneged its sacred role as steward of that land where our Creator put us, we First Nations people. We are and will remain sovereign.

I have, at home, a photograph of my maternal grandfather, who 'went on the spirit-road' ten years before I was born. Recently, a young nephew of mine, looking at that portrait, asked me, "Uncle, was your grandfather a Chinese?" I proceeded to explain to him that it was fairly evident, just by looking at external physical features, that our people are related to various peoples in Asia, but that our stories tell us that we come from the very soil of our land of America.

Since it is my very first trip to Asia, I do feel a special emotion thinking that it is almost certain that my distant Wendat ancestors and the distant ancestors of the Koreans were very close relatives, and walked and hunted and lived together in those ancient times. Most of our Amerindian people today feel offended when non-Indian scientists tell us that our ancestors came to America by crossing the Bering Strait, in successive waves of migration, the last one about 10,000 years ago. Besides the fact that we do not find the slightest trace of such migrations in our own stories, we feel offended because we know that the Euro-Canadian society, in order to justify and rationalize its often discriminatory policies and laws in relation to First Nations, needs to cultivate the notion, in its social discourse, that First Nations people are 'immigrants' too, and that their cultures, though admittedly interesting on the intellectual level and outwardly picturesque, do not carry or offer alternative ideas or remedies for the most obvious failings of the dominant social system at the philosophical, moral and spiritual levels. Simply, First Nations philosophical views and spiritual culture are seen and represented by the dominant culture as vestiges of the past, with very little or no practical value for the 'rapidly evolving modern world'. Therefore, the conventional Canadian wisdom about First Nations is that 'we' Canadians are all immigrants, or descendants of immigrants, and that the Aboriginal Canadians can find their own place in the great multicultural Canadian society, if only they can stop daydreaming and worrying about Mother Earth and their Brothers, the Animals, and understand the world as it really is and adapt to it. If they can't adapt—and help from Canada to 'its Aboriginal peoples' is getting disquietingly scarcer than ever—the same will continue to happen: they will disappear. But before going further into the topic of ideological differences between Canadian First Nations and the mainstream, we will conclude the subject of migrations. Because genealogical relationships between Orientals and Amerindians are so hard to deny, some of us have come to think that it is they, Koreans, Chinese, Mongolians, Japanese and others, who have migrated to Asia from an original American homeland, and not the other way, as scientists want us to believe. At any rate, I and some of my colleagues and friends, both Orientals and Amerindians, and also Euro-Americans, when pondering the striking, deep similarities between Amerindian and Oriental philosophies, cannot but think that the two have common roots, which their respective scholars and others have to do research into, in the hope of breaking the isolation that weakens isolated nations and peoples, and prevents humanity as a whole from forming positive self-concepts by recognizing its global unified spiritual nature; that is, knowing its unchanging place and role in the eternal Circle of Life.

While Canadians and other Euro-Americans have desperately striven to convince Amerindians that they should come to renounce their unenlightened life ways and world view, so as to come to see reality and life in the Euro-American way (the 'true, civilized way'), we Amerindians have thought very similarly about Euro-Americans. My nation, and others in the eastern part of Canada, have traditionally had a very special feeling about the sense of the history of contact between Euro-Americans and us. For my part, I think this is because we, in the East, were standing on the shore to receive them when they first arrived in our land, which they thought to be India, or Cipango (Japan). What we saw was not a wealthy, healthy, noble people; we saw a poor, unhealthy set of angry, suspicious, intolerant and violent men, already behaving themselves as the owners and the lords of our land, planting their crosses, shooting their firearms and hiding themselves in their forts from the ones who brought them food and cured them from their diseases, which immediately began to take a disastrous toll on our people. Then, as soon as they could go back to Europe to make a report to their masters, they treacherously lured our leaders and people on board their ships, apprehended them, and took them with them to Europe, where we now know they all soon died, even though we were told, some years after, that having seen and known the real civilization, none of them had wanted to come back to their hopelessly savage country of Kanatha (Canada), as my own ancestors named it to them.

The more we have known about the foundations of Euro-American civilizations, all along our history of contact with these civilizations, the less impressed we became by them and, simultaneously, the more our peoples, nations, have reflected on the foundations and the nature of our own civilizations, in order to have strength to resist and survive. That we have, indeed, survived is often seen as a wonder by outsiders. But to us, our survival is something natural, logical. The basic thought that always comes to us, when we reflect on the meaning of all this history, this pain, this organized process of destruction of our land, our air, our water, our food sources, our people, is: how can they truthfully believe that we will accept their ways as superior to ours? Why did they arrive at the necessity of leaving their own motherlands in the first place? Who would think of doing that, if not for very grave reasons, such as widespread diseases and war, and other related causes? Therefore it is they who need to see life in a different way, not we. We have to help them find a better way, the way of respect, the way Nature teaches us, the way we call the Sacred Circle of Life.

To explain the circular thinking of Amerindians, I will take an extract from the prologue of my recent book on the history of my nation:

> There is, in reality, for us humans, only one way to look at life on this earth, and it is as a sacred Circle of Relations uniting all beings of all forms and all natures. The great danger is to no longer see life as a great kinship system. Strictly speaking, there are no peoples, races, civilizations: there is only the human species, one species among so many other species of beings, a species even particularly weak and dependent on the other species and the families of beings that compose them: animal, vegetal, mineral, elemental, immaterial, supernatural. There is only one civilization adapted to human existence: the civilization of the Circle, the sacred Circle of Life. There are, in reality, only two types of human societies: those that see and live the Circle and those that have forgotten about the Circle.

The Europeans who had to leave their lands and proceeded to invade America and other continents towards the end of the 15th century, had forgotten about the Circle and had come to believe that life is a linear, evolutionary process, in which they, the European and Christian, are to lead the rest of humanity and nature itself in a certain enlightened direction. Their Bible itself told them that God intended man—again, European-Christian man—to dominate the Earth and all of creation, and to rearrange natural things and peoples according to European-Christian material and spiritual interests. Under that supposedly 'divine' authority, everything becomes the possession of man: all the non-human beings, such as air, water, plants, animals, earth and rocks, as well as non-European, non-Christian peoples and their possessions; even woman loses the high status she has in circular societies to merely become man's possession. In such social and spiritual disorder, how can anything but inequality, repression and destruction come to be the rule? To the traditional Amerindian, that, in a nutshell, is the nature and the logical result of linear thinking. It is also the history that he has known and that someday must come to change. Circular thinkers do not condemn Christianity or the actions of linear peoples. On the contrary, spiritual leaders in circular-thinking societies constantly affirm that all humans, all societies come from the Circle, for the Circle is the symbolic representation of life's creative process itself. They also affirm that humanity is a family and that if some family member loses or forgets about some important thing, it is the responsibility of other members of the family to make that member repossess such thing, or knowledge. Amerindian members of the human family are possibly among the ones who have retained the clearest consiousness that life is a Circle, a family of beings, and *not* an evolutionary, linear process in which beings repress, dominate and exploit one another.

To Canadian First Nations people, and to Amerindian and Aboriginal people generally, the history of the presence of linear thought in America, for 503 years, has been a nightmarish one. It is well known that during the 1st century of contact, we lost from eighty to ninety-five percent of our original population, on a hemispheric scale, mainly because of new, incoming diseases. It is also fairly well known, beyond America, that throughout the next five centuries, our surviving people were subjected to every imaginable attempt to crush their basic vital strength, which is their belief in themselves, their faith in Nature, the Earth, the Circle of Life. When physical repression ceased to be necessary because of European demographic and military superiority, it was misinformation, through the educational systems and through the media, that was used to discredit and de-legitimize, dispossess and further weaken our peoples, in Canada and in the rest of our continent. It is therefore normal that, throughout most of the world, we are today thought to have disappeared. I am not surprised, nor offended, that even many Koreans also think that Aboriginal Canadians, or Indians, as we have been called, have long ceased to exist and that Canada's population is mainly composed of descendants of French and English immigrants. The reality is quite different, mostly as regards Canada's Aboriginal population, now commonly referred to in Canada as the First Nations.

The First Nations population is today the fastest-growing segment of the Canadian population, in contrast to the original francophone and Anglo-Saxon segments, which are in many regions the oldest, or least self-regenerating segments of the Canadian population. For example, in Saskatchewan, where I now live, First Nations, thought to be on the verge of extinction at the beginning of this century, are on the way to becoming the majority population—this will likely happen by the year 2020. Also, First Nations governments, now recognized as a third order of government in Canada (that is, after the federal and provincial governments), are, especially in western Canada, considered among the most sophisticated systems of indigenous government anywhere in the world and as such, as important generators of concepts of future governmental systems and new social ideas on a world scale. Yet, as strange as such a turn of events and history may appear to outsiders, it is seen as only logical to people inside the Amerindian, or First Nations cultures, for all these developments accord with the words pronounced by many sages of our nations throughout the Dark Age that we have lived through. Those words can be summarized as follows: This way that the Strangers are living and the way that they are treating life cannot last for a very long time. One day, soon, the Strangers will be frightened by the consequences of their actions. They will not know what to do. They will then release the grasp that choked us and they will ask us for help. That is when our people will begin to get strong again and will begin to teach the world what we know, mostly why and how we have to treat each other, and all things that exist, as relatives.

Canada, like Korea and all countries, is a wonderful, beautiful country. What makes it special is not, like Korea and many other countries, an absolutely astonishing, visible human history, which so much overwhelms and moves a stranger like me. What is very special about Canada, of course, is its vast, vast expanses of pure, pristine nature, and all the life and moving beauty it contains. Canada is also a safe and very welcoming country. That spirit of welcome and appreciation for differences has been Canada's primary character trait, ever since my ancestors welcomed the Norse, Basque, French, Portuguese, English and other Europeans, lost on their shores, many centuries ago. Those Europeans may have been needy, desperate, sick, but we, the first Canadians, always proceeded quickly to make them feel good and happy again, and to trade with them and to inform them and learn from them, because we believed that around the Circle of Life, everyone possesses unique spiritual gifts, which are made to be shared to make everyone and all happier, wiser, more prosperous and therefore more able to strengthen others.

Canada is also a land where nature imposes its power on humans. I believe that our harsh winters have a lot to do with Canadians' marked propensity to empathize with other fellow humans, because we are all, individually, so defenceless before the power and the strength of Nature. And true Canadians love their winters, because they love that feeling of need for human solidarity. Québécois singer Gilles Vigneault wrote a wonderful song to express precisely this. "My country is not a country," says he: "it is winter.... My house is your house."

Canada's term for her special spirit of welcome, as coined by former Prime Minister Pierre Elliott Trudeau, is *multiculturalism*. It is also a symbol and a signal of welcome made to entice other people to come and become Canadians, for it takes a certain number of people to make such a huge country functional and prosperous. But Canada is largely oblivious of the fact that it really inherited that spirit of welcome and human solidarity from its First Peoples. More importantly, Canada has to come to realize that its First Nations people can and will help her live out to its full meaning her destiny as a country where a true democracy, in the circular sense of the word, will come to exist and be a model for the rest of humanity. A circular, or holistic, democracy will be one where all beings, human and non-human, will have their place and their rights in a universal relation of respect and interdependence. That, to me, and to many of my people, is the profound sense and vocation of Canada. At this moment, Canadian multiculturalism cannot have its full meaning, because Canadian thinking is still profoundly linear and the concept of multiculturalism does not agree with linear thinking. I, and many of my own people, believe that when our people, the true founding people of Canada, take our rightful place in Canada and in the world, Canada will begin to acquire its potential for being a truly multicultural country; that is, where all people are valued and treated equally, in consideration of the whole Circle of Life.

I am personally very heartened to see emerge, in Canada, institutions of learning controlled by First Nations people. I have the very good fortune to work as the Academic Dean of the first University College under First Nations control ever to exist anywhere in America. Our University College, situated in Regina, Saskatchewan, is called the Saskatchewan Indian Federated College (SIFC). I believe the SIFC is also the fastest-growing institution of higher learning anywhere in Canada. Founded in 1976 with seven students, we now have over fifteen hundred students, which come mainly from Saskatchewan First Nations communities, but also from most other regions of Canada. Two-thirds of our students are of First Nations origin, but we have increasing numbers of students of very varied origins, including many from Asia. We have a federation agreement with the University of Regina, which means that all our courses and credits have full validity in the Canadian university system. We claim that our educational standards are higher than those of mainstream institutions of higher learning, because we found our whole system in the circular vision of our ancestors and of our Elders. First Nations Elders are included in our regular staff. They counsel teachers, administrators and students, besides performing traditional ceremonies. In fact, they are the ultimate authority in the college.

Our college is a fully accredited member of the Association of Universities and Colleges of Canada. In spite of truly remarkable success in the face of strong adversity, we still have a very great deal of difficulty in convincing non-

Indian governments that our peoples are there to stay, that we contribute very significantly to the betterment of First Nations and of the general Canadian society, and that therefore they should help us a lot more. For instance, we still do not have a building. We rent space in the main university and have to situate many of our operations in very old, fragile, unhealthy mobile homes. We are very poor, but we do wonders, because we believe in ourselves, we believe in our future in the world. And we welcome you there. What we have, we will share with you, and we will grow together and go very far, together.

I would now like to finish here on the very joyful note of having made contact and friendship with you, the proud people of Korea. I feel very thankful for this. I also finish this presentation on a note of hope that the friendship between our peoples will be constructive, most fruitful and everlasting. May the Great Spirit bless you, your land and especially our greatest gift, all our children.

Ho! Ho! Attouguet! Kamsahamnida! Thank you very much!

Canadian Amerindian Nations of the 21ˢᵗ Century*

For 503 years, we, the real Nations of this land, have been asked, forced and expected to believe in the thinking and the ways of people who have had to abandon their own lands, have come here and have only been able to destroy our nations and our own land, which we call our Mother—503 years in which we, the real Nations of this land, have been, through the presence and the actions of the invaders, made to suffer every imaginable attempt to destroy us, our land and our livelihood. The quasi-totality of our nations have been effectively obliterated, exterminated, and the surviving ones have suffered the ultimate injustice of being pronounced extinct—at any rate, illegitimate—by the ones who have forged and still forge what passes for the history of Canada, or of any other 'legitimate' nation-state established by Europeans on our continent.

---

* Presented at the Annual Conference of the International Council for Canadian Studies, "Language, Culture and Values in Canada at the Dawn of the 21ˢᵗ Century", held in Ottawa, June 1–2, 1995.

Five hundred and three years, and we still do not believe, and I have the firm conviction that we will never believe, in the historical thinking and the ways that nurture and legitimize those nation-states.

In a recent interview with the magazine *Aboriginal Business* (December 1994), Alex Janvier, the rightly famous Dènè painter from Cold Lake, Alberta, explained the depth of his claim to the land as expressed through his art. "What I'm doing right now is negotiating my land back. I'm not going to pay a penny for it, but essentially, in my mind, I'm taking back the land. If somebody has a hard time with that, they had better put in their minds that all these beautiful plains were once covered with people like myself." He goes on to explain, "When I am claiming land, it's more like a spiritual claim. They [the dominant society] can have all the papers and deeds in the world, and they can have all the locks and so on, but they will never have the spirit of this land."

Janvier's claim of Indian ownership of the spirit of this land illustrates perfectly the traditional thinking of Amerindians on the whole issue of social and territorial justice in relation to the original American nation and on the history of contact itself. It also very eloquently tells the traditional Amerindian/Aboriginal/Inuit understanding of land ownership. When an Amerindian says, "This is my land", that person speaks about an emotional, spiritual relationship. That person is moved by the very same feelings that one has when speaking about one's parents and family members: this is my mother, this is my father, grandmother, brother, son, daughter, wife, husband, friend and so on. There is no reference to ownership; it's all about a relation of love and reciprocal belonging. "My country and my love: my mother and my land; America, my home", sings the great Buffy Sainte-Marie in her beautiful song *America, My Home*. On the other hand, that same phrase, "This is my land", pronounced by the average Canadian, would ordinarily have the resonance of a material, physical owning of the land. (Only very exceptionally would this statement carry that feeling of spiritual love for the true, caring, eternal Mother that the land really is.) What we have instead is that feeling that the land is loved and cherished only as long as it can fulfill dreams of material wealth, power and security. When the land becomes unable to do that any longer, a so-minded society moves on, or now, more simply, invents ways of creating material wealth that will be utterly dangerous for, and destructive of the 'environment', as the Earth has come to be called by people who are sensitive enough to eventually question those ways of treating Her.

As the word 'Canada' came from my ancestral Wendat language—more precisely from a variation as spoken by our relatives and allies who inhabited a political region that had its centre at Stadacona, the Quebec City of today—I will explain its meaning. I will as well go into the topic of Canadian history, in order to look at the situation of Canadian Amerindian/Aboriginal nations at the dawn of the 21st century, and attempt a forecast for times beyond. The actual word is *Kanatha* and it simply means principal town, or big village. In 1535 the town of Stadacona (as we just said, a capital in the geopolitics of the region) was described by its inhabitants to French explorer Jacques Cartier and his men as 'Kanatha', that is, their principal town. The Frenchmen, naturally using their feudal thinking, applied the name to the imaginary country of 'Canada', reigned over by Donnacona, an actual Headman of the people of Stadacona, whom Jacques Cartier enthroned in his writings as the Lord of Canada, and whom he set out to conquer, as was his sacred duty in his quality of Discoverer of new 'Indian' (read: pagan) lands in the name of King François I, a very Christian, European monarch.

On his first voyage the previous year, in 1534, Cartier had managed to lure on board his ship and take back to France, Donnacona's two grown-up sons. On a second voyage, the year after, unmindful that he and his crew had, over the winter, been saved from imminent death through scurvy (one-quarter of his men did perish) by the Stadaconans, the same French would-be-conquistador, through cheap gifts and other artifices, carried his plan through to capture and take away to France the Headman Donnacona, along with nine other persons of his lineage, among them two young women and two other Headmen. We now know that of these ten people, only one young woman survived beyond two years in France, even though Cartier, six years later, upon a third and last voyage, reported in Stadacona that being, by then, all famous and well-to-do in France, none of them had been interested in coming back to their poor, uncivilized Canada. A state of strict enmity set in from that time, which prevented France from carrying out any colonial projects in North America for the next sixty-five years. This was after the dispersal of all the Nadouek (Iroquoian) population in the St. Lawrence Valley had been caused, through the epidemiological phenomenon and, concurrently, the geopolitical catastrophe that customarily accompanied first contacts with incoming Europeans. Such historical events, to be sure, still not contained in standard works on Canadian history, help us to understand why France eventually lost out in its imperial struggle against Britain, in spite of a most strategic advantage it later acquired over that competing country by eventually winning the commercial and military alliance of the vast majority of Amerindian nations in northeastern North America. It also can help explain, and perhaps resolve, chronic problems of Canadian national unity.

The second Aboriginal groups (after the Stadaconan and other Nadouek of the region) to receive the name 'Canadians', or 'Canadois', from historians and French settlers were the Innu (Montagnais) and other Algonkians who came to frequent and inhabit the country named Canada by Jacques Cartier when the French, under explorer Samuel de Champlain and the Récollet missionaries, came back in the first decade of the 17th century to found a French colony at Quebec. Soon, when Quebec did become a fledgling colony, the name 'Canadiens' was transferred to the French 'habitants' themselves, the very ones whose descendants, three and a half centuries or so later, chose to repudiate that name for linguistic and other cultural and historical reasons and to call themselves 'Québécois', leaving the name 'Canadians' for English and other non-Aboriginal Canadians alone, even though in practice, an important number of Québécois affirm their loyalty to Canada and do call themselves Canadians first and then Québécois.

As for Canadian Amerindians (or Canadian First Nations people, the term in use in the Amerindian political discourse), there is among them universally, as we have already alluded to, a very definite sense of duty to resist being assimilated into the nation-states that have been constituted by Europeans and other immigrants on their soil. As we have also already asserted, their will to stay apart is not motivated by greed for the living space, and the wealth and power to be accrued from physical, material ownership of the land. In fact, Amerindian people have traditionally had a quite different agenda. Even though each of the two societies intends to bring the other to see life and the world as it itself does, the Amerindian society does this out of a sense of spiritual duty. And what is its claim to that duty? The answer is all contained in a basic dichotomy: life, as Amerindians very frequently say, is a sacred Circle of Relations uniting all beings, and not the linear process that non-Amerindians generally conceive it to be. What has made Europeans and others (except African slaves) abandon their motherlands and seek a living here and elsewhere is their loss of that knowledge about life. Through circumstances not of their making, they have come to think that life is a linear process. Peoples of the Circle have traditionally viewed this thinking as an aberration of the human spirit, which can only breed ever increasing social and ecological impoverishment, and which they, who, through simple good planetary fortune, have been able to conserve their awareness that life is a sacred Circle of Relations, have the responsibility to correct. Traditional Amerindians believe that there is not and must not be social, political or religious differentiation between races and cultures. In fact, Amerindian spiritual spokespeople, like all true spiritual people, profess that there is only one human family, beautiful and admirable in and for its infinite diversity of forms, colours, characters and talents. "Indian is not about colour of skin, origin, or even language; Indian is a state of mind and spirit", say the true thinkers of the Circle.

The reason Canada was created was that the Old World needed one. The creation of Canada signified extreme destruction 'and utter chronic misery' for the real nations of this land. With the incommensurable material wealth that was appropriated by the creators of Canada, Canada has fast become a very powerful and very envied nation-state in the world. Surprisingly for many Canadians, however, their dear Canada is now showing signs of physical exhaustion. Ever since Cartier, the first Canadian, so arrogantly 'conquered' and began destroying his imaginary Canada, the grasping frenzy of Canadians has taken its toll. It hasn't taken very long to bring this once so clean and healthy land to the verge of the collapse Old Europe knew then. And the people of the Circle knew this all along; even many clear-sighted Euro-Americans foresaw it and wrote about it.

What then is in store for the Amerindians of Canada, as we are about to leave the 20th century and the second millennium behind? Popular belief, instructed by conventional linear history and the media, is that we, who call ourselves Indians, First Nations, Amerindians, Aboriginal people, mostly in Canada and in North America, have long disappeared. We are popularly thought of as false, illegitimate nations, or merely tribes. We are inadequate as people, we are unreal; we are a "costly myth", as one well-known US media guru said a few years ago. The Oka crisis in 1990 so shocked public feeling, by raising the terrifying possibility that we might, in fact, be existing for real, that it has triggered a very severe backlash from the Québécois and Canadian societies. To me, the official 'Indian policy' of governments for the past five years has been, in summary: "Maybe it is true: maybe these people do exist. What the heck do we do with them? They might take back this country and re-establish savagery." Then some clever ones, approved by some of their chosen 'Indian leaders', said, "Here is the solution: we will give them self-government (our idea of self-government, of course). They will then turn towards themselves. The 'leaders' will grab what they will see and know are great opportunities for themselves. They can then all resume pretending they exist. Many will become civilized in the process, and we can all go back to Canadian business as usual." And so far, it seems to be going even more nicely than expected.

While all this is happening, every Amerindian person, and an ever-increasing number of 'Amerindians at heart', know that time is on the truth's side and that the facade is rapidly collapsing, showing the untruth behind. The earth's ecosystem is in grave danger, and this impacts Canada's economy, an economy ranked among the strongest worldwide, yet very threatened and rapidly declining; other no longer concealable facts are ever newer and greater threats to human health, the rise of youth violence and interracial strife, and many more social diseases only to be found in linear thinking contexts.

In 1492, the Old World needed a new one and began creating one. But so far, the creation has been only a physical, material one, and we all know that this creative process has reached the point of extreme danger. What now needs to be found is the spirit of the New World, the spirit of Kanatha. And, as

Alex Janvier says, "they will never have the spirit of this land." I also say that 'they', the ones who are irretrievably on the material, physical quest (and 'they' can be nominally 'Indian'), will never possess the spirit of my land. But as an Amerindian, I do have that sense of responsibility for sharing with conscious, respectful brothers and sisters my feeling about the spirit of my land. In fact, if I don't succeed in creating that strong, indispensable bond of reciprocal belonging between my land and my newly arrived brothers and sisters, what future is there for my own children and theirs? What respect do I have for my responsibility towards my ancestors, those of Stadacona, of Wendake and of so many other places where nothing, or so little, is left or known of them?

In closing, I will say that I believe that we Amerindians will not only survive, but we will attain once more the place of spiritual and ideological leadership which is our own, as people immemorially in love with and in stewardship of this land of ours. I believe that the world is in need of possessing the spirit of Canada, and of America as a whole. I believe that as long as a person (or a people) has not found and understood the spirit of the land he or she inhabits, he or she is in a destructive stance in relation to that land. I believe many of our Amerindian languages will be revitalized, will survive and will become worldwide subjects of study as avenues to find and understand the spirit of this Amerindian land of ours. I believe that we all come from, belong to and will come back to the sacred Circle of Life. I believe that Life will prevail! I welcome the times to come! Kanatha, we stand on guard for thee!

Attouguet! Meegwetch! Niaweh! Thank you from the heart!

Rebuilding First Nations:
Ideological Implications for Canada*

First, in the name of my Sioui Clan and my Wendat people, and of my colleagues, as well as our students and Elders of the Saskatchewan Indian Federated College, I want to greet the German and other German-speaking peoples and their Land, and convey to them our heartfelt wishes for happiness and prosperity, in the Great Circle of Peoples of our Mother-Earth.

Then, I wish to thank the Association for Canadian Studies in German-Speaking Countries for this invitation to speak, and my friends Ursula Mathis, the President, and Cornelius Remie, both of whom I had the great pleasure to meet last June, at the International Council for Canadian Studies Conference in Ottawa, and who thought it would be another special and very productive experience to come and participate in this other excellent and exciting conference in Grainau. Also, I wish to express to my new friend and colleague Elke Nowak

---

* Presented at the Annual Conference of the Association for Canadian Studies in German-Speaking Countries, held in Grainau, Germany, February 16–18, 1996.

and her colleagues my very deep appreciation for the personal dedication we all felt she and they showed in the preparation of this conference.

For some reason, I have had the sure feeling that this conference is going to have some special, positive consequences for the realization of justice for Canadian Aboriginal people as they themselves and an ever-increasing number of non-Aboriginal Canadians see that it has to happen. I think the reason I have this sentiment of hope is that this event, of very high and serious reflection on this very current and emotional Canadian topic, which is the survival and the evolution of Canadian Aboriginal peoples in future times, is organized in a country where we Aboriginal people know a true feeling of human solidarity exists about us. We know, by both intuition and experience, that the Germans particularly, and also many European peoples generally, feel real appreciation for our world view and our life ways. It is a good feeling for us Aboriginal Canadians, and Aboriginal people generally, to find ourselves in the company of people who do not feel threatened by us just because we look at life differently and therefore want to live our lives differently. It is, indeed, good to feel that the other person, the other people, does not carry that load of harmful, conventional, negative notions about us, and is able to listen and respond to us the way we should all be able to, as and among members of the same human family. Therefore, I reiterate my personal heartfelt gratitude to all who created this meeting of hearts, minds and spirits, in this very beautiful part of this German Motherland.

My People, the Huron-Wendat

My name is Georges Paul Emery Sioui. At the moment of contact with the Europeans, my people of the Wendat Confederacy had been, for several centuries, at the heart of the commercial, political and cultural world of a vast conglomerate of nations of Northeastern North America. I descend, on both sides, from a line of hereditary chiefs who, throughout history, played very important roles in the defence and representation of our and many other nations of the Northeast. My name, Sioui, means 'Those of the Rising Sun'. We trace our origin to the Big Turtle Clan. My clan name, Wendaye: te ('One who carries an Island on his back'), refers to our belief, shared by many Aboriginal Peoples in America and others throughout the world, that the Earth is carried by the Big Turtle who, at the beginning, offered to lodge on his back Aataentsic, the Woman who came from a celestial world and thereafter created the Earth, which we therefore respectfully call 'The Great Island on the Turtle's Back'.

French-Canadian History

After a century of exploring the Gulf of the Saint Lawrence River and the Saint Lawrence River itself, during which time they consciously brought about grave disorganization of the Aboriginal societies, the French knew enough about Aboriginal geopolitics to determine that they had to establish the base of their projected American colonial empire in the country inhabited by the Wendat and their five confederated nations. The Wendat called their country 'Wendake'. The French named it 'Huronia'. Writing in 1744 and referring himself to the commercial and military policy of Samuel de Champlain, Governor of the fledgling colony of Quebec, Jesuit historian F.-X. Charlevoix stated: "He [Champlain] intended, by means of those Huron Missions, to prepare the way for the Establishment which he projected to realize in their Country, situated very advantageously for Trade, from which discoveries would be pushed to the extreme limits of North America." "The Missionaries," goes on Charlevoix in the same chapter of his *Histoire du Canada*, "were convinced that by fixing the Center of their Missions in a Country (Wendake) which was at once the Center of Canada, it would be easy for them to carry the Light of the Gospel to every part of this vast Continent."

A mere twenty years later, that Country of Wendake, 'Center of Canada' and home to at least thirty thousand Wendat, which modern scholars have conventionally described as the most politically sophisticated and the most prosperous Aboriginal nation in Aboriginal Northeastern North America, lay in waste, its surviving population (about six thousand) all scattered. (Most were naturalized in neighbouring nations. Two groups maintain the Wendat identity to this day, one in the state of Oklahoma and one in the province of Quebec.)

In 1632, the Jesuit congregation arrived in force in Wendake to replace the more contemplative and less politically favoured Franciscans. This time corresponds to the beginning of severe depopulation of the Wendat (and, to a lesser extent, of neighbouring nations and confederacies) through epidemics; that time also brought a dire intensification of warfare, due in large part to political meddling of these same missionaries in Wendat affairs. The most serious immediate result was the emergence of opposed factions of Christian and conservative Wendat. This phenomenon had a paralyzing effect on the Wendats' capacity to resist the onslaught of their Iroquois enemies, intent on supplanting them and incorporating them into their society. The Iroquois, also strenuously fighting for their survival, had the better fortune of having European allies—the Dutch—who did not make religious conversion a condition for trade and therefore armed their Iroquois allies realistically. Not surprisingly, the Dutch, aided by much fewer Native allies, prevailed over the inconsequential, politically less advanced French of that era. The well-known result was that Europeans built and expanded empires on Amerindian soil, while the bulk of the Aboriginal population got consumed in the great colonial pyre.

It is important, when approaching the field of First Nations studies, in Canada or elsewhere, to remind oneself of how colonial settlement began, not with a view to condemn people who, at any rate, are long gone, but in order to determine in what measure, if at all, there has been, and continues to be, a positive evolution in mentalities. Should this be the case, we could, with justified human pride, let history lie at rest in the books, and pull it out when we need to show ourselves and others how far we have travelled since then. The French, in Canada, have written a very self-righteous history about themselves, as co-shapers of Canada as we know it, and about their history of contact with the First Peoples. Historically, however, it is they who have had the larger part to play, among European powers, in the overthrow of the social order elaborated and maintained by the Aboriginal nations and confederacies that constituted the demographic and political force of the Aboriginal country that first came to be called Canada. Is there today one single soul on Earth who may claim to be a direct physical descendant of the Erie, or the Attiwandaronk, or the Tionontate, or of so many of those strong and thriving Aboriginal nations that once lived in what is now Quebec and Ontario, where the French then chose to plant their 'Missions' and 'Establishments'? No. Not one single one. They have all disappeared, mostly under the better (than the English), more benevolent, rule of the French. And what fate do current Québécois political leaders eagerly say they reserve for the remaining First Peoples within 'their' envisioned country of Quebec? They promise that 'their' First Nations will be treated in absolute equality with all other Québécois. So, where is the positive evolution? Or are the concepts of evolution and disappearance of Earth peoples and Earth world synonymous? There is overwhelming evidence that under an unchanged Eurocentric rule, nothing is really changing or will change at all.

English-Canadian History

And how does non-French Canada look under this same prism of historical evolution as relating to Earth peoples and Earth world? Historically, the Anglo-Saxons had it easier than the French, in the sense that they were eventually able to appropriate the best expanses of commercial land in eastern Canada (principally in southern Ontario), left largely vacant after the destruction and the dispersals, under French rule, of the great Nadouek (or Iroquoian) confederacies and of their also populous Algonkian commercial and cultural allies. Quickly consolidating their strength on such a rich territorial basis, the Anglo-Saxons turned towards the West and proceeded to expropriate with increasing speed and ease the Aboriginal nations west of the Great Lakes, all the way to the Pacific Ocean. Treaties were signed by much disrupted nations fearing for their very physical survival, which they most often did not manage to maintain. The ones that did survive were thrown into reserves, in the care of governmental wardens chosen on the basis of the thoroughness of their colonial mentality, and of missionary congregations, the spiritual originators of that colonial mindset. Many Aboriginal nations and people in the West, and especially in the Northwest, are still living under that stark colonial rule, and fearing for their very physical survival, as I am speaking to you. First Nations east of the province of Quebec had virtually the same historical experience as those in French Canada: a very severe destruction at first, due to epidemiological depopulation, and new forms and dimensions of warfare related to European imperial struggles, followed by centuries of harsh colonial rule, until the present time, one in which Canada, in its new haste to get at the riches of the North, the last frontier, and to throw off the increasingly taxing burden of caring for its Indian wards (who are taking too long in assimilating, if they are ever going to) and their affairs, shows itself capable of convincing public confessions of past wrongs inflicted on Aboriginal Peoples and launches itself on a quest for finding Aboriginal leaders brave and impatient enough to take up the noble challenge of 'self-government', right now!

Our Overthrown Country

Wendat leaders of the 1630s are frequently reported by the Jesuits, in their famous *Relations*, to have described the efforts of the French, and other Europeans, as a strenuous, systematic attempt to "overthrow the country." And should it be surprising to you, my dear friends, to hear that that is the only way we can truthfully look at the history of our country and of our land since Europeans arrived? The words and the feelings of those Wendat and other Amerindian ancestors of ours have had, and still have, the same true and emotional ring in our hearts as they had in theirs.

This feeling of looking at our land as something that French, English and others have turned upside down is at once a sad and a happy one. Indeed, while it constantly reminds us of all the harm, the brutality and the senselessness that we have seen and experienced in our history of contact with colonial Europe, it also, on the positive side, keeps us awake to the sense of how things should be; that is, to our double responsibility of resisting, believing in the falseness of the physical and mental structures wrongfully built around us, and assuming our leadership in changing that state of things and thereby setting our country and our land right side up again; that is, restoring the work and the dignity of our ancestors, for the benefit and the better-being of generations of humans and other beings to come.

Now, do we, Canadian Aboriginal people, truthfully have any hope of re-establishing our own idea of order in our own land and if so, how would we go about that task? How can we even think of resisting accepting the Canadian ideas of truth, justice and order, when everything around us most of the time in our lives cries out to us that we should give up, that it is senseless to 'hold on to the past', that we must live with reality, that society, life, the world, will be good and fair to us, if we only believe in something that is outside of us, because *we* are outside of life and reality, outside of History?

Our Elders' Instructions

Yet our Wise Ones have always told us, their offspring, just as we too repeat to our own children:

> Our newly arrived Relatives are mistreating the Earth. They do not acknowledge that the Earth is our Mother. They came here with harmful habits. But they cannot forever behave as they are behaving. One day, soon, they will have to stop, because they will be afraid of the consequences of what they have done. That day, they will come to us and ask us for our help, because they know our understanding of life is better than theirs. That day, they and we will begin to live as relatives together. Not only will we learn from them, but they will learn from us also. But we will be the elder brothers and sisters, because we have known and lived with and from this Land, our Mother, ever since it was created by our Father, the Great Spirit, and all his female and male Helpers, whom we call our Grand Mothers and Grand Fathers.

And of late, our Wise Ones have also said to us, their younger Relatives:

> That time when we were told our newly arrived Relatives would come to us and ask us to teach them about our ways has now arrived. Let us hold on as firmly as ever to our ways, to our spiritual traditions, to our languages, and let us be eager to study and acquire all of the positive knowledge that they have. That way, our people will become able to once again occupy a leading position in our land. That way, we will help create a better, happier, safer world for all of us to live in, and our newly arrived Brothers and Sisters will help us do this, with all their hearts, minds and souls. When we all know how we must show respect for Life and when

we all understand that all life is a family, there will no longer be a need to discriminate against others because of their differences, or to mistreat other beings because they are not human. We will have achieved the means of peace, order, justice and harmony. This was the dream and the vision of our ancestors, who left us our Sacred Ceremonies, our Sacred Drum, our Sacred Pipe and our Sacred Circle.

The Circle

The Circle is at the centre of our Aboriginal thinking. We are taught at an early age that life is a Great Circle of Relations between all beings: humans, animals, plants, rocks, water, air, spirits, earth, sky, sun, moon, stars, planets, everything. We believe that the day, the lunar month, the year, even human life itself, are circular phenomena, and that there are cycles of many years, representing the circular reality. We also believe that all circular phenomena have four parts, or movements: spring, summer, fall and winter; morning, noon hour, evening and nighttime; infancy, youth, maturity and old age. Also, most things in nature are round, or rounded: the sun, the earth, the moon; the rocks, after prolonged action of the elements; plants, trees, fruits, seeds, vegetables, the bodies of humans and animals, the nests of birds, their eggs—in brief, almost everything is round.

Thinking: Circular or Linear

We believe that our circular thinking harmonizes with the order of Creation and that the thinking that Europeans brought with them to our land has been so destructive of life precisely because it is not in harmony with the Circle of Life. We call their thinking linear and believe that it is antithetical to our own. We are also told by our sages that all human societies have come from a circular tradition—because life can only originate from the Circle—but that some societies, because of particular constraints and events experienced along their historical path, have stopped knowing that life is a universal Circle of Relations and have started believing that life is an evolutionary process, which follows a straight line. Such societies have lost much of their spiritual awareness about life and have compensated for that loss by becoming matter- or possession-oriented. It is becoming more and more disturbingly obvious that this change in ideology bears consequences that are as fortunate for the few who manage to be in power as they are unfortunate for the very many who are excluded from any power. The thirst for possessions typically becomes limitless in linear societies, because of the spiritual distance; thus the indifference of power elites in relation to other beings, human or non-human, who are opposed to their interests or who represent an interest through their exploitability, and also because 'religious' ideologies are always present to sanction the limitless acquisition of possessions by the elites. It is not only the humans who then become either proprietors or property, but also, and more obviously, other non-human beings, formerly sacred and therefore equal to humans in dignity, become mere material property, to be used and discarded as fits the owner's need or fancy.

No one can now sensibly dispute the fact that the natural world, on which we humans depend for our very breathing and living, cannot sustain much more of the abuse caused by linear man's thinking. As for us Aboriginal peoples—and circular thinkers generally—we are ever more conscious that the ancestral Aboriginal vision is coming true—that is, that we are now beginning to play a primary role in bringing about a world spiritual consciousness in relation to life and the place of humans in the Great Circle. We also draw strong faith in this from the fact that we possess great capacity to unite spiritually because our own spiritual traditions are beginning to regain their former strength. This guarantees us protection from religious and political divisions, the two main evils that separate human beings within and between social entities, and allow destructive, repressive systems to stay in place. We Aboriginal Peoples may be scattered in isolated places all over our lands, and appear to be divided by very diverse languages and expressions of culture, but we probably are the most unified People on earth, because we have spiritual unity: we all understand the Circle. And what further increases our hope is that a lot of so-called non-Aboriginal people are joining our ranks every day as believers in the Circle. We Aboriginal Canadians happen to know that important numbers of Germans and German-speaking people are circular thinkers, just like us. So we know that we have an important, populous Sister-nation right here in Germany, and others close to here and elsewhere in Europe and in the non-Aboriginal world. So our numbers are not dwindling, as many still think they are: they are increasing. But that is our secret.

An Aboriginal Outlook on Canada

Canada, at this point in its evolution, cannot serve as an example of a country that treats its First People fairly or with sincerity. Its past has been too strongly colonial, which means that the average Canadian, especially one of old stock, or 'de vieille souche', is handicapped in his or her vision of First Nations by a sum of notions about 'Indians' received from several generations of colonial schooling and social conditioning. However, I believe that a distinctive positive character trait of Canada, in spite of its strong colonial heritage, stems from the fact that the basic Aboriginal right of its First Peoples has survived incomparably better within Canadian borders than in other Euro-American nation-states, especially when compared to what happened in the United States. Canadians, because of a much less repressive historical record, cannot and do not have as bold and imposing an attitude as their neighbours to the south about their right to own and occupy the soil. Canadians have a shyness and an honesty about their soil that comes from an undeniably stronger survival of the fundamental Aboriginal title than almost anywhere else in the colonial world. I believe that should Canada take—that is, legislate—this trait out of its character, it would become as charmless, arrogant, aggressive and shameless as most other countries that have a colonial past.

For this reason, and others, including that Aboriginal Canada has increasing numbers of supporters outside of its confines, I am of the opinion that Canada is the right place where you, dear friends, and we, and others can create, on a world scale, a place of true respect and responsibility towards Earth Peoples and the Earth world. Three main elements would enable this to happen: first, Canada's Earth world is not irreversibly damaged by linear thinking—it is still beautiful, wonderful, pristine and very, very vast; secondly, the Canadian system is not of the directly repressive type—as a matter of fact, I believe it is one of the most open and respectful among all the countries with a strong colonial legacy; thirdly, and most importantly, the Aboriginal or circular vision in Canada is still very much alive. But time is of the essence. Specialists predict that only three of the fifty-five Aboriginal languages still alive in Canada have a chance to survive more than one more generation. I would then like to stress that we do need to put our collective minds together to define exactly our common goals and work towards their attainment.

At this time, Canada must not be allowed to rush its Aboriginal citizens into taking over the administration of the social and political confusion that it has created over centuries. Nice discourses and manipulative invocation of governmental poverty must not be accepted as sound reasons for allowing what is already seen by enlightened individuals of all origins as the consecration of Western-style Aboriginal oligarchies and the consolidation of already often rampant poverty, even social misery and, what is even more serious, for causing an acceleration of the loss of the cultural and philosophical capital possessed by the Aboriginal people. Clearly, instead of the political expedients currently used by different levels of Canadian governments (both francophone and anglophone), what we need to bring about is the creation of educational tools and institutions needed by Aboriginal Canadians, and the strengthening of existing ones, so as to proceed to the educational exchanges we are talking about, between Aboriginal and non-Aboriginal Canadians and people generally. For the non-Aboriginal educational system, although admittedly very efficient in the suppression of Native cultures over past decades and centuries, has had the one positive effect of bringing the Aboriginal people into contact with the non-Aboriginal world and its mentalities. It is now the non-Aboriginal Canadians who need to know about the historical experience, the world view and the aspirations of their country's First Peoples.

An Aboriginal Challenge for Canada

What is really and urgently needed is a bilaterally initiated and promoted (by First Nations and non–First Nations Canadians) process of reciprocal education aimed at clearly and systematically defining the respective social and educational roles to be played by Aboriginal and non-Aboriginal elements of Canadian society, as well as defining the strategies of complementarity. Our people are firm in saying that the process of healing from past and ongoing social and moral wounds, which Aboriginal Canadians have collectively undertaken, must be pursued and amplified, as it is the will of our people to survive, recover and take the place that they have been prevented from taking, in Canada and the world. Many of our people affirm that even the time of one generation will not be enough to complete the healing process. The time and devotion of two of our generations is realistically what will be required for the Circle of our Nations to become whole and strong again, certainly not the few months or years that the federal governments is saying it has to take.

We, the First Peoples of America, are the Fourth Family of Nations, positioned at the East, around the Great Circle of Nations of Mother Earth. Many non-Amerindian sages, and many of our own sages, have said that the Great Circle of Nations of the Earth will not find its true, global vision of peace and brotherhood as long as the Fourth, so far forgotten Family of Nations will not be recognized, and allowed to sit at its place around the Great Circle of Nations. I believe that our world will keep being in disharmony as long as any one of its member-peoples is left out of the Great Universal Talking Circle, no matter how small and insignificant that member may appear to be. We will then, as a global human community, be in possession of our whole physical, intellectual and spiritual potential, and we will find the ways we still cannot find. And I believe that the true integration of First Peoples in Canada will be the commencement of the composing of our full human family worldwide. That is the vision and the challenge I propose for my country, Canada, for Canada, with the strong help that you are bringing and can continue to bring, my dear friends, possesses the greatness to meet this challenge.

Ho! Ho! Ho! Attouguet Eathoro! Thank you very much, dear friends and relatives! Merci beaucoup, chers amis et parents! Danke sehr viel, liebe Freunde und Verwandte!

Indien sans terre mais avec plume

Indien sans terre mais avec plume

Un Indien sans terre
Peut toujours manger,
Mais un Indien sans plumes
Est un Indien sans armes,
Sans voix,
Sans droit,
Même à la vie.
Grand Esprit, Merci
Pour mes plumes !
Pour dire, chanter, crier
Ce que je vois,
Ce que je crois,
Ce que je suis
Et resterai
Grâce à ma plume.
Mes plumes, Mes armes :
Toujours à mes côtés !

WHY WE SHOULD HAVE INCLUSIVENESS
AND WHY WE CANNOT HAVE IT[*]

Thank you very much, Elvi [Whittaker]. I first would like to acknowledge the Musqueam Nation. This is their territory, theirs in the sense of being their mother-territory, just as it has become the mother-territory of you who are from here. Also, greetings to the Aboriginal nations from this area. Then, my thanks go to my friend Dennis Pavlitch. As we were taking a group cruise on the Ottawa River during our stay in Ottawa at the last annual Conference of the Academic Deans and Vice-Presidents, he approached me for this conference. As we were on the river, Dennis and I quickly got acquainted and became friends. Seeing Dennis's size and the relative smallness of the boat, I very soon asked Dennis: "Please, Dennis, stay in the middle of the boat, or else you would

---

[*] Presented at the National Conference "Academic Freedom and the Inclusive University", held at the University of British Columbia, April 10–12, 1997. Published in *Ayaangwaamizin* (The International Journal of Indigenous Philosophy), Lakehead University (Thunder Bay, Ont.), Vol. 1, no. 2 (1997), pp. 33–47.

rock it pretty much." So, since he didn't rock the boat then, I promise I will not rock the boat this time either …

I would also like to greet all my fellow participants and fellow speakers; it is a very bold and challenging conference to organize and conduct. I congratulate the people who have been able to make it a reality and a success. The exchange has been very rich and always challenging.

I would like to recall the time, about eighteen years ago, when I organized the first National Conference of Aboriginal Writers in Ottawa, as an exercise of my duties as Officer of Literature and Communications at the federal Department of Indian Affairs and Northern Development. I had then asked the late, great British Columbia Indian artist, George Clutesi, to be our keynote speaker and special guest. As a then younger man, I was impacted by something George said in his speech. He recalled words often spoken by his own father: "Always remember that we were here first." That message, said that great thinker, was of great importance to him. And those words stayed with me, because they echo those of my own father and many Indian friends, Elders, relatives and other people. This, to me, does not mean that First Nations people have more rights than anybody else, but rather that we have different responsibilities than other fellow Canadians. I believe it means that we have a role and a responsibility to teach because we have known this land for much longer, because our languages, our voices are the voice of this land.

The teaching we must perform is about resisting being engulfed in the system that was transplanted here from Europe. I believe that this is a purpose in which all of us here, and all enlightened Canadians and world citizens, have to support one another and which we have to attempt to communicate to others: this purpose and this task of resisting being engulfed in the value system, the social vision that Europeans once proceeded to implant here, where we, the Aboriginal People, were already living. I believe it is important that non-Aboriginal people of this land explain to the world the circumstances in which the so-called Western civilization came to exist and the consequences of this process for the Aboriginal people and the land, and also the consequences expected under that system, or social vision. Because there is a very real danger for the economically weaker world, or so-called Third World, to be wrongly impressed by the Western system and vision, and to feel threatened by it, therefore to want to emulate it and thus to eventually commit our own grave deeds of abusing the life-strength of their own land, and cause the further deterioration and impoverishment of life on our planet generally. Therefore, it is important that we explain that the superiority of the Western social vision is only apparent; that appearance is only the consequence of Europeans arriving here with superior technical power and being thus able to produce this kind of civilization. It is very important to tell other peoples around the world that that Western way is in no way morally, intellectually or socially superior, as we are reflecting on our self-preservation as inhabitants of a common planet-home.

In this order of thinking, it is also very important for Canada to recognize and embrace its Native roots, because as we know, if we linger much longer on the old Euro-Canadian, socio-political paradigm, we will in short order lose the quality of life that we want to preserve; we will lose our country itself. Canada is threatened in its very existence because we still have not, as a people, reflected enough on the spiritual and intellectual nature of the place that we inhabit. Our universities have not been accepting of our true leaders, which are our spiritual and intellectual ones; that is, the ones we commonly refer to as our Amerindian/Aboriginal/Inuit Elders.

British Columbia is a Canadian province where, understandably, a lot more of the original spiritual substance and strength of our First Peoples has survived. I personally have always looked at British Columbia as a place with a special responsibility to practise that inclusiveness. Certainly, universities such as UBC must be at the forefront in causing this type of reflection to take place in Canada.

I would now like to tell you about our story of creation and explain why I feel that our People have the status and the role of Toads in relation to the larger society. In very ancient times our old Grandmother came down from an Upper World. The Big Turtle who had offered to receive her on his back immediately called a council of all the animals to find someone who would dive to the depths of the primordial ocean and bring back the magic, sacred mud from which the Earth, whom we call our Great Turtle Island, would be created. Of course, as always happens, the best divers all failed in that attempt: the Beaver, the Otter, the Loon and all the others. Then the lesser divers attempted and also all failed to bring back a mouthful of earth. In the end, the very humble Toad felt she must also try. She was gone longer than anyone and did reach the bottom of the sea. At long last, she surfaced and expired after opening her mouth, in which the Celestial Woman found the original earth. Through her very great powers, she was able to create a small island, which then began to expand into our Great Island, our Mother Earth.

Our people, and likewise Aboriginal people generally, do not feel they have any special right to be heard and seriously listened to, but they feel that people with no special power or social status, such as the Toad, do, on occasion, find the ways and ideas that allow the rest of the beings to survive and fare better. To us, the Toad is a useful symbol for representing folks such as ourselves, and here I mean all of us who wish to bring about the better living of humankind. Therefore, I would like to extend membership in this Toad clanship to all of you, all of us.

The Toad, then, embodies the thought of our profound need for inclusiveness. Here, I would like to recall words of another great Aboriginal thinker from these territories, the late Chief Dan George, of the Squamish nation, in about 1970. In one of his famous allocutions, which is a plea for inclusiveness addressed to the non-Indian society, he said:

> I must wait until you want something of me, until you need something that is me. Then I can raise my head and say to my wife and family, "Listen, they are calling ... they need me ... I must go." Then I can go across the street and hold my head high for I will meet you as an equal ... I shall not come as a cringing object of your pity. I shall come in dignity or I shall not come at all.

Those words of the great spiritual leader mean to convey to our fellow Canadians that the Aboriginal people of this land have yet to perceive that Canada cares about the unique spiritual and intellectual contributions that we could make in this county of ours, as people and as nations. Chief Dan George also expresses his belief that some day, our fellow non-Aboriginal Canadians will come to ask us to help them, to help Canada and the world with something that is us. That day will be one of pride and happiness, at last.

Those were some thoughts as to why we need inclusiveness and should practise it. Now: why can we not be inclusive? I will use another story, which I heard from my friend, the great Abnaki storyteller Joe Bruchac. It's about matricentrism, or circular thinking. It's the story of someone named Djee-djees.

The Abnaki, like ourselves the Huron, think that the world is a great island created by our old Grandmother on the back of the Big Turtle. Twins were born to that woman's daughter. They had the task of preparing the island for the existence of the human people and all the other peoples. One twin was inclined to prepare a very easy existence for the human species and the other meant to do his utmost to create a very tough world for us to live in. To make the story quite short, they eventually challenged each other and had a final combat, which the benevolent twin won, although the other did not die, for they both keep life in balance, just like the Yin and the Yang of the Chinese.

To the Abnaki, the name of the so-called good twin is Glooskabe. He has a very high rank among the Spirit-beings who created our earthly world. One day, long after his epic fight against the twin named Malsum, Glooskabe was walking about on the island, feeling very mighty and proud about his great work. By and by, he meets an old woman who, upon recognizing him, says, "Are you not the great Glooskabe, the one who created so many things in this awesome, beautiful world?"

"Yes, I am Glooskabe," answered the hero. "I'm the one no one can defeat."

Surprised and shocked at that bold answer, the old granny retorted, "Well, I think I know someone more powerful than you."

Quite surprised too, Glooskabe quickly inquired, "Who is that person? And where does that person live?"

"That person's name is Djee-djees, and he lives at the Place of White Rocks." Leaving the old woman, Glooskabe directed himself to the place indicated. Arriving there, he asked someone where the lodge of Djee-djees was. "This is where he lives," answered the woman, "and you are in luck, for he has just woken up from his nap."

Glooskabe entered the house and saw, playing on the floor, a little baby. Quite shocked and amazed once again, Glooskabe asked, "Is this the mighty Djee-djees?" The woman, instead of answering, simply left them together and went to do something by the doorstep.

Glooskabe began playing with the little child and copying his gestures and moves, so as to discover in what the power the old grandmother had said Djee-djees had consisted. Glooskabe was successful in the match until the baby picked up a toy and started playing with it and having fun. Looking for another toy and finding none, Glooskabe snatched the toy from the baby's hands in order to prove he could do the same or better. Of course, the baby then started to cry. He cried inconsolably and loudly, and louder and louder, until Glooskabe felt he could stand that crying no more and got up, half shouting, "You are more powerful than I am! You have defeated me!"

Just then, the woman came in, wearing a knowing smile. She picked up her baby and began rocking it. Almost immediately, to be sure, the baby stopped crying. The mother then began singing a lullaby, which has since become known and is sung the world over [here the speaker sings "Way-oh, way-oh Djee-djees", to the melody of "Rock-a-bye Baby"]. Quickly the baby fell asleep. Having tiptoed out of the house, Glooskabe reflects to himself, "It is true that the baby had defeated Glooskabe, but the mother (!) has defeated the baby." [laughter in the audience]

And that is why we cannot have inclusiveness at the university, but I will explain that in a little while [laughter in the audience] ...

My Aboriginal experience and my life's experience tell me that the great battle being waged in all the world society is not between Reds and Whites and Blacks and Cowboys and Indians and peoples and races; it's between man and woman. In this manner of thinking, I will refer to our own traditional Aboriginal world view as circular, which is something already familiar to most, if not all of you. On the other hand, I will describe as linear the traditional world view of Euro-Canadians and Euro-Americans generally, which is something that many of us are attempting to find alternatives to, because of the danger we feel is implicated in blindly remaining within this tradition. I say blindly because we would not be wise to disown the positive legacy of the reign of absolute linearity, which our present world obviously wishes to leave behind. My own way of classifying concepts in this regard is to associate inclusiveness with circularity, and oppose these concepts to exclusiveness and linearity. Likewise, spirituality and materiality, mother-centredness and father-centredness, universalism (circular) and parochialism (linear).

We Aboriginal people—as do Toads generally—think that there is much more survival value in mother-centredness than in father-centredness. I suggest you look at me as a living example of the superior survival value of mother-centredness. I will explain. When, in the middle of the 17th century, we became drastically depopulated through epidemics and wars, often caused by missionary interference, we were saved from complete extinction principally thanks to the fact that we had matricentrist, socio-political traditions. Some of you will know that Iroquois and Hurons are often described in anthropological writings as a foremost example of the strength and wisdom of matricentrist thought. Our wars, which we did wage just as cruelly as anyone, had, as their primary purpose, the replacement of lost members through capture of enemies. We used our alliance with the French to go and attack the English colonies to the south with the primary intent of capturing people, especially young and female, and ritually "give them a new life" in our nations, through adoption. As it was, Clanmothers had the principal say in these military undertakings, as they had the primary responsibility of maintaining and restoring the integrity and composition of the societies which, as woman-leaders, they headed. White and other captives were given over to Clanmothers who had called for and authorized war expeditions by approaching and commissioning war chiefs. The captives were then ritually and factually nationalized, and thence brought up and treated as full members of their social communities. Observers of our societies, as early as the 1740s, such as Peter Kalm, the Danish naturalist, wrote that southern tribes of Lower Canada, among which were the Huron, were composed in no mean part of Europeans formerly captured in wars against the British colonies. Those former captives, wrote Kalm, were now thoroughly integrated into their adoptive nations and lived a quiet, contented existence as Indians. In this manner, we, the Huron, became genetically mixed with a European nation that, unlike the French or the Spanish, as a rule did not show much inclination to mix with the Native peoples they colonized. Therefore, as I am explaining, some of our Aboriginal nations survived almost only because of our traditional mother-centred thinking. Had we then had leaders formed in the patriarchal, colonial institutions, as is so often the case nowadays, many of our nations would simply not have survived beyond the 18th century. Seeing those young captives, patricentrist leaders would have then said, as they often say today about some of their own people, "We have no use for these children: they are white, they are black, they are not Indian. They do not have a proper quantum of Indian blood." And we and other quite weakened, vulnerable nations would have soon disappeared. But as I am implying, our good fortune was that then we lived within a matricentrist, circular system, where people and other species are not disqualified and eliminated because of their not being what they are not.

I believe this has meaning for all various human peoples and families of peoples today. Our Elders teach us that the great human family is composed of four families of peoples, each having its position around the Great Circle of Life, each its sacred colour and each its unique gifts, to be shared with the others for the better faring of each and all. The Caucasians are at the North, the Native Americans at the East, the Asians at the South and the Africans at the West. Our Elders say to us that all peoples have first known and existed by the Circle, but that some, in the course of their journey, have arrived at forgetting that life is a sacred circle of relations and at thinking that life is a linear process, where only a select few men must have considerable or absolute power over everybody and everything else. The sacredness of creation then gets lost. Linearity implies father-centredness. In those societies, women, from their original position of dignity and even social primacy, become themselves servants in the possession of men, who are themselves servants of other masculine masters.

I believe that society as a whole is undergoing a reflection about how to recover a sense of balance. To me, mother-centredness means recovering balance between genders and in relation to all creatures generally, not because women should command—which is implied in words such as matriarchy—but only because women do have a very central role and the special natural capacity to create, educate and preserve society.

I do not agree with discourses accusing men, or women, therefore furthering enmity between genders. I simply think that our particular Euro-Canadian society has inherited the European patricentrist mode, and has been in it for many centuries and that it will be a long journey before we strike a new balance. Yesterday, Dorothy came up with an expression that I found useful. She talked about "stag effect" (men hanging out together and staying aloof from women). I would not want to be offensive to white male persons; in fact, it is an external description that can apply to me, if one wants to look at me that way. At any rate, I have been struck all along in this conference by the argumentative power that is being developed and used by feminist theoreticians. And the fact that some of these thinkers and scholars are themselves very strong male feminists augments my hope—in fact, deepens my belief—that in spite of our severe differences at times, we are all attempting to come back to a position of balance as human beings, because just like Glooskabe himself, we cannot deny the special nature and roles of women. We cannot deny Nature itself in any of its wise dictates and expressions.

Circular thinkers spontaneously know that woman is the central spiritual sustainer of their society. Also, they traditionally recognized a more important social value in the life of woman. For example, in our Aboriginal judicial thinking, where the criminal loss of a human life had to be compensated through material gifts, it took more gifts to atone for the wounding or the murder of an ordinary woman than it took to atone for the wounding or the murder of a common man. Woman, to circular thinkers, brings new life to the world. Therefore, she understands more the value of life, the price of life. She is life's primary caretaker.

We are not talking about the superiority of one gender, but about the complementarity between the two, based on spiritual observation of life and creation. In this regard, I wish to say that while I believe that the emergence of women-leaders in our Aboriginal political organizations is a good and very needed thing, I do not believe that it should stay like this forever. In functional Aboriginal societies of old, women were political leaders only very exceptionally. Again, we, as part of a colonial, patriarchal society, have been in the linear mode for several generations and many of our thinkers and leaders have been trained, principally through the Christian churches, to act and lead patriarchally. As

I said at first, the fight is not between races, it is between genders. I firmly believe that we will regain our balance, as an intelligent species that wills to survive, and that women will once again have taught men to respect them and themselves. I believe we are progressing towards a time when society will have been sufficiently redressed that genders can once again perform their proper roles. That is not possible at this time. As regards us Aboriginal people, I will simply relate to you that one of our male Aboriginal students at the master's level intends to write a thesis entitled "The Fatherless Nation". This idea aims at reflecting how much confusion has come to exist among our own societies regarding people, mostly males, losing the comprehension of their role and of their nature in relation to their own children and communities. This is a generation in which an incredible number of young women (and also some men) have to raise children alone and, of course, go through a lot of personal suffering. And as we all know, this harsh, sad condition is shared by large numbers of women in our Canadian and North American society overall. To be sure, very many men also suffer helplessly, with the children paying the real price.

Again attempting to suggest ideas that come from the traditional Aboriginal circular perspective, I will recall that women were not customarily in the actual leadership roles; rather, they were the ones who, in family and clan councils, drafted the agenda for male officers to discuss and act on. The women were also the ones who identified natural leaders at a very tender age within their lineages and communities, and eventually appointed them, and demoted them, did they not serve their people appropriately. I do not think that I am demeaning the role of women by saying these things. If there is so much abuse, sexual and otherwise (which, by the way, is unknown among circular-thinking peoples of all races), it means that this war between genders is very harsh and destructive. There is very much loneliness and suffering out there and we do not want to remain in this mode forever.

What I have heard during this conference is all about this war, which brings tremendous suffering to all of us. We heard about the "stag effect" and someone also said, "What about the doe effect?" I say that while we are in the current patriarchal phase, women often have to stick together. There is much loneliness, because respectful men are few and far between. I have a deep, special personal sympathy for women, which arises, I believe, from having witnessed my own mother's typical lifetime struggle against the usual triumvirate on reserves: the priest, the Indian agent and—who is the other guy? —oh yes, the chief, of course. My mother endured being looked at basically as an insane woman because she talked about women's right to education, because she challenged the authority of these three men and the validity of their system. Eventually, she became the first Indian woman to hold a PhD in philosophy, in 1988, at the age of sixty-eight. My experience was seeing my mother resisting all these people who misjudged and branded her throughout her life, and seeing her fall back on a matrilineal support system that allowed us, her seven children, to survive physically and spiritually. Looking back now, and ahead, I think this is all so typical of the effects that the gender war has on all of us, and in which women and children usually have to suffer the most.

There is a new generation of men being raised by the present generation of mothers, and these new men face a special challenge and condition, that of being misjudged and mistreated in their turn under the old patriarchal paradigm. This society is undergoing a deep crisis as to its values, as we all know. Our Elders say it is the spirit of the Earth that is anxious and moving her human and other children to act. For in the same way as patriarchal thinking has meant and caused the mistreatment of women, it has also conditioned societies and people to be insensitive towards what has been happening to the Earth; that is, in one word, its ruthless destruction by so-called "man", whom I call the linear, patricentrist man. We are, therefore, going to witness a more and more forceful change in values in our society in forthcoming years. And since I feel that change manifests itself in the physical visage of society, I will remark that that visage is obviously being transformed. People now frequently have multiple identities, especially in Western countries, making it harder and harder to distinguish so-called races by the facial and physical features of people. Personally, I see hope in this. It is a hopeful time to be living in.

In closing, I will express my hope to be contributing something useful to the development of the feminist discourse. Also, I will call on feminists to lend us help in developing our own Aboriginal theories of emancipation, so as to make all of us joint contributors to the common cause, the cause of our future happiness, seven generations down the road, as goes one of our favourite

Aboriginal sayings. I have often been inspired by feminist theoreticians and by minority thinkers, whom I am very attentive to as circular thinkers, particularly Black, Asian and indigenous generally, for they often have covered ground that we Canadian and North American Aboriginals still need to cover.

We have to help each other de-linearize and re-circularize ourselves. In this perspective, I believe it very important to root our thinking in our own continent. I believe we have to cease feeling and behaving like strangers to this land. I think we have to start using the spiritual leaders of the First Peoples of this land, the Aboriginal intellectual and spiritual leaders of our own Canadian land. We have to open our minds and our doors wider. It will take much too much time if we are waiting for First Nations to have all the necessary PhDs before we make room for them in the Canadian universities and before they can establish their own universities. I am myself, at present, very involved, as the Academic Dean of the SIFC (Saskatchewan Indian Federated College), in the very arduous process of creating such a place, where our respective societies can, at last, aspire to become unified and united, in mutual respect and in harmony. We do not, at this time, have the numbers of professionals and scholars from our own nations. We therefore need the universities to become more flexible and to accept the people that we recognize as our scientists, professionals and leaders, especially our spiritual leaders, who in a very deeply Canadian sense are also your own spiritual leaders. Incidentally, I am happy to report that the recently formed Canadian Federation for the Humanities and Social Sciences did support the principle that Aboriginal educational institutions have the freedom and the authority to give academic validity to the teachings of persons accredited as Elders by these institutions. It was under my own initiative and I was strongly helped and supported by many members of the Federation, in particular by one of its leading members, Dr. Chad Gaffield. Recently, UBC has played an important role and given a strong example in that sense, and much, much more has to happen in our country, if we wish it to become a much stronger and more unified country. Indeed, we feel that this way of recognizing the deeper Aboriginal roots of Canada has the power of effectively combating the racism that is still so much directed at us Aboriginal people, and that keeps conveying to us the harmful notion that we somehow did not have ways or the capacity of thinking out our lives before Europeans came here with their own thinking patterns.

I will now end with this very fundamental idea of circular-thinking folks, the one of creating relationships through adoption. I would urge the ones among you who have been formally adopted into Aboriginal nations, such as David Strangway and Elvi Whittaker, to bear your name proudly and use those names. I give you my assurance that Aboriginal people have always only hoped to naturalize newcomers to their land by adopting them, and thus take down the social and ideological barriers that artificially separate us. Just like my ancestors who practised adoption so spontaneously, I believe that that is what our being here together is all about: getting to feel that we are all rightfully, that is, spiritually, children of this land that gives us life and inspiration, and embracing these roots. For the time being, you will have to be satisfied with belonging to the very humble Toad clan, should you feel you want to.

That is what I wanted to say to you today. My dear friends and relatives, I thank you very much for listening to me.

Why Canada Should Look For, Find, Recognize and Embrace its True, Aboriginal Roots.
The Time of the Toad*

Ses préjugés ont empêché la société non aborigène de reconnaître la profondeur, le raffinement et la beauté de notre culture. [...] Mais cela doit changer, sinon il y aura d'immenses souffrances dans ce magnifique pays que le Créateur nous a donné.
Chef Eli Mandamin (Kenora, Ontario, le 28 octobre 1992)

Dès le premier moment où des Européens l'entendirent prononcer par un chef de Stadacona en 1534, le mot « Kanada » a été synonyme d'abondance infinie, de tranquillité, d'espoir et de majesté naturelle indicible. « Canada » signifiait alors, et continue de signifier et d'être imaginé dans le monde comme un très grand pays situé dans le Nord du merveilleux nouveau continent de l'Amérique, où tout est mieux, plus libre, plus juste, plus propre, moins frénétique, plus sécuritaire que partout

---

* Presented at the 24th Annual Conference of the Association for Canadian Studies, held at Memorial University of Newfoundland, June 6–8, 1997.

ailleurs dans le monde. En fait, nous, les Canadiens, savons que tout cela est vrai. Nous aimons passionnément notre pays et ferions tout en notre pouvoir pour le garder tel qu'il est.

Malheureusement, nous sommes en train de perdre le Canada qui nous est cher et nous ne le savons que trop bien ; il semble que rien de ce que nous avons pensé à faire au cours de ces dernières décennies si inquiétantes n a pu ralentir la désintégration. Dans cet article, je suggère que si le Canada veut préserver son existence et bâtir des fondements vraiment solides pour son avenir, il doit porter une attention très sérieuse à sa civilisation aborigène authentique et profonde. Je soutiens qu'une conception euro-canadienne de la genèse et de la croissance du Canada, et le processus éducatif qui la soutient, sont des facteurs importants dans notre échec à créer une identité et un pays forts. Basant ma réflexion sur des légendes « canadiennes » immémoriales, j'expliquerai la nécessité d'utiliser la conscience circulaire des peuples aborigènes du Canada et j'examinerai les façons dont tous les Canadiens peuvent incorporer cette vision à leur pensée socio-politique et a leur mode de vie. Penser le Canada à l'aborigène, c'est construire un pays plus fort pour tous les Canadiens.

The following thoughts are offered in friendship, kindness and honesty to my colleagues of the Association for Canadian Studies and to my fellow Canadians of all creeds and origins. First, I am greeting the land of my relatives, the Beothuk, whose spirits are here with us and whose blood runs in many of us, their Red relatives. Lest we forget in this year of the celebration of the 500th anniversary of Giovanni Cabotto's landing on this beautiful island of Newfoundland, I wish to recall that 1497 also marked the beginning of the 332-year history of the extermination of the Beothuk as a national and human entity. This said, I wish to express my joy, as an Aboriginal person, that the Island of Newfoundland does comprise two Micmac communities in its human population. For me, it means that the Aboriginal flame is alive and strong in this great island and it makes things right and hopeful. Then my greetings go to the people of Newfoundland, whose friendly and generous spirit I've already had several opportunities to appreciate on this first brief visit to their island-home. I feel that the good old Canadian spirit of simple and healthy cordiality and hospitality is particularly well preserved here. May it always stay like this to remind us all of what Canada is really about! Lastly, in the name of my institution, the Saskatchewan Indian Federated College, my warm greetings to my colleagues of the Association for Canadian Studies and of all the Learned Societies, and my very special thanks and congratulations to Memorial University for holding this large and important conference.

Canadians have various viewpoints on whether their elected governments should or should not actively and systematically address Aboriginal issues with a view to preserving and enhancing the integrity of Aboriginal cultures. Many Canadians think that Aboriginals should be looked at and treated as other Canadians. Many others say that Canada should actively assist Aboriginal Canadians in reaching their own particular societal goals. Many of those who are of this first opinion think that Aboriginal people should abandon their culture in favour of the Canadian culture, just as all other immigrants are expected to do. "What is relevant about Aboriginal cultures in a modern world such as our own?" they often ask. Others, less patient, say that Aboriginal people should not be encouraged to live at the expense of Canadian taxpayers, as they 'almost all' do. Others still, more radical, do not think it is possible to 'elevate' Aboriginals to a civilized state and argue that governments should adopt a hard line and adhere to it. These Canadians have no moral problem with maintaining as large a number of Aboriginals as necessary in the Canadian penal and correctional institutions, at a cost to Canadian taxpayers of $120,000 per year per inmate. This stance is obviously irrational, racist and highly corrosive to our individual and collective well-being and self-esteem.

As to the reasons why other Canadians look favourably upon their Aboriginal fellow country-people, these are also diverse. Many Canadians are motivated by a guilt complex and typically think, "We should give them every chance to survive the extreme chaos we have created for them. After all we have done to them, how can they still be so patient with us?" Others, more practical, look at the question from the standpoint of its social and economic consequences. "If we, as a society, invest the right quantity and quality of resources," they think, "our economy will eventually start benefiting. Besides, there are many human lives to be saved." A third group with a favourable disposition are ideologically motivated. They think their country should recognize the richness inherent in 'its' various Aboriginal cultures, and that Canada could only be more prosperous, more distinctive and more culturally attractive for it. A fourth, like-minded category of Canadians extends this thinking further and says that Aboriginal cultures are what is truly and deeply Canadian about Canada. They believe that our educational system should expose Canadians of all ages to the history, the cultures, the current realities and the aspirations of Aboriginal Canadians, in order for mainstream Canada to receive and integrate this virtually untapped cultural wealth, which is as much Canada's own as are the riches of Canada's subsoil and offshore resources.

While the latter viewpoint is obviously the most enlightened of the ones described, I would like to suggest that even it does not have the capacity to make Canadians understand why it would be worthwhile for their country to make a decisive attempt to uncover, valorize and exploit the philosophical and social riches of its ancient and modern Aboriginal civilization. In this regard, I would like to express my belief that should Canada decide to take this approach, it will not succeed by the precipitous creation of self-governments. Without the prior due process of national cross-cultural education in Aboriginal history, philosophy and current issues, the current self-government tactic will only result in further isolating the Aboriginal population from the rest of Canadian society, thereby increasing the potential for violence. Even more importantly, the result will be the creation and consolidation of classes based on wealth and corruption within Aboriginal societies, and thus the final erosion of a most valuable social and philosophical resource still possessed by Aboriginal societies, and therefore part of Canada's ancient heritage.

Like all Canadians—and this certainly includes my Huron-Wendat people and all Canadian Aboriginal people—I feel a deep and growing concern about our chances of maintaining national unity, and consequently the quality of our national standards of living, which we are intent on extending equally to all segments of the national population. I would like to suggest that Canada has only superficially recognized and even less explored the wealth of social and political ideas belonging to its Aboriginal peoples and thus only part of its own intellectual and spiritual human heritage. I am basing my reflection first on my belief that some of those Aboriginal ideas and practices have great potential for renewing Canada's socio-political vision and for strengthening the bonds uniting all Canadians, and second on my desire, as an Aboriginal Canadian and an academic, to see my own socio-political heritage recognized, embraced and put to serious and respectful use by my country, Canada.

Above all, Aboriginal people believe in inclusiveness. In fact, we know that this belief and our practice of inclusiveness are truly the factor that has made our survival possible over the last five centuries. In spite of all the enlightened predictions by successive generations of scholars and administrators that we would rapidly and eventually disappear, not only are we still here, but we are now recovering strength in numbers, and in social and economic status in all parts of this country to which we belong in our own special way.

All Aboriginal folks have stories that affirm their faith in inclusiveness. Just as the people of Newfoundland have a very valid claim that even though they may be the least affluent Canadian province, they are the most generous when it comes to helping other Canadians in need, my people, the Huron-Wendat, have this story, among many others, to also say that the apparently powerless should never be discounted by the more imposing. We believe that the great island of America was first created as a small island on the back of the Big Turtle by a Spirit-ancestress of all humans. But to begin creating that island, someone had to dive to the depths of the primordial Sea in order to bring back a little of the sacred mud, which First Woman would spread on the Big Turtle's back, and which would then grow into the Great Island on which powerful spirits would create all the different Peoples of Beings, including the Human Beings.

As customarily happens, the most adept divers all tried in turn to obtain some of the precious earth from the bottom of the sea and all failed. At last, seeing the despair among all her fellow aquatic creatures, the Toad, very humbly and with only sheer goodwill, said that she now also had to try. Of course, she was gone the longest of all underneath the great, very deep waters, and eventually swam back up, very weakened, but carrying in her mouth the blessed mud, which was then very thinly spread around the carapace of Big Turtle and which started to become the revered Mother-Earth, which we now all inhabit. (Of course, in time we of the mainland lent some earth to the folks of Newfoundland, so they could one day be part of Canada ... and yes, preserve there the true Canadian spirit. This part of the story ceases to be Aboriginal mythology.)

Respectfully and seriously, I would ask you, dear colleagues and fellow Canadians, to look at your fellow Aboriginal Canadians as the toads in our great Canadian story. For it now seems that our best divers have all been failing in the attempt to find the sacred ingredient for the creation of a true, durable, unifying basis for us all to stand on and build happy, healthy, constructive lives for ourselves and our children's children as Canadians and as members of the great human family. I would like to propose that we have reached the end of a first phase in Canada's history. I would call that period the phase of innocence. During that time, Canadians have begun their existence as Canadians and have been mostly preoccupied with discovering and exploiting the resources of their new surroundings. It has been an intense age of character formation, with its attendant carefree, often wasteful material discovery. Canadians are now realizing with innocent surprise that their material space, while still bounteous, is by no means inexhaustible. We are now at the point where the spirit of our Motherland is commanding us to exercise our maturing minds, hearts, bodies and spirits to find the deeper meaning of our collective existence; that is, to understand how we are going to create a spiritual, and no longer simply material country for ourselves, in which all our fellow human and non-human creatures will also have a place and a future. That is the wisdom of our Mother Earth, which is also the wisdom of the Old Toad, whom we Hurons call our Grandmother and respect accordingly. I would, indeed, propose that we Canadians begin approaching the Toad to dive for us. She will likely bring to us the very simple, but very essential matter out of which we will collectively create the solid, durable, unifying rock and earth bottom for the Canada that we all carry in our hearts and souls.

Aboriginal people have a well-known phrase to express the idea of inclusiveness: the Sacred Circle of Life. In our traditional vision, this represents the cultural ability to see and honour the universal chain of relations uniting all things that exist. We have always resisted and will always resist the biblical precept that man, even to the exclusion of woman, has been created to dominate our sacred Mother Earth. If it were so, why are there so few men in actual positions of domination? Furthermore, why is it that so much destruction has come through the domination of so few men? And why are those men mostly of one ethnic background? Surely, our Great Creator would not have willed so much confusion, oppression and destruction.

It is a fact well known to anthropologists that traditional Aboriginal people everywhere firmly believe that they are safeguarding the sense of truth and justice—the integrity of Life itself—on behalf of other humans who have lost this sense, and on behalf of all the other beings and entities equally belonging to the Sacred Circle of Life. Are we able to look at the toad as our equal, we lofty and mighty otters and beavers, kingfishers, eagles and loons? Are we able to believe that the toad should try to dive for us? There is a pressing need for us to create a true foundation to stand on, as a human community named Canada, isn't there?

I would like to inform you of the human outcome, long after the original toad brought back the primordial mouthful of mud, and made possible our eventual existence as humans on this Great Island named America. We Hurons call ourselves Wendat, which means Dwellers of the Island, partly because we think, in our own ethnocentric way, that we were the First People to be created on the Great Island on the back of the Big Turtle. One thing that we still remember clearly in our hearts' memory is that our first emotion, upon emerging from an underground world, was one of infinite wonderment at the sheer beauty of that motherly earthworld, prepared for us over eons of time by the eternal, powerful Spirits of the Universe, under the direction of the Great Creator, who is both male and female. Every thing, every fellow being that we saw and observed through our senses, had so much beauty and meaning. In fact, all of our thinking and feeling immediately came to be centred on understanding the purpose, the life-spirit of every simple being belonging to every single family of beings. That is why the Aboriginal genius is steeped in the awareness of Life's circularity, or inclusiveness, and that is also why five centuries of the harshest possible experience of contact with the most linear civilization on earth have not managed to effectively break our Aboriginal faith in our primordial vision, nor our sense of responsibility towards fellow humans who have forgotten about their own Aboriginal vision, which is the common human spiritual origin and legacy.

Aboriginal nations all believe that they were created right here, on this Great Island, and none has any memory of having emigrated here, as many scholars maintain. Aboriginal people and scholars believe that it is unjust and inconsequential for a society to use its scientific constructs to force some of its (mostly Aboriginal) members into assimilating its historical concepts and thus its own social mythology. It is a means of cultural genocide. We Wendat, after being created on this Great Island, remember living our lives in numerous parts of it. Eventually, we opted for a more sedentary, agricultural existence and elected to live in the lands situated between the present cities of Toronto and Quebec, the Saint Lawrence and Trent valleys, and the Georgian Bay areas, in present-day Ontario and Quebec. That is mostly where we lived when Europeans started deserting their homelands and landed on our and other shores.

Most Canadians have been taught in schools and universities that my ancestors, the Wendat (or the Hurons, as the first French immigrants disparagingly named us), were a rustic, though friendly tribe of Indians who fell prey to and were basically exterminated by their terrible Iroquois enemies. The narrative continues that this would certainly have happened without the overall blameless presence of the Europeans who, at least, recorded all that patently inglorious history in their various histories of Canada. These histories are all largely unanimous on the score of the "destruction of the good Huron by the bad Iroquois", which I termed a cornerstone of conventional Canadian history in my book *For an Amerindian Autohistory* (McGill-Queen's University Press, 1992). In 1994, Les Presses de l'Université Laval published in French my doctoral dissertation, "La civilisation wendate", under the title *Les Wendats. Une civilisation méconnue* (an English translation has since been published by UBC Press in 1999). This book is a survey of Wendat history since the time of their shift to agriculture, a sedentary lifestyle and systematic matricentrism; that is, roughly one thousand years ago. The difference between the conventional, Eurocentric picture and the one arrived at through my method, which I have named *Amerindian autohistory*, is both startling and inspiringly provocative.

Through this paper, I have mostly wanted to deliver to my colleagues of the Association for Canadian Studies, and to my fellow Canadians, the essential ideas I found and brought back up when I dove down into the deep, mysterious sea of my people's self-consciousness, aided in important ways by the tools created and the information honestly recorded by successive generations of non-Aboriginal specialists in our history.

My first observation in this regard will be that roughly half a millennium before the European accident, the Wendat consciously and strategically placed themselves at the centre of what soon became a multinational, multi-ethnic, multilingual governmental arrangement that was to produce rich intercultural life, prosperous commerce and formidable political alliances for quite a numerous and populous society of nations. Most interestingly, even though this same society of nations was quickly blown apart through epidemic diseases from Europe and through religious and political colonial manoeuvring, this national political arrangement is what today's Canada has been trying so hard to replicate ever since Confederation. Of course, I and many Aboriginal and non-Aboriginal thinkers ascribe this unconscious Canadian and Euro-American emulation to the resilience and the power of the deeper Aboriginal spirit of this land, percolating freely into the social ethos and national ideals of Canada and its people.

My second observation is that our neighbours to the South consciously adopted several political ideas and governmental symbols of the Hodenosaunee (Iroquois) Confederacy, and that inspiration carried them far in their own Eurocentric vision of domination. Now, I wish here to be genuinely respectful of my Hodenosaunee relatives and recognize that it was their confederacy that made for the physical and spiritual survival of many remnants of Aboriginal nations, including many Wendat, and that much of our own socio-political legacy, which was akin to theirs, has been in this manner amalgamated with their own and with so many others. This said, I wish to suggest that the ways in which we organized our own Wendat Confederacy and built a large, multi-ethnic society around it not only bears upon Canada in being able to provide governmental, legal and political inspiration, but is, ultimately, more refined and universally applicable than the Iroquois-inspired American model. A Wendat-derived social model could enrich our country and many other modern nation-states who face—and are sometimes overwhelmed by—the disintegration of traditional national identities, their replacement by plural identities, and the need to integrate (as opposed to assimilate) an array of newly immigrated members, themselves often displaced as a result of colonial practices and legacies in their countries of origin.

The most inspiring feature of Wendat and Aboriginal social and political practices was inclusiveness on the basis of respect and even studious admiration of differences as the challenge of something new from which to understand and grow. The Wendat Confederacy comprised two founding nations, the Bear and the Cord, and three smaller nations. Every nation was composed of up to eight clans and every village contained families, or clan segments, belonging to any of the eight clans. Each clan segment of each village lived in its own longhouse and had its own council, upon which no village council or national council or confederacy council could impose any decision, except through open discussion and gentle persuasion. The confederacy was a very decentralized governmental structure, operating on the belief that the interests of the larger collectivity took precedence over personal ones. The collectivity repaid individual loyalty by allowing every child, every individual to learn through free experience of one's power of reasoning, and eventually, through living and working for the common good. Also, the community was always aware of the needs, ills and unfulfilled desires of any and all of its members (which bring us to the realms of medicine and psychiatry, but this is not our topic here).

As said above, the Wendat Confederacy itself—and in this it differed significantly from its Hodenosaunee counterpart—was the hub around which gravitated a large body of other nations, many of which are of quite distinct ethnic stocks. But the Wendat language was used by all, and archaeology confirms oral tradition in that trade, and not war, had been the predominant orientation of this great 'pre-Canadian', multicultural civilization.

Inclusiveness, decentralization, welcoming protection and use of differences, responsibility to the collective before personal interest, and circular consciousness: these are ideas that grew out of the spiritual soil obtained by the primordial Toad. Let there be a time of the Toad again in this new, maturing Canada. Canadians need a base; an island; a real, durable country, with a spirit. The spirit of the Old World has not worked here. It will not work here. This land has its own spirit. Let us recognize and embrace it, for it is our own, as Canadians. But first, let us ask our Grandmother the Toad to dive for some sacred mud, for that is the only soil from which a true Canadian spirit will grow. And there are no other divers left.

Attouguet Eathoro! Thank you, friends and relatives!

Canada and the First Nations:
The Need for Two Feet to Stand On*

Honoured Elders, dear friends and relatives,

First, I would like to express many heartfelt thanks to the Association for Canadian Studies for having the idea and going through all the needed efforts to organize this special conference, which puts an important emphasis on Canadian Aboriginal Peoples in this anniversary year of the Association for Canadian Studies.

For many, maybe all of us here, the topic and the purpose of a conference such as this one are not just another interesting academic exercise; the future and identities of Aboriginal Peoples in our great Canadian land are matters that, as persons, occupy our minds, hearts and souls on a constant basis. As people so disposed, we breathe, think, dream, pray and live with the purpose

---

* Presented at the 25th Annual Conference of the Association for Canadian Studies, "Futures and Identities : Aboriginal Peoples in Canada", held at the University of Ottawa, May 31–June 2, 1998.

of seeing our Aboriginal people given the mere chance to play their role as the people they are in this great country and in the world, and thereby to survive. For there is no survival for the ones not allowed to participate, to give of what they are, as opposed to accommodating themselves to the socio-cultural ideals and priorities of the more powerful. As one moved by that purpose, our survival, and wishing to find means to reunite our minds and hearts in the spirit of this conference, my style for this presentation will be markedly autobiographical. I believe this is because I have been taught as a child and throughout my life by our Elders that our human hearts are like sacred drums, which beat to inspire and create human trust, peace and harmony when the words we speak with our spirits are both kind and honest. I will use this sweetgrass, which speaks from the kind and honest heart of our Mother-Earth, so that my thoughts and words reflect my respect for our good, wise, loving Mother and the Great Circle of Relations [simple ceremony of burning the sacred sweetgrass, to bless the work we are doing].

I will now tell you a few things about where I come from, as a person, before singing to you a song I wrote this year and have entitled "Singing Indian". I am the second child and first son of two traditional Huron-Wendat: Georges and Éléonore Sioui. Sioui is the French rendition of the name Tseawi, meaning 'Rising Sun'. My ancestors were hereditary Headmen and Headwomen of the Wendat, Keepers of the Wampum Archives and traditionally entrusted with the external affairs of our confederacy. They acted as *Garihoua Dandionxra*, or Keepers of the Peace, often translated as "war chiefs" in the conventional historical discourse. They had a determining influence among a vast Commonwealth of Native Nations (including Iroquoian, Algonquian and Siouan speakers) who, at the time of the coming of the Europeans, used the Wendat language in their commercial and diplomatic dealings. Like many of you, my upbringing was marked by a very committed effort on the part of my extended family to pass on to the young an understanding of our history, and to impart to our young minds and spirits a sense of why and how we, in our turn, had to protect the life-flame of our people and of all our fellow Aboriginal people because, as we were made to understand, the life-flame of our people is the life-flame of humanity itself. There is but one human people, one heart, one prayer, one song.

My song, "Singing Indian", expresses that our universal song is a song of sadness, because it is little understood, therefore little respected, but it is also a song of pride because we are united. It is also a song of hope, because it is ancient and it is about Life. The word 'Indian' means singing, praying, standing up for Life, for the truth of Life. In that deep sense, all of us are born with an Indian heart. Some regrettably lose it.

Singing Indian

Sing, my brother, sing, my sister,
Sing the great Indian song of sadness,
The beautiful song the Old Ones have sung,
Sing it on down the times to the young,
There's no tree if you cut out the roots,
There's no life if you take out the truth,
That's our fate and that's our fight,
Who else will keep the flame alive?
Sing, my brother, sing, my sister, …
… There's no life if we don't sing the truth.

I hear every Elder,
Read the words of writers,
See the mind of painters,
Watch the dance of dancers:
There's only one song,
There's only one pain,
The pain of Mother Earth,
Song of her Indian child.

In the soul of speakers,
Of the music makers,
In the heart of actors,
Of every son and daughter,

> From ocean to ocean,
> From North to South,
> From Nation to Nation,
> There's only one heart,
> There's only one song,
> There's only one dance,
> There's only one prayer,
> There's only one word,
> There's only one pride,
> That pride is to feel
> United as children
> Of our Mother Earth
> And cry out together
> The love and the pain,
> For that is the song
> We'll forever sing.
>
> Sing, my brother, sing, my sister, …
> … If we don't sing the truth.

I will now tell you about where I've been, where I presently stand as an Aboriginal academic and why I chose this title for my presentation. I remembered, when I first went to university, that my parents had once told me, when I was six years old and already beginning grade three, that I would one day need to write other books about Canadian history in order to help change the perceptions of non-Indians about our people, perceptions that had been created by the history books then utilized, and that had been and were still the root cause of the suffering, poverty and slow but sure disappearance of our people.

Many years later, while beginning university studies, I told teachers of my goal to write the history of my people, and I was answered that the history of Indians had all been written down long ago, that it belonged in the past and that history could not be changed, or rewritten, especially if one had only had an oral tradition. I then remembered that some of my people had often said that the time would come when we could help the non-Indians by communicating to them our feeling about life and about historical truth. Elders said that newcomers were still very blinded by notions that they had brought over from Europe, notions that had not worked there—in fact, that had caused them to leave from there, and that had to do with disregarding the sources of life themselves and that had made them jeopardize their very future for the sake of acquiring material wealth. I later came to know that that way of thinking was named linear and was directly opposed to our own traditional circular thinking, which tells us that Life is but one great family of beings, each one of them to be acknowledged and respected, because the same Spirit of Life inhabits all beings equally. Life has spirit and Life is a great sacred Circle of reciprocal relations. The human being is only one among an infinite number of species of beings, and has not been created to dominate the Earth. Many circular-thinking people have now come to disbelieve that tenet, so fundamental in linear (patriarchal) religious traditions.

I then realized that the time when our non-Indian relatives would be ready to listen to us too had not arrived, and as a temporary alternative to the study of history, I took up the study of languages for the next three years. During another nine years, I lived off the land, travelled, consecutively became the editor of two Aboriginal magazines—the first, founded by my mother, the *Kanatha* magazine and the second, the *Tawow* magazine, at the Department of Indian and Northern Affairs—and subsequently Assistant Director General of the Cree Board of Health and Social Services of James Bay. Among these many great experiences, the most determining one was to get to know many First Peoples Elders and, with their caring and help, to begin finding answers to my ever-present spiritual, intellectual and life concerns.

Eventually, this brought me back to university in 1982. That same year, I, together with friends and relatives, was arrested in a provincial park in Quebec while doing a traditional fast. Because of the Elders' teachings, I was able to lay the foundation of what came to be well known in Canada as the *Sioui Case* after we obtained a resounding victory in the Supreme Court of Canada, in May of 1990. During those years, I also did my graduate studies. I obtained my master's degree in 1987 and my doctoral degree in 1991. In 1985, I met my wife and we founded the family I so much love. Much of all of this I owe to the help and guidance of our Elders.

In 1989, I had the good fortune to see my master's dissertation published by Les Presses de l'Université Laval, under the title *Pour une autohistoire amérindienne. Essai sur les fondements d'une morale sociale*. That book came out in English in 1992 as *For an Amerindian Autohistory*. The second part of the original French title was not used. It translates, "Essay on the Foundation of a Social Ethics". That part is very important, because it refers to the Aboriginal circular view of life. The basic idea of the book is that in our social reality, as modern Canadians, there is no social ethics adapted to the deeper unchanging needs of humans and their non-human relatives. The social ethics that we do have is a short-sighted, materially based one. It is essentially the one once brought over from Europe which, obviously, is not working out here either in this land that we still call 'Indian' in its entirety, out of an awareness of a responsibility to protect her.

My book proposes, fundamentally, that we collectively rediscover the real Aboriginal social ethics of this land that we all share, and that we go through the collective effort of adapting it to reality as it has unfolded and will continue to unfold around and within us. Concurrently, the book suggests that it is the newcomers who eventually and naturally become assimilated into the basic civilization of the land they migrate to and that, therefore, in spite of superficial appearances, it is the non-Aboriginals who are in the process of becoming 'Indian', and not the opposite. Here we are in the realm of essential values, not of material culture change. So this book is a very different reflection from the usual discourse that stresses victimization, since it puts the Aboriginal civilization in a position of honour and responsibility. It aims at relieving living people of guilt, resentment, fear and other harmful feelings, and therefore has the potential of uniting people, instead of replicating the 'divide and conquer' intent and effect of conventional books about Indians. That is the power of circular thinking. That is why I personally highly honour my First Peoples' spiritual and intellectual traditions.

That is also why I believe that until all of us are reunited in the true circular spirit of this land, neither First Peoples nor Canada will walk together firmly on two legs. Instead, we will continue to walk on just the only leg we have had so far, the legal-political leg. We need the other one: the intellectual-spiritual leg. And to me, the most important element in achieving this unity of hearts and souls is the way we will choose in the near future to enable the First Peoples of this country to recapture the deep sense of where they come from historically, so as to know where they want to go, always keeping in mind their responsibility as intellectual and spiritual guides of their fellow Canadians. Very importantly also, in order to develop true sympathy and care for their new fellow Canadians, Aboriginal people need to know of the hardships and pain that forced people to leave their own motherlands and seek a new life, here and elsewhere. Knowing history, therefore, is to me the cornerstone on which a positive sense of First Peoples' identity will be built, and the foremost element in our collective acquisition of the power to stand and walk on two legs, all together, as the great country that we are.

As both an Aboriginal person and a professional historian, I am not happy to see my people and my country limping along on their quite strong legal-political leg, while I know that some basic physiotherapy would give us our other spiritual-intellectual leg and allow us to walk normally and compete advantageously in any international or world championship race. As a person, I am not happy either to see many of our political leaders, both Aboriginal and non-Aboriginal, give in to the easy solution of isolating us from one another by creating forms of separate societies, which our spiritual and intellectual leaders, as a rule, do not approve of. Again, basic knowledge of First Peoples' history demonstrates that our real philosophy always has been about sharing, mutual assistance and intelligent integration of the positive knowledge of others, be they other Aboriginal nations or immigrant European or other nations. The fact that we had very functional multinational, multilingual, socio-political arrangements in pre-European times is beginning to be well documented and awaits more research by First Peoples academics. I predict that in time, that body of research will blossom into a new, Canadian-grown, very rich historiographical field. It will happen when new Aboriginal-inclusive institutions of learning begin to exist and prosper and make of us a country with two strong, solid legs to stand and walk on.

My second book on Canadian and First Peoples history is my doctoral dissertation, defended at Laval University on September 30, 1991. It is a reflection on how one Aboriginal nation, my people, the Huron-Wendat, had organized their life and their relations with their Aboriginal neighbour-nations. It gives a concrete example of how circular-thinking people view and live life. It is also an illustration of how circle societies can quickly be destroyed when linear societies are forced to leave their own lands and come to create a new place for themselves in the midst of indigenous, circular-thinking peoples. My book *Huron-Wendat. The Heritage of the Circle* covers my people's history over the last one thousand years. Like the first book, it also states our feelings and sense about history and life, while aiming at relieving present and future inhabitants of our land and the world from lingering negative, divisive feelings about one another, feelings produced by past and current linear historical writings. That book, out in French since 1994 (and since published in English at UBC Press), is based on the first doctoral dissertation in history ever defended and published by a Canadian Amerindian.

Now, I wish to tell you about teachings of Elders that have had a very decisive influence on how I have oriented my life and my own personal struggle as an Indian person. As a young individual, like so many of us, I was drawn to wanting to put a stop to the cultural, social, economic and spiritual misery of my people by going into politics and fighting it out against our perceived enemies, both inside and outside of our communities. I ran for the leadership of our nation when I was twenty-three years old. My 'group' (notice the similarity to non-Aboriginal party politics) was not elected, but we did obtain some gains in favour of the ones we saw as the discounted elements of our population, namely, the traditionally oriented. What caused my personal eventual disenchantment with that linear style of politics was noticing that it was divisive, and that people who had gotten along well together, former friends or even relatives, sometimes became staunch enemies. Our community, instead of becoming stronger, became weaker, and our cultural opponents, mostly on the outside, had fun watching what happened and knew very well how to take advantage of that state of affairs. In other words, as Elders put it, we were making the wheels of the linear system turn, to the great disadvantage of everyone, of the entire community (the circle of Life).

Eventually, at about the time I turned thirty, I began searching for the spiritual guidance of Elders. I travelled extensively, east, south, west and north, seeking and obtaining that guidance. Consistently, the Elders told me and my seeking comrades: "Do not waste your strength on politics or religion. Our people are not good at those things because those things are not ours and they are all about fighting and power. Try to stay away from alcohol. Lastly, stay grounded in your Indian culture and go and perfect your formal education." I have since striven to follow the advice of the Elders on all those counts.

Today, some twenty years later, I believe there is one Elders' teaching I have understood particularly well, and that is how high a value our Aboriginal nations have always put on education, and how strongly our First Peoples have traditionally believed that their people's place in their land was one of intellectual and spiritual leadership and responsibility, but that the only way Aboriginal people are going to take back our rightful place and keep it is by placing that same primary value on education. This means staying firmly grounded in our traditions, languages and spiritual values, and therefore being unconditional and forceful in claiming our right to high-quality education at all levels for every one of our citizens. I believe that through the invalidating effects of the linear system, our people have been severely debilitated and that we have lost the use of some of our limbs. I believe that that is how we have come to compensate by walking on only one leg, the political-legal one. Using very powerful mental and emotional resources, many of our people have become incredibly strong and articulate political leaders, and this has been a very important means of our survival during the very harsh times we have known since the European accident. However, now is a new time, when some of the old predictions are clearly coming true; namely, that the day will come when the newcomers will begin to be scared by the consequences of their actions here in our land and start coming to our people for advice. That time has indeed come and that is why our spiritual leaders are telling us how to go about readying ourselves for playing our own due role in the world, a very important and honourable role.

My experience, mostly as an educator and an educational administrator, is that the doors of the places where we will obtain the credentials that will put us in those positions to act are simply waiting for us to open them. They will open all the more easily if we approach those places in the manner prescribed by our traditional leaders; that is, with kindness, honesty, pride and humility. Very importantly also, many of those places of learning have yet to be created. In my experience, very many individuals in academia and in our larger society have come to strongly believe that this country urgently needs to establish Aboriginal-inclusive and Aboriginal-controlled places of learning where the people of Canada can come and meet their Aboriginal fellow Canadians in a non-political, academic setting and learn to understand and appreciate the essential civilization of their land of adoption. This meeting of hearts in an Aboriginal social, intellectual and spiritual setting is seen as possibly the prime factor of a much needed new strengthening of the Canadian spirit towards the building of a true, united, more deeply conscious Canada. Thus the strengthening of First Peoples through the development of First Peoples' education may very well mean the strengthening of Canada itself. I believe that Eurocentric attempts to assimilate First Peoples will keep producing failure and resistance, and that these will be produced at a higher and higher social and economic cost for Canada, not to mention the far more regrettable intellectual, cultural and spiritual loss for our country and the world. I strongly believe that we need to create those places of Aboriginal learning, in every region of this beautiful country, where we will begin to truly converse and make ourselves intelligible to one another, therefore able to empathize together, and proceed to create great, durable things together and for one another, as true societies do. Such is my lifetime desire for my Aboriginal people, for my country, Canada, and for all our relations, the Great Circle of Life.

Ho! Ho! Attouguet Eathoro! (Thank you from the heart, friends and relatives!)

Favoriser l'intégration.
Point de vue matricentriste[*]

Avant-propos

Historiquement, les sociétés matricentristes, telles les sociétés amérindiennes, ou indigènes, au plan mondial, ont eu beaucoup plus de facilité à intégrer leurs nouveaux venus. Selon moi, Huron traditionaliste, cela est dû à la reconnaissance et à l'utilisation, dans ces sociétés, de la capacité naturelle des femmes à voir la vie dans sa réalité circulaire, c'est-à-dire comme une chaîne de relations complémentaires entre des êtres de natures extrêmement variées, mais égaux. C'est le cercle sacré des relations, prémisse philosophique connue des Amérindiens traditionalistes. Dans cet ordre d'idées, en quoi les Amérindiens, les Indigènes, peuvent-ils continuer à être

---

[*] Communication présentée au Colloque international *Définir l'intégration ? Perspectives nationales et représentations symboliques*, organisé par l'Association internationale des études québécoises et l'Institut d'études politiques, tenu à Aix-en-Provence, France, du 24 au 26 mars 1999. Publié dans le livre des Actes de la Conférence, *Définir l'intégration ? Perspectives nationales et représentations symboliques* (sous la direction de Yannick Resch), Montréal, Éditions XYZ, 2001.

une source d'idées sociales nouvelles et utiles pour la France, l'Europe ? En échange, comment leurs nations subjuguées conçoivent-elles obtenir un appui idéologique des Français, des Européens ?

L'être humain, en tous temps et en tous lieux, n'a jamais pu ni ne pourra jamais, sauf à son péril, échapper à la nécessité de rattacher sa réflexion et ses actions à la nature et à ses lois. Je voudrais, dans cette présentation, offrir à mes frères et sœurs français, européens, euro-américains et autres, un point de vue huron et amérindien sur les façons dont ma tradition ancestrale et ma perception historique peuvent aider à mieux comprendre comment nous, humains, nous sommes dissociés des lois naturelles, particulièrement lorsqu'il est question d'intégrer l'« autre » à notre nous national/étatique ou, simplement, collectif, ainsi que comment retrouver une sagesse et une connaissance utiles nous venant de notre commun héritage circulaire (ou matricentrique), lorsque nous comprenons la nécessité et l'urgence d'humaniser nos processus d'intégration d'autres qui viennent vers nous.

Comme la grande majorité de nos nations amérindiennes et indigènes, au plan mondial, ma nation, la nation wendate, jadis nommée huronne par les Français, a connu une expérience coloniale extrêmement dure, presque fatale. Si j'ai dit « la grande majorité » c'est que j'entends que pour les autres nations, cette expérience a été effectivement fatale et qu'elles ont donc cessé d'exister à un moment donné sous les coups de l'assaut colonial. D'ailleurs, plusieurs collectivités indigènes – et amérindiennes – disparaissent du portrait vivant de l'humanité chaque année. Bien que cela soit d'un intérêt tout au plus secondaire pour l'entité politique humaine non indigène, dans son ensemble, nous, indigènes, nous y intéressons intensément et constamment. Parce que nous voyons nos peuples disparaître à un rythme effarant dans la grande fournaise coloniale, et même postcoloniale, oui, c'est là l'une des raisons de notre intérêt, mais nous en avons d'autres que je dirais encore plus importantes. J'en résumerai un grand nombre en parlant de la certitude qui loge dans chacun de nos cœurs que nous sommes les peuples ancêtres de l'humanité, les Premiers Peuples (et non pas le « quart-monde » comme le monde indigène est fréquemment appelé), et que, un peu comme des aïeuls que peu veulent écouter, nous pouvons et devons aider ceux qui ont perdu leur orientation et leur sagesse et, donc, leur capacité de recouvrer le sens de la nature et de ses lois. En d'autres mots, les indigènes, contrairement aux non-indigènes, ne peuvent se voir premièrement et simplement comme d'impuissantes et amères victimes, puisqu'ils sont d'abord animés par un sentiment sûr de leur devoir et de leur rôle extrêmement importants de préserver la conscience originale de l'humain et possiblement d'y ramener leur semblable dit civilisé. « Sans la présence de l'Indien, dira typiquement un *máma* (guérisseur) kogi de la Colombie, le monde serait déjà fini. Si un jour l'Indien oublie ses croyances, dit-il encore, le monde s'éteindra ».

Nos sages nous disent souvent que nous, plus jeunes ou moins initiés, ne devons pas penser que ce que nous appelons coutumièrement notre culture indienne, « *the Indian Way* », nous appartient en propre. En fait, nous a-t-on dit et redit, il ne faut pas tomber dans cette habitude d'imaginer, de penser et de dire que les choses et même les personnes n'existent vraiment et pleinement que si elles sont possédées par quelqu'un, ou par soi. En réalité, nous a-t-on répété, nous ne sommes que de passage dans ce monde matériel et ne pouvons donc rien posséder. C'est l'absence du Tien et du Mien, observé par l'écrivain philosophe Armand de Lom D'Arce, baron de Lahontan, chez ses hôtes hurons et algonquins. Le baron de Lahontan fut, à la fin du XVIIe siècle, l'un des plus grands amis qu'eurent jamais les Indiens. Écrivain à l'origine des Lumières et, donc, de la Révolution française, il fut proscrit, excommunié et expatrié pour s'être porté au secours de mes ancêtres dans sa vie et par ses écrits.

Pour nous éviter l'écueil de cette notion de possession, nos Sages nous disent plutôt qu'il n'y a, en réalité, qu'une façon de comprendre et de voir la vie et que c'est comme une chaîne unissant tous les êtres de toutes les espèces. Ils symbolisent cette chaîne, cette complémentarité et cette égalité universelles par un Cercle, qu'ils appellent « le Cercle sacré de la vie ». Ils nous disent aussi que tous les peuples humains ont, durant un certain temps, eu cette même tradition et cette même connaissance, cette même capacité de voir la vie pour ce qu'elle est, un Cercle, dont on a documenté les traces matérielles et visuelles dans les dossiers archéologiques de tous les peuples du monde.

M'appuyant sur l'enseignement intime et constant des Aînés de nos nations amérindiennes, j'ai dit, dans deux livres, que certains peuples, à cause de contraintes qui ont été particulières à leur trajectoire historique, en sont venus à oublier que la vie est un Cercle sacré de relations, et à croire qu'elle est plutôt un processus qui évolue et progresse de façon linéaire vers un futur inconnu. J'ai décrit cet abandon de la pensée circulaire comme un accident idéologique, une sorte de déraillement hors des lois de la nature. J'ai aussi écrit que cette pensée humaine originelle circulaire était matricentriste, c'est-à-dire fondée sur la reconnaissance que notre bonheur humain, notre sécurité humaine à long terme dépendent de notre reconnaissance du lien filial nous unissant à la Terre, nourricière de nos corps, de nos intelligences, de nos cœurs et de nos esprits. De même que nous dépendons de notre Mère, la Terre, pour notre vie, notre équilibre et notre bonheur, de même reconnaissons-nous dans nos femmes, nos mères, nos grand-mères, nos tantes, nos filles, nos sœurs, nos amies, ce même don propre à la femme de la conscience des besoins vitaux supérieurs des sociétés et de la science, et des moyens pour y répondre. Aussi ces sociétés originelles à pensée circulaire inventent-elles leurs institutions à partir d'une foi souveraine dans le caractère et dans les dons sacrés de la femme, porteuse et donneuse de vie. Ces sociétés, que nous nommons, globalement, indigènes, c'est-à-dire non étatisées, sont matricentristes, c'est-à-dire qu'elles placent la femme au centre de leur pensée et de leur organisation sociopolitique, contrairement à ce que font les sociétés linéaires, qui sont patricentristes, typiquement coloniales ou autocolonisantes, et qui relèguent la femme à une position de productrice-reproductrice-objet ; ces sociétés linéaires peuvent ainsi, avec la bénédiction de religions patriarcales, les dominer et les exploiter impunément.

La France, et l'Europe prise globalement, sont de plus en plus durement aux prises avec le problème de l'intégration de gens et de groupes d'immigrants et de minorités qui réclament des droits et une existence à part entière en tant que Français, en tant qu'Européens. Du point vue amérindien circulaire que je suis en train de décrire, je vois une extrême importance pour la France – et les pays européens – de juger honnêtement et sévèrement leur héritage idéologique patricentriste, linéaire et colonisateur, simplement parce que je puis affirmer que la pensée circulaire matricentriste confère une viabilité infiniment supérieure aux sociétés qui l'embrassent ou qui ne s'en sont point départies.

J'illustrerai mon propos par l'exemple de la survivance de ma propre nation huronne-wendate grâce, à son attachement à sa cosmologie matricentrique originelle et de son affaiblissement critique depuis qu'elle commença à recevoir, de façon forcée, l'éducation linéaire patricentrique, surtout depuis un siècle. Ma nation wendate, en réalité une puissante confédération à l'origine, fut vite reconnue par les premiers explorateurs français comme la nation maîtresse d'un commerce très étendu et florissant et la nation-cœur d'un réseau vaste et complexe de relations diplomatiques, politiques, sociales et culturelles. Dans mon livre *Les Wendats. Une civilisation méconnue*, j'ai expliqué les origines et la formation de cette grande société multinationale et multilingue, il y a environ un millénaire, ainsi que sa pensée civilisationnelle et son fonctionnement intime. J'ai aussi démontré comment, en l'espace bref et apocalyptique de 35 ans, les maladies épidémiques d'origine européenne et l'assaut colonial, donc patriarcal, détruisirent plus des trois quarts de notre population, jusqu'à la dispersion finale des survivants, en 1649-1650.

Ce fut sa pratique gouvernementale matricentriste qui sauva ma nation de l'extermination complète. En effet, en cette période très sombre de notre histoire, les mères de clans et leurs conseils eurent recours à leurs pratiques traditionnelles de la capture et de l'adoption, qu'elles intensifièrent. Les guerres que se livraient les Amérindiens étaient des guerres motivées par l'honneur et visaient essentiellement le remplacement par des captifs de leurs gens perdus ou capturés. Des guerriers habiles et valeureux étaient commissionnés par les mères de clans pour aller enlever des gens à l'ennemi, surtout des jeunes gens et des femmes. Les hommes mûrs étaient parfois torturés ou exécutés, ou encore réservés pour d'éventuels échanges de captifs avec les nations amies ou ennemies. Mes ancêtres capturèrent ainsi et intégrèrent nombre d'individus de nations amies, amérindiennes ou européennes, ainsi que nombre d'ennemis et d'enfants d'ennemis, non seulement iroquois, mais aussi de leurs alliés européens, c'est-à-dire anglais, hollandais et autres des treize colonies ancêtres des États-Unis. Les observateurs européens du temps exprimèrent toujours leur surprise de voir que ces captifs devenus adultes étaient en tous points à l'aise dans leur identité d'adoption, se retrouvant, selon l'expression alors courante, « ensauvagés » et ne manifestant aucun désir de retourner vers leur société d'origine. D'autre part, les Amérindiens capturés par les sociétés patriarcales et linéaires européennes, même en bas âge, finissaient immanquablement par retourner à leur société de départ.

Je retiens de ma culture quatre enseignements que je crois pertinents pour le propos de l'intégration des minorités en France, ou n'importe où. Premièrement, il est un fait extrêmement bien documenté et difficilement discutable que les sociétés indigènes, donc matricentristes, ont de tous temps, et en dépit de leur relative simplicité matérielle et technologique, exercé un puissant attrait sur nombre d'individus des sociétés coloniales qui les envahirent et les dépossédèrent. Un exemple évident et pertinent pour la France serait les fameux « coureurs des bois », hommes français qui trouvèrent leur libération américaine en découvrant la réalité du respect de la vision individuelle dans ces sociétés du « bon sauvage », comme on nomma nos sociétés, et fréquemment en s'y intégrant, pour créer et former le peuple métis. Deuxièmement, si elle était alors devenue linéaire et patriarcale, tel qu'elle l'est effectivement aujourd'hui devenue jusqu'à un certain degré, ma nation aurait perdu ce pouvoir de survie qui lui a permis de résister à l'assimilation, voire à l'extinction. En effet, des chefs acculturés et patricentristes auraient trouvé inacceptable l'inclusion de ces enfants étrangers et notre nation se serait éteinte à assez brève échéance. Troisièmement, je crois qu'il est oiseux et illusoire de parler de volonté réelle d'inclusion positive des étrangers, surtout s'ils sont pauvres, dans une société à pensée linéaire, puisque ces sociétés sont par nature matérialistes, élitistes, racistes et androcentristes. Quatrièmement, et en dernier lieu, les sociétés traditionnelles européennes (tel qu'en a parlé monsieur Stéphan Hessel ce matin) ont l'occasion et doivent saisir la chance de délinéariser leur pensée et, donc, leurs pratiques sociales au contact de tous ces gens qui arrivent chez elles ou sont déjà parmi elles, souvent conscients que la richesse française et européenne vient en partie de la colonisation des leurs. Très souvent, ces gens portent en eux des traditions circulaires collectivistes et matricentristes, capables de regénérer l'Europe, si conservatrice de schèmes idéologiques, de pratiques sociales, politiques et économiques périmées qui empêchent la circulation de son énergie vitale, donc l'utilisation positive de son gigantesque et merveilleux héritage culturel, idéologique, scientifique, en un mot, humain.

Ce fut un Français, le baron de Lahontan, qui, par ses fameux « Dialogues » avec mon ancêtre huron Kondiaronk (Adario), commença à inspirer la philosophie des Lumières, flamme originelle de la Révolution française, au tout début des années 1700. La Hontan, penseur tout à fait central dans l'histoire de la France et qui pourtant attend encore sa juste reconnaissance dans son pays, et son ami Adario, de même que d'autres « philosophes nus », tels qu'il les appelait, s'entendirent sur des idées qui devaient guérir la France, l'Europe, de maux sociaux et spirituels graves qui les faisaient souffrir et qu'elles avaient transportés au Nouveau monde, et dont les principaux étaient l'obsession du Tien et du Mien, l'existence de religions et de patries, l'oppression de l'individu par les élites, le non-respect de la Terre, mère de l'humain, et l'exploitation des enfants et de la femme par l'homme.

Assez tôt, les idées de Lahontan, d'Adario et de leurs amis philosophes indiens eurent des répercussions décisives sur l'ordre sociopolitique qui avait prévalu en Europe et dans l'Occident. À quelque neuf mois de l'avènement d'un nouveau millénaire, j'aurai voulu, dans cette brève présentation, donner une explication renouvelée de l'origine d'une rencontre idéologique productive entre deux civilisations, l'européenne et l'amérindienne, l'une pensant et parlant par un Français et l'autre par un Huron, deux peuples indéfectiblement alliés depuis leur première rencontre physique, au XVIe siècle. L'explication renouvelée dont je parle identifie comme point focal de cette rencontre idéologique, vers 1700, l'opposition diamétrale entre une vision du monde gravement linéarisée, virtuellement incapable d'inclusivité, et une autre, préservée dans sa circularité originelle, sympathique et ouverte à l'autre, et disposée à lui recommuniquer les moyens de sa guérison. Les remèdes identifiés par La Hontan et Adario il y a trois siècles et qui ont alors commencé à guérir la France, l'Europe, l'Occident et le monde sont les mêmes que l'on doit redécouvrir et réappliquer, avec toute la vigueur et la résolution nécessaires, à une France, à une Europe, à un monde apparemment trop souvent indifférents à leur bonheur et à leur sécurité présents et futurs. Ce sont : l'esprit de partage et de sollicitude envers les faibles et les dépossédés, le remplacement des religions et des patries par la spiritualité circulaire et matricentriste, la compassion et le respect envers notre Terre-Mère et ses autres enfants non humains, qui sont donc aussi nos parents, et, élément de la plus haute importance et rattaché à tous les autres, la compréhension des raisons pour lesquelles nous devons permettre à la femme de réintégrer sa place centrale dans nos familles, dans nos sociétés, dans notre monde. En tant que

Huron de tradition, c'est ce que j'entends le plus fondamentalement lorsque je dis, comme je l'ai fait au début de cette présentation, que l'être humain ne pourra jamais, sauf à son très grand péril, échapper à la nécessité de rattacher sa réflexion et ses actions à la nature et à ses lois.

Puisque, dans ma culture, il doit toujours y avoir un échange, je vais terminer en énonçant ce que, personnellement, je souhaiterais que mon peuple reçoive de nos parents français, européens et autres, si tant est qu'ils trouvent ou jugent utiles les propos que j'ai tenus. D'abord, je révélerai que nos nations amérindiennes, à l'échelle du Québec, du Canada ou même du continent américain, ne montrent jamais que de faibles signes qu'elles peuvent se remettre des coups physiques, émotionnels, intellectuels et spirituels extrêmement violents qu'elles ont reçus et continuent de recevoir sous l'égide paternaliste coloniale qui perdure. Où qu'on aille, on reconnaît une même détresse, qu'on essaie de cacher, d'oublier ; partout, c'est le stress angoissant de la peur de la disparition, manifesté tristement dans des taux effarants de suicide juvénile.

Mais il y a un nouvel espoir, à l'affirmation duquel je participe très activement depuis plusieurs années en tant que responsable des études. Il s'agit de l'émergence, difficile mais résolue, d'institutions éducatives dirigées par nos nations selon notre propre vision du monde et de ce que doit être notre éducation. Les résultats sont édifiants. Nos gens qui ont la chance d'y avoir accès (ils sont encore relativement très rares, vu le peu de ressources que les gouvernements mettent à notre disposition) y trouvent non seulement une fierté souvent perdue de leurs racines, mais aussi, et par conséquent, une guérison personnelle émotionnelle et physique. Dans cet important développement social et intellectuel, l'Ouest canadien est nettement plus avancé par rapport au Québec, à l'Ontario et aux provinces maritimes. Il y a quelques mois, je suis devenu président du collège universitaire que je considère à l'avant-garde en Amérique du Nord. Il s'agit de l'Institute of Indigenous Government, à Vancouver. Si je suis venu au Salon du Livre de Paris, à titre d'auteur invité, puis comme conférencier à cette importante rencontre sur les études québécoises, c'est que je sais dans mon âme huronne qu'il y a une sympathie spéciale pour mon peuple qui se trouve d'ordinaire plus abondamment et facilement dans le cœur des Français et d'autres Européens que dans celui de mes concitoyens québécois et canadiens, pour des raisons évidentes, surtout historiographiques et politiques. Ma passion pour notre Institut est telle que j'en ai parlé au président Jacques Chirac, en lui remettant ma carte d'affaires, durant les brefs instants que j'ai pu être en contact avec lui. Il s'est montré content et intéressé lorsque je lui ai dit que je cherchais à recruter des étudiants français. Et l'échange que je veux vous proposer, chers collègues et amis français, québécois et autres, c'est de m'aider, de nous aider à faire croître et prospérer l'Institut que je dirige ainsi que les autres qui existent aussi, tel que le Saskatchewan Indian Federated College, à l'Université de Régina, où j'ai été doyen aux études durant quatre ans, ainsi que d'encourager la création d'institutions d'éducation similaires pour que nos peuples amérindiens puissent continuer ou, pour certains, recommencer, à faire entendre dans le monde, et pour son bénéfice, leur propre voix.

Nos nations amérindiennes redécouvrent, depuis une vingtaine d'années, qu'elles ont autrefois été des sociétés qui valorisaient plus que tout la communication et la connaissance. Dans nos communautés à pensée circulaire, tout individu, tout enfant avait un accès libre et abondant aux conseils que l'on tenait quotidiennement et aux sources de savoir qu'étaient les sages et les spécialistes de tout type de connaissances. Ce ne fut qu'avec l'avènement de l'oppression coloniale que ces sources furent confisquées, saccagées et que l'on nous plongea de force dans l'obscurantisme, donc la pauvreté et la misère sociale. Par conséquent, nous avons aujourd'hui un besoin vital de pouvoir développer à nouveau notre culture de la connaissance, qui doit éventuellement nous redonner le pouvoir d'exercer le rôle qui nous appartient dans la grande société humaine, c'est-à-dire, tel que l'exprime le guérisseur kogi de la Colombie, de même que tous nos chefs spirituels, le rôle de gardiens des racines les plus profondes et les plus oubliées de notre humanité commune. C'est là notre rôle à nous, que beaucoup de soi-disant spécialistes tentent aujourd'hui de nier et de s'approprier, mais que personne d'autre que nous-mêmes ne pourra jamais assumer. Le don que je désire de votre part pour nos nations, chers amis et parents, est votre compréhension et votre appui dans notre effort de revivre, grâce à une éducation basée sur notre vision, nos croyances traditionnelles propres. Nous avons besoin de votre participation dans nos écoles et nos institutions. La validation qui vient de vous est pour nous vitale et inestimable. Ensemble, nous

nous donnerons des lumières nouvelles, à l'instar de Lahontan et d'Adario. Nous nous comprendrons et nous nous entre-intégrerons, dans le grand cercle universel que nous devons former, sous le regard humanisant de nos mères, nos femmes, nos filles, que nous écouterons, que nous protégerons.

Ho! Ho! Ho! Attouguet Eathoro! (Chers amis et parents, grand merci de m'avoir écouté!)

L'Amérindien philosophe[*]

Georges E. Sioui est membre de la nation des Hurons-Wendats. Il est né en 1948 à Wendake, le Village-des-Hurons, près de la ville de Québec. Titulaire d'un doctorat en histoire de l'Université Laval, il est président de l'Institute of Indigenous Government à Vancouver, après avoir été pendant plusieurs années Academic Dean au Saskatchewan Indian Federated College de Régina, le premier collège universitaire au Canada a être dirigé par les Premières Nations. Il a publié Pour une autohistoire amérindienne *et* Les Wendats. Une civilisation méconnue, *tous deux édités par les Presses de l'Université Laval (Québec) et traduits en plusieurs langues. Sioui est également militant. En 1982, il s'est volontairement laissé arrêter avec quelques amis et parents par des agents de la conservation de la faune du Québec qui voulaient lui interdire d'accomplir un rituel annuel de purification. Cette cérémonie se déroulait dans un parc provincial dont la création, en 1906, avait nécessité l'expulsion des*

---

[*] Ce texte a paru dans la revue *Arguments*, vol. 2, n" 2, p. 17-31. Entrevue avec Georges E. Sioui. Propos recueillis par Francis Dupuis-Déri.

Amérindiens qui possédaient pourtant cette terre en vertu de la Proclamation royale de 1763. Sioui et ses frères remporteront leur cause en 1990 devant la Cour suprême du Canada. Enfin, il est également poète et musicien.

Comment synthétiseriez-vous, en quelques mots, le cœur de la philosophie amérindienne ?

La philosophie amérindienne est caractérisée principalement par un mode de pensée circulaire, c'est-à-dire que cette philosophie entend reconnaître les relations qui unissent entre eux tous les êtres. Ajoutons également qu'il n'y a pas de séparation entre sacré et profane, ni d'éléments permettant de légitimer la domination des espèces par une d'entre elles qui serait supérieure aux autres. L'idée biblique selon laquelle l'être humain a été créé par Dieu pour dominer le reste de la création, qui n'existe que pour servir ses intérêts, est étrangère à la philosophie circulaire.

Cette pensée circulaire amérindienne rappelle d'autres modes de pensée non européens, comme la philosophie de la « négritude » telle que développée par Aimé Césaire et Léopold Senghor et qu'ils opposaient à la pensée rationaliste des colonisateurs français.

La pensée circulaire n'est pas la propriété ni le produit exclusif des Amérindiens, et j'irais même jusqu'à affirmer que, malgré l'hégémonie que semble détenir la pensée linéaire européenne sur l'ensemble de la planète, sans doute quatre-vingts pour cent des êtres humains ont une vision circulaire du monde et de la vie. Allons encore plus loin : il n'y aurait pas eu naissance de sociétés humaines si la nature circulaire de la vie n'avait pas été reconnue. Après avoir traversé une série de contraintes environnementales et climatiques, certaines sociétés ont oublié momentanément l'idée de circularité pour adopter une approche linéaire qui a la malheureuse capacité de détruire. Pourtant, si l'on retourne aux sources, toutes les grandes philosophies et les grandes religions s'accordent sur l'unité fondamentale des êtres humains. Ce sont là des vestiges de la pensée circulaire propres à chaque culture. C'est en parlant avec des bouddhistes, des hindous, des chrétiens ou des musulmans que l'Amérindien réalise que, pour des raisons historiques, il a retenu plus que quiconque cette capacité de comprendre ce qu'est l'humanité : une espèce unifiée dont tous les membres sont apparentés.

La pensée circulaire offre à l'individu la capacité d'entrer en communication avec les animaux ou les plantes même s'ils nous paraissent mystérieux au premier abord. Alors que, pour d'autres traditions, l'idée de se concevoir l'égal des animaux, des plantes ou des pierres semble humiliante, il s'agit, chez les penseurs du Cercle, d'une idée sécurisante qui apporte la paix.

Contrairement à la philosophie occidentale, la philosophie amérindienne est de tradition orale. Cela ne constitue-t-il pas une faiblesse ? Cela n'a-t-il pas pour effet, par exemple, que la philosophie amérindienne ne puisse que difficilement « compétitionner » avec la philosophie occidentale sur le plan de la rigueur, des systèmes, des appareils théoriques ?

La pensée amérindienne paraît si étrangère qu'elle semble à première vue caricaturale, à tout le moins dans sa forme et dans sa symbolique. Certains affirment dès lors que ce n'est pas une vraie philosophie. Il est plus facile de la discréditer en rejetant sa prétention à être philosophique plutôt que de tenter de saisir toutes les implications qui en découlent. Quant à l'idée de « compétitionner » que vous évoquez, ne faut-il pas savoir quel est le but de la compétition ? Les systèmes philosophiques rationalistes occidentaux semblent « compétitionner » pour obtenir des résultats généralement négatifs en politique, mais aussi dans les relations humaines en général : domination de l'environnement avec tout ce que cela entraîne de crises présentes et à venir, domination de la femme et des enfants, rejet des aînés et négation de la sagesse pratique acquise par toutes les sociétés. Si c'est là le résultat d'une telle compétition, ce n'est certes pas une compétition très positive…

Enfin, une philosophie de tradition orale a tout aussi besoin d'être rigoureuse qu'une philosophie qui s'appuie sur l'appareil artificiel – ou disons même sur la béquille – de l'écriture.

Mais ce n'est pas le même type de rigueur. La transmission orale de la parole, du savoir et de la sagesse nécessite beaucoup de rigueur et de systématisation sociales parce que tous les membres de la communauté sont concernés, et non pas seulement un cercle fermé d'initiés ou d'érudits, comme c'est le cas avec les traditions écrites.

Il y a pourtant un problème particulier à la philosophie amérindienne : les rares sources écrites ont été rédigées par des Français qui vivaient en Nouvelle-France. La tradition philosophique amérindienne prend donc racine en partie dans des sources qui lui sont en quelque sorte étrangères. Cela pose effectivement problème.

Par ailleurs, ces écrits ont souvent été rédigés par des Français qui avaient l'assurance que les sociétés qu'ils décrivaient allaient disparaître sous peu. Les auteurs ont donc fait preuve d'une sorte de négligence politique et auraient sans doute été beaucoup plus discrets sur certains éléments s'ils avaient connu la suite de l'histoire. On peut donc relire ces textes avec des yeux contemporains et en dégager des éléments très utiles. On procède, en quelque sorte, à de l'archéologie spirituelle ou intellectuelle. De plus, on peut dire que le cœur de la pensée amérindienne reste tout de même vivace chez les anciens encore vivants, et cela permet d'orienter notre recherche archéologique.

Dans votre livre Pour une autohistoire amérindienne, *vous puisez abondamment dans les textes du baron de Lahontan.*

C'est que ce baron français, que des revers de fortune conduisirent en Amérique, passera, comme il le dit lui-même, « les plus beaux jours de [sa] vie avec les Sauvages de l'Amérique ». Son livre *Dialogues curieux entre l'auteur et un Sauvage de bon sens qui a voyagé* a été publié au début du XVIIIe siècle puis réédité une dizaine de fois et traduit en anglais, en flamand et en allemand. Lahontan y donne la parole à Adario, un Wendat-Huron identifié comme un « philosophe nu ». Or c'est à travers l'interprétation que Lahontan en fait d'eux que les « philosophes nus » influenceront Rousseau, Voltaire, Chateaubriand, Diderot et Leibniz, avec qui le baron entretenait une correspondance.

Dans ma tradition, Lahontan, mais aussi d'autres penseurs de sa trempe, nous ont beaucoup marqués. Je me souviens que, chez mes parents, nous avions un vieil ouvrage des écrits du baron de Lahontan. Je n'ai jamais su comment ce livre avait traversé le temps et s'était conservé. On le citait parfois en disant combien des gens comme lui avaient compris la réalité de leur temps.

Plus tard, je me suis aperçu que Lahontan était souvent considéré comme un auteur ayant utilisé les Amérindiens pour parler de sa propre société française et, surtout, la critiquer. On en venait même à affirmer que ses écrits ne correspondaient en aucune façon aux discours que de vrais Amérindiens auraient pu tenir sur leur propre société ou sur les sociétés européennes. Mon réflexe, en tant qu'Amérindien, fut de réhabiliter Lahontan, car, en l'absence de sources qui viennent enrichir notre autoperception, des écrits comme les siens deviennent très importants.

Dans mon premier livre, j'ai donc voulu démontrer que Lahontan tenait un discours qui représentait authentiquement la philosophie amérindienne. D'ailleurs, Lahontan avait eu de toute évidence un contact significatif avec les Amérindiens, car il reprenait des éléments centraux de la philosophie amérindienne comme la santé, la nature, la territorialité. De tels axes de réflexion n'auraient pu surgir d'un esprit informé uniquement par le contexte européen de l'époque.

La pratique de la critique est un élément essentiel de la tradition philosophique européenne. La tradition française, par exemple, est riche de penseurs extrêmement critiques de l'organisation politique et sociale de leur propre pays. Or, à la lecture de vos livres, il semble que vous vous refusiez à critiquer ne serait-ce que le moindre aspect de la culture et du mode de vie des Amérindiens. Cela s'explique bien sûr par une volonté explicite de votre part de brosser une image positive des Amérindiens qui ont trop longtemps été décrits de façon très négative par les historiens euro-américains. Mais cela justifie-t-il pour autant un tel discours lénifiant ?

Il est normal que la critique s'abatte sur un historien qui essaie de réinterpréter l'histoire. Souvent, ce sont des Européens comme Tzvetan Todorov qui se révèlent être les meilleurs alliés des Amérindiens qui, comme moi, veulent réécrire l'histoire de l'Amérique. On m'a souvent reproché de présenter un tableau idéalisant de la culture et de l'histoire amérindiennes, mais cette critique me paraît pour le moins simpliste. Il est facile de prétendre que mes thèses reprennent à leur compte le mythe du « bon sauvage ». Je ne prétends pourtant pas que les sociétés amérindiennes étaient des sociétés idéales. Les guerres menées pas les Amérindiens étaient ainsi inhumaines et cruelles, comme le sont toutes les guerres. De plus, il est malheureux de constater que les sociétés amérindiennes ont connu et connaissent encore l'abus politique.

Mais par-delà l'invention des mythes, il ne faut pas oublier que, si elles n'étaient pas parfaites, les sociétés amérindiennes traditionnelles n'en ressemblaient pas moins pour les arrivants européens à de petits paradis en comparaison des sociétés du vieux continent. Cela est d'autant plus vrai lorsqu'on se souvient à quel point les Français qui venaient s'établir en Amérique fuyaient l'Europe, où ils se sentaient victimes d'une société dans laquelle ils n'avaient plus leur place.

Ainsi, l'Europe a découvert en Amérique une chose qu'elle recherchait très intensément : la liberté. C'est d'ailleurs surtout vrai pour la France, qui a toujours été ce pays qui questionne, qui est à l'avant-garde de la pensée humanitaire, qui est le refuge des éprouvés et des laissés-pour-compte de l'humanité. C'est un peu la raison pour laquelle les Français idéalisent souvent les Amérindiens. Grâce au mouvement des Lumières, la France a pensé la liberté, et c'est en Amérique qu'elle l'a trouvée. Les philosophes européens, grâce aux récits des explorateurs de l'Amérique, ont réalisé qu'il était possible de maintenir des systèmes équilibrés « sans foi, sans roi, sans loi ». Cette découverte a donné à certains penseurs européens une immense confiance en la nature humaine.

Il est intéressant de noter que ce mythe du « bon sauvage », qu'on m'accuse souvent d'entretenir, est un pur produit de l'imaginaire européen. Autant la version positive du mythe du « bon sauvage » est en partie une création de l'imaginaire européen, autant sa version négative l'est-elle aussi, car il y avait bien sûr une élite coloniale et cléricale chargée d'exporter le modèle social européen en Amérique. Pour un livre signé par Lahontan, combien d'écrits de Jésuites décrivent les Amérindiens comme des êtres sans moralité, des guerriers barbares, des cannibales ?

Ce sont ces récits méprisants qui deviendront les sources de l'histoire officielle. Les Amérindiens ont trop souvent intériorisé ces clichés dégradants, développant une image dévalorisante d'eux-mêmes. Mon travail de réécriture de l'histoire consiste bien sûr à offrir aux Amérindiens la possibilité de définir leur identité en des termes positifs. Pour ce faire, je mets en perspective les textes méprisants en les comparant à d'autres sources de l'époque, comme les écrits du baron de Lahontan. Ce travail n'est pas salutaire seulement pour les Amérindiens, mais également pour tous ceux qui sont venus nous rejoindre en Amérique, car nous sommes plusieurs à penser que nous restons en contrôle de cette terre que nous avons habitée durant si longtemps. Nous avons toujours la responsabilité d'améliorer la façon de vivre et de penser des gens qui y vivent.

Cette empathie n'est pas surprenante lorsque l'on sait qu'Adario lui-même disait : « Je ne méprise point les Européens, je me contente de les plaindre ».

Prenons l'exemple de la Nouvelle-France, celle où vivait Adario. Comme je viens de le mentionner, les ancêtres français des Québécois essayaient d'échapper à l'emprise de ceux qui les avaient victimisés en Europe. L'expression « s'ensauvager » correspondait à la fois à une volonté réelle des Français arrivant en Amérique de découvrir une nouvelle façon de vivre et à une pratique à laquelle les autorités cléricales tentaient de s'opposer.

Les Amérindiens ne pouvaient donc ni vraiment mépriser l'Européen ni même le haïr puisqu'ils voyaient avant tout en lui une victime. Ce qui troublait profondément les Amérindiens, c'était de découvrir que, pour des raisons que personne ne semblait en mesure d'expliquer, les nouveaux arrivants appartenaient à une société où des individus qui ne démontraient aucune sensibilité quant au sort de leurs compatriotes occupaient des positions d'où ils dominaient le reste de leurs semblables. Les Amérindiens refusaient l'autorité et les inégalités et ils s'expliquaient mal qu'un Européen puisse accepter que ses idéaux individuels et collectifs soient réprimés, ou encore que certains Français souffrent de pauvreté alors que d'autres vivaient dans l'opulence à la vue de tous, insensibilisés par leur système.

Ce refus de l'autorité de la part de l'Amérindien est, je dirais, métaphysique. Ainsi, le temps n'est pas une contrainte pour lui. L'Amérindien ne conçoit pas non plus l'éducation comme un processus visant à refaire ou à transformer l'enfant. L'Amérindien considère d'ailleurs l'enfant comme un individu entier qui a un esprit et un sens en lui-même et pour lui-même. Dans la culture amérindienne, l'éducation ne peut pas devenir une forme de répression, car l'enfant n'est pas compris comme un être imparfait qui doit être réformé ou baptisé pour le laver de ses imperfections.

Nous revenons au mythe du « bon sauvage »?

En quelque sorte. Il est possible, à ce point de notre entretien, d'articuler plusieurs éléments que nous avons abordés. J'ai parlé un peu plus tôt des deux portraits historiques du « bon sauvage », l'un positif, l'autre négatif. Le mythe du « bon sauvage » s'inscrit également dans un cadre philosophique. Plusieurs se sont empressés de noter que ces fils de la nature, qui vivaient au jour le jour en harmonie apparente avec leurs semblables et leur environnement, n'avaient aucune compréhension de la notion de progrès, si chère aux philosophes des Lumières. On avait dès lors beau jeu d'affirmer que les Amérindiens n'étaient pas « progressistes » au sens européen du terme. Mais si l'on intègre le concept du « bon sauvage », à première vue caricatural, dans l'ensemble théorique de la pensée circulaire, on réalise dès lors que le mythe est en accord avec une conception spiritualiste ou idéaliste de l'individu, par opposition au matérialisme européen. Le mythe du « bon sauvage », articulé avec soin, s'inscrit donc dans un discours philosophique cohérent.

Tout comme le « bon sauvage », l'individu moderne rationnel et autonome relève lui aussi du mythe et de la caricature, et il peut être présenté sous un jour positif ou, au contraire, négatif. Pour l'Amérindien, le mythe de l'individualisme moderne n'a que peu d'attrait car le progrès prôné par le Prince au nom de la liberté se traduit souvent, dans la pratique sociale, par une perte individuelle de la liberté, chacun étant soumis à un mode de vie aliénant qui ne profite qu'à quelques individus situés au sommet. Il n'est pas surprenant qu'Adario plaignait les Européens : ils sont esclaves de principes, de l'argent, d'un monarque, et ce, souvent au nom de la liberté. C'est la servitude volontaire.

Il ne faut pas en conclure qu'il n'y a rien de valable dans la culture européenne. Le mythe du progrès, par exemple, s'inscrit dans une valorisation du mouvement qui, selon les Amérindiens, caractérise le mode de pensée européen.

Les Amérindiens, par leur nature contemplative, cherchent à comprendre le sens des choses, des gens et des cultures. Selon la philosophie amérindienne, le chiffre 4 est celui de l'équilibre : il y a quatre temps de la vie, quatre moments du jour, quatre directions, quatre couleurs sacrées et quatre grandes familles de peuples avec chacune leur position autour du Cercle. La position du nord correspond à la famille de peuples européens à laquelle est associée la couleur blanche et l'élément de l'air, qui représente le mouvement. Les Européens sont les maîtres du mouvement, pour le meilleur et pour le pire. C'est ainsi que nos Anciens ont toujours dit que leur venue n'était pas accidentelle. Les Européens iront probablement sur d'autres planètes, car c'est le mouvement qui donne sens à leurs rêves et à leur histoire.

Nos anciens affirment également que le temps du mouvement tire à sa fin. Nous avons reçu le plus de bénéfices possible de cette ère du mouvement, de cette façon européenne d'agir.

Si l'on se fie à la direction de la course du soleil, nous devrions arriver à une nouvelle ère. Ce serait à la position de l'est, c'est-à-dire précisément celle des peuples amérindiens, d'occuper une place prépondérante. Contrairement au mode de pensée européen principalement linéaire, l'Amérindien croit que nous sommes Un, tous unifiés dans le grand Cercle de la vie. Cette conception métaphysique a bien sûr des répercussions politiques : la démocratie ne doit pas comprendre seulement les êtres humains, mais aussi tout ce que l'on conçoit comme êtres existants.

Il semble y avoir une tension inhérente à la philosophie amérindienne en ce qui a trait à l'individu. Quelle est la marge de manœuvre pour l'individu, dans cette philosophie circulaire où tout dépend de tout ?

Les penseurs du Cercle ont toujours eu une jalousie sans borne, et même légendaire, pour leur liberté individuelle, en autant que cette liberté signifie la liberté d'être responsable pour soi-même et pour les autres. C'est véritablement le « un pour tous et tous pour un ». Par ailleurs, quelle liberté peut-il rester à l'individu appartenant à une philosophie linéaire lorsque l'on force celui-ci à croire en des systèmes philosophiques et politiques qui ne protègent que les intérêts des gens les plus puissants et les plus habiles à perpétuer le système ?

Si la pensée occidentale a fourni les justifications nécessaires à certains individus pour légitimer leur propre autorité, la pensée occidentale a également donné naissance à des tendances dites « progressistes » qui rêvent d'un monde meilleur. Il y a ainsi une riche tradition messianique, héritée en partie du judaïsme, mais qui se retrouve en philosophie politique chez les penseurs utopistes, libéraux et marxistes.

Pourquoi attendre des messies quand on peut exercer son jugement et sa raison par soi-même ? Les messies interviennent dans des systèmes où l'humain a été opprimé intellectuellement et spirituellement. Les philosophies progressistes promettent des messies libérateurs parce qu'il y a eu une oppression prolongée. Cette stagnation idéologique, spirituelle et sociale ne peut se résoudre que dans une révolte.

L'Europe, justement, a souvent connu la révolte et même la révolution. Quelle place occupe l'idée de révolte dans la pensée amérindienne ?

Le penseur linéaire sait dans son tréfonds que le monarque, le dictateur, le politicien fourbe est là pour rester et que, même renversé, le système le « réincarnera ». Il n'y a plus de place pour la foi, l'espoir. Intrinsèquement, le penseur circulaire n'est pas enclin à la guerre. Sa foi en la nature et envers le Créateur lui dit que les choses, si on leur donne le temps et l'espace, vont reprendre leur place dans le grand ordre naturel. En général, l'Amérindien ridiculise le dirigeant abusif ou corrompu. Si cela ne suffit pas à corriger la situation, il remplacera ce dirigeant selon une volonté qui vient du peuple, et ce, en dépit des systèmes politiques colonialistes imposés et dont on doit s'accommoder.

Par ailleurs, et pour revenir à cette idée de messianisme, il faut souligner qu'elle renvoie également à la question de la distance entre les êtres humains et Dieu. Chez les peuples indigènes, nous n'avons pas l'assurance de pouvoir parler facilement à Dieu, prétention que l'on retrouve chez les membres de clubs fermés et d'organisations religieuses. De plus, nos Anciens nous demandent souvent : « Pourquoi est-ce qu'on demande tant à Dieu »? Et ils ajoutent : « Où est la responsabilité de l'être humain ? Où est la reconnaissance du pouvoir de raison et du pouvoir d'action de l'être humain »?

Vous faites souvent référence aux Anciens. Il y a donc, outre les textes comme ceux de Lahontan, ces Anciens toujours vivants et qui sont comme les gardiens de la philosophie amérindienne ?

Oui. Je retrouve chez eux cette disposition à ne pas faire de divisions nettes entre les nations, les gens, le monde humain et non humain. Je retrouve toujours ce même besoin culturel de reconnaître ce qui coexiste avec les êtres humains, c'est-à-dire le Cercle de la création. Il y a toujours, dans la pensée des anciens, cette flexibilité très grande à accueillir et à inclure les autres qui coexistent avec nous. De cette approche viennent d'ailleurs les problèmes que les anciens rencontrent dans les institutions d'éducation et les institutions universitaires, qui sont très rationalistes et qui privilégient une pensée linéaire. L'université est un lieu où les disciplines sont très compartimentées. Or, chez nous, l'interdisciplinarité va de soi. Cette interdisciplinarité repose sur une conscience non pas seulement intellectuelle et physique, mais également spirituelle et émotionnelle, les quatre composantes de l'être humain. On dit d'ailleurs souvent que, quand une institution d'enseignement amérindienne décerne un diplôme, le diplôme est double, car l'éducation reçue s'est adressée à toutes ces quatre composantes de l'étudiant.

Une telle approche entre en complète contradiction avec le monde universitaire contemporain, qui se veut séculier et distinct de toute allégeance religieuse.

Il ne faut pas croire que « spiritualité » et « religion » sont synonymes. Pour nous, la religion est un concept négatif. Par contre, vivre avec une conscience spirituelle veut simplement dire qu'on cherche toujours à appréhender la vie dans son ensemble, incluant le monde non humain. Notre place en tant qu'humain est égale à la place qu'occupent toutes les autres composantes de la création. L'être humain n'occupe pas, dans la création, une place de domination. Cette démarche spirituelle peut inclure des prières (surtout expressions de gratitude pour la vie, le grand cercle, « le grand mystère) au début de réunions, par exemple.

Avez-vous reçu une éducation catholique ?

Oui. J'ai été baptisé, comme mes ancêtres l'ont été depuis la colonisation, mais il n'y avait pas dans ma famille d'insistance sur la pratique religieuse, ni sur les croyances et les dogmes. La spiritualité amérindienne prévalait. Je m'affirme catholique si cela signifie vivre et laisser vivre, aimer les autres et ne pas les juger. Mais je me dirais alors au même titre musulman, bouddhiste, juif, etc. Je ne crois pas aux religions ébauchées par les êtres humains, je ne crois pas aux drapeaux ni aux frontières, je ne crois pas aux étiquettes qui nous isolent des autres êtres et de la vie elle-même.

Avec l'arrivée des Européens en terre d'Amérique, c'est tout un processus de colonisation politique et culturelle qui se met en place et dont seront victimes les Amérindiens. Pourtant, vous prétendez dans vos livres que le mode de pensée et la culture de l'Européen nouvellement débarqué subissent eux aussi une transformation au contact de l'Amérindien.

Les Amérindiens affirment que celui qui migre doit forcément adopter la philosophie propre au nouveau territoire. La culture euro-américaine est bien sûr une sorte de prolongement de la culture européenne, qui a connu un incroyable métissage au contact de l'Amérique. C'est ce que je nomme le processus d'« américisation » par lequel les Européens qui arrivent en Amérique s'assimilent aux schèmes mentaux et idéologiques des Amérindiens. Dès le début de la période coloniale en Amérique, les Amérindiens ont voulu intégrer les Européens dans leur système de parenté et leur cercle de relations, ainsi que les éduquer afin qu'ils adoptent leur mode de pensée. Bien sûr, tout cela fut perçu par les autorités coloniales et religieuses comme une attaque contre l'ordre établi. Encore aujourd'hui, la philosophie amérindienne va à l'encontre de toutes les théories politiques ou sociales occidentales, et il est sans doute normal qu'elle soit mal accueillie. Elle remet en cause les idées de progrès, de profit et de croissance telles qu'elles sont généralement définies dans le contexte européen.

Néanmoins, si l'on prend l'exemple de l'Euro-Québécois, on retrouve cette tendance à vivre et à laisser vivre qui est en définitive très amérindienne. Des siècles de résidence en terre d'Amérique ont permis aux Euro-Américains de s'imprégner d'un individualisme étranger à l'Europe. En Amérique, la liberté est quelque chose de non négociable, individuelle plutôt que collective. Cette vénération de la liberté s'explique en partie par la présence des grands espaces. Ils permettent d'explorer une certaine solitude inconnue des Européens, qui vivent sur un continent entièrement occupé par l'homme. Les Euro-Américains, tout comme les Amérindiens, ont besoin d'espace, de silence. Il est extrêmement important pour eux de savoir qu'il existe, quelque part, une place où ils peuvent se retirer loin des yeux scrutateurs du système.

En observant le Français, le Québécois peut découvrir ce qui, de lui, s'est transformé au contact de l'Amérindien et de l'Amérique ; et le Français, en observant son cousin québécois, peut comprendre à quel point l'Amérique a le pouvoir de modifier l'état d'esprit d'individus historiquement issus d'une certaine culture française. Malheureusement, les Québécois oublient trop facilement ce qu'ils ont reçu au contact des Amérindiens. Les Québécois « de souche » s'affichent aujourd'hui comme étant les « autochtones » de l'Amérique, et c'est une des raisons pour lesquelles nous n'utilisons pas ce mot. Pour se distinguer des nouveaux arrivants qui débarquent d'Asie ou d'Afrique du Nord, par exemple, les Euro-Américains s'arrogent notre identité profonde en se déclarant « autochtones ». C'est l'enseignement de l'histoire tel qu'il se pratique depuis plusieurs générations qui a rendu possible une telle appropriation symbolique. Le Québécois a retenu de ses cours d'histoire que les Amérindiens acculturés vivotent dans quelques réserves dont l'emplacement est incertain. C'est en partie après avoir constaté cette méconnaissance que j'ai décidé d'écrire une autohistoire amérindienne. Même si la population du Canada ne compte qu'environ 1,5 % d'Amérindiens recensés (mais on dit qu'il y a peut-être jusqu'à 15 % de gens métissés qui refusent de s'identifier comme Amérindiens), il est aussi important pour les Québécois que pour les Amérindiens de réapprendre l'histoire amérindienne. L'ignorance de la présence de Mohawks au Québec est un facteur qui permet d'expliquer pourquoi la crise de 1990 à Oka et à Kanesatake a été si dramatique.

Dans le monde d'aujourd'hui, qu'en est-il de la politique amérindienne ? Est-ce que cette philosophie circulaire, que vous nous avez présentée, s'incarne dans les pratiques sociopolitiques des Amérindiens contemporains ?

Ceux qui revendiquent l'étiquette de « progressistes » ont accepté d'adopter les normes politiques euro-américaines. Les leaders politiques sont, dans l'ensemble, des gens qui ont acquis une habileté à se servir des systèmes politiques canadien et québécois et même à les contourner. Ils ont appris à jouer le jeu et ils tiennent un discours isolationniste, c'est-à-dire qu'ils ont intégré des concepts exclusivistes comme celui de « race », qui n'ont rien à voir avec la tradition amérindienne. Ces dirigeants amérindiens ont également appris qu'ils pouvaient manipuler les gouvernements (de la générosité desquels les Amérindiens dépendent très souvent pour leur survie matérielle), en laissant planer sur la société dominante la menace d'une révolte violente.

Mais les exigences formulées dans cette situation ne représentent trop souvent que les intérêts de l'oligarchie au pouvoir. Grâce à l'ignorance, feinte ou réelle, de ces gouvernements en ce qui concerne la vraie tradition amérindienne, certains chefs amérindiens se maintiennent au pouvoir beaucoup trop longtemps. Voilà, à mon sens, une des bonnes raisons pour lesquelles les gouvernements québécois et canadien devraient mettre plus d'efforts à promouvoir une meilleure connaissance, chez tous leurs citoyens, des cultures respectives des Amérindiens et des non-Amérindiens. Cela devrait être entrepris loin des arènes politiques où les leaders n'ont que trop de raisons de cultiver l'isolationnisme.

Les « progressistes » sont particulièrement influents dans les parties du territoire qui ont été le plus en contact avec les institutions sociales et politiques euro-américaines, comme au Québec, par exemple. Ces « progressistes » prônent la création d'une classe moyenne amérindienne. Cette idée rebute beaucoup les traditionalistes, qui ne la prennent d'ailleurs pas tellement au sérieux : cette idée de « classe » n'a pas de place dans la civilisation du Cercle. Adopter cette idée équivaut à donner son assentiment à une société qui ne donne pas de place à la redistribution de la richesse. Créer des classes signifie ouvertement qu'on ne se préoccupe pas de la pauvreté qui en résulte, qu'on déresponsabilise les gens sur les plans social et environnemental.

Le mot d'ordre devient : que chacun s'occupe de sa classe et que les autres se débrouillent. L'attitude typique des gens de la classe moyenne à propos des pauvres ne se résume-t-elle pas justement à « Qu'ils fassent comme moi s'ils veulent réussir »?

Approfondissons la question de l'autorité politique dans les communautés amérindiennes d'aujourd'hui. Plusieurs auteurs, dont vous-même, mais aussi des textes de l'époque de la Nouvelle-France, évoquent une philosophie politique et même une culture politique amérindiennes de type anarchiste, c'est-à-dire qu'il y aurait de l'ordre, de la cohésion et de la solidarité mais point de chefs exerçant leur autorité et leur domination sur leurs semblables.

De toute évidence, la situation politique sur les réserves est présentement en décalage avec cet idéal. Quel est le rôle de l'intellectuel amérindien face aux politiciens amérindiens qui ont adopté une philosophie politique et des comportements politiques très éloignés des valeurs amérindiennes traditionnelles ?

Il n'y a presque pas de place pour l'intellectualité amérindienne dans les communautés amérindiennes, ni d'ailleurs dans la société dominante. Il n'y a pas réellement de place pour des discours plus informés qui auraient été mis à l'épreuve dans des cercles savants et des cercles traditionalistes. Il y a aussi un phénomène de répression dans nos sociétés à l'égard des traditionalistes. On les écarte parce que leurs discours et leurs réflexions vont trop radicalement à l'encontre des systèmes imposés à nos sociétés par la société dominante. Pire : quand l'intellectuel amérindien parle et écrit, il se met souvent en situation de rupture vis-à-vis de sa propre société. Il est alors obligé de s'en aller, car il ne trouve pas de place chez lui. Il existe donc un phénomène d'exil intellectuel amérindien. Et la société est prise de court quand elle veut s'expliquer.

Il est intéressant de noter qu'il y a de plus en plus d'Amérindiens diplômés en sciences administratives ou en médecine, mais encore très peu en sciences humaines. Cela se comprend facilement, car les possibilités sont plus grandes en sciences pures. De plus, les Amérindiens viennent souvent de familles peu conscientisées, peu au fait de leur propre culture. Je pense que je suis encore le seul Amérindien francophone à avoir terminé un doctorat en histoire... La même chose se constate dans toutes les disciplines qui occupent des positions clés dans la réorientation philosophique d'une société et dans sa façon de se voir et de se comprendre.

Le Canada est le lieu d'une curieuse collision : les souverainistes du Québec et les Amérindiens en quête de plus d'autonomie s'affrontent, alors que leurs projets sont d'une même nature. Allons plus loin : ces deux groupes voulant défendre et promouvoir leur culture respective, n'y aurait-il pas moyen qu'ils s'entendent plutôt qu'ils s'affrontent ?

Malheureusement, les discours ne se situent pas seulement sur le plan des principes culturels... L'accession du Québec à la souveraineté se pense également en termes de contrôle et d'exploitation maximale des ressources disponibles. Et il y a des nations amérindiennes qui ont aussi des ambitions économiques entrant en conflit avec les aspirations du Québec. C'est pour contourner ces blocages politico-économiques que les intellectuels devraient se détacher des discours politiques et s'acquitter réellement de leurs devoirs d'intellectuels. L'expérience montre malheureusement que les intellectuels des deux côtés glissent trop facilement dans le champ politique. Si l'on créait des lieux de rencontre plus isolés de la tourmente politique, et si l'on parlait honnêtement autour d'une table, il y aurait certainement place à des compromis.

J'ai d'ailleurs toujours regretté que le Québec ne devienne pas un leader quant aux relations entre les Euro-Américains et les populations indigènes. Je viens du Québec et j'y ai beaucoup d'intérêt émotif et historique. Pour moi, le Québec pourrait presque naturellement jouer un rôle de leader, car le contact français a été beaucoup plus humaniste que le contact espagnol, portugais, hollandais ou anglais. Lahontan en est une preuve. Mais les politiciens québécois ont perdu ce fil historique...

The Spiritual Revolution: Looking after the Earth from an Indigenous (Matricentrist) Perspective*

[The one-day vision quest fast, at the age of seven is] a time when the child learns to let go of his/her mother and the mother also learns to let go of her child when the child is put out in the bush to be cradled by Mother Earth. The child is taught that the physical Mother is not his/her real mother, but only the mother who cares, teaches and guides the child. The child learns who his/her real mother is, and that is Mother Earth. She/he begins the process of learning to respect the Earth for its teachings and spirituality. Mother Earth is the child's first teacher and all things upon Mother Earth are considered sacred. Mother Earth must be

---

* Conference given at *Millennium Symposium on Science, Society and Human Rights: Implementation of the UNESCO Declaration on Science and the Use of Scientific Knowledge in the 21st Century*, University of Regina, August 2000. Georges Sioui has dedicated this paper to the memory of Gordon Wasteste, Dakota-Saulteaux sprituralist and scholar.

treated with respect and kindness as our Mothers and Grandmothers for they are life carriers who bring new life into this universe.[1]

About ten springs ago, when I was still a doctoral student in my home province of Quebec, I went to spend some days on my friend's trapline, as I used to do a few times every year. Alfred, an Innu Indian, does not know how to read or write but, of course, has amazing knowledge about his Nature-home, the boreal forest. And like many people finely attuned to Nature, he is soft-spoken and a man of few words. I remember us striking up a conversation after a long silent trek in mountains that had recently been clear-cut, which had made us both reflect on the fate of those formerly very beautiful forests, rich in all kinds of animal and other life, including human.

"The White Man is destroying everything," had said Alfred, in the resigned, matter-of-fact, sad manner of Indians talking when "no one else" is present. I remember forming the project of using that simple phrase of Alfred's as the title of an eventual paper, which I have not yet written (and which, I believe, could be this one, with another title). Of course, realizing our great fortune of being where we were, feeling the wonderful warmth of the sweet spring sun and thinking that we were very likely to get a few moose by taking advantage of the thick ice crust on the snow in the early dawn of tomorrow, our powerful Indian humour swiftly changed our mood back to happy.

The first book of the Amerindian autohistory of this continent, yet to be written, has to do with the reasons for the European immigration here. Far too many books purporting to be about the history of this continent after the arrival of Europeans have focused (and still are doing so) on the history of contact between the European and the Amerindian civilizations. Invariably, and understandably, their purpose is to account for the 'changes' that have resulted from the 'shock of cultures' for all the peoples involved. The obvious and, again, understandable end goal of all such official histories, even when their tone is sympathetic to the invaded and damning of the invaders, is to

---

[1] Marie Eshkibok-Trudeau in, "Circular Vision—Through Native Eyes," in *Voice of the Drum*, edited by Roger Neil (Brandon : Kingfisher Publications, 2000), p. 20.

ever more firmly establish the superiority of the Europeans' civilization and therefore their right to be here and to further their 'conquest'/'development'/ 'conversion', which my friend, Alfred, sitting and smoking quietly amidst the debris of his dear forest-home, unresentful, looked at and called "the White Man's work of destruction".

The Europeans left home because they needed to. I have always had a problem with references to 'the various cultures' that came here—and went elsewhere in the 'discovered' parts of the planet—and began to 'co-exist' with 'the other, indigenous ones'. I and many of our Elders and other teachers (not strictly indigenous) very firmly believe that people truly possessing and practising a culture (more often in the spiritual sense, nowadays, at least in an urban context) are rooted in their ancestral land and territories, which means that people who, for any reason, have uprooted themselves from their own territories and countries cannot for long sustain their culture. If they wish to retain, or to regain, the quality of mind, body, heart and spirit consciousness that is implied in the word 'culture', they will soon seek to re-root themselves by getting 'naturalized' to a living Earth-culture belonging to their new Motherland.

It is not man and his governments, it is the spirit of the Earth that creates and nurtures human cultures in every sense. A true, viable human culture is circular in nature: it has not lost consciousness that Life is the vibrant, pulsating expression of the great Circle of relationships linking all beings together, material and immaterial. A culture that has lost such knowledge has replaced it with the belief that Life is a linear process, where time, as designed by man, can be used to make Nature's laws serve man's selfish interests and artificial needs. Cultures have to be spiritually rooted in natural Life; they cannot exist in the abstraction of the Circle.

An abysmal sense of insecurity is what drove Europeans and others from their Old World homes. It originated in the antique demise of the original Mother-centred, human cultures and Earth spirituality and in the parallel, gradual fragmentation of humankind into patriarchal nation-states and man-centred religions. With this upsetting began an age of untold violence perpetrated by man against the Earth and all femininity, that is to say, against himself, since life originates in the feminine nature. That is why the Europeans had to leave home and how they eventually landed here, on this continent, whose original peoples traditionally honour and think of the Earth as a mother, who not only nurtures the human physically, but even more importantly, inspires, teaches, guides and educates him or her.

> The Lakota [the 'Sioux Indian'] was a true naturalist—a lover of Nature. He loved the Earth and all things of the Earth, the attachment growing with age. The old people came literally to love the soil and they sat or reclined on the Ground with a feeling of being close to a mothering power. It was good for the skin to touch the Earth and the old people liked to remove their moccasins and walk with bare feet on the sacred Earth. The soil was soothing, strengthening, cleansing and healing.
>
> That is why the old Indian still sits upon the Earth instead of propping himself up and away from Her life-giving forces. Kinship with all creatures of the Earth, Sky and Water was a real and active principle …
>
> The old Lakota was wise. He knew that man's heart away from Nature becomes hard; he knew that lack of respect for growing, living things soon led to lack of respect for humans too. So he kept the young people close to its softening influence.[2]

The "old Indian" (Standing Bear conceded that many of his people had become less soft-hearted, that is, assimilated to the linear world view) believed in the Earth. He knew that the Earth not only was a true nurturing Mother, possessing like himself a mind, a heart, a body and a spirit, but also a wise teacher who, because she was listened to, imparted to him all the knowledge and wisdom that were needed to live a happy, healthy life. Because of his faith in the Earth, the old Indian knew limitless abundance and security. Leaving his Mother-home was, for him, unthinkable. The Earth becomes abandoned by Her human children only after man has cut her in pieces, called countries, and devised social and religious and scientific dogmas that have justified the rape and the destruction of Her being and of Her subdued, desecrated children,

---

2 Chief Luther Standing Bear, in T. C. McLuhan, *Touch the Earth*, cited in G. E. Sioui, *For an Amerindian Autohistory* (Montreal and Kingston : McGill-Queen's University Press, 1992), p. 25.

human and otherwise. Torn away from Nature and imprisoned inside man-made structures, man becomes hard-hearted, de-humanized. He will help the happy few powerful further their conquest of Nature, which implies the destruction of what still remains of the Earth-world of the "old Indian".

The material power of America (politically concentrated in the North) is wrongly praised as the product of the human genius at its most morally valorous. America, the sacred Amerindian continent, was, in 1492, a place of unimaginable physical richness. (In fact, it still is so, after 508 years of senseless plunder.) Such abundance, coupled with such insecurity and want in the European, could not but trigger the fast production of material wealth, science and technology of such power that it has taken this brief half-millennium to replace all of that once sheer, all-bountiful beauty, health and strength with ubiquitous ugliness, disease, poverty, social loneliness and crime. Where is the genius in this? Where is the greatness of all the science and technology that have been developed?

The word 'science' comes from the Latin *sciere*: to know. How did 'the White Man' (understand: the linearized man, and he or she can be of any ethnic background) get to know what he knows? Is his heart connected to his Mother's heart? The world is in need of a spiritual revolution. It has become a cliché to say that the planet, and therefore its inhabitants, are in for a not-too-distant future of untold poverty and misery if we human beings do not improve our consciousness of Life and of how we endanger and threaten Life. The kind of Earth-education referred to by Marie Eshkibok-Trudeau, in my opening quotation, is one hint as to where to look for such teachings and how to re-infuse them into our lives and social practices.

Now that the exhaustion of our Mother Earth's physical resources is in sight, for those who care to look at the facts, the time has come for effecting the true encounter that needs to occur between the Old World and the New. Efforts to carry over and impose here the patriarchal, linear vision of Old Europe must cease. The spiritual revolution, which until now has been upheld mostly by Amerindian and other indigenous peoples, consists in re-educating the world about circular, that is, matricentrist and Earth-conscious thinking and acting.

There is still unbounded spiritual abundance to be gained from attention to and understanding of the myriad teachings of Mother Earth. Translating those into healthy, secure, happy living through spiritual awareness and belief is not difficult: it is simply about cultivating a personal and collective state of mind. Science, the product of knowing, has to set for itself the overall goal of producing security in the heart of man. Science, the product of knowing, must cease to be the main agent and cause of violence done to Mother Earth and Her children, man being one of them.

There is a spiritual revolution afoot. It is the Indigenous revolution. It really started on October 13, 1492, the first day after the European landing, when the wisest people of our nations (first of the Caribbean Islands) realized what the future now held for the peoples of *Abya Yala* (Carib word for America). However, I believe it began to be a movement about twenty-five years ago when our spiritual leaders felt they could come out from their long-repressed, underground teaching places, as a new generation of their people felt that an important Indian prophecy was being fulfilled: many non-Amerindians, often very educated and spiritually enlightened ones, began to search out the Amerindian sages (Elders) and ask them to take a leading role in the spiritual guidance of the global society.

The resurgence of belief in an 'old' spiritual world view has now become strong enough to cause the emergence of educational and other social institutions (such as healing societies, retributive justice systems and sentencing circles). One such educational institution, certainly the oldest anywhere, is the Saskatchewan Indian Federated College (SIFC), at this University of Regina, where I had the privilege of working as Dean of Academic Affairs and Associate Professor of Amerindian Studies for many years in the recent past. The SIFC is one such beacon where the "old Indian", or indigenous spirit, sends out a signal to the world that an Indigenous spiritual revolution is, in fact, afoot. And as for all great movements of liberation, the sheer existence and daily survival of such places as the SIFC is a pure miracle performed by the human spirit. The SIFC, and other similar places of learning, would not exist without its Elders, because prayers are the only thing that cause such miracles and that keep the revolution existing at the spiritual level, thereby safeguarding its respectability in the eyes of a society that apparently has insurmountable indifference, indeed aversion, towards the indigenous existence.

I left the SIFC in 1997 to be on sabbatical leave for one year, and then chose to take up the challenge of the presidency of the Institute of Indigenous Government (IIG) in Vancouver, a then four-year-old, public, post-secondary educational institution politically and administratively controlled by BC First Nations. The IIG's mission statement says that the institute exists in order to "empower Indigenous Peoples to exercise their right of self-determination in their territories in ways which fully reflect Indigenous philosophy, values and experience throughout the world". To me, one of the quintessential teachings of the Elders, as regards formal education, is that indigenous students, in their own places of learning, do not have to fear losing their culture or their soul just because the mainstream society has constructed the notion that there is such a thing as 'White Man's knowledge', especially in academic realms where non-mainstream people have traditionally been discouraged from entering and pursuing professions, namely, those related to science and mathematics. The Elders tell students that as long as they keep a firm grounding in their people's traditional spiritual values and practise them, there is no possible contradiction between safeguarding any cultural traditions and acquiring any type of knowledge, as all knowledge is the product of the genius, effort and suffering of all peoples equally. It also needs to be mentioned that education towards leadership in such realms as administration, health, sciences and engineering is now strongly requested by a new generation of leaders who have an increased awareness of and pride in their identity and want to achieve self-governance in those very crucial domains. Furthermore, indigenous Elders teach that indigenous people have a special responsibility to apply their own unique sensitivity for and knowledge of Nature towards redefining the goals and fundamental premises of all the sciences (as well as all the other disciplines), that is to say, to infuse the indigenous, matricentrist, Earth-revering spirit into science.

That, essentially, is the spiritual revolution, such as we intellectual and spiritual leaders in indigenous-controlled institutions live it. It is extremely important that indigenous people and students be allowed, through adept and honest teaching and mentoring, to lose their fear of sciences and mathematics, particularly, in order to realistically tackle the task of achieving autonomy ('self-government') through education.

Conclusion

I often think back to an experience I had here in Regina, while I was working at the SIFC. I was asked by the Royal Canadian Mounted Police (RCMP) to give, over a period of six months, a series of twenty-five, four-hour presentations to as many different groups of about twenty-five young Canadians of all cultural backgrounds, recruited by the RCMP.

The aim was to provide these young people (aged twenty to thirty-five, men and women) with specialized, cross-cultural instruction, to help them cope with future duties to be performed in and around rural and urban Canadian Aboriginal communities. Needless to say, since most of them had had little or no direct exposure to Aboriginal people's cultures, there was always a tangible level of anxiety in these sessions, especially in view of more and more social and political unrest in Aboriginal Canada ('Indian country') as a whole.

From my own vantage point as an Aboriginal educator, I was always both pleasantly and sadly impressed at how these young fellow Canadians cheered upon learning about the existence of this 'Indian college' (the SIFC), so close to the RCMP headquarters in Regina: pleasantly because it was always so easy to collectively see the utmost importance of creating such places of learning, so eagerly wanted by both Aboriginal and non-Aboriginal Canadians, and where 'Indian education', a traditionally dismal failure in the mainstream educational institutions, was a success story worthy of widespread mention; sadly because of my harsh daily experience, as an Aboriginal academic and educational administrator, of seeing the SIFC encountering such inexplicable resistance on the part of governments to allow our growth to take place, when so much social benefit was there simply to be received by the province and the country. And the same continues to hold true at the IIG, where I am working today, as President. But we keep struggling, we keep praying.

My friends the RCMP recruits, after a mere couple of hours of exchanging, very readily became recruits also in the Indigenous spiritual revolution. To this day, I am convinced that all six hundred or so of them quietly militate for the creation of at least one 'Indian' university college in every Canadian province and territory, where 'the revolution' can come to be so strong as to create a new Canada, healthy, unified and secure because it is rooted in Mother Earth and Her teachings.

Attouguet Eathoro!
Thank you, my dear friends and relatives, for listening to me!

FOR AN AMERINDIAN AUTHOHISTORY: THE FOUNDATIONS OF A PROPERLY AMERICAN SOCIAL ETHICS*

Respected Elder and old friend of my people, Chief William Commanda, dear friends and colleagues of Saint Paul University, dear friends old and new:

Being here with you is my great privilege and a pleasure that makes my heart happy and thankful. I wish to thank Saint Paul University for creating and supporting this important and unique lecture series and especially Daryold Corbiere-Winkler, my new Anishnabe brother, who has the rare courage and belief required for daring to create this opportunity for change in our hearts and spirits, as Canadians and as humans, and who has extended to me a very cordial invitation to his university.

As my name, Sioui, means 'Rising Sun', I can relate to the intent of this lecture series called "New Sun". I know that in our hearts we all wish and hope to see the new sun of a new day, a new beginning, a new time. We are all longing for a renewed reality where there will be truth, justice, love, beauty that will strengthen our hearts and souls, that will enrich our lives, that will make us feel free and rejoice. Free from so many lies that assault us, free from so much

---

* Conférence de la série « New Sun Lectures » à l'Université Saint-Paul, Ottawa, 25 février 2001
Lecture in the "New Sun Lectures" series at Saint Paul University, Ottawa, February 25, 2001.

ugliness that insults the divine soul within us at so many moments, free from all the injustices that our human heart recognizes so unmistakably, free from all the hate that so much contradicts the infinite capacity for love with which our Great Creator equipped our hearts when He gave us this life. Praying for humility, honesty, courage and kindness, it is in the spirit of this new hope that I will talk about my book, *For an Amerindian Autohistory*, and about my life and dreams.

This book is an MA dissertation that I submitted in 1987 to the Department of History of Laval University, Quebec, where I also did my PhD in history. The text quickly caught the attention of the Laval University Press and was published at the end of 1989. The original title, which, I think, is also of interest, never appeared in full anywhere. It was (translated from the French): "For an Amerindian Autohistory: Essay on the Foundation of a Properly American Social Ethics". It was the two words "properly American" that were left out in all the various editions and translations. However, as I will explain for the first time here tonight in all these fourteen years, those two words carry a lot of meaning in relation to the contents of the book.

I am the grandson of four Huron grandparents (nowadays, we say Huron-Wendat). In the days when I grew up, being Indian (we now say mostly Aboriginal or Amerindian) was by no means fashionable. You could not get rich, or richer, by declaring your aboriginality and getting all the benefits attached to the status, as many have done in recent years, especially in some southern or otherwise well-to-do reserves. In fact, my parents encountered enormous social and economic difficulties because they committed, in 1946, the social sin of marrying their own traditional people. When we were, for too many years, in deep trouble as a family of seven children, struggling daily with poverty, social rejection, alcoholism and other related social stigmas still known by so many of our families, I heard some of our own people unfeelingly say to my mother, "You should have done like us and married a White guy. Now look how you are!"

Poor and marginalized as we were, there was an unexplainable, unconscious pride in our home, like the discreet red glow of a very slowly rising sun (I can find no other image). Even though we understandably had only very rare occasions to discuss our identity or our history, I have come to realize that my education at home made me a strong believer in our role and our message as First Peoples. Also, and very importantly, my parents made me deeply conscious of our responsibility as First Peoples of this land vis-à-vis our non-Aboriginal relatives. My own particular upbringing, maybe because I was first of five sons, carried a sense of duty to be a uniting force by connecting all people to the spiritual roots possessed by our people. It is to this educational and spiritual concept, which I received as a traditional Huron, that the words "properly American" relate.

"The Foundation of a Properly American Social Ethics" implies several ideas and beliefs. First, the phrase implies that we, traditional Aboriginal people, refuse to adhere to the social dogma according to which this present-day society has its foundations in the social ethics brought here from Europe. For how could a happy, harmonious and viable society be founded on a social ethics that caused our Euro-Canadian relatives to have to leave their original homes and that caused here in our land such environmental and human upheaval in so short a time? The phrase "the foundation of a properly American social ethics" also implies that traditional Aboriginal people do not believe that our national society is, in fact, founded on European social ethics, for the reason that the Aboriginal civilization of this land is much too ancient to simply have given way (or to ever do so) to another foreign, uprooted, unproved, unwarrantable civilization. The phrase also signifies that Aboriginal people generally, as well as many non-Aboriginal people, believe that in order to achieve the dreams of change that we all share, it is urgent that our society become acquainted with Aboriginal social ethics through a deep, serious effort at educating itself about its First Peoples' civilization, thereby basing its future evolution on the foundation of a properly American social ethics.

My essay, *For an Amerindian Autohistory*, is a statement of my belief that Aboriginal people must look at themselves as leaders in their own land at the levels of philosophy, spirituality and education. It is, as well, a statement about the sense and the direction in which I believe Aboriginal people can and must lead society. The reason the book is not of a recriminatory nature, as my much regretted friend and spirit-relative Bruce Trigger has noted in his preface, is that it leads to the realization that Aboriginal people cannot and must not think and act socially as victims because, as leaders in their own right, they do not have the luxury of a lot of time to dwell on the sad and tragic aspects of their history. Also, the book proposes a formulation of how we are to make sense of our history and how we are to relate to it in a positive, that is, altruistic way, instead of self-pityingly.

An important premise of 'autohistory' is that having lived here on our soil since the beginning of time, so to speak, we possess an intimate understanding of the mind, the moods and the spirit of this land, our Mother-Earth, and therefore cannot be in danger of losing the sense of our spiritual and emotional relationship with our land, even after a terrible accident, such as the chance arrival of the Europeans after 1492.

Seeing the arrival of the Europeans as an accident, instead of a 'shock of cultures', a 'meeting of two worlds' or 'the beginning of a period of contact' is one illustration of how 'Amerindian autohistory' is a new historical and philosophical paradigm, allowing for a fundamentally different way to look at ourselves and at society. For, in that accident, the ones who hit and wounded us, and damaged or destroyed our possessions also got very seriously wounded. In fact, more so than we did, because their vehicle was so frail and weak and ours, so strong and solid. Besides, they had neither medicine nor food with them. So we do have a duty to walk over to them and help them, care for their sick and their wounded, attend to their dying and bury their dead, for they are helpless, not even knowing where they are and what or whom they hit. We cannot only complain that someone hit us and look after our own. They came in a makeshift craft and what they had with them was barely enough to sustain their lives, for they had fled from something, somewhere. They collided with very rich people in a very rich land who had everything. We are still rich. They are still poor. It is as though no time has passed. We have to go over to them and help them, console and reassure them, inform and teach them, for they are our human relatives and we can improve our lot even further from what they know, from what they think and feel. But first, we have to give them confidence and trust in us by helping to relieve them of their trauma, their fears, their bad memories, the guilt or anger that they may have. We have to think of how to heal them, while attending to our own wounds which, in the context of that accident, can be seen as mostly physical.

The new paradigm of Amerindian autohistory allows Aboriginal people to situate themselves in relation to their post-European history by seeing and characterizing it as no more than an accident. Many people of diverse backgrounds have found that approach useful, mainly because it allows the dispelling of myths that have made traditional Canadian historiography highly hazardous to our capacity to empathize with one another on the basis of mutual recognition and the collective searching for truth, as a society should do to function well. The two main myths that I discuss in the book and that are impossible to recognize as such when old paradigms are used are the myth of the superiority of European civilization and the myth of the consequently normal—even desirable—disappearance of Aboriginal peoples. In contrast, the autohistorical approach, because it establishes the permanency of essential Aboriginal values over the long term, enables us to appreciate the unique resiliency of Aboriginal people's belief in their own value system, understood and adhered to by many non-Aboriginals and supported by the evidence of the failure of the value system that Europeans once strenuously tried to impose on the Amerindians. All of this substantiates the urgent necessity of denouncing those myths.

For an Amerindian Autohistory has known a rather rare success as an academic book about Indians. Surprised at first, but guided by the feedback received from a continuous flow of letters and comments from appreciative readers, I have come to attribute this attention to the existence of a long-standing desire in the heart of the common person of seeing an end to the historical glorification of the coming of White people to this land, whose 'savage' inhabitants needed to be discovered so they could be saved from their senseless, godless existence. I strongly believe there is no longer any room for such fables in the psyche of an evolved nation, as Canadians wish to think of themselves. Accordingly, the autohistorical method is meant for anyone to use as a prism through which any aspect of our history, any facet of our societal nature can be looked at in another way, an Aboriginal way, be it environmental, educational, social, cultural, medical, historical, economic, religious, legal, or in terms of international relations, gender relations, inter-generational relations, intercultural relations and so forth.

I now wish to conclude by sincerely saying that this book, and its follow-up, *Huron-Wendat. The Heritage of the Circle*, are part of my ongoing humble attempt to comply with the duty that was passed on to me by my Huron-Wendat forebears, of helping to reconcile all peoples that the Great Spirit has willed to live together on this great island on the Turtle's back (the American continent). I have just revealed to you what I have thought was the best way, for me as a Huron, to remove the walls that have for too long separated too many of us. I am sure that by now, you have realized that Hurons have a special concern about history, for some reason. That's one way of trying to heal our society and the world. Others do the same through athletics, politics, diplomacy, arts, teaching and in very many other ways. I will end by expressing my very many thanks to Saint Paul University, the "New Sun" series and to all of you for providing me with this rare, wonderful chance to speak and converse between us from the heart.

Ho! Ho! Ho! Attouguet! I thank you, friends and relatives, for listening to me!

America, my Home

America, my Home
(To my friend Buffy Sainte-Marie)

Je ne change pas
Je n'ai jamais changé
Je ne changerai jamais
Je suis L'Amérique
Je suis l'extase devant la Création,
Amérique que l'on blesse
Amérique que l'on souille
Ma mère, l'Amérique,
Ma mère, pour toujours

Quatre Amériques, une seule Grande Île sur le dos de la tortue[*]

Tout comme il y a des choses que les Blancs comprennent à l'exclusion des non-Blancs, il y a des choses que nous, Indiens, comprenons aussi comme Indiens, à l'exclusion des non-Indiens[1]. L'une de ces « choses » sue et comprise par tous les Indiens est que nous avons la tendance, le désir et, donc, le pouvoir de nous voir et de nous concevoir collectivement comme un seul peuple, une seule famille aborigène de l'Amérique. Nous pouvons avoir entre nous des différends au plan politique, en plus des différences réelles souvent immenses de nos origines géographiques et linguistiques, cela ne nous empêche nullement d'être et de nous

---

[*] Conférence prononcée le 15 avril lors du *Sommet des écrivains des Amériques*, tenu au Salon international du livre de Québec, 12 au 15 avril 2001. Une version modifiée de cette conférence a été publiée dans *Les Cahiers de l'idiotie*, vol. 1, n° 1 (2008).

[1] Ici, j'utilise les mots « Blancs » et « Indiens » seulement comme lieux communs, étant entendu que ces catégories ne correspondent en rien de généralisable dans la réalité.

sentir tous « Indiens » et, donc, de nous comprendre « sans même nous parler », comme les gens disent parfois. Et cela va beaucoup plus loin que le simple réflexe de s'unir entre opprimés pour se renforcer mutuellement et survivre ou, encore mieux, vivre : il s'agit du sentiment intuitif et indestructible d'être tous enfants naturels désirés et bien-aimés d'une même Mère-terre (« matrie ») qui, parce qu'elle est Mère, est une, infiniment vénérable, et indivisible, et de n'être encombré dans ce sentiment par aucune réminiscence d'être venus d'ailleurs. Cette chose que l'Indien comprend, finalement, est qu'il est uniformément et universellement chez lui, ici, en Amérique.

Ne serait-ce que pour nourrir notre imagination d'« américitude », il serait intéressant d'entrer dans le sujet des histoires mythiques de la création du monde selon diverses familles de peuples autochtones de l'Amérique, tel que l'a fait si brillamment Claude Lévi-Strauss, parmi d'autres penseurs, dans plusieurs ouvrages. Mais, comme on s'y attend, ces histoires reflètent la très grande diversité des peuples américains aborigènes, de même que l'extrême antiquité de leur existence sur leur continent. Plutôt, notre propos est de découvrir comment et pourquoi les peuples autochtones de l'Amérique conçoivent l'unité idéologique et spirituelle fondamentale de leur continent et comment, cinq siècles après l'impact de l'accident de l'arrivée européenne, ils se conçoivent la vocation de réaffirmer cette intégrité première dans un contexte moderne et futuriste de la migration continue et incessante vers eux de quantités toujours grandes de nouvelles personnes de toutes provenances possibles.

Puisque nous nous trouvons, ici à Québec, dans le territoire original de mon peuple huron-wendat[2], où nous avons toujours une petite réserve, je commencerai ma présentation en vous relatant comment nous, Hurons-Wendat, voyons traditionnellement l'origine de notre existence. Ainsi, nous rejoindrons la vision philosophique, sociale et politique, comme j'ai déjà dit unitaire, de tous les Amérindiens. Au commencement, il n'y avait pas de terre, seulement la mer infinie, habitée par les animaux et les oiseaux marins. Les ancêtres des

---

2 Les Stadaconas, habitants de ce territoire lors de l'arrivée des Français, se sont fondus à leurs alliés wendat (appelés Hurons par les Français) lors de leur abandon de leurs pays du Saint-Laurent, après le troisième et dernier passage de Jacques Cartier.

humains habitaient un monde céleste. Un jour, les animaux de la mer virent descendre quelqu'un du ciel. Les outardes volèrent et firent de leur dos et leurs ailes une surface où put reposer cet être, qui était une femme. En conseil, les animaux décidèrent d'accepter l'offre de la Grande Tortue de prêter son dos comme première demeure de la femme tombée du ciel. Puis le plus humble plongeur, le Crapaud (certains disent que ce fut l'*ondatra*, ou rat musqué), fut celui qui finalement réussit à obtenir un peu de terre prise aux racines d'un arbre tombé du ciel en même temps que la femme, Aataentsic, la Grand-mère des Wendats et de tous les Amérindiens. Ensuite, les animaux étendirent la précieuse substance sur la carapace de la Grande Tortue, et une Île commença à se former et à grandir, jusqu'à devenir le continent de l'Amérique. Aataentsic était déjà enceinte d'une fille, qui bientôt vint au monde, grandit et fut imprégnée par l'esprit de l'Homme Tortue. Elle eut deux fils, l'un bienveillant et l'autre malveillant, qui eurent la tâche de préparer le monde pour les êtres de toutes les espèces qu'ils créèrent, y compris les humains de la Grande Île. Pour nous, Hurons, l'Amérique est donc une Grande Île que la Grande Tortue porte sur son dos et, vous l'aurez deviné, lorsque la terre tremble, c'est que la Grande Tortue veut changer de position.

Comme tous les gens qui ont un cœur indien, c'est-à-dire qui ont beaucoup d'émotion filiale pour la terre, nous appelons notre Grande Île notre Mère-terre. Comme tous ces gens, Amérindiens et autres, qui vénèrent et honorent la Terre, nous n'appartenons pas de cœur aux États-nations qui se sont formés sur notre sol. L'identification à un État-nation est fondée dans un sentiment de possession de la terre. Or toute notre conscience nous dit que c'est nous qui appartenons à la Terre qui nourrit nos corps, nos âmes et nos esprits ; comment celle dont nous dépendons pour tous nos besoins pourrait-elle nous appartenir, nous qui sommes ici avec elle pour un peu de temps seulement ? Notre conscience nous dit aussi que tous les autres êtres ont la même vie que nous et que, lorsque nous adhérons à un État-nation, nous nous élevons, comme humains, au-dessus de nos parents non humains (les animaux, les plantes, les pierres, l'eau, l'air, même les astres, etc.) et nous les traitons aussi comme nos possessions matérielles, ce qui implique les détruire, les décimer, insensiblement, puisque cela fait partie de nos droits de membres de l'État-nation.

Nos Sages nous ont toujours parlé du grand Cercle sacré de la vie, nous expliquant que tout ce qui existe, matériellement et immatériellement, fait partie égale de ce cercle. Cette façon de voir le monde et la vie exige la transmission aux jeunes générations d'une sensibilité qui rend capable d'un respect révérenciel envers toute forme, toute expression de vie. J'ai souvent utilisé l'expression « pensée circulaire » en référence à cette disposition culturelle qui confère une qualité spirituelle aux gestes, aux paroles et aux pensées. Lorsque nous parlons de « sociétés à pensée circulaire », nous nous référons aux sociétés typiquement « indigènes », qui continuent de valoriser une éducation traditionnelle qui donne à leurs membres cette capacité de voir et d'honorer tous les êtres dans leur interdépendance et leur complémentarité. On ne peut amoindrir la force du cercle sans amoindrir en même temps la qualité et la force de son propre être. C'est en ce sens que la vie, dans un tel cadre, revêt une qualité spirituelle. Les gestes, les paroles, les pensées ne sont pas sans conséquence : ils doivent avoir la dimension spirituelle, sinon c'est la qualité de toute la vie qui est affectée, y compris la nôtre.

Le concept de pensée circulaire est indissociable de la pratique sociale la plus essentiellement indigène, donc amérindienne, que je nomme *matricentrisme*. La société matricentriste reconnaît le principe de la centralité de la femme comme mère originatrice du corps social et éducatrice de son cœur et de son esprit. Il ne faut pas ici parler de matriarcat, puisque ce concept implique une domination de l'homme par la femme. Plutôt, l'idée que je défends est que les sociétés et les personnes à pensée circulaire, à cause de leur acceptation révérencieuse de la nature et de ses lois, savent que la femme détient, par rapport à l'homme, la place prépondérante dans les domaines sociaux où se joue l'équilibre ainsi que la santé et la survie spirituelles de la société. La pratique matricentriste et circulaire est collectiviste, c'est-à-dire attentive à l'existence, aux qualités et aux besoins des autres êtres, tandis que la pratique patricentriste et linéaire est individualiste et utilise la force matérielle et politique pour placer et maintenir l'homme dans une position et un rôle de domination, non seulement par rapport à la femme, mais aussi par rapport à tout l'univers non humain. C'est là l'essence du conflit qui commença à exister en terre américaine, il y a 509 ans, lorsque les puissances les plus patriarcales de l'Europe vinrent entrer en collision avec la civilisation matricentriste et circulaire la plus intacte de la planète. Pour l'ensemble de nos peuples de l'Amérique, les conséquences de cet accident furent et continuent d'être tragiques.

Je voudrais maintenant que nous considérions comment certains penseurs amérindiens regardent l'histoire postcontact de leur continent et comment une vision amérindienne de cette histoire est capable de nous fournir, à nous, modernes, des solutions à nos impasses sociopolitiques et idéologiques présentes et à venir. Puisque notre génie propre (notre compréhension indienne des choses) nous commande d'affirmer et de renforcer l'unité et l'intégrité de notre continent, notre observation nous fait voir aujourd'hui quatre Amériques, superficiellement différentes à cause de leur couleur linguistique et culturelle européenne respective : une Amérique anglophone, une francophone, une hispanophone et une lusophone (c'est-à-dire de langue portugaise). Mon frère innu et moi participons de l'Amérique francophone ; mes frères dakota et déné vivent en Amérique anglophone ; nos sœurs kogi et quechua sont héritières de l'Amérique hispanophone et nos autres parents kayapó et yanomami ont comme deuxième langue le portugais dans leur Amérique lusophone. Pour nous, Amérindiens, ces différences ne sont qu'accidentelles et, plutôt que de nous diviser, nous aident à nous rejoindre dans notre indianité. Pour les Euro-Américains en général, ces mêmes différences relèvent d'une mythologie sociale extrêmement sérieuse. Des oppositions, voire des guerres se sont livrées et d'autres se trament à tous les jours au nom de différences culturelles ou religieuses, en réalité superficielles, oppositions et guerres dont la rhétorique ne réussit jamais à cacher le vrai motif, qui est la possession matérielle du territoire et des biens qu'il produit pour l'élite patriarcale.

Mon regard personnel sur chacune de nos quatre Amériques euro-américaines est le suivant, à commencer par la quatrième, lusophone : le Brésil est une société faiblement métissée où les peuples amérindiens continuent à disparaître le plus rapidement, c'est-à-dire au rythme d'au moins une entité humaine survivante par année. Par « métissage », je veux dire le mélange du sang et de la culture matérielle entre Euro-Américains, principalement, et le peuple aborigène amérindien. Je ne partage pas l'opinion d'autres observateurs selon laquelle le phénomène de métissage, en Amérique, exige une amalgamation de deux cosmovisions d'où l'euro-américaine ressort la prépondérante, en regard à la simple réalité du déséquilibre démographique entre les deux populations. Au contraire, je soutiens, à l'instar de plusieurs autres observateurs, pas exclusivement amérindiens, que la cosmovision européenne, parce qu'elle est sans racines, ici, en Amérique, est destinée à flétrir et, donc, à céder devant la réaffirmation et la redéfinition moderne de la pensée autochtone de l'Amérique profonde. J'ai exprimé ce concept par l'expression « américisation de l'Amérique[3] ».

L'Amérique hispanophone, la plus métissée des quatre, est, avec la précédente, celle où il y a eu le moins de compromis politique entre l'Europe et l'Amérique. Le rapport en fut un de conquête directe et brutale et continue de l'être, notamment dans les pays hispanophones à forte population amérindienne, tels la Bolivie, le Mexique, le Pérou, le Guatemala et l'Équateur. Par ailleurs, cette absence de distanciation politique, nécessairement accompagnée d'une profonde arrogance culturelle, eut pour résultat la constitution d'États-nations où les populations autochtones survivantes sont marginalisées économiquement et politiquement, mais sont beaucoup plus exemptes de la marginalisation additionnelle aux plans social et racial dont sont affligées les populations autochtones du nord du continent, c'est-à-dire celles des États-Unis et du Canada (l'Amérique française, constituée essentiellement par le Québec, doit être regardée différemment). On pensera naturellement à la multitude de peuples autochtones « mis en réserves » dans ces deux pays.

L'Amérique anglo-saxonne et l'Amérique francophone[4], toutes deux nordiques, sont assez différentes des deux autres. Leur histoire s'est distinguée par une certaine distanciation idéologique qui a permis (et ce, beaucoup plus dans le cas de l'Amérique française) une certaine idéalisation des premiers peuples, même s'il est certain que cette admiration ne fut parfois rien de plus qu'un outil rhétorique inventé et utilisé pour critiquer et attaquer « les plus respectables »

---

[3] Notamment dans mon livre *Pour une autohistoire amérindienne*, paru aux Presses de l'Université Laval en 1989 et réédité par elles en 1999 sous le nouveau titre *Pour une histoire amérindienne de l'Amérique*. Traduction anglaise parue aux McGill-Queen's University Press, Montréal et Kingston, 1992.

[4] Une petite enclave anglophone, telle Bélize, dans un univers hispanophone, ou une autre, francophone, telle la Guyane française, en Amérique du Sud, ne possèdent pas la force ni le rayonnement culturel voulus pour imposer leur caractère foncier différent dans le contexte majoritaire qui les englobe.

institutions des mères-patries. Dans les faits, les peuples amérindiens qui eurent à interagir avec le colonisateur britannique eurent un allié commercial et militaire toujours socialement et racialement distant, dont l'intérêt était ouvertement matériel. Aussitôt et toutes les fois que la balance démographique pencha en sa faveur, l'Amérique anglo-saxonne institua un procédé rapide de « mise en réserve des Indiens », accompagné d'un également rapide procédé parallèle d'extinction des droits territoriaux qui, dans le cas particulier des États-Unis, entraîna la répression directe et violente et la dépossession finale des peuples autochtones, surtout aux mains du nouveau compétiteur étasunien, après la conquête britannique, en 1760.

Quatrièmement, l'Amérique française (c'est-à-dire la Nouvelle-France, ancêtre du Québec), eut un effet physique tout aussi désastreux que les trois autres sur les populations autochtones parmi lesquelles elle s'implanta à cause de pratiques militaires génocidaires dans certains cas, mais surtout en considération des épidémies, très souvent aggravées par le fait de l'insistance française – et néo-française – sur la « conversion religieuse » par leurs nombreux et fervents missionnaires, qui aussi furent parfois jugés et condamnés par nos peuples pour leur ingérence néfaste dans nos affaires politiques et commerciales.

Malgré cet aspect du contact entre la France et l'Amérique, résultat d'ailleurs normal et attendu de l'arrivée subite et violente d'envahisseurs linéaires et patriarcaux parmi une civilisation circulaire et matricentriste, la France s'est distinguée en Amérique par un contact idéologique unique et privilégié avec l'Amérique aborigène. En effet, c'est en Nouvelle-France, sa colonie laurentienne dont Québec fut la capitale dès 1608, que des penseurs français élaborèrent le discours sur le bon sauvage à partir d'échanges philosophiques qu'ils eurent avec les « philosophes nus », hurons, algonquins, iroquois, miamis et autres. C'est dans l'œuvre écrite du baron de Lahontan, spécialement dans ses *Dialogues* avec le chef huron-wendat Kondiaronk, que cette rencontre philosophique entre les deux civilisations est la mieux illustrée. Bien que, tel qu'énoncé antérieurement, les écrits du genre de ceux de Lahontan aient parfois été un moyen de mettre en question les institutions politiques, sociales et religieuses européennes, la matière sociale et philosophique trouvée dans la réalité civilisationnelle du Nouveau monde et reconnue comme véridique par plusieurs penseurs européens éminents de l'époque ne peut pas être mise en doute. Comme l'a remarqué le grand ethno-historien américain Wilcomb E. Washburn[5], « l'utilité de l'argument pour les Européens ne prouve pas que le "bon sauvage" soit un mythe ».

La France, selon moi, a donc eu un contact plus intime avec l'Amérique profonde que les autres puissances coloniales européennes. Cependant, la raison de mon plus ample traitement de l'Amérique française dans le contexte de ma présentation ne s'arrête pas là. Encore plus fondamentalement, je veux proposer que cette histoire de contact particulière à la France et à la Nouvelle-France, devenue le Québec[6], jointe au fait que le Québec est une société nord-américaine affluente, fait de l'Amérique francophone un lieu-refuge potentiel de réflexion continentale et mondiale sur toutes les questions touchant la civilisation profonde de l'Amérique ainsi que la responsabilité et la vocation de cette Amérique comme penseur de la politique globale. Voir l'Amérique francophone de cette façon ne serait-il pas plus utile et positivement prometteur que de continuer à assister impuissamment au déroulement sempiternel et improductif de la vieille querelle franco-britannique en cette terre américaine, où et d'où s'est déjà accompli tant de réunification entre des humains artificiellement divisés par leurs vieux souvenirs des « vieux pays », et entre ces mêmes humains et la Mère-terre ? Utiliser et adopter l'autoperception amérindienne et voir quatre Amériques, au lieu d'une (dominée par les États-Unis), deux (celle du Nord et celle du Sud) ou trois (celles du Nord, du centre et du Sud) serait pour tous les Américains un moyen de commencer à comprendre leur histoire et donc de définir les paramètres sociaux, politiques et économiques qui permettront à l'Amérique de se reconnaître collectivement et de mieux préserver et cultiver son rôle mondial propre dans les temps à venir. Adopter une autoperception proprement américaine, c'est, je le propose, commencer à découvrir et reconnaître avec affection et compassion notre famille américaine, dont la majorité,

---

5 Wilcomb E. Washburn, « A comparative view of the "Noble Savage" in English, Spanish, Portuguese and French eyes », *Revue France-Amérique*, 1998, p. 531-538.

6 Mon but, ici, n'est certes pas d'idéaliser le rapport politique moderne entre le Québec et ses peuples autochtones. Qu'on ne pense qu'aux difficultés presque incroyables expérimentées par ceux-ci dans la résolution de crises récentes, au fond banales, impliquant les Mi'kmaq de Listiguj et les Agniers (Mohawks) de Kanesatake (Oka), par exemple.

surtout l'hispanophone et la lusophone, écrasée sous son impossible fardeau colonial, n'a pas même le droit de rêver d'inclusion. Voir l'Amérique d'un point de vue amérindien veut dire s'enrichir d'une vision alternative pour approcher nos impasses américaines politiques, sociales, écologiques et autres. Se donner une vision proprement américaine veut dire finalement débarquer spirituellement dans le Nouveau monde et répondre, une fois les cauchemars oubliés, au geste d'inclusion et au sourire des gens qui étaient descendus sur les grèves, prêts à accueillir, à échanger, pour vivre encore mieux tous ensemble.

On parle de plus en plus d'« américanité », particulièrement dans le contexte de la création d'un marché continental de libre-échange. En 1992, année du cinquième centenaire de l'arrivée européenne, j'ai écrit dans le livre *Indigéna*[7] un article que j'ai intitulé « 1992 : la découverte de l'américité ». « Américité » veut circonscrire ce qu'est l'Amérique dans l'esprit de ses peuples aborigènes et vient se juxtaposer au terme « américanité », qui réfère à ce qu'est l'Amérique aux yeux des nouveaux-venus. J'ai proposé le terme « américité » à cause de la connotation dominatrice du terme « américanité », de même que du verbe « américaniser » et du substantif « américanisation », tous impliquant que l'Amérique, c'est-à-dire les États-Unis (qui s'arrogent ce nom qui appartient à tous les Américains), a le pouvoir, donc le droit, de penser que le monde entier veut vivre son rêve matérialiste et consommateur et de se conduire en conséquence. « Américité », « américiser » et « américisation » sont la contrepartie amérindienne à ces trois termes. Ils impliquent que le pouvoir « américanisateur » des États-Unis doit aussi être regardé du point de vue des premiers peuples américains. Comment ce pouvoir s'est-il constitué ? Et donc, la réponse à cette question étant bien connue, doit-on être intimidé ou impressionné par un pouvoir ainsi construit ? Enfin, est-ce qu'un pouvoir ainsi construit possède les bases morales qui font la respectabilité qui a toujours conféré la permanence ? Après cinq siècles d'« américanisation » de l'Amérique et du monde, il existe un fort courant de pensée mondial selon lequel il est temps de réfléchir aux sources et aux racines de la vie elle-même, qui sont dans la Terre, qui est une. Il faut américiser l'Amérique. Il faut réparer et soigner le monde entier.

---

[7] *Indigéna. Perspectives autochtones contemporaines* fut un livre et une exposition artistique marquants, réalisés en 1992 par deux artistes autochtones, Gerald McMaster et Lee-Ann Martin, du Musée Canadien des Civilisations, à Ottawa.

Mais qu'en est-il des « Indiens » ? Sont-ils toujours là pour accomplir ce grand rôle qu'on peut, par ailleurs, facilement concevoir comme leur appartenant ? La réponse est qu'en dépit de toutes les prédictions et attentes coloniales, nous assistons depuis quelques décennies à une forte résurgence culturelle, spirituelle ainsi que politique et économique de tous les peuples autochtones des Amériques, sans exception. Un élément indispensable de cette renaissance américaine est l'appui reçu de gens non autochtones de plus en plus nombreux et influents, appui qui n'est pas totalement étranger au débat sur le « bon sauvage », débat aussi vieux que le premier regard européen sur l'Amérique mais qui, aujourd'hui, a gagné une ampleur inédite en raison de la crise environnementale et sociale aiguë qu'ont causé l'européanisation, puis l'américanisation de l'Amérique. Maintenant, des rencontres de plus en plus fréquentes et importantes de représentants indigènes, dont les Amérindiens des quatre Amériques, ont lieu, sous les auspices des Nations Unies, tel le Groupe de travail sur les droits des peuples indigènes, qui se rencontre à Genève, ainsi que les rencontres visant la création et le renforcement d'institutions d'éducation supérieure contrôlées par les peuples indigènes, dont les Amérindiens.

La tenue en Amérique française du Sommet des Amériques (ou « Sommet des quatre Amériques » ou « de l'Amérique », si l'on veut se référer à la vision que j'expose) a, pour moi, Huron et premier et principal allié historique de la France, une signification profonde en même temps qu'elle représente une occasion historique. Au mois d'août sera commémoré à Montréal un traité de paix unique dans l'histoire de l'Amérique. Ce fut le 4 août 1701 que fut ratifiée la Grande Paix de Montréal, qui mit fin à un siècle de guerres génocidaires entre la France et ses 38 nations amérindiennes alliées contre les Britanniques et les cinq nations iroquoises. Cette paix fut orchestrée par mon ancêtre, le chef Kondiaronk, le même qui, par les écrits de Lahontan, eut une influence prépondérante dans l'avènement d'une idéologie politique renouvelée en France et qui fut l'origine américaine de la Révolution française.

Mon peuple huron-wendat a vu naître cette ville de Québec, où s'ouvrira dans quelques jours le Sommet. Cette ville, où est né le Canada, est tout près du lieu où mon peuple vit dans sa Réserve, depuis 364 ans. Je suis également fier d'être citoyen amérindien du Canada, un pays qui a, dans les deux dernières décennies, élevé le statut de nos peuples autochtones par plusieurs décisions juridiques importantes, dont l'*Arrêt Sioui*, une victoire en Cour suprême du Canada, qui a primordialement impliqué ma famille, puis tous les Hurons-Wendat. L'occasion historique dont je parle et que représente la tenue de ce Sommet en Amérique francophone existe en vertu du fait de l'expérience américaine particulière à la France, que j'ai décrite, et du statut minoritaire du Québec au Canada et en Amérique anglophone. Cet état de minorité entraîne une capacité d'empathie vis-à-vis de la condition similairement vulnérable des peuples autochtones. Je crois qu'il y a ici une chance de créer une nouvelle réflexion sur les raisons et les voies à prendre pour effectuer un abandon des visions sociales et environnementales exclusivistes, androcentristes et patriarcales. Une approche circulaire, inclusive et matricentriste sera plus propice à nous mettre collectivement en possession de tout le potentiel humain et non humain dont nous sommes particulièrement comblés en tant qu'héritiers de ce monde encore nouveau. C'est ce que nous devons et pouvons faire si nous voulons libérer l'énergie vitale, présentement étouffée et méconnue, de notre merveilleux continent.

J'ai voulu, dans cet exposé, proposer à tous mes frères et à toutes mes sœurs de nos quatre Amériques d'épouser le combat spirituel et idéologique amérindien pour rendre à notre continent son intégrité première et véritable d'une seule Amérique, une seule Grande Île sur le Dos de la Tortue, Mère-terre de tous ses enfants, passés, présents et à venir, ceux d'ici et ceux venus de tous les coins du monde.

Ho! Ho! Ho! Attouguet! (Merci, amis et parents, de m'avoir écouté !)

Kondiaronk Seawiaga Sastaretsi et la Grande Paix de Montréal de 1701[*]

Mon ancêtre le Chef Kondiaronk Seawiaga mourut le 2 août 1701 et fut inhumé le lendemain, 3 août, sous l'Église de Montréal. Il avait environ 75 ans. Son nom chrétien était Gaspard.

Kondiaronk Seawiaga portait le nom et titre héréditaire de Sastaretsi, qui voulait dire premier chef, ou premier ministre de la Confédération wendate, appelée huronne par les Néo-Français. Depuis des temps immémoriaux, les Wendats constituaient le cœur de la géopolitique amérindienne de la région, qui fut le berceau de la Nouvelle-France et du Canada.

Kondiaronk fut le premier de son pays mais, comme tout leader authentique, il fut davantage le dernier des siens, en ce sens que sa vie fut, jusqu'à son

---

[*] Written on the occasion of the Tricentenary of the death of Kondiaronk, my ancestor, principal leader and creator of the Great Peace of Montreal, a treaty signed in 1701, which put an end to ninety-two years of warfare between the French and the English alliances and that was ratified by thirty-nine Amerindian nations. This important historical event was commemorated in the Saint-Joseph Basilica in Montreal on August 2, 2001.

dernier moment, un sacrifice constant et personnel pour son peuple, wendat et amérindien, menacé d'extinction, ainsi que pour toute la communauté humaine de son pays.

Adolescent, Kondiaronk vécut la dispersion de son peuple et de son pays wendat à cause de la guerre et d'épidémies. Durant sa vie, il vit un nombre effarant de ses congénères amérindiens consumés dans le grand brasier colonial.

L'historien jésuite Charlevoix a décrit Kondiaronk comme un dirigeant « de mérite, de génie, de valeur, de prudence et de discernement ». Kondiaronk utilisa ses dons naturels et son éducation wendate et amérindienne pour orchestrer, sur plusieurs décennies, avec l'aide de nombreux autres leaders algonquiens et de dirigeants français éclairés, une paix universelle et définitive qui pût mettre fin à deux siècles de guerre et de désordre généralisé.

Le Chef et l'Ancêtre que nous honorons spécialement aujourd'hui fut l'âme de la Grande Paix de Montréal. Mille trois cents chefs et porte-parole de 39 nations amérindiennes observèrent le signal qu'il donna, en 1701, et vinrent signer le Traité de Paix. Comme leur frère et grand leader Kondiaronk, ils entreprirent ces longs voyages au mépris de leur vie, sachant qu'une épidémie faisait rage dans la région montréalaise. Plusieurs n'arrivèrent jamais ici. Kondiaronk lui-même succomba à l'épidémie deux jours avant la signature du Traité, après avoir fait un discours d'adieu qui émut toute l'assemblée des chefs et des Montréalais et fit pleurer même ses plus anciens ennemis (les chefs de l'Hodenosaunee, ou des Cinq-Nations), maintenant devenus des frères dans la Grande Paix.

Tous ensemble, Gens des Premiers Peuples et Français, ils plantèrent l'Arbre de Paix, s'invitant les uns les autres à continuer à jeter souvent les yeux du côté de la plus haute montagne, le Mont-Royal, où métaphoriquement se tient, au sommet, ce grand pin blanc. Métaphoriquement aussi, Kondiaronk Seawiaga et les autres cocréateurs de la Grande Paix de Montréal invitèrent tous les gens de toutes les nations ainsi que nous, leurs descendants, à « ne plus jamais quitter la lumière de la Paix ».

Les funérailles de Kondiaronk Seawiaga eurent lieu le 3 août 1701 et furent dignes du grand homme d'État qu'il fut. Au terme d'une cérémonie de condoléances officiée par les Roianer (Chefs civils) iroquois, l'orateur tsonontouan (sénéca) Aouenano résuma tout le sens de l'œuvre du leader wendat et de la

Grande Paix pour toutes les générations à venir en ces mots : « Le soleil est aujourd'hui éclipsé. C'est la mort de notre frère Kondiaronk qui en est la cause. Nous vous prions de ne point vous trouver dans les ténèbres ; au contraire, nous vous prions d'avoir le même esprit, les mêmes sentiments qu'il avait, de ne faire dorénavant qu'un seul corps, de ne manger que dans une seule marmite […] ».

Les mots et les sentiments de Kondiaronk et des autres qui nous ont légué la Grande Paix, il y a trois siècles, n'ont rien perdu de leur noblesse et de leur importance. Les yeux tournés vers l'Arbre de Paix et le Mont-Royal, il faut les redire souvent et ensemble, car nous avons toujours le même besoin de paix : « Ô ! Grand Créateur, Dieu, Maître de la Vie, Ô ! Esprit de notre douce et merveilleuse Mère, la Terre, nous vous disons merci pour la vie et pour notre famille humaine et nous rendons hommage à nos Ancêtres et à nos Chefs, qui ont vécu et sont morts pour que nous vivions ensemble en Paix : Kondiaronk, Callière, Aouenano, Anjelran, Koutoualibwé, Courtemanche, Joncaire, Teganissorens, Maricourt, Onanguicé, Gruyas, Chichicatalo, Vaudreuil, Meskouadoué, madame de Champigny et tant d'autres, et tous ceux qui ont lutté et luttent dans l'esprit pour la justice, le respect, l'amour, sans lesquels il n'y a jamais eu de Paix ».

Kondiaronk, le chef huron

Kondiaronk, le grand chef huron
Tu fus Premier de ton pays,
Tu guidas toutes les Nations,
On te nomma Sastaretsi
Tu naquis dans un monde de guerre,
Tu vécus pour sauver ta terre,
De tous tu reçus le respect,
Tu partis en nous donnant la Paix.
Oh ! Kondiaronk Adario,
Premier ami d'Onontio,
Tous les gens de tous les pays
Saluent ta mémoire aujourd'hui,
La Paix est toujours la vainqueure,

Kondiaronk Seawiaga Sastaretsi

Pour toujours tu vivras dans nos cœurs.
Mille six cent vingt-trois,
Quand ta vie commença,
Un chef nous était né,
C'était ta destinée,
La mort allait frapper
Ton pays renversé,
Vers toi se sont tournés
Nos peuples dispersés.

À la paix, à la guerre,
Tu as guidé tes frères
De quarante nations,
Toi, le grand chef huron.
1701 en juillet
Nous vint le temps de la Paix,
1,000 Chefs vont à Montréal
Quand tu donnas le signal.
Wyandots et Outaouacs
De Michillimackinak
Kiskakons et Sakis,
Saulteux, Poutéouatamis,
Nipissingues, Abénakis,
Mascoutins et Miamis,
Ouinipégons et les Cris,
Kickapous, Ménominis,
Algonquins et Iroquois,
Attikamekw, Illinois
Avec leur frère français.
Ont planté l'Arbre de Paix.

mai 2001
© Paroles et musiques de Georges E. Sioui

Ho! Ho! Ho! Attouguet! (Grand merci, amis et parents, pour m'avoir entendu !)
Etsagon! (Gardons notre courage !)
Niaweh Kowa! (Grand Merci !) (en agnier, ou mohawk)
Kitche Meegwetch! (Grand Merci !) (en algonquin)

L'AUTOHISTOIRE AMÉRINDIENNE :
L'HISTOIRE MISE EN PRÉSENCE DE LA NATURE*

D'abord, je voudrais honorer le peuple allemand, son histoire et sa terre et dire que, comme Amérindien et Huron-Wendat, je ressens, comme toutes les fois que je suis venu en Allemagne, une attention spéciale portée aux choses chères à mon peuple et une empathie réelle pour ce que notre histoire a été depuis notre rencontre accidentelle avec l'Europe, il y a 509 ans. Ensuite, je veux exprimer ma joie d'être ici avec vous tous dans ce coin de terre allemande que je ne connaissais pas, et aussi ma gratitude envers les personnes et les organismes qui ont rendu possible cette remarquable réunion. Je voudrais remercier particulièrement monsieur Denis Laborde, qui m'a contacté il y a deux ans en rapport avec ce colloque, et qui a maintenu avec moi un lien qui est maintenant devenu de l'amitié. Finalement, je dis également merci à messieurs Hans Medick et

---

* Communication prononcée au Colloque international *Désirs d'Histoire(s) – Das Verlangen nach Geschichte(n)*, organisé par le Conseil national de recherche scientifique (CNRS), la Mission historique française en Allemagne et le Max Plank Institut für Geschichte à l'Université d'Erfurt, 7 au 9 juin 2001.

Alf Lüdtke qui, avec Denis Laborde, ont trouvé les moyens de matérialiser ma présence ici.

Zuerst, wenn auch ich weiss, dass es schwierig zu glauben ist, dass ich ein Indianer bin, ich sage Ihnen, dass meine vier Grosseltern Indianer sind. Also, wie konnte ich anders mich identifizieren? Ich bin ein Wendat. Je parlerai à partir de mon point de vue amérindien et, croyant comme les miens et certainement comme vous tous que nous possédons tous la même nature humaine, j'espérerai que tous mes frères et sœurs puissent trouver dans mes propos résonance à leur vie et à leurs rêves, ainsi qu'une plus grande solidarité entre nous tous.

J'ai naguère écrit, dans mon livre *Huron-Wendat. Une civilisation méconnue* : « Il n'y a, en réalité, pour nous humains, qu'une façon de voir la vie sur cette terre, et c'est comme un cercle sacré de relations entre tous les êtres de toutes formes et de toutes espèces […] Il n'y a qu'une civilisation propre à l'existence humaine : la civilisation du Cercle, le Cercle sacré de la vie. Il n'y a, en réalité, que deux types de sociétés humaines : celles qui voient et vivent le cercle et celles qui ont oublié le cercle ».

Je voudrais aujourd'hui expliquer la même idée en énonçant une croyance qui résume toute la pensée amérindienne : ce qui fait qu'on est Amérindien[1] est la confiance sereine que la Nature est l'expression vivante d'un ordre transcendant créé par une Intelligence infinie capable et désireuse de pourvoir aux besoins de tous les êtres, y compris les êtres humains, lesquels ne doivent, ni n'ont besoin de se substituer à cette Intelligence, sous peine de compromettre leur propre équilibre, voire leur existence, à l'intérieur de cette même Nature. Trois corollaires découlent de cette croyance. Un premier est que les humains ont ou n'ont pas cette croyance, donc ce respect et cette confiance aveugles dans la Nature. Un deuxième corollaire est que ceux d'entre nous qui, à cause des contraintes qui ont déterminé leur histoire, ont échangé leur foi originale en la Nature pour une foi en l'homme (terme excluant ici la femme) ont besoin de recouvrer le sens d'une cosmovision originelle qu'ont eue toutes les sociétés humaines, avant leur perte de cette foi. Le troisième et dernier corollaire est que cette déconnexion de la Nature (que je nommerai « pensée patriarcale et linéaire » et expliquerai

---

[1] Chaque fois que je me réfère aux Amérindiens en rapport avec la cosmovision, je me réfère aussi aux peuples indigènes du monde entier.

à l'instant) signifie une négation simultanée du droit d'être des sociétés et des individus qui luttent pour sauvegarder ou pour recouvrer leur connexion spirituelle avec la Nature et, donc, une guerre physique et psychologique à finir, livrée par le monde non indigène au monde naturel et indigène.

Pensée patriarcale et linéaire

La plupart des penseurs occidentaux qui ont affirmé la supériorité morale des sociétés matriarcales[2] par rapport aux sociétés patriarcales, tel Johann Jakob Bachofen, l'ont fait en concluant qu'il est, en définitive, dans l'ordre des choses que le matriarcat s'éclipse éventuellement pour faire place au règne patriarcal, stade plus avancé dans l'évolution de l'humanité[3]. Ma riposte à cette proposition, qui, selon moi, n'est pas assez radicalement contestée dans les sciences humaines, a été, et est toujours, que puisque comme toute vie, la vie humaine ne peut se concevoir dissociée de la Nature, comment peut-on regarder comme une accession à un stade plus avancé une telle rupture initiant un état de guerre total et permanent contre les sources mêmes de la vie ? Comment, en ce sens, parler d'évolution ?

Comment, aussi, ne pas avoir des questionnements fondamentaux vis-à-vis de l'Histoire ? C'est dans cet ordre d'idées que j'ai inventé le terme « autohistoire » et écrit ma dissertation de maîtrise qui, en 1989, est devenue mon premier livre, *Pour une autohistoire amérindienne. Essai sur les fondements d'une morale sociale*.

Le procès de l'Histoire

Traditionnellement, les Sages de mon peuple ont éprouvé une vive inquiétude vis-à-vis de l'Histoire écrite par les Blancs au sujet de nous, notre Terre et notre

---

2 J'emploierai plutôt les termes « matricentriste » et « matricentrisme », qui n'impliquent pas une domination de l'homme par la femme mais un rapport de complémentarité dans un contexte de centralité sociale de la femme.

3 S'il-vous-plaît voir le livre de J.J. Bachofen, *Le droit de la mère dans l'Antiquité [Das Mutterrecht]* (Paris, Groupe français d'études féministes, 1903), et la mise en relation de certaines de ses idées avec les miennes dans mon livre *Pour une autohistoire amérindienne. Essai sur les fondements d'une morale sociale*, Québec, Presses de l'Université Laval, 1989, p. 22-27.

histoire avant et depuis leur arrivée, accidentelle, chez nous. Généralement, l'histoire avait dépeint les Premiers Peuples, les Amérindiens, comme naturellement cruels, stupides et paresseux et, donc, méritant amplement le dur sort qu'ils subissaient. Ces préjugés à notre endroit avaient été méticuleusement cultivés sur plusieurs générations dans l'esprit de nos concitoyens non indiens par leurs éducateurs, d'ailleurs presque toujours de pieux et doctes religieux. Le succès était plus que complet et le problème indien avait été merveilleusement réglé. Les missionnaires et autres religieux faisaient assister les Indiens[4] à tous les pèlerinages et offices religieux, et l'hymne national entonné par les chœurs de chant des réserves indiennes devenait facilement une apothéose du progrès et de la foi pour les auditeurs canadiens touchés par une si exemplaire et si miraculeuse conversion.

Cependant, éduqué à l'intérieur de deux clans traditionalistes, je connaissais l'injure ressentie par nos Anciens. Comme tous les gens censés négligeables, nous avons vu l'Histoire comme un grand rouleau compresseur opéré par les élites politiques et économiques, et utilisé par elles pour niveler le monde naturel et ceux qui maintiennent avec lui une connexion spirituelle. Mais comme l'espoir doit et peut exister, nos parents et nos Anciens ne nous enseignèrent pas la révolte ni l'irrespect. Leur discours prenait parfois un ton de prophétie et de prière.

> Les Blancs[5], disaient-ils, ont été obligés de s'en aller de leurs pays. Lorsqu'ils sont arrivés ici, nos ancêtres les ont accueillis. Ils étaient malades et nous les avons soignés. Nous les avons aidés à se faire une vie ici, à nos côtés. Ce sont les gouvernements et les églises qui ne veulent pas que nous vivions en paix et en harmonie tous ensemble parce que nous serions alors maîtres dans notre pays et les gouvernements blancs ne pourraient pas nous voler nos biens et toutes nos richesses naturelles pour s'enrichir. C'est pour cela qu'ils bourrent la tête des enfants de mensonges à notre

---

4 Ce vocable était, dans les années 1950, en train de devenir à la mode et était le remplacement « politiquement correct » de celui de « Sauvages », utilisé depuis le début de la période du contact. Je me souviens que les traditionalistes trouvaient suspecte cette nouvelle supposée politesse et préféraient continuer à s'autodésigner en français comme « Sauvages ». Ce jeu de mots et de politesse n'a jamais cessé et continue aujourd'hui.

5 Cette désignation, englobant tous les non-Indiens, était alors d'usage très général.

endroit, dans les écoles, pour nous rabaisser et nous faire haïr. Mais le Bon Dieu[6] ne permettra pas que ça continue pour toujours. Le temps est le père de la vérité. Et puis, il y a bien des gens qui comprennent le bon sens et la justice et qui nous appuient. Nos ancêtres l'ont prédit : un jour, les Indiens vont cesser de souffrir. La terre aussi, elle souffre, les animaux aussi, ils souffrent. Les hommes n'ont pas le droit de faire ça à la nature. Un jour, il faut que ça finisse. Quelque chose arrivera bientôt.

Désir d'histoire, droit d'être

Ma mère, une grande penseure et une illustre combattante pour le retour à la santé de nos peuples écrasés par la grande logique de l'histoire blanche, n'avait été qu'à l'école primaire. Avec des moyens minimes, elle retourna aux études à 50 ans et, tout en terminant d'élever seule sept enfants, elle devint la première Amérindienne canadienne à obtenir un doctorat en philosophie. Éléonore Sioui, il y a 25 ans, parla au monde du « droit d'être[7] » de nos peuples et de tous les peuples frappés à mort par le rouleau compresseur du « progrès ». Car il ne s'agit pas d'autre chose : dans la logique linéaire et patriarcale, il n'y a jamais eu de compromis possible. Dans quelque partie des Amériques (ou du monde colonial) que l'on regarde, le dossier historique est on ne peut plus clair et abondant sur ce point : le seul choix permis aux envahis (je ne veux employer ni le mot « vaincu » ni le mot « conquis ») a été celui de consentir, sous peine de brutalité intensifiée, à oublier d'avoir été et à jouer le rôle de faire-valoir dans le glorieux récit historique et social de l'envahisseur sans racines et culturellement destructeur.

Deux pensées sont en présence : l'une inconsciente ou, au mieux, indifférente à situer l'humain à l'intérieur de la Nature, et l'autre dont la conscience d'être doit consister en la connaissance sans cesse renouvelée de la place de

---

6 Nous avions alors déjà perdu notre langue (huronne-wendate) et n'utilisions pas encore les termes français « le Grand Esprit », ou « le Créateur ». Parfois, les vieux, ainsi que mon père, disaient « le Grand Maître », pour se référer à l'Être Suprême. Comme toutes les nations amérindiennes, nous avons, depuis une trentaine d'années, parcouru une longue route à la recherche de notre vraie spiritualité.

7 Notamment par la voie de la revue *Kanatha*, qu'elle créa en 1973 comme organe d'information et de communication du Centre socioculturel amérindien, qu'elle créa la même année.

l'humain dans le Cercle sacré des relations vivantes entre tous les êtres. Dans la logique des rapports coloniaux, donc patriarcaux et linéaires, perpétués dans la soi-disant ère postcoloniale, il n'y a pas de possibilité de communication bilatérale, donc de coexistence. En contrepartie, les sociétés « d'accueil », à pensée circulaire matricentriste, n'ont jamais eu d'autre réflexe culturel que celui de reconnaître ceux qui vinrent entrer en collision avec elles comme des humains qu'elles devaient aider à reprendre vie et racine et qui, de plus, possédaient des dons, des connaissances et des potentialités susceptibles d'aider à élaborer une existence commune plus diversifiée, plus riche et plus intéressante.

L'autohistoire amérindienne, ou l'histoire en présence de la Nature

L'autohistoire amérindienne, telle que je l'ai conçue dans mon essai portant ce titre, et celle de tous les peuples en mal de revivre après le passage sur eux de l'infernal rouleau compresseur, est un nouveau paradigme historique venant de l'Amérique amérindienne. Je dis même qu'elle est une nouvelle science, proposée en remplacement de l'histoire conquérante, coloniale, linéaire et patriarcale. Cette nouvelle science diffère fondamentalement de la vieille histoire, dont l'exercice est le traitement des faits et des événements afin d'arriver à une vérité historique. Bien que cet exercice doive avoir son temps et son lieu, il doit être précédé et contextualisé dans un but premier de tendre vers une Histoire assujettie aux lois de la Nature, c'est-à-dire élevée au statut de réflexion morale globale. Les enjeux sont extrêmement sérieux. Il n'y va pas seulement de la destruction du monde naturel et des sociétés qui le révèrent, mais aussi de ceux qui continuent de prononcer la sentence de mort de ce monde. « L'humain, ai-je écrit dans mon deuxième livre, n'a le choix qu'entre deux attitudes possibles : reconnaître la dignité et l'interdépendance de toutes les formes de vie ou les détruire toutes, à l'exception d'une certaine classe (patriarcale et linéaire) de son espèce, elle-même trop spirituellement appauvrie et affaiblie pour survivre[8] ».

Remise à l'intérieur de la Nature, c'est-à-dire approchée du point de vue amérindien et indigène, l'histoire devient quelque chose de très différent de la traditionnelle histoire linéaire telle que la pensent, l'écrivent, l'enseignent et en

---

8 *Huron-Wendat. Une civilisation méconnue*, p. 343.

parlent la plupart des spécialistes non Indiens. D'abord, il faut énoncer la différence radicale entre deux façons de concevoir le temps. Cette chose appelée « le passé » est une idée non indienne. Pour les autochtones, généralement, l'histoire est une réflexion sur les valeurs morales et sociales essentielles et celles-ci sont inextricablement liées aux lois de la Nature, observées, pour ainsi dire, depuis le début des temps, sans interruption. Pour un Amérindien de tradition, tout ce qui existe ou arrive doit être regardé en référence aux lois de la Nature. Ces lois étant immuables, il est impossible de regarder une chose ou un aspect quelconque de l'histoire comme quelque chose de figé à l'intérieur d'une interruption du temps, parce que ce qui arriva alors, ou ce qui est en train de se produire à chaque instant détermine comment nous (tous) allons vivre dans les temps qui viennent. Hier est aujourd'hui et demain est hier : le temps est un, la vie est une. Vivre comporte une responsabilité spirituelle et l'histoire doit être élevée au statut de réflexion morale car toute chose, tout événement, doit être regardé en référence aux lois de la Nature.

Jadis, mes ancêtres wendats parlèrent de la venue des Européens dans leur pays et du grand désastre qui s'ensuivit comme du « renversement du pays ». L'ordre immémorial qu'ils avaient élaboré au long d'incomptables siècles d'observation respectueuse du caractère et de la nature de leur Terre-mère dut faire place au désordre et à une destruction incontrôlable parce qu'elle était perpétrée par une civilisation qui s'était sortie du cadre des lois naturelles et, donc, avait perdu la capacité d'apprécier ce qu'elle avait trouvé accidentellement en notre pays. Il est logique que nos Premiers Peuples n'aient jamais perdu le sens de ce qui leur arriva alors, ni de leur histoire, ni, par conséquent, d'une responsabilité de faire en sorte que cesse un jour le désordre apporté chez eux et de remettre leur pays à l'endroit. La réalité de l'immensité, voire de l'impossibilité apparente de cette tâche n'a jamais découragé, ni ne découragera jamais, l'être humain dans son désir d'être, son désir d'histoire. Voilà un sens important de notre solidarité humaine.

Une éthique « proprement américaine »

Le titre original de mon autohistoire était : *Pour une autohistoire amérindienne. Essai sur les fondements d'une morale sociale proprement américaine*. Ces deux derniers mots ont été omis dans le titre éventuel du livre. La spécification « proprement américaine » implique plusieurs idées, plusieurs croyances qui sont de nature à inspirer tous ceux qui sont à penser leur propre autohistoire. Premièrement, le titre ainsi mis en entier veut dire qu'en tant qu'autochtones traditionalistes, nous refusons d'adhérer au dogme social selon lequel la société dominante est fondée sur l'éthique sociale apportée chez nous d'Europe. Car comment une société harmonieuse et viable pourrait-elle être fondée sur une éthique sociale qui a jadis forcé nos frères et sœurs euro-américains à délaisser leurs foyers originels et qui a causé tellement de destruction humaine et « environnementale » chez nous en si peu de temps ? Également, ce titre en entier signifie que les autochtones traditionalistes, en fait, ne croient pas que les sociétés euro-américaines soient fondées sur l'éthique européenne, pour la raison que la civilisation autochtone de notre terre est beaucoup trop ancienne pour avoir simplement cédé la place (ou pour jamais la céder) à une autre civilisation déracinée, qui n'a pas fait ses preuves et n'a jamais montré sa viabilité. Ce titre signifie aussi que les peuples autochtones, généralement, ainsi que de nombreux individus non autochtones, croient que pour réaliser les rêves de changement que nous avons tous, les sociétés non autochtones doivent déployer un effort sérieux pour s'éduquer au sujet de la civilisation des Premiers Peuples, posant ainsi des fondements pour leur évolution future sur une éthique sociale « proprement américaine ».

Mon essai *Pour une autohistoire amérindienne* est l'expression de ma croyance que les peuples autochtones doivent se voir comme leaders dans leur propre pays sur les plans de la philosophie, de la spiritualité et de l'éducation. Loin de se limiter à « examiner l'envers d'une question dont l'endroit reste inchangé[9] », le nouveau paradigme de l'autohistoire établit le sens et la direction dans lesquels les peuples autochtones peuvent et doivent éduquer la société globale. La raison pour laquelle le livre n'est pas de nature récriminatoire, tel que l'a observé mon regretté frère et ami l'ethno-historien Bruce Trigger dans la préface, est qu'il amène à faire voir que les autochtones ne peuvent, ni ne doivent penser ou agir socialement comme des victimes parce que, comme leaders de plein droit chez eux, ils n'ont pas le luxe de beaucoup de temps pour s'attarder sur les aspects

---

[9] Je me réfère au questionnement, fin et utilement provocateur, élaboré par les concepteurs de cette présente conférence.

tristes et tragiques de leur histoire. Aussi, le livre propose une façon de voir un sens à notre histoire et de nous y rattacher de manière altruiste, au lieu de nous apitoyer sur notre sort.

Une prémisse importante d'*Autohistoire* est qu'ayant vécu sur notre sol depuis, pour ainsi dire, le début des temps, nous possédons une compréhension intime de l'esprit, des humeurs et de l'intelligence de notre Terre-mère et, donc, ne pouvons pas être en danger de perdre le sens de notre relation spirituelle et émotionnelle avec elle, même après un terrible accident, tel que fut l'arrivée fortuite des Européens après 1492.

Voir l'arrivée des Européens comme un accident plutôt que comme un « choc des cultures », une « rencontre de deux mondes » ou le « début de la période du contact[10] » constitue une illustration de comment l'autohistoire amérindienne est un nouveau paradigme historique et philosophique permettant une façon fondamentalement différente de regarder la société et nous-mêmes en tant que peuples. Car lors de cet *accident*, ceux qui nous frappèrent et nous blessèrent et endommagèrent ou détruisirent nos biens furent eux aussi grièvement blessés. En fait, plus grièvement que nous, parce que leur véhicule était frêle et faible et le nôtre, très fort et solide. De plus, ils n'emmenaient avec eux ni nourriture ni remèdes. Nous avions donc un devoir d'aller les trouver et de les aider, de soigner leurs blessés, leurs malades, de nous occuper de leurs mourants et d'enterrer leurs morts, car ils étaient sans recours, ne savaient pas même où ils étaient ni quoi ni qui ils avaient frappé. Nous ne pouvons pas simplement nous plaindre qu'on nous avait frappés et nous occuper seulement des nôtres. Les étrangers vinrent dans une embarcation de fortune et ce qu'ils transportaient était à peine suffisant pour subvenir à leurs propres besoins vitaux, car ils avaient dû s'enfuir de quelque chose, quelque part. Ils entrèrent en collision avec des gens très riches de terres très riches et qui avaient tout. Nous sommes encore riches. Ils sont encore pauvres. C'est comme si le temps n'avait pas passé. Nous devons aller les trouver et les aider, les consoler et les rassurer, les informer et leur enseigner, car ils sont nos parents humains et nous pouvons améliorer davantage notre sort en apprenant ce qu'ils savent, en sachant ce qu'ils pensent

---

10 Trois expressions fréquemment utilisées dans le discours spécialisé pour parler de l'événement du « contact » entre l'Europe et l'Amérique.

et ressentent. Mais, d'abord, nous devons les faire avoir confiance en nous en les aidant à se guérir de leurs traumatismes, de leurs peurs, à se débarrasser de leurs mauvais souvenirs, de la culpabilité ou de la colère qu'ils pourraient avoir. Nous devons trouver la manière de les guérir, tout en nous occupant de nos propres blessures, lesquelles, dans le contexte de cet accident, peuvent être considérées comme surtout physiques.

La vocation américaine et mondiale de l'autohistoire

Le nouveau paradigme de l'autohistoire amérindienne (ou l'histoire mise en présence de la Nature) permet aux peuples autochtones de se situer vis-à-vis de leur histoire posteuropéenne et de caractériser celle-ci comme rien de plus qu'un accident. Diverses personnes de diverses origines ont trouvé cette approche utile surtout parce qu'elle permet de dissiper des mythes qui ont rendu l'historiographie traditionnelle hautement débilitante de notre capacité d'empathiser entre humains à partir d'une reconnaissance mutuelle et d'une recherche collective de la vérité, comme toute société normale doit faire pour bien fonctionner. Les deux principaux mythes que je discute dans le livre et qu'il est impossible de reconnaître comme tels lorsqu'on utilise les vieux paradigmes, sont le mythe de la supériorité de la civilisation européenne, et son corollaire, celui de la disparition normale (voire désirable) des peuples autochtones. Par contraste, l'approche autohistorique, parce qu'elle établit la permanence des valeurs sociales autochtones essentielles dans la longue durée, nous rend capables de reconnaître l'étonnante résistance et la foi des peuples autochtones en leur propre philosophie sociale, d'ailleurs comprise et adoptée par de nombreux non autochtones et validée par l'évidence de l'échec du système de valeurs que les Européens s'acharnèrent jadis aveuglément à imposer aux Amérindiens. Tout cela tend à établir l'urgente nécessité de dénoncer ces mythes.

Un autre mythe que l'autohistoire amérindienne permet de cerner et de disséquer est celui de la moralité du pouvoir occidental, investi surtout dans les États-Unis. Nous avons déjà vu que la réflexion autohistorique s'éloigne des discours récriminatoires et stériles qui positionnent l'Amérindien dans un rôle figé de victime toujours potentiellement quémandeuse ou vengeresse.

Vu à l'aide du prisme autohistorique, le discours « américain » (ce mot réfère aussi au continent) sur les Premiers Peuples devient un outil d'analyse du pouvoir américain et occidental. Il devient alors possible de dénoncer la fausseté et l'indésirabilité du « rêve américain ») ou de l'« américanisation » du monde. Si ce rêve n'est possible que par une intensification de la spoliation de la Nature, il faut neutraliser les termes « américanisation », « américaniser » et « américanité » et les remplacer par ceux d'« américisation », « américiser » et « américité » et définir ceux-ci comme traitant du transfert de la civilisation américaine profonde, c'est-à-dire *amérindienne*, aux nouveaux venus d'Amérique et au reste du monde. Comment le pouvoir « américanisateur » des États-Unis et de l'Occident s'est-il constitué ? Les peuples heurtés ou détruits dans ce processus doivent-ils se sentir intimidés ou être impressionnés par un pouvoir ainsi construit ? Est-ce qu'un tel pouvoir possède les bases morales qui font la respectabilité qui a toujours produit la permanence ? Après cinq siècles d'« américanisation » de l'Amérique et du monde, il existe un fort courant de pensée à l'échelle américaine et mondiale selon lequel il est temps de se pencher sur les sources et les racines de la vie elle-même, qui sont dans la Terre et dans l'esprit de la Terre. Il faut américiser l'Amérique. Il faut réparer et soigner le monde entier.

Pour une autohistoire amérindienne a connu un succès assez rare pour un livre savant sur les Amérindiens. Surpris au début, mais guidé par la réponse de nombreux lecteurs, j'en suis venu à attribuer cet intérêt à l'existence d'un désir ancien et durable dans le cœur des gens de voir une fin à la glorification de la venue et de l'œuvre des Blancs dans nos pays, dont les habitants sauvages avaient censément besoin d'être découverts et sauvés de leur existence insensée et sans Dieu. Je crois fermement qu'il n'y a plus de place pour de telles histoires dans la philosophie de nations modernes soi-disant développées.

Certains penseurs nous ont dit que le matriarcat a dû nécessairement céder la place au patriarcat pour que le monde évolue, c'est-à-dire qu'il est un jour devenu nécessaire de dissocier l'histoire, donc l'homme, de la Nature. Pour ma part, je pense et je dis, en accord avec de nombreux sages que j'ai connus, amérindiens et autres, qu'un retour aux valeurs humaines premières et vitales, c'est-à-dire aux sociétés matricentristes plus petites, égalitaires et viables, est nécessaire et inévitable. Je veux voir dans la vigueur des mouvements et de la pensée féministes et environnementalistes une preuve absolument sûre de l'engagement irréversible de la reconnexion de l'humain avec la Nature. C'est dans le même esprit que je vois dans le présent colloque la confirmation qu'un grand travail à accomplir se présente à nous tous : celui de faire individuellement et collectivement notre autohistoire, en nous ancrant les pieds, les mains, le cœur et l'esprit dans la Nature, que tous nos ancêtres ont vénérée.

Je désire conclure en disant que mon livre, dont j'ai parlé, ainsi que celui qui l'a suivi *Huron-Wendat. Une civilisation méconnue*, sont l'expression de mon effort continu d'accomplir le devoir que m'ont transmis mes parents et ancêtres hurons-wendats, celui d'aider à réconcilier tous les peuples que le Grand Esprit a placés ensemble sur la Grande Île sur le Dos de la Tortue, tel que nous appelons notre continent et, par extension, le monde. J'ai exposé pour vous ce que je crois être la meilleure voie pour voir disparaître les murs qui ont séparé beaucoup d'entre nous pendant et depuis trop longtemps. Les Allemands n'ont-ils pas récemment posé un grand geste en ce sens ? Tous ensemble, il faut continuer.

Ho! Ho! Ho! Attouguet Eathoro! Liebe Freunde, ich danke Innen sehr mich zu hören gehabt!
(Chers amis et parents, merci de m'avoir écouté !)

Québécois et Canadiens dans l'ordre historique amérindien[*]

Chers frères et sœurs du Canada, du Québec et d'autres lieux,

Le Canada que nous connaissons et chérissons aujourd'hui, ce pays rêvé de tolérance, de sécurité et de promesse, est d'abord le résultat du travail d'innombrables gens, ancêtres des citoyens des Premiers Peuples d'aujourd'hui. Non seulement est-il vrai, comme on l'entend souvent dire de nos jours, que ces antiques « Canadiens » préservèrent avec clairvoyance et succès la qualité du corps physique de leur Terre, mais aussi qu'hommes et femmes édifièrent avec leur cœur et leur esprit un ordre politique, économique et social singulièrement bien harmonisé avec l'esprit et le corps de cette terre, qu'ils aimèrent telle une mère. Voilà la source de l'existence du Canada – et du Québec.

---

[*] Texte présenté à la conférence « Identité et citoyenneté dans le Québec contemporain » tenue à l'Université McGill les 8 et 9 mars 2001. Publié dans le livre *Repères en mutation* sous la direction de Jocelyn Maclure et Alain-G. Gagnon.

Un ordre territorial. Combien de Canadiens, de Québécois ont-ils déjà même pensé que leurs concitoyens autochtones puissent eux aussi posséder un paradigme, avoir une idée culturellement héritée de la façon dont devrait continuer à évoluer le Canada si les grands écueils sociaux et écologiques qui se pointent à l'horizon du futur doivent être évités ? Ma conscience historique, informée par ma connaissance de l'éducation offerte dans mon pays depuis son contact avec l'Europe au chapitre de la civilisation amérindienne, me dit qu'encore peu de Canadiens – et de Québécois – sont susceptibles d'avoir ce questionnement au sujet des autochtones. Sinon, nous verrions notre pays activement à l'œuvre, par la voie de la création de maisons d'éducation supérieure contrôlées par les autochtones, afin d'intégrer le savoir de ceux-ci à tous les champs de la connaissance moderne. Au lieu de cela, notre société, soi-disant inclusive et évoluée, continue de gaspiller l'important héritage humain et philosophique conservé tant bien que mal grâce à la fière résistance des Premières Nations.

Un ordre géopolitique maintenu mentalement par les Amérindiens. En fin de compte, ce n'est qu'hier qu'a été tronquée notre vie civilisationnelle par l'arrivée européenne. Comment donc pourrions-nous même avoir commencé à oublier l'harmonie de son fonctionnement ? N'avons-nous pas constamment sous les yeux et devant tous nos sens le contraste atterrant de ce qui hier commença à détruire et à remplacer ce que nos ancêtres nous avaient légué ? N'avons-nous pas toujours, et de plus en plus fréquemment, été encouragés par de nouveaux frères et sœurs d'adoption à ne jamais troquer notre foi et notre héritage au profit de celui du nouveau venu ? Nos pères et mères ne nous ont-ils pas constamment prédit avec exactitude le temps non lointain (maintenant arrivé) où l'étranger viendrait nous dire qu'« il a besoin de quelque chose qui est nous[1] », signal déjà présent que nous commençons à exercer notre rôle de Premiers Peuples, maintenant que nous sommes complètement entourés d'un auditoire captif, venu chez nous et en mal d'un réenracinement spirituel, que de plus en plus de gens nous disent devoir recevoir de nous, pour ne plus être des étrangers sur une terre dont nous sommes tous enfants ?

---

[1] Expression du grand Squamish, le chef Dan George, en 1970.

Comme tout pays, le Canada a été construit à partir de l'héritage matériel, intellectuel et spirituel des peuples qui ont eu leurs foyers dans son territoire avant qu'il ne fût Canada. Le Canada, cependant, est une terre spéciale, en fait sacrée, dans le sens que ses peuples originaux n'ont pas le souvenir de s'être livré des guerres de dépossession pour des raisons économiques ou religieuses (peut-être en partie à cause du retrait récent des glaciers et, donc, de sa relativement brève habitabilité depuis lors). Les conflits (d'ailleurs de faible envergure) qu'ils ont connus furent généralement des conflits d'honneur, impliquant vengeance et réparation. Dans mon ordre d'idées, j'emploie le mot « sacré » en référence au fait que le territoire du Canada n'est pas entaché d'une histoire de guerres massives impliquant armées, conquêtes et génocides économiques et religieux. Les prédécesseurs du peuple canadien furent des gens qui utilisèrent leur temps et leurs ressources physiques et mentales pour connaître intimement leur Terre-mère et, donc, penser des cultures et une civilisation d'ensemble qui fussent en accord avec la nature, la pensée et le langage spirituel de celle-ci. Regardé sous cet angle, le Canada que nous avons aujourd'hui est la création d'autres gens qui durent délaisser leurs pays et leur histoire et qui trouvèrent ici l'héritage riche, pur et propre que déposèrent généreusement dans leurs mains ceux qu'ils étaient destinés à mépriser ; ils tentèrent de les déposséder et voulurent les assimiler à une civilisation en laquelle ils ne purent jamais croire. De ce point de vue aussi, il est possible de concevoir la présence, chez les peuples autochtones, d'une foi vivace, bien que réprimée et encore dissimulée, en leur capacité et en leur responsabilité de rétablir en son essence l'ordre que leurs ancêtres avaient créé de concert avec les lois de la Nature[2].

Dans mon livre *Huron-Wendat. Une civilisation méconnue*, j'ai expliqué comment le Canada est l'héritier d'un trésor civilisationnel wendat-algonquien, entre autres, qu'il méconnaît. Cet ouvrage expose la démarche philosophique, sociale et territoriale pluriséculaire des Wendat préeuropéens, qui eut pour résultat de créer une société multilingue et multiculturelle de nations, qui éventuellement constitua la force sur laquelle la France fit tourner sa stratégie impériale en Amérique du Nord et sur laquelle les fondateurs du Canada assirent

---

2 En 1636, un chef wendat avait décrit l'action désordonnée des Blancs comme « le renversement du pays ».

leur imposante création. Longtemps avant l'arrivée des Français chez eux, les Wendat avaient créé un « pays », qu'ils nommaient Wendaké (Huronie pour les Français du XVIIe siècle).[3] Le Wendaké était un territoire d'étendue assez restreinte (moins de 600 kilomètres carrés), mais une véritable clé géopolitique, puisqu'il était au croisement des principales routes naturelles de commerce. Renommés pour leur génie politique et commercial, les Wendat, qui constituaient la plus importante confédération du Nord-Est, avaient élu d'établir le foyer de leur civilisation, le Wendaké, à l'endroit géographique qui leur offrait une proximité stratégique aux nombreux peuples algonquiens du Nord, affiliés culturellement et politiquement à une multitude d'autres peuples, de familles linguistiques souvent disparates. Pour conserver et amplifier des réseaux commerciaux et politiques qu'ils avaient cultivés depuis des siècles, les Wendat se concentrèrent rapidement au Wendaké, à partir des années 1250-1300, plutôt que d'opter pour les terres agricoles plus au sud, plus fertiles et moins sujettes au gel hâtif. Bien que proprement wendat sur les plans culturel et linguistique, le Wendaké fut une création à laquelle participèrent aussi, et de façon importante, plusieurs peuples algonquiens circonvoisins, pour lesquels le Wendaké devint, et pour longtemps (c'est-à-dire jusqu'au début de sa destruction, vers 1630), un territoire d'échanges privilégiés et fraternels de plusieurs natures : éducative, cérémonielle, médicale, sacrée, diplomatique et, bien sûr, matérielle.

Ce fut dans l'esprit du Français Jacques Cartier que commença à germer la notion euro-américaine d'un Canada. Entendant Donnacona, Premier Chef des Stadaconas[4], désigner sa ville et sa contrée par le mot « Kanatha », Cartier parla dans son journal du « Seigneur » et du « Royaume » de « Canada » qu'il lui revenait donc de supplanter et de soumettre, si son statut de découvreur officiel au nom du roi de France n'était pas qu'une vaine prétention. Pour ce faire, Cartier, lors d'un deuxième voyage l'année suivante (en 1535-1536), mit à exécution un plan qui consistait à capturer Donnacona ainsi que plusieurs (neuf) autres personnes de sa lignée, portant ainsi un coup fatal à l'ordre immémorial du pays.

---

3 Wendaké signifie « presqu'île» ou « pays à part ». Ce pays petit mais très stratégiquement situé se trouvait à proximité des villes actuelles d'Orillia et Penetanguishene, à une heure et demie au nord de Toronto.

4 Amérindiens du site et de la contrée entourant la présente ville de Québec.

Un état de méfiance et d'inimitié s'installa, qui allait avoir des conséquences très lourdes sur toute l'entreprise impériale française en Amérique, surtout du nord, mais aussi du sud. Cartier ne put jamais fonder de colonie française durable sur le Saint-Laurent et ce ne fut que 62 ans plus tard (en 1603) que la France, excédée par son ample implication militaire en Europe, put faire une nouvelle tentative de peuplement dans la Nouvelle-France qu'elle désirait créer. En 1603, Samuel de Champlain, qui fonda Québec en 1608, ne vit que des vestiges de nombreux « Andatha » (villes) répertoriés par Cartier le long de la rive nord du Saint-Laurent. Le Canada amérindien avait cessé d'exister après les trois passages de Cartier. Le Canada imaginé par Cartier, c'est-à-dire un Canada soumis à l'empire français, pouvait donc prendre naissance. Avant d'être des Français, les premiers « sujets canadiens » de la France furent les nouveaux occupants innu (« montagnais ») et algonquiens des contrées abandonnées par leurs prédécesseurs stadaconas, hochelagas (Amérindiens centralisés à Hochelaga, maintenant Montréal) et autres. Bien sûr, ces « Canadiens » ne s'autodésignèrent jamais comme tels ; en effet, même les Amérindiens du Canada actuel continuent de se considérer membres de leur nation autochtone d'abord et ensuite, peut-être, Canadiens[5].

Que ce soit à cause de la faiblesse économique relative de la France en Europe, à l'époque, et donc de la symbiose peut-être forcée des Néo-Français et des Amérindiens (condition qui ne fut pas celle des Anglais ou des Hollandais[6]), ou encore à cause d'un caractère plus porté à l'analyse et à la contemplation philosophiques, il reste difficile de nier que l'âme française a plus d'affinités que l'anglo-saxonne avec l'âme amérindienne, ou l'âme primitive, prise globalement. Passablement nombreux furent les jeunes Néo-Français qui, d'instinct, « s'ensauvagèrent » de très bon gré[7], c'est-à-dire se fondirent culturellement et ethniquement au peuple autochtone de leur nouveau pays, le Canada. Si l'on se réfère à l'apport prioritairement français à l'élaboration historique et

---

[5] Beaucoup de gens des Premières Nations continuent de refuser d'être appelés « Canadiens ».

[6] Par contre, les Écossais et les Irlandais, encore animés d'un esprit clanique, donc « primitif », ont aussi connu ce rapport avec les autochtones, d'une façon différente puisqu'ils étaient eux-mêmes des conquis.

[7] J'ai créé le mot « (s'américiser) amé » dans mon livre *Pour une autohistoire amérindienne*, publié aux Presses de l'Université Laval en 1989.

littéraire du concept du « bon sauvage », il est, selon moi, possible de noter que le caractère français recèle des traces sensibles de la pensée dite primitive, définie comme non étatique[8] dans l'œuvre de penseurs de la taille d'un Pierre Clastres et d'un Claude Lévi-Strauss.

Deux géographes québécois, Jean Morisset et Eric Waddell, ont récemment publié un livre intitulé *Amériques*, dans lequel ils décrivent de façon brillante et vivace la grande expérience française de métissage en Amérique. Le livre, qui est une synthèse de l'œuvre écrite et de la vie de bourlingueurs des deux professeurs, cerne donc de façon révélatrice le caractère intime du « Franco » en Amérique, traditionnellement trahi par l'appareil officiel du savoir et donc connu seulement par lui-même, défilant le rêve d'une Amérique connue par lui seul et égrenant le drame d'une assimilation dont lui seul sait la fausseté. Tout cela m'amène à parler du Québec dans le Canada, selon l'ordre historique amérindien.

En dépit d'expériences néfastes, voire tragiques, avec les Français, telles que celles du temps de Cartier, puis de la destruction du Wendaké et des autres grandes confédérations amérindiennes du Nord-Est, surtout attribuables à la faiblesse économique de leur allié français, les Amérindiens originellement ligués à la France – et ils furent la grande majorité – ont toujours voué aux Français et aux Néo-Français une amitié spéciale et une loyauté inébranlable. Je veux ici illustrer mon propos par un événement charnière dans l'histoire de l'Amérique du Nord, la Grande Paix de Montréal de 1701, dont le tricentenaire sera célébré dans cinq mois, le 4 août 2001, ici, à Montréal. Ce faisant, j'avancerai aussi ma croyance, partagée par plusieurs des miens, que les Amérindiens ont, de fait, cultivé et maintenu stratégiquement le pouvoir français parce que c'était là le meilleur moyen dont ils disposaient pour maintenir leur ordre à eux, pour remettre, donc, éventuellement, leur pays à l'endroit.

La Grande Paix de Montréal, conclue en août 1701, marque la fin de 92 années de guerre presque ininterrompue entre les deux alliances, la franco-wendate-algonquienne et l'hollando-anglo-iroquoise[9]. Ce conflit fut véritablement un holocauste du côté amérindien (même chez les Iroquois) puisqu'il fut

---

[8] Je rappelle cette vision philosophique par l'expression « pensée circulaire » dans mes deux ouvrages précités.

[9] Les Anglais supplantèrent les Hollandais en 1664.

nourri et intensifié par une horrible dépopulation causée par les pathogènes venus d'Europe. Le maître d'œuvre de ce grand traité de paix fut Kondiaronk Sastaretsi[10], chef principal des « Hurons du Détroit » dont l'historien jésuite Charlevoix, son contemporain, dit que « jamais Sauvage n'eut plus de mérite, un plus beau génie, plus de valeur, plus de prudence et plus de discernement ». Né à l'aube de la destruction de son pays, le Wendaké, vers 1625, Kondiaronk fut un chef de guerre extrêmement habile et un diplomate de tout premier ordre qui, en dépit d'une force militaire wendate très réduite par les guerres et les épidémies, mena, dans la plus pure tradition de son peuple, toute l'action militaire et politique des Français et de leurs nombreux alliés amérindiens.

De son vivant, il vit des nations populeuses de ses congénères entièrement consumées dans le feu déclenché par l'invasion européenne ; Kondiaronk et ses contemporains furent témoins de la mort d'un nombre incroyablement élevé de leurs gens. Avec frayeur et une tristesse insondable, ils contemplèrent la fin de leur monde[11]. Providentiellement, ils purent mettre au point une stratégie qui leur permit de confier à la garde des Français la flamme chancelante de leur survie, c'est-à-dire de l'ordre ancestral qui devait être protégé. La vision, la stratégie et certainement la prière de Kondiaronk et de tous les siens furent d'arrêter cette guerre séculaire par une paix générale, incluant toutes les nations de leur alliance ainsi que les Iroquois et les Français. Le rêve devint réalité. Kondiaronk et les autres dirigeants amérindiens réunirent leurs 38 nations dans un traité de paix qui a perduré jusqu'à notre temps. Bien qu'ils fussent leurs ennemis ataviques, leurs congénères iroquois y trouvèrent aussi leur protection, leur survie et la réorientation de leur carrière politique en tant que force amérindienne devant jouer un rôle de premier plan dans une grande stratégie de protection et de redressement de l'ordre amérindien continental. De façon également très importante, la Grande Paix de Montréal confirma la préséance

---

10 Sastaretsi était, dans la confédération wendate, le plus haut titre héréditaire, désignant le chef suprême du pays.

11 Kondiaronk lui-même s'éteignit à Montréal, le 2 août, victime d'une épidémie qui sévissait dans presque tout le pays. Son discours d'adieu la veille de sa mort, devant les autorités coloniales, la population néo-française de Montréal (environ 2 000 habitants), de nombreux visiteurs canadiens ainsi que les 1 300 délégués de 38 nations amérindiennes, la majorité venant de contrées très lointaines, causa une vive et rare émotion. On lui fit des funérailles d'État. La Grande Paix de Montréal fut ratifiée le 4 août, le lendemain de ses obsèques.

des Français, par rapport aux Britanniques, comme alliés privilégiés de toutes les nations amérindiennes, parce qu'ils étaient liés à elles d'un lien d'amitié et de parenté et non seulement pour des considérations matérielles.

Conclusion

Dans le cadre de cette importante conférence sur la question identitaire québécoise et canadienne, il m'a paru important, en tant qu'Amérindien et historien, d'exposer un point de vue venant d'aussi loin que je puisse aller dans ma tradition. L'opposition généralisée des Amérindiens québécois et canadiens au projet séparatiste québécois ainsi que les motifs de celle-ci sont connus dans le reste du Canada et dans le monde.

Nonobstant toute cette controverse, j'ai voulu dans cette présentation situer la question de l'identitaire québécois dans une perspective de longue durée. J'ai voulu établir que *d'un point de vue amérindien traditionaliste*, le Canada, tel que nous le connaissons et tel que nous le vivons aujourd'hui, a été une création française, dont les Québécois – et les Franco-Canadiens – sont et doivent être les premiers héritiers non autochtones. Cette préséance a été reconnue historiquement et confirmée par toutes les nations amérindiennes dans l'alliance fondatrice. Je crois que le Canada, pour survivre comme meilleur pays du monde, doit prendre conscience de son obligation de fonder son identité dans la civilisation profonde qui fut et est la source de son existence, c'est-à-dire dans l'ordre respectueusement créé par ses peuples autochtones, de concert avec la Nature (le grand Cercle de tous les êtres) sur une période d'au moins 10 000 ans. Me basant sur les enseignements tout aussi anciens que j'ai reçus, j'affirme aussi l'obligation du Canada de reconnaître la place spéciale du Québec ainsi que celle du Canada français dans l'histoire (plurimillénaire) et dans l'espace de ce grand et beau pays. J'affirme aussi l'obligation du Canada de traiter honnêtement et humainement avec le Québec et de cesser de fournir au Québec des motifs de le percevoir comme un arrogant fier à bras, le défiant de passer à l'acte de séparation. Un Québec humilié et acculé à cette ultime solution sortira du Canada, au grand détriment de celui-ci. Personnellement, je ne veux même pas imaginer la pauvreté culturelle et sociale d'un Canada sans le Québec.

Par ailleurs, je ne crois pas que notre pays trouvera un vrai équilibre social, une vraie prospérité à long terme simplement en utilisant ses avantages naturels et en poursuivant une course effrénée et opportuniste vers les grands marchés et la seule richesse économique. Je pense aussi que cette voie recèle de profondes et graves déceptions. Je crois plutôt que c'est d'abord dans une compréhension plus profonde et plus respectueuse de son histoire et de son héritage philosophique, spirituel et humain que le Canada trouvera les voies de sa stabilité et de sa vraie identité, donc de sa fierté comme nation présente et future.

Finalement, revenant à nos propres problèmes philosophiques et existentiels amérindiens, je me dis : qui sait ? Un Québec bien compris, apprécié et traité avec une dignité d'égal par le Canada voudra peut-être faire de même, ou encore mieux, pour ses propres « Québécois », les Premières Nations de son territoire, et ainsi donner l'exemple que lui seul est capable de donner aux autres Canadiens en ce sens.

Ho! Ho! Ho! Attouguet! (Amis et parents, merci de tout cœur de m'avoir écouté !)

Le racisme est nouveau en Amérique[*]

Louis-Armand de Lom D'Arce, baron de Lahontan, vint en Nouvelle-France en 1680, alors qu'il était encore jeune homme. Il sut se gagner l'amitié et la confiance des Amérindiens et se familiarisa à un rare degré avec leur pensée, leurs coutumes et leur sens de leur propre histoire. Son œuvre littéraire fut souvent proscrite en France, son pays natal, à cause du caractère révolutionnaire de ses idées sociales et religieuses. Il est surtout connu pour ses Dialogues avec un Sauvage, *où il s'entretient avec le chef huron Adario (l'illustre Kondiaronk) sur les lois, la religion, la médecine et la moralité. Les idées sauvages (« amériquaines »), dans les* Dialogues, *sont plus avancées, plus justes et plus humaines que celles de l'Europe. Lahontan fut un précurseur du renversement de la monarchie française. Dans le texte qui suit, Lahontan a été « rappelé » du monde des esprits pour éclairer une société moderne aux prises avec le « racisme », une aberration sociale venue d'Europe et pour laquelle la sagesse sauvage*

---

[*] Publié dans le livre *Écrire contre le racisme : le pouvoir de l'art*, Montréal, Les 400 coups, 2002, p. 18-24.

possède une explication et un remède : son attitude philosophique envers la Terre et la féminité.

Chers frères et sœurs sur cette belle et merveilleuse Terre, c'est avec beaucoup de reconnaissance et d'émotion que j'ai reçu, au beau pays où j'habite, votre message m'exprimant votre croyance que je puisse « contribuer », avec mon cercle d'amis, « quelques conseils sages » pour l'allégement d'un désordre dont souffre votre grande société canadienne et amériquaine, qui va se généralisant et que vous appelez « racisme ». Il y avait longtemps que j'avais cessé de penser que les écrits que j'ai laissés en quittant ce beau et merveilleux monde terrestre pourraient un jour avoir quelque utilité pour « nos enfants de l'avenir », comme mes amis canadois, hurons et autres, m'ont appris à les appeler, de notre temps terrestre.

Ce fut toujours avec bonheur et une plaisante nostalgie que je vis certains de nos frères et sœurs de notre beau pays des âmes être « rappelés », comme nous disons, c'est-à-dire recevoir le signal, avec l'« essence » d'une réincarnation éphémère parmi les « gens de terre », comme nous vous appelons avec amour et tendresse. Le but de ces retours est toujours d'aller alléger et garantir la vie de nos descendants qui cheminent au ras le ventre de la merveilleuse Terre Mère. Quant à moi, j'avais même perdu la mémoire de beaucoup de choses que j'avais faites, dites et écrites ici-bas. Par moments perdus dans ma délicieuse existence d'esprit, j'ai souhaité, en tous cas, que rien de mes pensées et actes terrestres ne puisse jamais faire ombrage à personne qui fût venu vivre sur terre après moi. Et voici que le Grand Esprit (je pourrais, bien sûr, dire Dieu) m'a rappelé ! Je suis tellement chanceux !

En recevant le message, le signal et l'essence, j'ai tout de suite convoqué mes amis les plus proches. Puisque maintenant je sais que mes livres, dont j'ai maintenant le contenu frais à l'esprit, ont continué d'être lus et mes idées, débattues, après mon départ pour le Grand Pays des Âmes, je sais aussi que je ne surprendrai pas ceux qui me connaissent en révélant que j'habite, dans le Pays des Âmes, une Province huronne très fréquentée aussi par des Algonquins et autres Sauvages, en plus de Français et autres hommes blancs et femmes blanches au cœur sauvage, comme moi. Mon âme ensauvagée n'avait attendu que la libération de mon trépas, en France, pour s'y envoler et rejoindre ma chère Kiwaydinokway, ma douce épouse nipissingue, ainsi que mes chers frères et sœurs amériquains, chez qui j'avais connu tant de vérité, de liberté, donc de félicité, dans leurs simples et chaleureux villages, il y a à peine 300 ans.

Mes amis (ceux que j'ai appelés « philosophes nus » dans mes livres) et moi nous sommes réunis chez notre frère aîné, le grand Kondiaronk Adario, qui a toujours un excellent brasier, les mets et les boires les plus enchanteurs et, dans son grand calumet, les meilleurs de tous les tabacs. La nuit, de jeune automne, était des plus délicieuses et le bonheur se lisait dans tous les yeux et émanait de toutes les lèvres. Durant le temps de notre entretien (dans notre monde, nous ne sommes pas contraints par ce que nos parents terrestres appellent « le temps »), nous n'entendîmes de musique que la grande et parfaite symphonie de l'univers.

Tout le message que j'ai reçu, puis partagé avec mes frères et sœurs sauvages, tourne sur les mot « haine » et « racisme ». C'est là un mot que nous ne connaissions pas, pas même moi qui ai appris la langue française au sein de ma douce mère. Toutefois, j'ai compris très clairement les quatre mots explicatifs : injustices, exclusions, discriminations et persécutions. D'abord, j'ai exposé à notre feu, c'est-à-dire à notre cercle, ou conseil, la nature de la requête qui justifiait mon rappel sur terre. Cela causa un émoi. En effet, mes confrères et consœurs canadois s'unirent en un seul sentiment que le pays de leurs descendants, qu'ils avaient jadis laissé avec l'assurance qu'il redeviendrait sauvage et libre, avait plutôt évolué dans un sens contraire et dangereux : étrangement, les idées et les problèmes qui avaient fait fuir les étrangers de leurs pays semblaient avoir maintenant remplacé les idées et les façons de faire naturelles à cette terre amériquaine de refuge et de salut.

> Nos peuples, dit, ému, le grand Poutéouatami Onanguicé, ont eu entre eux des différends et des guerres, mais jamais, de mémoire sauvage, personne n'a vu, ni n'aurait toléré, qu'un autre être humain soit méprisé, persécuté et privé de nourriture, de logis, de vêtements chauds ou présentables, ou de sa liberté, ou encore de sa dignité, à cause de la couleur de sa peau ou de ses croyances, origines, idées ou habitudes de vie, pourvu qu'il ou elle respecte celles d'autrui. Une telle chose, qu'on nous nomme « racisme »,

est une aberration et une injure au Grand Esprit et à l'esprit de nos ancêtres, qui ne la souffrirent pas de leur temps, en leur pays.

Ici, Onanguicé regarda Adario, le grand chef wendat, et alla lui remettre la pierre de parole. Cette pierre (c'est-à-dire l'esprit de celle-ci), présentement gardée par Kondiaronk, avait été passée de gardien à gardien depuis bien avant le temps que les Portugais avaient capturé un grand nombre de nos gens, dans l'île des Béothuks (Terre-Neuve) (Corté Réal fit cette capture en 1501).

Mon oncle Donnacona que voici, qui était grand capitaine à Stadaconé[1] lorsque Jacques Cartier arriva avec 110 autres Français, reprit notre hôte Adario, nous a souvent raconté comment ses gens et lui-même traitèrent ces pauvres visiteurs qui ne voulurent pas s'en retourner chez eux et comment ceux-ci les traitèrent en retour. Ce fut le commencement d'une histoire triste qui, un jour, suivant la volonté du Maître de la Vie, devra changer pour le mieux. Voulez-vous parler, mon oncle ?

Le vénérable Donnacona qui, en 1536, fut si traîtreusement capturé avec les siens par Cartier et dut mourir de tristesse, en France, moins de deux ans après, offrit au cercle son regard noble, quelque peu mouillé par moments, et dit ceci :

Nous ne sommes pas allés chercher ces gens dans leur pays pour qu'ils viennent ici, mais nous fûmes heureux de penser que nous allions les aider à demeurer chez nous, puisqu'ils ne désiraient pas s'en retourner d'où ils venaient. Ils souhaitaient beaucoup que nous leur échangeassions nos fourrures d'animaux contre leurs objets de verre et de métal, que nos gens trouvaient beaux et, parfois, utiles. Nous nous disions que, sûrement, nous allions apprendre d'eux des choses que nous ne connaissions pas et qu'ensemble, nous formerions un jour une nation encore plus forte et plus heureuse, sans jamais compromettre notre liberté, qui était infinie et que nous placions au-dessus de toute chose dans notre vie, puisqu'elle nous signifiait l'amour même de l'Être qui nous donne la vie.

---

1 Aujourd'hui ville de Québec.

Le premier été que nous les vîmes à Honguedo (appelé aussi Gaspé par nos voisins mi'kmaq), je fus très choqué de la façon dont ils m'enlevèrent mes deux fils, Domagaya et Taignoagny, pour les emmener en France. Toutefois, mes gens et moi nous avisâmes que nous ne devions pas montrer notre peine et notre inquiétude, mais plutôt prendre le risque les voir revenir l'année suivante, puisqu'on nous en donnait l'assurance, et, ainsi, avoir l'avantage de savoir comment on vivait en ce pays d'Europe, auquel ces gens ne semblaient que peu attachés.

Tard l'été suivant, mes deux fils revinrent, ce qui causa une très grande réjouissance chez nous, à Stadaconé et dans tout le pays auquel Sieur Cartier et ses compagnons se référaient maintenant comme « le Canada » (ce mot de notre langue, que nous prononçons "Kanatha", signifie chef-lieu, ou ville principale).

Le retour de Domagaya et de Taignoagny effaça pour un moment la peine et l'inquiétude que leur enlèvement nous avaient causées. Toutefois, rien ne pouvait changer notre sentiment que ces étrangers avaient peine à dissimuler leur irrespect pour notre peuple. Dès les premiers instants, l'année précédente, ils s'étaient comportés comme si nos terres leur appartenaient, comme si notre existence les gênait. C'était très étrange, même incompréhensible. Cependant, depuis le retour des deux enfants de ma sœur (lesquels j'appelle mes fils, puisqu'ils sont de la lignée de notre mère), nous avions appris des choses bouleversantes au sujet des Français et autres peuples d'Europe, des choses qui auguraient mal pour la suite de leur présence chez nous et qui s'avérèrent encore plus néfastes dans les temps ultérieurs. Le « racisme », dont nous avons à parler, n'est qu'un aspect d'un problème beaucoup plus sérieux et grand, car il s'agit de la continuation de la vie même des enfants de nos descendants. Mais s'il faut commencer à nourrir ce feu[2], je vais dire comment je vois cette chose appelée « racisme ».

Le lendemain de leur retour, mes deux fils parlèrent en conseil de quantité de gens qu'ils avaient vus en France réduits à quémander un

---

[2] Expression amérindienne qui veut dire : tenir conseil, c'est-à-dire réchauffer les siens en partageant les richesses et les secrets de son cœur.

peu de nourriture à des compatriotes français à qui rien ne manquait, lesquels se montraient très souvent insensibles à la peine et à la misère de ces gens, qui étaient de leur propre peuple. Ils parlèrent d'une autre chose tout aussi monstrueuse, dont il me fut malheureusement donné de témoigner cette même année de 1535, puisque je fus moi aussi, en ce temps-là, capturé, comme un animal qu'on prend au piège, par Cartier et ses compagnons et emmené en France pour bientôt y mourir, de maladie et de chagrin. Cette expérience horrible fut d'observer que plus quelqu'un avait le teint foncé, plus il devait s'attendre à être traité durement et injustement par ses propres compatriotes au teint plus pâle que le sien. Les gens d'Afrique, qui sont par nature très foncés, sont dans ces contrées ordinairement esclaves de gens au visage un peu ou beaucoup plus pâle que le leur. Les paysans, eux, qui sont souvent basanés, doivent faire 1 000 courbettes devant d'autres qui s'appellent « nobles » et attendent d'eux ce respect forcé, qui doit s'accompagner d'une infinité de formules de politesse feinte, de gestes et de comportements serviles devenus comme naturels aux Français, mais qui, à nous, gens d'ici qui n'avons rien de plus cher que notre indépendance, nous inspirèrent toujours une grande pitié mêlée d'une colère que nous dûmes toujours contenir, vu notre état d'otages gardés en demi-liberté, comme des animaux dont la vie vaut plus que la perte. « Qu'adviendra-t-il de notre cher et pauvre peuple » ?, nous dîmes-nous des milliers de fois. Notre peuple a la peau comme l'écorce intérieure du bouleau blanc. Notre peuple qui a offert à ces hommes aux visages plus pâles que les siens le plus beau et le plus cher de lui-même sans pouvoir jamais toucher leur cœur. Notre peuple sans qui ces pauvres étrangers seraient morts comme des bébés laissés dehors, le premier hiver, avant notre enlèvement, qui eut lieu au mois des fleurs[3]... leur premier hiver qui fut notre dernier, puisque des dix que nous étions, nul ne revint jamais ici, chez nous.

Mahorah, ma fille, dit encore Donnacona, raconte, si tu veux, ce qui se passa lorsque, toute jeune fille, nos grands-mères voulurent unir les

---

[3] Mois de mai dans plusieurs langues amérindiennes.

Français et notre peuple et, par ma main, t'offrirent en mariage au sieur Jacques Cartier le 17 septembre 1535[4].

J'étais celle par qui les deux peuples devaient devenir un seul, tel que vous, mon oncle, l'aviez dit en m'offrant au capitaine Cartier. J'étais si jeune, et le destin que j'envisageais m'émouvait à l'extrême. Mon seul grand désir était de rester parmi les miens et de dédier toute ma vie à aider à créer une vie nouvelle et heureuse pour mon mari et pour son peuple. Ce jour-là fut le plus beau de ma vie, mais les suivants virent mon âme chavirer dans le malheur. La cérémonie de notre mariage fut si belle : jamais je n'avais vu tant de solennité, tant d'espoir et de joie sur les visages des miens. Pour m'exprimer leur affection et m'assurer de leur aide pour toujours, mes gens, tous les gens, me comblèrent de présents et des paroles les plus douces et les plus touchantes. J'étais heureuse, j'étais forte, j'étais prête. Nos Sages m'avaient dit d'avoir une patience, une tendresse infinies pour celui qui avait pris ma main devant tout mon peuple et devant mon oncle, Donnacona, notre Agouhanna (Sage et Premier Chef).

Lorsque vint le soir et qu'il fut temps de partir avec mon époux, il reprit ma main et me mena dans une barque, où je m'assis à son côté. Deux hommes ramèrent la barque jusqu'au bateau principal. Le sieur Cartier ne me regardait pas. Il conversait avec les deux rameurs et partageait avec eux des rires qui, pour quelque raison, me donnaient froid. Nous arrivâmes au bateau et on me fit monter la première, par une échelle de corde, sans m'aider, sans me parler. La nuit était fraîche et j'avais froid. Rendue à bord, je fus conduite à une pièce où quelques hommes dormaient et d'autres s'occupaient à différents travaux, certains à ce qui me semblait des jeux. L'odeur dans cette pièce, comme dans le bateau, était désagréable, voire étouffante. Mon mari me conduisit à une autre pièce très petite, m'y enferma, puis partit sans me regarder et ne revint plus de toute la nuit. Par un minuscule hublot, je voyais sur la grève de Stadaconé les feux de mes gens qui se réjouissaient. Je finis par m'endormir, l'âme inquiète.

---

4 Ce mariage eut vraiment lieu ce jour-là, à Québec. Personne ne s'y est jamais arrêté. J'en parle aujourd'hui pour la première fois dans l'histoire de notre pays.

Au milieu de la nuit, je fus éveillée par deux hommes ivres. Ils entrèrent où j'étais en vociférant. L'un d'eux, assez vieux et le regard méchant, voulut me pousser vers mon grabat. L'autre, plus jeune mais très laid, m'arracha à lui et me serra si fort que je criai, tentant de prononcer le nom de celui auquel je venais d'être mariée. Je ne m'attirai que des coups des deux hommes. Ils voulurent m'arracher mes vêtements, mas je me sauvai. Je montai vivement une échelle et réussis à trouver un petit recoin où, tremblante de peur et de froid, je passai le reste de la nuit. À l'aube, je réussis à me trouver un autre endroit où je restai cachée jusqu'au lendemain soir sans me faire voir. De ma cachette, je vis mon mari, visiblement fâché, qui me cherchait avec d'autres hommes. À la fin, ils abandonnèrent, croyant sûrement que j'avais sauté à la mer et nagé jusqu'à mon village. C'est ce que je fis lorsque vint la nuit. Arrivée à la grève, non loin de Stadaconé, je restai là de longues heures, presque sans vie. Je pus enfin me traîner jusqu'auprès de ma très vieille grand-mère, Taréma. J'appris que personne ne savait ce qui m'était arrivé. Ma grand-mère fut si triste que je pleurai longtemps, sans pouvoir m'arrêter, jusqu'à ce que je m'endorme. Je dormis très longtemps.

Mes deux frères capturés l'année antérieure par les mêmes hommes nous avaient dit, à leur retour, que les hommes blancs sont susceptibles d'utiliser leur force et leur statut de mâles pour violenter les femmes et les déshonorer. Ils ont été témoins en France que ces sortes de crimes restent impunis lorsque les victimes sont pauvres. Or puisque pauvreté, teint foncé et croyances différentes vont généralement ensemble, ces femmes sont des victimes de ce que l'on nomme « racisme », tout comme je sais maintenant très bien que je l'ai été, ainsi que mon peuple, de multiples autres façons.

Ce qui, cependant, mérite d'être remarqué par-dessus toute autre chose, en parlant de « racisme », est que celui-ci n'a pas existé ici avant l'arrivée des Européens. Nous aurions pu, lors de leur venue, craindre que nos relations avec eux pussent tôt ou tard tourner mal pour des causes qui font normalement s'opposer entre eux les humains, tel que nous l'étions alors aux Gens des Cinq-Nations, maintenant appelés les

Iroquois. Je veux dire à cause d'une envie pour des choses qu'une autre nation possède, ou pour une injure que l'on reçoit et que l'on ne juge réparable que par la guerre ou pour quelque erreur ou tromperie dont les humains sont si capables. Mais jamais n'aurions-nous pu penser être un jour méprisés, maltraités, volés à cause que nous ne croyons pas aux mêmes choses. Non, et d'ailleurs, je l'entendis dire pour la première fois par notre frère Lahontan : les choses monstrueuses dont nous parlons ici et qui ont justifié que ce même frère soit rappelé au Monde d'En-Bas pour aider nos descendants à les enrayer, ne nous furent pas connues avant le temps où vinrent les Gens plus pâles que nous.

Mahorah, soudain habitée d'une grande tristesse, cessa ici de parler. Le grand pacifiste tsonontouan Téganissorens se leva pour venir prendre, de ses mains, la pierre de parole. Le très grand et cher ami iroquois du huron Kondiaronk s'exprima ainsi :

Frères et sœurs, nous savons tous que ce grand mal maintenant appelé « racisme » par les enfants de nos descendants sur terre, même s'il est venu de la France et de l'Europe, n'a pas de relation avec la couleur plus pâle de la peau de nos parents européens. L'humain, comme tout dans la nature, est une créature du Grand Esprit, et rien dans la nature n'existe uniquement comme force du mal. La dureté et la douceur, le beau et le laid, le froid et le chaud, le clair et l'obscur s'équilibrent toujours et la vie triomphe tôt ou tard.

Nos chers ancêtres, dont nos oncles Donnacona, Domagaya et Taignoagny, et plusieurs autres qui virent la France, nous ont parlé d'un déséquilibre sérieux dont souffrent beaucoup de nos parents européens et d'autres continents. Lahontan, parmi nos autres frères et sœurs adoptifs, a souvent été éloquent sur ce sujet, et nous comprenons tous pourquoi c'est lui qui, cette fois-ci, ira transmettre le message de notre monde aux Gens de Terre. Ce débalancement vient d'une négation par l'homme de l'essence féminine dans sa société. La nature est une mère. L'homme d'Europe et ceux d'autres continents, pour des raisons certainement comprises par le Grand Esprit mais non par nous, se sont éloignés de cette Mère. Confiants en une fausse sécurité obtenue grâce à une exploitation excessive des dons matériels et de l'affection de leur Terre Mère, ils sont devenus insensibles et durs envers celle-ci. La femme, compagne de l'homme, naturellement plus liée et sensible que lui à la Terre, ne peut être indifférente à l'irrespect de l'homme pour la source de la vie de tous les êtres. L'homme, quant à lui, voit aussi la femme, cet être de la nature, comme une chose de plus à exploiter et à contrôler, donc à opprimer, ce qui revient à dire détruire. Cette société dénaturée est en guerre contre elle-même. En fait – et cela est au cœur de notre message –, le monde terrestre connaît une guerre qui va se globalisant. Cette guerre a de multiples formes, presque toutes rattachables aux luttes pour la suprématie économique et religieuse, mais elle est, en réalité, une guerre unique que les hommes font aux femmes, à la Terre et à tous les humains qu'ils parviennent à dominer, lesquels sont majoritairement de teint plus foncé que celui des Européens, c'est-à-dire ceux d'Europe et ceux d'Amérique. Le « racisme », ce comportement dominateur et oppresseur sanctionné par des lois injustes et par de condamnables religions, n'est, au fond, qu'une manifestation parmi beaucoup d'autres d'un problème beaucoup plus grave et plus grand car, comme l'a dit notre oncle Donnacona, il s'agit, en vérité, de la continuation de la vie même de nos descendants.

Les peuples sauvages ne méprisent, ni ne maltraitent, ni ne déshonorent leurs filles et leurs femmes, comme nous le vîmes faire à notre sœur Mahorah. Nos mères, nos filles, nos femmes sont les maîtresses de nos foyers, de nos villages et même de nos pays. Nos sœurs nées Françaises, ici présentes, ont toutes décidé de devenir et de demeurer Sauvagesses à cause de la grande liberté qu'elles ont trouvée chez nous et de l'autorité et du respect qu'elles ont connus en devenant nôtres. D'ailleurs, nos Anciens nous ont tant de fois parlé du profond et cruel ressentiment que conçurent les Robes Noires envers nos vénérables et regrettées aïeules à cause du respect dont ils virent celles-ci être l'objet parmi nos peuples et à cause de l'autorité qu'ils les virent posséder et exercer. Ces hommes censés bons et sages virent même en cela une preuve finale d'un empire absolu du « Diable » sur notre existence, et nous traitèrent en conséquence.

À ce moment, Téganissorens capta le signe qu'une femme voulait parler. Il se leva et alla lui porter l'esprit de la pierre. « Parlez, ma sœur. Pour moi, j'ai dit tout ce que je désirais dire. Je vois aussi que mon frère Lahontan s'apprête à faire son voyage vers le merveilleux monde de nos descendants. »

Mon nom avait été Marie Dupré de Longlac, dit une femme aux traits dont la sérénité étonnait, même dans ce monde d'esprits. À dix hivers, la guerre m'avait rendue orpheline et je suis devenue Huronne du clan du cerf. Ma mère, voyant que j'aimais être toujours occupée, me donna le nom de son arrière-grand-mère maternelle, qui nous quitta cette année-là. Je devins Nyandakon, Celle-qui-marche-toujours. Ma première vie chez mes parents français avait semblé me promettre à une existence bien commune, une vie de paysanne vite et totalement chargée d'une nombreuse progéniture et complètement soumise à un mari autoritaire, comme toutes les Françaises ordinaires. Devenue Huronne, je fus destinée par ma mère et les autres femmes de notre *owachira* (famille clanique étendue) à occuper une place importante dans notre clan et dans notre village. Je n'eus que deux enfants, de deux mariages différents, et, à 35 hivers, on me demanda de commencer à siéger au Conseil des Anciennes, où l'on cultiva une habileté que j'avais souvent montrée pour la cause de la paix et de l'expansion du commerce de notre nation. Peut-être avais-je eu ce don de patience et de pacifisme à cause des tragédies qui détruisirent ma première famille et tant d'autres, parmi tous les peuples du Canada sans exception.

Je connus, au cours de ma vie de Huronne, de nombreuses femmes européennes capturées jeunes par les Sauvages. Je n'en vis jamais aucune qui ne fût pas, avec le temps, devenue heureuse dans sa vie de Sauvagesse et qui voulût retourner à son peuple européen d'origine, toute libre qu'elle fût de le faire. Plusieurs de ces femmes sont ici même à ce feu et sont de ce village. Mes frères et mes oncles qui ont parlé avant moi ont parlé avec sagesse et bienveillance. Le mal dont nous avons à libérer nos chers descendants n'a pas de racines en terre huronne, iroquoise, siouse ou algonquine. Cette chose monstrueuse et néfaste, à laquelle on a donnée le nom de « racisme », vient, tel que l'a dit notre frère Téganissorens, de la tyrannie des pères. Je me souviens d'un très beau feu tenu dans notre village au temps où j'étais jeune femme, aux premiers jours de mon premier amour, à la saison où le soleil commence à amollir la neige. Mon oncle Lahontan avait aussi nouvellement trouvé l'amour de ma cousine Kiwaydinokwé, la beauté nipissingue que, jeune enfant, son peuple avait donnée au mien pour reconsacrer notre antique amitié avec lui. Mon oncle, en ces beaux jours terrestres, partageait un bonheur semblable au mien. Je me souviens que les Sages, à ce feu, s'entretinrent longuement sur le sujet de la domination imposée par l'homme sur la femme. Comment l'homme peut-il créer une société saine, prospère et heureuse, dirent les Sages, alors qu'il se fait la guerre à lui-même, c'est-à-dire à son complément, qui est la femme ? Je me souviens que cette discussion fut reprise à de nombreux feux, tant locaux que publics, pendant longtemps, et qu'une bonne partie de la sagesse de ce temps, que l'on continuera toujours d'honorer, fut assise sur ce principe sauvage et amériquain de l'égalité et de la complémentarité des hommes et des femmes, qui ne sont, en réalité, que les deux moitiés d'un même être humain.

Cette remémoration de ma chère nièce Nyandakon me toucha très spécialement puisqu'elle me fit me replonger en pensée au temps de ce feu, si magique pour mon jeune cœur s'éveillant à l'amour et si important parce qu'il commença à causer un grand et durable rapprochement de toutes nos gens qui, plus que jamais auparavant, trouvèrent un sens à cette grande aventure amériquaine dans laquelle le Grand Maître (et la Grande Maîtresse) (Dieu, si vous voulez) nous avait tous placés. Je me souviens que ma plume qui, en ces temps, manquait d'encre souvent, en trouva, par ce feu, une quantité qui ne s'épuisa jamais.

Il fallut à ce moment que je parte pour cet important voyage, décidé au Pays des Âmes, en réponse à votre appel à l'aide, chers amis et descendants sur cette belle et merveilleuse Terre. Je ne partis pas, toutefois, sans aller embrasser, dans notre logis, ma belle et très chère Kiwaydinokwé, celle qui fit de moi un Huron pour toujours. Eh bien, chers frères et sœurs, nous avons quelque temps pour tout remettre à l'endroit. Commençons notre travail ! Voici de l'encre et des plumes. Nous allons écrire contre le racisme.

China's Northern Ethnic Minorities and Canada's Aboriginal Peoples: How Both Countries Can Inspire and Help Each Other[*]

Dear friends and relatives:

It is, indeed, a rare joy to be once again with colleagues and friends who once received me, my wife and my son so warmly, six years ago, here in their beautiful Chinese and Inner Mongolian land and here in this unique and great University of Inner Mongolia. Once again, I get the magical feeling that the physical distance separating homelands of peoples becomes somewhat of an illusion when the heart is touched by the warmth of other hearts. And being here and meeting my Chinese friends once more confirms to me the truth of my

---

[*] Keynote address given at the special Symposium on Comparative Studies between Amerindians and China's Northern Ethnic Groups organized by the Inner Mongolia University, Hohhot, China, July 11–13, 2002. In spite of recurrent political troubles between the country and some of its ethnic minorities (and in this, China is certainly not alone as a nation-state that has indigenous people and/or vulnerable minorities among its citizenry), this author wishes to respectfully suggest that it is wise to look deeper and see whether China has some things to teach other nation-states as to relationship with such minorities.

people's own saying: "Friends one day, friends forever". I feel it as one of life's special gifts to be reunited with my friends Vice-President of the University of Inner Mongolia and Professor Hugjiltu and Professor Xu Bingxun, and with Mr. Zhao Yung and our new friend, Mrs. Song Min, who visited me and my family two months ago in our Canadian home, and my young fellow-historian Wang Songtao, and many more people whom we have met in this great and friendly Autonomous Region of Inner Mongolia. I am, indeed, very grateful for this invitation to Inner Mongolia University and for the constant effort of Professors Xu and Hugjiltu and their colleagues to keep alive the vision that we share; that is, the vision of causing our respective countries to expand their knowledge about their ethnic minorities—in this instance, the ones of their northern regions—and to allow these Chinese and Canadian minorities to deepen their appreciation of their similitudes and particularities. In this way, both countries stand to be enriched and strengthened by the development of the unique and sometimes largely untapped human potential possessed by their northern peoples and other ethnic minorities. As Professor Hugjiltu writes in his preface of the Chinese translation of my book *For an Amerindian Autohistory*, "there is a need for in-depth exploration of the commonalities shared by northern Amerindians and Mongols and other northern Chinese in the areas of linguistics, social and cultural anthropology, genetics, and so on".

For many years, I have been an admirer of the Chinese, and I would like to tell you why. Because of the antiquity of their civilization, the Chinese are capable of a high degree of acceptance of their minorities, and therefore often refer to their global society as "a family of peoples". As a member of a Canadian Aboriginal nation, I believe that my country, as well as many others, must reflect on this. I first came to China in 1996, in my function as Academic Dean of the Saskatchewan Indian Federated College at the University of Regina. In coming to China, my two mandates were to visit Chinese institutions of higher education for Chinese ethnic minorities, and to reactivate agreements signed several years before by our respective institutions to foster the exchange of students and academic personnel and to create and sign other exchange agreements with other Chinese institutions of higher education for minority nationalities. During that five-week trip, accompanied by my wife and my nine-year-old son, I visited the Central University for Minorities in Beijing, the South-Central University for Minorities in Wuhan, a Cultural Institute of the Naxi nationality in Lijiang and this University of Inner Mongolia. Apart from the academic work, which was very stimulating, I was able to meet and warmly exchange over wonderful, friendly meals with many scholars from a vast array of minority peoples. They also were active in every academic discipline, from linguistics to engineering, to architecture, to anthropology, to nuclear physics and so forth. To me, this was the beginning of a revelation. On the other hand, I also began to comprehend why we, on our own Canadian side, were not able yet to respond to the opportunity of the intended academic exchanges. From my viewpoint as the Academic Dean of the only Aboriginal university-level college in Canada, I saw the road ahead as a very long and rather lonely one, at least for an initial time.

I wish to come back to the words I just used: the beginning of a revelation. I remember hearing my mother remark, when I was maybe twelve, "The Chinese say that they cannot afford to waste a single brain." And she mused on: "When one thinks that they have so many people." It is, of course, quite normal, when you are a proud and therefore a downtrodden Indian, to find a defence for your people in the example or in the words of some other people, especially as powerful as or more powerful than your oppressor. And to illustrate the great value that Indians have traditionally put on education, as well as how deeply felt were my mother's words, I must tell you that at that moment my mother only had a grade six education, but that much later on, at sixty-eight years old, she became the first Canadian Amerindian woman to earn a PhD in Amerindian philosophy and spirituality. It would also take many years before I got my first opportunity to go to China and find out whether, and how genuinely, its practice matched its reputation in terms of giving its ethnic minorities access to higher education.

As Dean of Academics I had taken a vivid interest in the Chinese connection that our college had created years before, jointly with the Chinese, and especially in the very serious efforts made by the latter to reactivate the initial commitment by coming to our college several times over the years of my deanship.

My colleagues and I were always very impressed by the high professional and personal quality of all of the delegates, who invariably represented several different national minorities of their country as well as the Han majority. I made it part of my professional functions to help plan and arrange the visits of those Chinese delegations to our college, to Indian reserves, as well as to cultural and academic events occurring in the surrounding region. I guided those officials and attended to their needs during all of their visits, and they reciprocated with the greatest kindness and warmth, as well as cordially inviting our own people and colleagues to visit their country and educational institutions for their national minorities. As required by their national tradition, they also always gave presents to their Canadian counterparts and to dignitaries, among which were our Indian Elders, or sages. In that way, I personally received many fine cultural objects, always given most humbly and respectfully, and also several books (most of which I unfortunately cannot read, since they are in Chinese, which lack I hope to remedy some day), and films describing China's educational and developmental work in relation to their minorities. One of the authors I thus discovered was the great Chinese anthropologist Fei Hsiao Tung, former president of the Chinese Association of Sociological Research, who dedicated much of his professional and personal life to the social, cultural and economic advancement of the Chinese national minorities in the immediate wake of the Chinese Liberation. Born in 1910, Professor Fei was trained in social anthropology at the London School of Economics. Reading part of Professor Fei's writings on the People's Republic of China's goals, accomplishments and social philosophy in relation to its ethnic minorities has answered many questions I had had about China's vision of itself as a multinational modern state. I have realized how serious that country is about creating a harmonious society internally if it is to become a world leader in every important respect in times to come. I am now convinced that China lives by Shou-En-Lai's precept of "divided, we all suffer; united, we all prosper". "China," explains Fei Hsiao Tung, "is trying to achieve modernization in her own way, and in the process, is paying full attention to the fact that she has many nationalities and doing her best to reduce and eventually eliminate the cultural and economic differences among them."[1] "The Han people,"[2] write Professors Xu Bingxun and Wang Songtao in their beautiful book, *Inner Mongolia*,[3] "are encouraged to respect the social customs of the minority peoples, and usually live in harmony with Mongols and other minorities and bear in mind the utmost importance of the unity of nationalities." "As a matter of fact," remark the two authors, "a new concept of mutual dependency has taken root in the hearts of all these different nationalities."[4] One of the greatest honours I have ever received is to be asked by my colleague and *gege* (elder brother) Ben (Professor Xu Bingxun), of this university, in 1996, if I would allow him to translate my first book, and then to receive from him several copies of the actual book in Chinese, a brief four years later. Now, that is an act of a rare spirit! What determination! What commitment and what belief!

If I say all this about my brother Ben, it is not primarily because that translation represented a huge task, besides his myriad other tasks, or because it was a difficult translation—which it indeed was, as I know that many words, concepts and realities contained in it are not readily translatable to Chinese. If I am taking this opportunity to publicly acknowledge him, it is really because that book is a tough, bold book which, even though it has brought me surprising notoriety in North America and even worldwide as an Amerindian historian and philosopher, has encountered a high degree of resistance, often downright rejection, from various schools of historical and ethnological thought in Canada and North America. Why? Because one of its basic postulates is that the world view that is native to America and that I demonstrate to be more attuned to natural laws and true human needs than others transported there from Europe, has superior survival value than those same foreign thought systems. That is the reason that I have been so gratified by the intellectual gesture of the Inner Mongolia University when it proposed and undertook to translate my book, and that is why I shall forever commend the intellectual openness and honesty

---

1 F. H. Tung, *Toward a People's Anthropology* (Beijing : New World Press, 1981), p. 86.

2 The largest nationality in China, with approximately 92 percent of the total Chinese population.

3 Xu Bingxun and Wang Songtao, *Inner Mongolia* (Hohhot : Inner Mongolia University Press, 2002).

4 Ibid., p. 23.

of Professor Xu, a great and true scholar. That translation allowed my ideas to break out of the North American context where they had been and continue to be enthusiastically received by many publics, both in French and in English, but where they were and continue to be reproved by the academic establishment, on mere ideological (and not academic) grounds. In other words, what caused my joy about the Chinese translation by Inner Mongolia University is that at long last, I and many other thinkers and scholars (both Amerindian and non-Amerindian) could feel that a vital connection had been made with a very important country of a faraway continent, so far removed from America both physically and ideologically that a healthy, normal scholarly discussion could be, if not simply initiated, then enlivened, on topics that are of direct interest and concern to Canadian Aboriginal people and people from the fifty-six Chinese nationalities, and that truly integrate these ethnic minorities into the debate. Before getting to the heart of my topic, I need to express to you how I feel about the way it has been between us Amerindian people and Canada, the country that has formed around us and that is ours in so many special ways. As you well know, it has been very tough going, but there is also a lot of good to be said, and a lot of very worthy and exciting challenges to take up for any and all of us. First of all, Canada is a new country. Because of the quite severe initial demographic upsetting that the First Peoples have undergone through no real fault of the European incomers (except in a few war-related contexts, such as the willful spreading of smallpox among our people by means of infected blankets during the war led against the British by Odawa Chief Pontiac), Canada has very rapidly grown to be quite wealthy. If it had not been for European pathogens (microbes), it would have been easy for our peoples to maintain their demographic advantage and to uphold their life ways and social systems, and to forcibly or willingly integrate the newcomers into their own societies and cultures. However, the catastrophic impact of the epidemic diseases and the consequent speedy implantation on our soil of completely foreign thought systems soon made our people be seen and treated as a problem and an embarrassment for the White people in their glorious march towards 'progress'. Our passive and sometimes active resistance was seen as a sign of stupidity, and racist treatment and behaviour at the hands of the immigrants became the usual fare and expectation of our people. The Canadian state left it in the care of various Canadian churches to devise and implement educational philosophies and systems, which had the very deleterious effect of solidly entrenching that racism in the minds of a great number of Canadians, besides, of course, the other destructive effect of drastically undermining our capacity to maintain our existence as First Peoples. We are still very much in that condition.

However, in the past decade or so, Canadian churches and governments have begun to see the great damage that past policies and practices have caused to Canadian society, and particularly to Canadian Aboriginal people. A report produced in 1996 by the Royal Commission on Aboriginal Peoples revealed a dismal picture. The stark reality is that Aboriginal Peoples in Canada are engaged in a final stage of cultural extinction. To illustrate this: it is scientifically quite likely that fifty out of the fifty-three surviving Amerindian languages will no longer be spoken within only one more generation. Also, I could go into the horrible statistics of Aboriginal youth suicide, Aboriginal incarceration or Aboriginal longevity, but I have wanted to concentrate on what we can do together to find solutions.

As I already remarked, Canada is a rich country, and I would not stand for Canada being accused of stinginess when it comes to attempting to redress the condition of its Aboriginal citizens and avert or remedy the social catastrophes that loom in the not-too-distant future, or are already happening. If one looks at the statistics of the financial assistance provided by Canada to Aboriginal organizations for all kinds of purposes, one is bound to be impressed and likely commend the government and revert to blaming the First Peoples for not having the will or the good sense to get out of their misery amidst such governmental generosity and cleverness.

What I really mean to say here is that my country, Canada, has the means and also very good intentions in regard to the preservation and the advancement of its Aboriginal nations, but that it needs to elaborate a vision to see those good intentions bear fruit. What I am humbly suggesting, based on my personal and professional experience, is that when one opens up to someone else's views and ways of doing, the inspiration one gets is often magical and sometimes miraculous. I am an academic in my own right and I have come to China before and have felt true, genuine sympathy from the Chinese for my Amerindian and Aboriginal people. I have gained some knowledge about China's own vision in relation to its ethnic minorities and have long reflected on how my country and China could and should work together and inspire each other. In my own personal estimation, no other country possessing Aboriginal, indigenous or minority cultures has as clear an idea about where, why and how it wants to meet its future with that segment of its citizenry as China has; I also estimate that no other country has such a rich background of experience as regards its ethnic minorities as China has. Consequently, there are some things that I wish to see happen in respect of the foregoing. I see it as very important, indeed vital, and potentially very productive as well as mutually beneficial in every way for both countries, that efforts and resources be allocated by both countries, in proportion to their respective capability, to allow educational and other leaders of their respective nationalities and peoples to meet and reflect together on what policies, what assistance, mostly what vision espoused by their respective central/federal governments are capable of promoting the welfare, development, productivity and happiness of the ethnic minorities/Aboriginal peoples, instead of their under-development, unhappiness and disappearance from the human cultural scene.

As I am touching on the topic of cultural enhancement versus governmental neglect, I would like to share with you a personal reflection that has stayed alive in me ever since I visited Chinese minority regions, people and educational institutions six years ago. I am aware that my words can be interpreted as an idealization of the Chinese way of interacting with its minority nationalities. However, I believe in my right and my duty to express what I have felt when I came here, because my honest purpose is to help construct 'better-being' for my weak, worried Huron and Indian people, and for the whole human collectivity. What particularly struck me upon meeting and exchanging with the numerous national minorities academics and professionals I met during that first five-week trip and what has even made me feel envy, as a Canadian Indian, was that there was in them and around them a complete absence of that painful stress of knowing that as you speak, as you breathe and live, your own people are disappearing, every day closer to the end. Again, there is always the danger of generalizing and idealizing, but I do feel that I have to reveal to you that the stress of feeling your own kind disappearing is a weight that traditional Amerindians constantly feel and carry in their hearts and souls.

I now wish to lay special emphasis on the development of education as the single, most determining factor whereby minorities are made to feel included in a country's life and march towards its future. An official Chinese *Survey of China's Policies Regarding the National Minorities* (1995) informs us that the population of minorities has tripled since Liberation—that is, in roughly fifty years. Reading that document and others, one easily sees that the way China goes about effecting internal unity among its family of fifty-six nationalities is truly and genuinely through affording all of them every possible means to access quality education at all levels, especially at the higher ones, as a way of developing each nationality's economic potential. I personally have long held that Canada, a country rich in resources as well as in an Aboriginal heritage, should foster the creation of Aboriginal colleges and universities in every one of its regions, thus enabling Aboriginal people to have access to high-quality, high-calibre training in every field. When I and others have spoken about this, on various occasions and in many places throughout our country, we have been wholeheartedly supported by large numbers of non-Aboriginal and Aboriginal Canadians. Again, opening up to views and ways of others, especially successful ones, such as China in this instance, can be extremely beneficial for a young country like Canada that needs and strives to attain a vision leading to 'harmony' and 'mutual dependency' in relation to its Aboriginal nations. As for China, it has created, in about fifty years since Liberation, thirteen colleges, specialized schools and universities for its minority and ethnic nationalities. In 1994, China could boast of having already trained two million national minority cadres, of which 75 percent had received an education "higher than senior middle school, 40 percent were under the age of 40 and 26 percent were women". "In national autonomous areas," says the same source, "the proportion of national minority cadres is constantly on the increase."[5] I wish to further clarify my thinking by stating my belief that the greatest survival value for any people

---

[5] *A Survey of China's Policies Regarding the National Minorities*, issued by the Government of the Peoples' Republic of China, 1995, pp. 186–191.

lies in education, for it allows individuals to feel personally and collectively valued, as well as included in things much greater than just themselves and their communities. This said, I know quite well that I stand to be educated by others, among which I include my Chinese friends, about things that my own country, Canada, does better or has the potential of doing better than China or other countries. As an individual from one of the many endangered Canadian Aboriginal peoples, I am often too involved in my own people's struggle to be able to appreciate the positive things that may be there close to me. And increasing one another's awareness in that sense is also a form of mutual help that comes with communication.

Now that I have exposed my views as to the importance for both Canada and China of working together to find ever better ways to utilize and develop the human potential represented in the cultural and intellectual heritage of their ethnic and Aboriginal minorities, I wish to address more directly the topic that is central to this symposium: that is, the development of comparative studies between the Canadian and the Chinese northern ethnic minorities. I think it is no accident that this symposium is occurring in this northern Chinese region of Inner Mongolia. Indeed, Canada being a northern country, there are obvious reasons why many of its Aboriginal people would view Inner Mongolia and adjacent northern spaces in China as visually, materially and climatically similar to their own familiar, Canadian northern landscapes. And of course, northerners of all regions share ways of feeling, thinking, living and doing, all reflected in their cosmology, their beliefs and their value systems.

The North is the new and the last earthly frontier. Modern technology now enables man to search for and extract the earth's resources in any northern region where they may exist, disregarding Nature's harshest and most subtle laws. In Canada, there is a lot of economic activity in the North and this will go on for several decades. "Go north, young man" is a common saying, which many people have already heeded. Big money will soon have upset the ecological balance in our beautiful, wonderful North. And consequently, big money will soon have irreversibly perturbed, if not destroyed, the wonderful cultures of peoples who have learned to co-exist with all the other beings that make up the great, sacred Circle of Life. As in many other regions the world over, Aboriginal peoples of the Canadian North are made to choose from among plans of so-called development of their land the ones that appear least destructive of the way of life it took them many thousands of years to patiently, scientifically elaborate. Some of the 'big money' is then made to fall into the hands of our northern Aboriginal brothers and sisters, but I wish to leave it up to you, up to us as a collectivity of academics and humanists, to observe, investigate and decide whether that money, which may appear abundant, is being used or will be used to foster and promote the true well-being of northern Aboriginal people in Canada. I have personally lived and worked in the North—I maintain very strong links with my fellow Aboriginal people there—and I, among many other professionals and people of all walks of life, am extremely worried about what has been happening to those northern Aboriginal communities. The rapid deterioration of their physical and mental health is a cause for much immediate concern.

Bringing a different perspective, when approaching those realities, is of vital importance for the true interests of both of our countries. I believe that the creation of a branch of Comparative Studies between our respective northern ethnic minorities is imperative. In the course of becoming friends and colleagues and of learning how we can assist and inspire one another, as well as other citizens of both our countries, we are bound to discover wondrous intimate links and common traits shared by northern peoples of our two countries. We do know that common ancestors of Mongols, Daur, Wenki, Oroquen and certainly many others hunted and lived together and intermarried in remote epochs, at times here in Asia and at other times in northern North America. We need to create and expand studies of our deeper history on both sides and thus, possibly, let the people of the last frontier, the northern peoples, show the world the path of our spiritual and mental unity as humankind. I could not possibly find a more meaningful and beautiful a way to express this idea than by quoting the words of my brother and colleague Professor Hugjiltu in his preface to my book:

As man is rapidly evolving, as we are creating material progress, we have an even greater need to build the mansions of ethical progress. Material modern life is created by human beings, but mankind should never destroy its most beautiful possession using the excuse of the need to modernize. That beautiful possession is the splendid and excellent traditions created, protected and developed by all peoples and all nations in the long course of human history.[6]

Dear friends and relatives, let us use the reality of our deep human brotherhood and create, here in this strong, beautiful, ancient land of Inner Mongolia, the new fire that will strengthen and enrich our common human soul with the wise knowledge of our common ancestors telling us that we indeed are a great family of peoples and nations. I am convinced that concrete efforts such as this symposium on Canadian and Chinese northern ethnic minorities and Aboriginal peoples, is a timely and intelligent gesture to help our two countries initiate a new era of spiritual and intellectual globalization of the world.

In closing, I once again wish to thank wholeheartedly the Inner Mongolia University, and particularly Vice-President Hugjiitu, for keeping the vision alive and realizing this very important symposium. Thank you for the great honour of your invitation. Thalerhala! [Thank you in Mongol] Xie-xie! [Thank you in Chinese] Attouguet! [Thank you in Wendat!]

Friends and relatives, I give you my warmest thanks for listening to me.

---

6 Quoted by Professor Hugjiltu in his preface to the book *Comparative Studies Between Amerindians and Northern Ethnic Groups in China* (Proceedings of the July 2002 Conference), p. 12.

FAIS-TOI HURON (BECOME A HURON): AMERICIZING AMERICA*

It is both a real pleasure and a privilege to be back in this beautiful city of Chicago, which I have always found humanly warm and friendly. Nine years ago does, indeed, feel like yesterday, because of the many wonderful memories which we keep, as a family, such as the joys of exploring these pretty surroundings with our little boy of five years old, of listening to the greatest jazz music in the world and of making exceptionally good friends such as Helen Tanner, Olive Dickason, Francis (Fritz) Jennings, Fred Hoxie, Alfonso Ortiz, Henry Dobyns, Jay Miller, Torao Tomita, Corky McClerkin and truly, many others. What a marvelous, magical time! We love Chicago!

Also, what a joy to be back at one of the world's greatest, richest libraries, the Newberry. I feel so thankful for the existence of that scholars' and learners' paradise, and to the ones who once enabled me to spend such fine and valuable

---

* Presentation at the Conference "Indian-French Encounters in New France", held at the Newberry Library, Chicago, February 22–24, 2001.

time here. I also deem it a great privilege to visit with the Alliance française and to get acquainted with its community. Finally, I am very happy to be here, at this exciting Symposium, with my two friends and distinguished colleagues, David Buisseret and Laurier Turgeon. And what a pleasure to be reunited here, after nine years, with my Turtle clan-sister Helen Tanner and other old friends (I am realizing one can still be young and be an old friend). My many special thanks go to Caria Zecher and her excellent team, who have used such kindness and patience to achieve this unique gathering.

Dear friends:

As a Huron-Wyandot, a Native American nation which destiny (I, of course, mean the Great Spirit) placed in the colonial alliance of the French, the theme and object of this Symposium are of special interest to me. One thing peculiar to my people's history of contact with the Europeans is that the Wendat (named "Huron" by the French), having been centrally situated in the pre-European geopolitics of the Northeast, were chosen by the French to be their first and main Native ally. Having secured the very powerful and very populous Wendat-Algonkian alliance, the French, even though the less powerful European contender, could realistically foresee that they would gain hegemony over the Dutch, and then, from 1664, the British, in Northeastern North America. Most likely, you and I would be speaking French and Huron today. Quite unfortunately for all of them, however, the unforeseen effect of the new presence here of European pathogens was the speedy disintegration of the Wendat and other powerful confederacies and nations of the region. This truly spelled the end of France's ability to create a French empire in North America. As a traditional Huron-Wyandot (U.S. rendition of the word Wendat), I will, therefore, speak as an historical ally of the French. I will also speak as a professional historian.

But first, I must say that because Indians have a conception of time which is absolutely different from the European understanding of time, an Indian cannot write or express orally such a thing as conventional, linear History. The thing that is named "the past" is a European construct and is not part of the

Amerindian psyche. To Indians generally, History becomes a reflection on values and values are inextricably connected to the laws of Nature, observed since the beginning of time, so to speak, and without interruption. In that regard, the interest taken by Indians in aspects of history, such as the relations between Indians and French in New France, will be different from the way Euro-americans are interested in the same aspect of history. For a traditional Amerindian, everything that takes place has to be looked at in reference to the laws of Nature. These laws being immutable, it is impossible to look at an aspect of history as something frozen within an interruption of time, because what happened then, or what is happening right now, at every moment, determines how we and all of us are going to live in times to come. Yesterday is today and tomorrow is yesterday: time is one, life is one. Living carries a spiritual responsibility and History has to be elevated to the status of moral reflection, because everything and every event has to be looked at in reference to Nature's laws.

All along, our societies have faced an ideological impasse because of our different understanding of time, of history, therefore, of life. As to myself, in order to elaborate a common ground where we can come and reflect together, I have devised an approach to history which I have named the method of Amerindian Autohistory. It is offered as an alternative to the old historiographical paradigm of "who did what to whom, when, how and why," and to help us shed all the negative feelings that come with that old mindset and that paralyze our humanity, on both sides of the racial divide, and which should not exist in the first place. It contains an important key proposition: the role of America's First Peoples is to "Americize America".

In December 1989, Les Presses de l'Université Laval published my Master's dissertation with the title, *Pour une autohistoire amérindienne. Essai sur les fondements d'une morale sociale.* In the summer of 1988, I had come to the Newberry Library to attend Seminars and do research as a first-year doctoral candidate and had had my first opportunity to discuss my professional theories in a larger, world-class setting. Not so accustomed then to the non-Amerindian world taking a serious interest in our traditional Amerindian historical views, I was pleasantly surprised to find myself helping to feed a different, more universalistic discussion about those ideas. In 1990, I completed a preliminary English translation of my book and sent a copy here to Fred Hoxie, who shared it with Duane Champagne, at UCLA, and others. Fred, Duane, Helen Tanner and others gave me more feedback, which greatly helped me to think from a wider perspective. I then knew that the world could listen, wanted to listen. I had found my place. I had found hope for my people and for myself.

I began to feel positively challenged by the debate which I was helping to create, especially by the resistance in some non-Amerindian thinkers to my formulation of the old Amerindian concept of the historical, ongoing responsibility of the Native American to "Americize America", that is, to impart a deeper sense of spiritual rooting in the non-Native society, as an attempt to break down racial and religious barriers that have too often kept us divided from one another. This Amerindian concept is contained in two words that form part of the original title of my MA dissertation and were left out of the book title in French and of subsequent translations (so far, in English, Chinese and Japanese). Those two words are: "properly American", from the original MA dissertation title which translates in English as: *For an Amerindian Autohistory. Essay on the Foundations of a Properly American Social Ethics.* Why were these two words left out? We can simply guess that the thought that Canada's or the United States' social ethics *may* not be Canadian, or American, does not come naturally at all to the average reader in our countries, nor is it likely to strike the editorial Board of a mainstream North American University Press as carrying much commercial potential. To me, however, the text is not well circumscribed if these two words are not included in the title. For me, it is a question of not making a compromise on the essentials of my people's discourse. However, an author does have to consider the realities of the publishing world, which means to be ready to make compromises in order to be published.

The concept of *"le Bon sauvage"* or "The Noble Redman" has sprung essentially from and been cultivated by the French genius. As a Huron, a people which has otherwise had a deeply painful historical experience with its European counterpart, the French, I take a very vivid interest in the legacy that has originated in the philosophical exchange between my people and the French. The reason for my interest has very little to do with the romanticism with which history and literature have characterized our relationship with the French at the ideological level. My interest has its real connection with ongoing, present-day, historically uninterrupted concerns, which all Aboriginal people have about their own struggle with a restrained existence and about the global welfare of all of us who compose the Great Circle of Life.

In his *Dialogues avec un sauvage*, published in the early 1700s, the Baron de Lahontan has the exasperated Huron chief Kondiaronk (Adario in the *Dialogues*) reply to his constant, insistent entreaties to become French and Christian: "My brother, believe what you will, have as much faith as it pleases you, you will never go to the Good Land of Souls unless you become a Huron". A lot has been written and keeps being written to deny the authenticity of Lahontan's *Dialogues* with Adario. On this, I will say one thing: as a Huron born from four traditional Huron-Wyandot grandparents, the essential dialogue reported in Lahontan's writings has always been part of our ongoing historical and philosophical reflection, and way of thinking and feeling as Hurons. I am, therefore, not concerned about the form which Lahontan has given to his *Dialogues* with Adario and many other "philosophes nuds" (naked philosophers), Huron and Algonkian: my own soul knows that the sense of the argumentation is authentically ours.

It was primarily their encounter with the Huron that provided the French with new sources of ideas which they, more than other Europeans, were culturally predisposed to welcome and utilize. I have suggested, in my book *Amerindian Autohistory*, that the French Revolution has direct origins in the thought of Chief Kondiaronk and of his Wendat and Algonkian congeners. It, of course, took time before these new "wild American ideas" found their way and their place into the psyche of the French populace. Upon publishing his *Dialogues*, in Holland, Lahontan had to become an expatriate and was excommunicated by the Catholic Church in his native France.

However, the French idea of *"le Bon sauvage"* antedates Lahontan. It seems that the Wendat world, early on in their American adventure, struck the French as a social configuration from which they were able to draw acceptable analogies with what they thought of as an ideal society at the time, that is, a monarchical setup *"en puissance"*, with potential for familiar social stratification. Upon first assessing the geopolitics of the Northeast, the Jesuits, in the early

1630s wrote that the Huron were the aristocracy of the land, while the Iroquois were the nobility and the hunters, such as the Algonkians, the peasantry. Here, I must hasten to say that the Huron, as to them, had a contrary view about such order. I have explained in my second book, *Huron-Wendat. The Heritage of the Circle* that the Huron, having, like all Aboriginal societies, a spiritualistic world view, saw the hunting peoples at the top of the overall social order and saw themselves in a lower grade because of a perceived loss, by farmers, of an ideal state of proximity to the spirits of animals and the supernatural realm as a whole.

In 1535, one century before the Jesuits, Jacques Cartier credited himself with having discovered the "Kingdom of Canada", in the name of the King of France. The people of Stadacona (today's Quebec City) talked to the explorer about their "Kanatha" meaning their chief-town, which Cartier at once fancied to mean a whole country, his famed "Kingdom of Canada", of which Stadacona was the capital. The Indians that he associated to that town were the Stadaconas, cultural and linguistic kin, and political allies of the Wendat, then living in present-day Ontario, some one hundred miles or so north of Toronto. In his journal, Cartier named Donnacona, Headman of Stadacona, "Lord of Canada". In 1534, Cartier and his men saw in the people of "Canada" an ingenuous and generous people, who saved them from annihilation through scurvy and who obviously were moved to help the French survive that winter by a noble heart, rather than by interest. Even though Cartier paid them back with arrogance and deceit (he was there, after all, to conquer any heathen power he encountered), the memory of Canada's Kingdom lived on after him in France, as well as the memory of that kingdom's non-existent gold, diamonds and other riches, an invention of Cartier attempting to convince the French royalty to send him back in an obsessive search of a passage to the Orient and its wealth.

Because of what Cartier and his men saw on the Saint Lawrence in 1534 and on his two subsequent voyages, in 1535 and 1541, Canada began to germinate in the minds of Frenchmen. When France sent Samuel de Champlain to found New France, in 1603, the aboriginal country of "Kanatha" had ceased to be. Its inhabitants had been displaced through epidemics and the political upheaval that followed Cartier's upsetting visits. Archaeology has revealed that most of the Stadaconans and other Laurentians had resettled among or close to the Wendat in Wendake (the "Huronia" known by the French). Champlain eventually found the trace and the location of the ancient inhabitants of Cartier's Canada. To Champlain and his fellow Frenchmen, they were now the "Huron", with whom Champlain quickly understood he had to strike up an alliance, for they were the people at the heart of a vast Aboriginal commonwealth, which was to be the foundation for any ascendancy that France was to have in North America. And more for worse than for better, the great Wendat-Algonkian Alliance was to remain unfailingly loyal to the French.

Among the clerics who knew the Huron most intimately is Recollet Friar Gabriel Sagard. Writing in 1623, at a time when the Huron Confederacy was still thriving and populous, Sagard captured much of the social and psychological traits that were to be used throughout the remainder of the 17th century to fashion the French construct of "*le Bon sauvage*", a tool that many fine European minds would utilize to expose perceived abusive, oppressive or nonsensical (especially legal and religious) characteristics of their European society. Such influential thinkers as Montesquieu, Rousseau, Diderot, Châteaubriand, Montaigne and Leibniz adeptly picked up on credible descriptions of societies free from the obsession to possess, so typical of European civilization, or exempt from the use of legal coercion against their members and actually practicing fraternity, equality and liberty, and not just preaching about such social principles. A friend and correspondent of Lahontan, Baron Wilhelm Gottfried von Leibniz, the famous German philosopher, declared that the world had been wrong all along after Aristotle had affirmed that mankind did not have the ability to build functional, orderly societies without strong, coercive governments. At an earlier date, basing himself on European accounts of Amerindian life, the monumental French philosopher Michel de Montaigne had refuted Plato on similar grounds. The fundamental precepts of the European civilization got severely shaken and the world went through an ideological and social revolution, which is still going on and which I have termed: *the americization of the world*, the essential vocation of America, in which the most strategic part is being played by the descendants of America's First peoples.

The Huron chief Kondiaronk has left more than one type of legacy. We have seen how, through the writings of his philosophical ally and cultural interpreter

Lahontan, his thought can conceivably have had an incidence on an ideological revolution in France and then, in Europe, which, in time, triggered actual social revolutions, such as the French revolution, which in turn, had an incidence on the course and the outcome of the American Revolution. Kondiaronk was born around 1625, in the thick of a war that lasted ninety two years, from 1609 to 1701. During his lifetime, he saw most of the people having made up his Native world die out through war and epidemics. As First Headman of his people and First Leader of a Council-fire that included almost all native Nations of the Northeast, his brilliant military and diplomatic career was dedicated to the achievement of a global peace which would include the French ally and the Iroquois, both his enemies and his kin. Having seen native power wasted away as so many Nations were drastically depopulated, he and the numerous chiefs of the Indian-French alliance maneuvered politically, in the last years of the 17th century, to transfer to the French Governor of New France, in Montreal, the guardianship of the collective Amerindian strength, thus, of the survival and the future of all the Native Nations of the Northeast and of many others beyond. In that manner, the French became the arbiters in all contentions and the keepers of the peace. That great Peace Treaty was concluded and signed by the delegated leaders of thirty eight Indian Nations, in Montreal, on August fourth, 1701. On August 1st, the great Kondiaronk, mortally sick from an epidemic disease which the Indian delegates had known was raging in the Montreal region, gave a long last speech that moved many people to tears, even his lifetime enemies, the Iroquois, the very ones who, the next day, carried his coffin and performed the traditional Hodenosaunee Condolence ceremony for "their departed brother, Kondiaronk". (Following the Headman's wish, catholic funeral rites were also observed, so as to create unity between all traditions present.) French Governor de Callières ordered a state funeral, which was attended by one thousand three hundred Indian delegates and most of Montreal's two thousand inhabitants. In August of this year, Montreal will commemorate the signing of the Peace of Montreal, a Treaty that has left a healing legacy up to our times and that still serves today as a most significant illustration of one of the most positive expressions of the meeting of the European and the Amerindian ideologies.

There should never be a question that overall, the meeting of Europe and Aboriginal America was highly destructive from an aboriginal viewpoint.

However, as I have been trying to illustrate in this presentation, these two worlds did achieve proximity, at the philosophical level, essentially because of the specific nature of the relationship that the French elaborated with Native America. From my own Indian and Huron-Wyandot vantage point, I perceive the historical relationship of my people, and of all Native American people with the French as a vehicle. The French ideological construct of the Noble Redman, because it incorporates a lot of otherwise unrecognized positive truth about Native Americans, continentally speaking, is a vehicle and a passport that has been used, such as the Huron have historically done, and can still be used by all to move around in this new Euro-American world and go about the business not just of surviving, but of fulfilling the responsibility that Native Americans have traditionally claimed was theirs, the one of Americizing America and consequently, the world. My Wendat ancestors once said to the Jesuits, in 1636, that they and their people had come to establish their European missions and world in the heart of Native America (meaning their country of Wendake) in order to "overturn the Country". It is only logical and natural that the basic hope and strategy that we, and all Native American people, have had ever since is all about bringing back order in this land of ours, getting our Country right side up again. To achieve that purpose, we have to convince all Americans, all Canadians, everyone that has come to live with us, as we once convinced Baron de Lhontan to do, to become Huron, that is, ever truer Americans. US judge Felix Cohen, fifty years ago, expressed his credo in that philosophical vocation of the Native American: "When we have gathered the last golden grain of knowledge from the harvest of Indian summer, then we can talk of Americanizing (meaning: assimilating) the Indian. Until then, we might do better to concentrate our attention on the real job of the New World, the job of Americanizing [we would say *Americizing*] the White man".

Ho! Ho! Ho! Attouguet Eathoro! My friends and relatives, thank you very much for listening!

Bridges

Bridges

You may have all the locks and chains,
All the iron doors,
All the bulldozers
And all the dynamite,
But
You
Will always
Be
An
Outlaw
On my land,
You may hate me for speaking up,
You may dispossess, crush and
Discriminate me,
Try to starve me,
Post me up as "unwanted",
Wish me to apologize for existing,
All you do here is illegal,
My land has not been in order
Since your disorder began.
You have no other decent, dignified choice
But to meet me halfway
On the bridges I have built
Before and since you came
And on others we need to build
Together.

Canada: Its Cradle, Its Name, Its Spirit*

The Stadaconan Contribution to Canadian Culture and Identity

I am a Huron and a Canadian Indian. I am well aware that my nation originates essentially from the Wendat, once proprietors of a small country located in present-day Ontario, and that the name 'Huron' was given by the French to the Wendat as a way to belittle, negate and ultimately dispossess them. However, I am able to fully assume the history that made me and my people what we are today, that is, Huron. That name allows us to see the whole picture of where we have been, where we are and where we want to go. To me, Huron means being Canadian in a uniquely profound way, a sacred way. Being a Huron means being directly related to the Stadaconans, the people who were there before

---

* To be published in 2009 by Indian and Northern Affairs Canada (INAC) in the second volume of the book *Hidden in Plain Sight. Aboriginal Contributions to Canadian Culture and Identity*.

Quebec City existed, just like the rocks, the trees and the Saint Charles and Saint Lawrence rivers. The Stadaconans were those of my ancestors who, in 1535, gave Jacques Cartier a cradle, a name and a spirit for the country he fancied he had discovered: Kanatha.

I guess my dear reader already has a sense that if asked to talk or write about "Aboriginal Contributions to Canadian Culture and Identity", I can really get going. I will use the opportunity to share with my fellow Canadians some of my secret Huron knowledge about what the most ancient Canadians, the Stadaconas, did in order to help create a country that would, from then on, have to include Cartier's people and, as they already knew, so many other Europeans. I use the words "have to" because the French and others (such as the Basques) showed clear signs, by 1535, that they were going to keep coming here, many to stay. We knew this from at least two of our own Stadaconan youth who had been deceitfully captured by Cartier the year before and brought back home to Stadacona in 1535 on Cartier's second voyage.

At this point, some readers may object that the Huron, reputed to have come from (what is now) Ontario to (what is now) Quebec about 115 years later (1650), when their country was definitively destroyed "by the Iroquois", cannot claim to be ethnically related to the Stadaconans. I would answer that recent archaeological findings have confirmed our *returning* to Quebec in 1649–1650. It was, indeed, a return home for many of our families who had their roots as Stadaconans but had had to flee from their ancestral 'Quebec' lands as a result of the first impact of the French and European invasion in Cartier's time. More than any other Amerindian group, the Huron of today, though few in number, carry the heritage of the Stadaconans, just as they are the principal carriers of the spiritual and intellectual heritage of many of the great Nadowek (Iroquoian) peoples and confederacies who have disappeared: the Tionontati or Tobacco, the Attiwandaronk or Neutral, the Erie or Cougars, the Wenro, the Susquehanna, the Hochelaga and others.

Cartier first used the word 'Canada' in his log book in 1535, on his second voyage, to designate both the town of Stadacona (now Quebec City) and the country whose centre it was, which extends approximately from Trois-Rivières to l'Île-aux-Coudres. The previous year, Cartier's three ships had entered the

Gulf of the Saint Lawrence and had encountered two groups of Amerindians: Mi'kmaq (Micmacs) and Stadaconas. These people possibly journeyed far away from their homes with other people from 'Canada'. The Stadaconans camped at present-day Gaspé and were catching lots of fish and smoking them.

On Friday, July 24, 1534, Cartier had a large cross made carrying the inscription "Vive le Roi de France", and planted it at the entrance to Gaspé Bay. Donnacona, whom Cartier would identify a year later (September 8, 1535) as the "Seigneur du Canada", paddled up to Cartier's ship with three of his sons. This historically important moment was described in some detail by Cartier. First, we learn that the Stadaconan leader and his people did not come as close to the French as they had during the initial days of this one-week encounter. Rather, Donnacona's canoe remained at a distance while he addressed the French to explain to them that, as Cartier understood, "all the land was his" and that his people opposed the making and the planting of that object that the French called a cross and collectively worshipped. (We know from many early sources that Aboriginal people were then able to and, in fact, did enforce their strict prohibition that the Europeans cut even a twig or to take anything from their land without their permission.) We also learn that even though very far away from their homes and immediate country, these first Canadians shared territorial rights and therefore land stewardship with the Mi'kmaq. Also importantly, we learn that these Frenchmen, far from being affected by this defensive act against their intrusion, had a subterfuge ready to use that was intended to make the Native people understand that the French did not believe they had to respect the political order that the First Peoples had already established on their lands. At the end of Donnacona's harangue, which Cartier found lengthy, he showed the Stadaconan leader an axe, feigning a wish to barter it for a bearskin that the Chief wore. The latter, moved by this gesture, came closer to the French ship, "believing he was going to get [the axe]". Upon this, one of the sailors grabbed the Stadaconans' canoe, which allowed two or three Frenchmen to get into it and force two of Donnacona's sons to climb into Cartier's boat. Fear of French arms, and the vulnerability of the women and children present may have been a factor in the lack of Stadaconan resistance to the treacherous act of the French, to whom the Aboriginal people had given no motive whatsoever to conduct themselves in such an underhanded manner.

The French, on board their ship, made "a great show of love" for their two captives in presence of their people gathered in many canoes in the Gaspé Bay. Cartier then responded to Donnacona's speech about the cross and about Aboriginal 'ownership' of the land by explaining (again deceitfully) that the cross was only meant to be a landmark for future visits, which they intended to make soon, and that, at any rate, they would then bring with them all sorts of gifts, of iron and otherwise, for Donnacona's people. This, of course, meant that the French, despite the strange way they had acted by seizing Donnacona's sons, still felt that they had to pay for using the land and, furthermore, had to account to the Aboriginal people for that use and for their presence. The Stadaconans considered all the components of this new necessary relationship: the love and solicitude the French showed for their two captured "*sauvages*", their promise to bring them back soon and the strategic knowledge about the French these two young men would bring back. The Stadaconans then decided that they would, in time, be able to control and contain those newcomers. They showed themselves to be happy enough about everything. They even promised that they would not cut down the cross. Thus ended, on July 24, 1534, this prelude to France's Canadian adventure.

Over the next year they spent in France, Cartier's two Stadaconan captives, Domagaya and Taignoagny, studied the French in order to understand their motives and their aims, and devised their own Aboriginal strategy. Most certainly, the two young men, probably drawing maps, had spoken to Jacques Cartier and other French about their "Kanatha", that is, their "chief town", which was Stadacona (present-day Quebec City). Little did they know that the French would use this descriptive word as the name of a country, an actual 'kingdom' called 'Canada'. Nor could the two Stadaconans imagine that their father, Donnacona, had been made a European-style monarch in this new land, which the French fancied and planned to conquer (steal). Certainly, these two sons of an important Aboriginal Headman could not have foreseen that their father, too, would soon be deceitfully and forcefully captured by Cartier and his men, on May 3, 1636, and would die in France less than two years afterwards, sick and mortally sad for his lost people and country.

However, much happened before Donnacona's capture that is very significant as regards the Stadaconan contribution to Canada's culture and identity.

As promised, Cartier did return on a second voyage the following year. Cartier's three ships left Saint-Malo on May 19, 1535. Taking advantage of their two Amerindian guides' knowledge of the geography of the two coasts from the entrance of the gulf right up to Montreal (Hochelaga) and beyond (Cartier is explicit about that knowledge and assistance), the French took their time to reconnoitre (they, of course, said "discover") the country, where they saw human settlements and met inhabitants in every part.

The French were intent on visiting three 'countries', namely, Canada, Saguenay and Hochelaga. Cartier's account and other evidence (including our own oral tradition) indicate that Donnacona's sons, already well trained in the region's geopolitics, had reasoned that such an exploratory plan, still to be approved by leading Stadaconan councils and their allies, could potentially develop into an eventual alliance between their people and the French. They first took the French to Canada's chief town, Stadacona, where Donnacona, their father and First Headman, lived. Donnacona was a man whose authority the French already knew extended at least as far east as Gaspé.

Cartier and his people believed that during their year spent in France, Taignoagny and Domagaya had become naturally imbued with a sense of French cultural and religious superiority in relation to their own people, and would therefore, once back home in Canada, be perfectly prepared to help the French conquer their own land and peoples. To Cartier's dismay, the attitude of the two young men changed radically from the moment they set foot on their own soil once again. Understandably, that evening and night of September 8, 1535, was spent in intense discussion and long-awaited revelations about the French and their land. The Aboriginal people of the region had, by this time, been aware of and mystified by the Europeans for almost four decades.[1]

Fixated on the idea of finding a passage to the Orient, its gold and its other riches, the French were determined to visit Hochelaga and, at a later date, Saguenay, another very rich 'kingdom,' according to the two Stadaconan captives and guides. During the trip back, the Stadaconans had agreed that they would lead the French to Hochelaga. However, Donnacona and other council

---

1 Two centuries or so after the Vikings ceased coming to the region, vivid memories of them were certainly still present. This time, however, the newcomers behaved in very different, much more aggressive, ways than had their Norse predecessors.

leaders did not think the time was appropriate. Not only was the season too advanced to travel much more, but there were also strict protocols to be learned and observed regarding the laws of a particular territory, the respect to be paid to its leaders, customs of different Aboriginal nations, the advance notice to be sent to another country that one wished to visit, and many, many other things to be aware of.

The French had only been in 'Canada' for six days when, on September 14, they began pressing their two former captives to lead them to Hochelaga. On the next day, Taignoagny, whom Cartier resented more than he did Domagaya, informed the French captain that the Headman Donnacona was annoyed to see the French constantly bearing arms, to which Cartier replied that he (Taignoagny) knew very well that this was the way in France and that he would therefore let his men bear arms. Still, the Stadaconans remained cheerful and optimistic that they would eventually find common ground and make the French see their real interests, which meant using the friendship that was being offered them to create a larger, more affluent and powerful society from the uniting of the two peoples.

On September 16, Donnacona and five hundred of his people (roughly the population of the town of Stadacona) approached Cartier's two main boats anchored in the harbour of the Saint Charles River. The leaders entered Cartier's boat to once again try to impress on the French that they should not navigate towards Hochelaga (today's Montreal) at this time (they, of course, thought of another time, likely the following spring). Taignoagny, once again acting as the spokesman for the Stadaconans, withdrew his offer to guide Cartier, stating that his father, Donnacona, did not wish him to go because the Headman had said, "*La rivière ne vaut rien*" (the river forebode nothing good). The French explorer answered that his mind was set to go anyway, adding that should Taignoagny change his mind and agree to accompany them as he had promised, he would receive gifts and attention from the French that would make him happy. At any rate, Cartier explained, his aim was only to make a quick trip to see Hochelaga and then return to Canada.

Taignoagny remained firm in his refusal to go, and the visit ended.

The next day, the Stadaconas staged a very sensitive and solemn effort to make the French reconsider their plan to go to Hochelaga and especially to appreciate the great solidarity that would result from uniting their two peoples. They attempted this by actually marrying Jacques Cartier to the highest-ranking of their marriageable young women. To this day, an account other than Cartier's own has never been presented to Canadians about this very meaningful event in their country's history.

I have personally witnessed wedding ceremonies and other similar ceremonies still practised by Canadian Aboriginal peoples whose spiritual ways are almost identical to ours. I will take the reader through Cartier's account of what happened to him, the young maiden and the people of Canada that day. First, we are told that the people of Stadacona walked up to the French boats at low tide with large quantities of eels and other fish, as gifts for the French. Then there was much chanting and dancing, which usually occurred at such visits, Cartier said. What Cartier did not see, at this point, was that these particular songs and dances were preparatory to a specific ceremony that was about to take place. As well, the abundant quantities of fish and the prevailing festive atmosphere that was described indicate that the whole town (very likely with many guests and visitors from neighbouring places) was present for a very important event—a ceremony ordained after much praying, chanting, council-making and, quite likely, fasting, under the highest spiritual leadership.

Then the Agouhanna (a title carried by Donnacona, which implies very high standing in society) had his people (likely the other leaders) stand to one side and drew a circle on the sand, inside of which he had Cartier and his own principals stand. Donnacona then made a long speech in front of the thus reunited French and Stadaconans. While he spoke, the Headman "held the hand of a girl of about ten to twelve years old" whom, after he had finished speaking, he presented to the French captain. At this point, all of Donnacona's people began to "scream and shout, as a sign of joy and alliance". Now the fact that Cartier accepted the girl was affirmed by the loud, festive reaction of the throng. At any rate, was not Cartier and all of these Frenchmen, in the eyes of the Amerindians, much too long deprived of normal social relations, including those of a man with his wife, or the companionship of a woman, as sadly seen in their disorderly behaviour and appearance? Could so many negative traits in the present state of their intercultural relations not be modified by beginning to create a normal human life, a society, around these angry, rude, rowdy strangers?

Following this ceremony, two younger boys were given to Cartier in the same official way, upon which the Stadaconans made similar demonstrations of joy.[2] Cartier then officially thanked Donnacona for these presents. Finally, a crucial detail was given by Taignoagny: the "girl" (in Aboriginal cultural terms, as well as in French social and cultural terms, she is a *young woman*) ceremonially given (again, in the Aboriginal social frame of reference, that gift was a wife) to Jacques Cartier was "Lord Donnacona's sister's own daughter". This, in the matrilineal system of these Nadowek (Iroquoians), meant that the young woman was called "my daughter" by Donnacona, because she belonged to the same clan as he did, as opposed to his own children, who belonged to their mother's clan.

Thus, the young woman was the highest, as well as the purest, gift that could possibly have been offered to the first man among these Frenchmen. The Stadaconans probably thought, given these gifts and a chance to establish a normal life in this new land, who would care about an oppressive monarch back in problem-ridden France and about the lifelong odious obedience that was owed him: this land was Donnacona's, this was a pure and abundant free country, this was *Canada*. Most surely and naturally, there was a burning desire in many French hearts present to make the Canadian way of thinking their own.[3] Unfortunately, of course, it was, for that time, impossible. It was almost entirely a matter of religious prejudice.[4]

Cartier had his human gifts "put on board the ships". He gave no details about what occurred to the three young Stadaconans thereafter, except that the "older girl", had, three days later, fled the ship and that a special guard had been arranged so that the two boys would not do likewise. When finally "found" by Donnacona and her own family, the young woman explained that she had

---

2 With a high-ranking young wife given to him by the First Headman of the land and two young boys, one of whom was Donnacona's own son, did Cartier not have prime human material with which to start up a very good life in "Canada"? The Stadaconans certainly thought he did.

3 The "*ensauvagement*" (irresistible attraction of the free life of the "*sauvages*"), mostly of the French "coureurs de bois" probably was the most marked trait (and simultaneously the one most damned by the religious authorities) in French-Indian relations throughout the next two centuries. It produced Canada's Métis nation.

4 Cartier exhibited his deep European religious conditioning and unfeelingly uttered a very dark sentence regarding the original Canadians when, pondering what little he knew about their spiritual beliefs, he simply wrote : "One must be baptized or go to hell."

escaped because "the pages had beaten her", and not, as the French contended, because her own people had tried to make her (and the two boys) leave the French. Cartier showed reluctance to take the young woman back until, he said, the Stadaconan leaders (her family) begged him to do so. (To them, at least, Jacques Cartier and she were husband and wife.) She was accompanied to the ship by her father and other relatives. Nothing further is said about her.

Cartier tells us that Taignoagny said to him, after the bride-giving ceremony, that these three human presents had been given in order to keep the French from going up to Hochelaga. I have already presented my reasoning, based on the available evidence, which includes my own culturally informed perception, about the Stadaconas' motives for trying their hardest to create unifying bridges between themselves and the French. At any rate, I believe Cartier's blinding obsession about going to Hochelaga is self-evident. The last-ditch attempt of the Stadaconas to make him stay, on the next day, and the strange but accurate warning that he received about having to prepare for wintering right away, are further proof of Cartier's foolhardiness and spite toward his Aboriginal hosts, friends and benefactors.

On September 18, 1535, the Stadaconans, again attempting to avert misfortune for the French, turned to supernatural forces. Cartier described how this was acted out before his eyes.

First, three men clothed themselves in black and white fur (Cartier disparagingly says dog skins) and wore long horns on their heads. The three men hid in a canoe and, momentarily, rose up as their craft approached the boats. The spirit-being in the middle began to make a "marvellous" speech directed at the French, even though the three "devils" never even took notice of the French, as they floated past the French boats. The canoe was steered back to shore. Upon arriving, the three beings dropped to the bottom of the canoe, as though they had died. They were then carried to the woods in the canoe by Donnacona and other men. Every single Stadaconan followed their leaders into the forest and disappeared from sight. Then began a half-hour "predication" by the three spirit-beings. At the end of this, Taignoagny and Domagaya came out of the woods and, after the Catholic way they had observed, walked towards the French, their hands joined as if in prayer. "Showing great admiration," they advanced with their eyes lifted towards the sky and pronounced the words

"Jesus, Maria, Jacques Cartier," as though (my interpretation) asking for protection for Cartier and his men. At that moment, the French captain, seeing their grave countenance and having witnessed their "ceremonies", inquired "what the matter was, what new things had occurred". The two young men answered that there was "pitiful news", that nothing foreboded well (*"il n'y a rien de bon"*). When pressed further by Cartier, his two usual interpreters told him that Cudouagny (likely the Great Spirit for the Stadaconans and possibly the Hochelagans) had spoken in Hochelaga and, through the three spirit impersonators mentioned above, had announced that there would be so much ice and snow that they (the French) would all die. (Actually, twenty-five sailors died of sickness and hardship over the winter. At one point, Cartier himself became quite certain that all, including himself, would die. We will later see how they were saved by their hosts.)

To be sure, Cartier made light of the Stadaconans' way of trying to make him stay and to persuade his companions to start preparing for their first Canadian winter. "Go tell your messengers that your god Cudouagny is a fool who does not know what he talks about," retorted Cartier amid laughter from all the French who were there. "If you just believe in Jesus, he will keep you from the cold," added a sailor. As a way of restoring balance in the communication, the two youths then diplomatically asked Cartier whether he had had Jesus' word on the matter, to which the captain curtly replied that his priests had asked him (Jesus) about it and learned that the weather was going to be all right. Taignoagny and Domagaya gave many thanks to Cartier for this exchange and returned to fetch from the woods their own townsfolk who, as Cartier detected, could not conceal their disillusion, even amidst their cheers, shouts, chants, dances and other expressions of joy.

The next day, on September 19, Cartier's smaller vessel left for Hochelaga. The round trip lasted twenty-four days, during which the rest of his men, back in Stadacona, mostly used their time bracing for imagined attacks from the Stadaconans. As for the Stadaconans, they continued to demonstrate the same goodwill and humanity towards their strange visitors, bringing them victuals and waiting for their visits, which were, in fact, quite infrequent. Because the French did not visit very often, they began suffering from a lack of fresh food, especially meat and fish.

The rest of the story of Cartier's second voyage to Canada is better known. In brief, things soon turned very bad for the French, as foreseen by the Stadaconans. From mid-November, the cold was brutally felt by the ill-prepared Frenchmen. In December, the whole crew was hit hard by scurvy. By mid-February, eight sailors were dead. By mid-April, twenty-five had succumbed to the scourge and another forty were dying; of 110, "there were not three healthy men," wrote Cartier. "We were so overtaken by the said disease," confided the explorer in his chronicle, "that we had almost lost all hope of ever returning to France."[5]

Most readers will already know that people stopped dying in Cartier's fort thanks to a remedy (very likely, the white cedar) that the Stadaconans gave the French and taught them how to prepare. The credit for this human solicitude and actual salvation from sure catastrophe, however, was entirely given to God, the Europeans' God. The surviving crewmen, further strengthened by the fresh meat and fish that the Amerindians brought them every day, got better so rapidly that in less than three weeks, they were ready to set sail for France. However, as many readers must also know, they did not depart from Canada before realizing a very pressing dream: that of capturing Donnacona, Domagaya and Taignoagny, along with two other prominent Headmen and two other young Stadaconans, one of whom was another pubescent girl. To succeed in laying his hands on these people, especially the leaders, Cartier had to act his wiliest and also use force, as he proudly recounted in his journal. We know that ten Stadaconans, probably all belonging to Donnacona's immediate family, were in the possession of the French when they left for France on May 6, 1536. Among them were Donnacona, Taignoagny, Domagaya, the other two Headmen, another girl "of about ten", (almost certainly) Cartier's Canadian wife and his two given sons, and lastly, two other persons of unknown gender or age.

One of Cartier's promises made to appease the Stadaconans after so callously and treacherously stealing their leaders and people was that he would bring back all ten of them "in ten or twelve moons" (as, in fact, he had done with his first two captives). When he finally came back, without his captives,

---

5 Since mid-November, the Stadaconans also had lost about fifty people. Cartier, reflecting the knowledge of his epoch, could and did blame the "Canadians" for his people's sickness. Today's science, however, informs us that, rather, the Stadaconans' disease was caused by the Europeans' presence, because they were beginning to be struck down by "contact epidemics".

five years later and was asked by the Stadaconans what had become of their Agouhanna and other people, Cartier, still his deceitful self, replied that Donnacona had died and was buried in France (which was factual), but that all the others had remained there, where they were now married and had become *"grands Seigneurs"* (great Lords). We know from Cartier's own chronicle that eight more of his captives had died by then (French archival sources confirm that they all died within two years), except a girl of about ten (at the time of her capture).

This time, in August 1541, the French arrived in Canada to find an Aboriginal population in a state of virtual panic. Diplomacy was still present, but was mostly dictated by fear. The French had brought heavy weaponry and were ready for any eventuality. They were here to create a French colony. The Canadians' country would be theirs, for civilized Europeans were not bound to virtues practised by 'savages'.

However, for now, the task proved too great, support from France was not quite sufficient and the enmity of the First Peoples was too overwhelming. Cartier's third and last voyage ended in failure. However, the French (and Basque) presence in the Laurentian region increased year by year, because of the wealth of fur and fish. Hochelaga and Saguenay endured, but Canada's peoples, directly and forcibly affected by the European invasion (not just the sheer human pressure, but even more by the ever-present, devastating new epidemic diseases), had to seek refuge, which archaeology in the last few decades has revealed (again confirming our own traditional belief) they mostly found among the Wendat of present-day Ontario (in the Lake Simcoe–Georgian Bay area). According to leading archaeologists,[6] the original Canadians joined the Wendat Confederacy in the last decades of the 16th century, becoming its Nation of the Rock (maybe in remembrance of Stadacona: the place of the Big Standing Rock).[7]

---

6 For sources, readers may consult my book *Huron-Wendat : The Heritage of the Circle* (Vancouver : University of British Columbia Press and Michigan State University Press, 1999).

7 Because of the imposing rocky promontory it presents, Quebec has historically been called "Canada's Gibraltar". I encourage readers to consult a remarkable book on the city of Quebec edited by Serge Courville and Robert Garon, *Québec, ville et capitale* (Ste-Foy : Les Presses de l'Université Laval, 2001) (in the series *Atlas historique du Québec*).

Conclusion

No foundation can forever rest on lies, especially lies rooted in racial prejudice. While it is necessary to find the reasons and to understand why the French, like many Europeans at the time, perceived reality and other peoples as they did and acted with corresponding spite and inhumanity, it is equally necessary to help today's heirs to that ancient society (which means most of us, in greater or smaller measure) shed any lingering thinking and behavioural patterns related to that inheritance. We are long past the time when Europeans came here needing new places and new conditions for a renewed lease on life. However, after providing the same 'Canadian' generosity and contributing the very best of themselves and what they have, our Aboriginal peoples are still being deceived, mistreated and visibly destroyed as peoples in this great, rich and powerful country. One can take the Stadaconans' history of contact with Europe and, thereafter, non-Aboriginal Canada, and apply it exactly to the historical and present-day experience of any other Canadian Aboriginal group or nation. After all the political, social, academic and religious rhetoric, the very real fact remains that Canada, born in 1534 with an Aboriginal spirit, given an Aboriginal name in 1535 and tenderly cared for in an Amerindian cradleboard by the people of Stadacona, has seen and caused its Aboriginal peoples to waste away ever since its birth, while everyone else who has come here has, as Jacques Cartier and his men were, been cared for, healed and helped to find a new life. Can we now stop saying that this was, and will continue to be, the price to pay for a true civilization, until Canada's 'Indian problem' has been settled?

In this essay, I have mainly wanted to suggest to my readers and fellow Canadians that a better understanding of the way things happened in their country at the beginning of the contact between Aboriginals (the first Canadians) and Europeans is necessary if one is to also understand why all Canadians are still collectively afflicted by an immense incapacity to empathize, communicate and construct as we should the kind of secure, happy future that we all desire for our children and their descendants. As an Aboriginal historian, I believe an ignorance of history is the major reason for the glacial indifference of mainstream society that is still felt by most of my Aboriginal fellow citizens and is known and denounced by many non-Aboriginal Canadians and others, and is the major reason that so impedes us collectively from tackling and conducting our many common affairs in normal, empathetic, intelligent ways.

Finally, I am grateful for this opportunity to write about our peoples—their very many important past, present and, maybe especially, potential future contributions to our great and dear country's culture and identity. I also wish to greet and thank my readers for their time.

Long live my country, Canada!

Les Algonquins en 1857[*]

C'est pour moi un très grand honneur que m'a fait la Commission de la Capitale-Nationale, par la voix de mon ami et collègue monsieur Pierre Anctil, de me demander d'écrire et de prononcer, en cette belle et importante occasion, une adresse dans laquelle je veux expliquer comment vivait et pensait le peuple algonquin anishnabe au temps où Ottawa fut choisie pour être la capitale nationale du pays que nous habitons et auquel nous vouons tant d'affection, le Canada. Je veux aussi parler de la permanence et de l'importance pour nous tous d'une pensée maintenant de plus en plus reconnue dans notre pays, celle des Algonquins et des autres peuples autochtones.

Je me fais un devoir protocolaire et insigne de mentionner que nous nous trouvons sur le territoire sacré et jamais cédé du peuple des Anishnabe, que

---

[*] Je me dois d'exprimer un grand merci à ma collègue de l'Université de Trent, Paula Sherman, une grande Algonquine, dont la thèse de doctorat m'a aussi servi d'inspiration pour écrire ce texte.

nous connaissons beaucoup mieux sous le nom d'Algonquins. Je me sens doublement honoré du fait que les Algonquins, nation avec laquelle ma propre nation huronne-wendate a de tout temps été très étroitement et cordialement liée, m'ont donné leur amicale confiance pour écrire et livrer cette adresse.

« Nous aurions tous pu vivre très bien ensemble », a souvent dit le Chef et le Sage William Commanda de la communauté algonquine (Anishnabe dans sa langue native) de Kitigan Zibi, tout près de la ville québécoise de Maniwaki. Monsieur William Commanda, né le 11 novembre 1913, a reçu un doctorat honorifique de l'Université d'Ottawa en octobre 2005. Le docteur William Commanda est aussi le Chef suprême du gouvernement indien de l'Amérique du Nord, le mouvement précurseur de tous les arrangements modernes d'autonomie gouvernementale approuvés par le gouvernement fédéral conjointement avec les Premières Nations. Le Chef et Sage William Commanda a également fondé, en 1969, le Cercle de toutes les nations, un organisme de portée mondiale voué à la sensibilisation et à la lutte contre la discrimination raciale et à la défense de notre Mère-Terre. Il a aussi créé et promeut toujours très activement, avec un nombre impressionnant de gens qui l'affectionnent et le suivent, le projet de l'Île Victoria, dont le but est d'établir en ce cœur spirituel du pays de ses ancêtres un centre international pour la mise en valeur de la philosophie algonquine et pour la sauvegarde de la rivière des Outaouais.

Lorsque le Chef Commanda dit « Nous aurions tous pu vivre très bien ensemble », il se réfère aux anciennes Ceintures de Wampum sacrées dont il est le Gardien depuis quarante ans. Il se réfère particulièrement à la Ceinture dont il traduit le nom par « Ceinture de l'Amitié » ou « Ceinture de Bienvenue ». Il s'agit d'une Ceinture datant du début des années 1700, faite de perles de wampum et représentant trois personnages: l'Anglais, l'Amérindien et le Français, les trois se tenant par la main. Cette entente, sacrée aux yeux des Amérindiens, fut conclue solennellement en ce temps-là. Les symboles de l'unité et de l'amitié sont de toute importance, mais celui de la centralité de l'homme des Premiers Peuples l'est encore davantage. En effet, l'idée exprimée dans ce positionnement de l'autochtone représente l'ordre social, politique et spirituel qu'ont élaboré les Premiers Peuples au cours de longs âges d'écoute et d'observation révérencieuses des lois et des enseignements de leur Mère-Terre et de tous les peuples non humains, qui l'ont aussi pour Mère et Parente dans l'ordre du Grand Cercle de la Vie.

Dans la logique ancienne mais constamment renouvelée des Premiers Peuples, leur position centrale dans la Ceinture de l'Amitié signifie la responsabilité qu'a l'Amérindien de guider ses frères et sœurs nouvellement arrivés chez lui, dans leur entreprise de se créer un nouveau foyer et un nouvel avenir sur cette terre étrange et inconnue. « Ici, nous pouvons tous vivre très bien, ensemble », pense et dit le personnage au centre de la Ceinture à ses deux frères qui, savait-il déjà trop bien, avaient besoin d'apprendre à oublier des différences qui devaient perdre leur sens dans le pays de l'Indien. Or cette place au centre de son pays devait être niée aux Premiers Peuples, du moins pour un temps encore, un temps d'une grande dureté et d'une misère presque impossible à imaginer, où ce seraient les Ceintures sacrées elles-mêmes qui perdraient presque tout leur sens.

Le Chef William Commanda explique que certains enseignements et certaines prophéties sont contenus dans les Wampums et sont transmis parmi le peuple par les Gardiens des Wampums. L'une de ces prophéties est que les Anishnabek (les Algonquins) savaient qu'un autre peuple allait arriver pour vivre ici et qu'il fallait incorporer ces nouveaux venus à l'ordre social, spirituel et politique existant. Le chef explique qu'il était inconcevable pour les Anishnabek qu'un pays aussi riche et généreux que le leur ne puisse pas faire bien vivre aussi tous ces gens qui allaient venir se joindre à eux. Les connaissances et la sagesse combinées des deux familles de peuples laissaient aussi entendre les prédictions des Anciens ne pouvaient que renforcer la capacité de tous les gens de bien vivre ensemble, mais cela, aussi longtemps et tant que la position du centre resterait celle des peuples autochtones. Or les nouveaux venus s'approprièrent cette responsabilité de protéger l'ordre du pays autochtone et le résultat de ceci a été « la désacralisation de la Terre », dit le chef Commanda.

Dès les premiers moments de leurs contacts avec les Européens, les Amérindiens montrèrent ce grand empressement d'affirmer l'importance de leur position de primauté dans tout ordre social et politique à élaborer en vue d'incorporer les nouveaux venus. En 1534, à Gaspé, l'explorateur Jacques Cartier dut donner des explications aux Amérindiens pour avoir coupé un arbre, dont il avait fait une croix. Trompeusement, Cartier déclara que sa croix n'était qu'une balise pour guider les voyageurs (européens) ultérieurs. En 1823, le développeur Philémon Wright, l'un des réputés fondateurs de la ville de Hull, faillit lui aussi à l'honnêteté lorsqu'il dut expliquer ses procédés de « développement » aux Algonquins, occupants et gardiens immémoriaux du territoire que Wright était en train de dévaster.

> Les chefs s'assemblèrent, rapporte Wright, et obtinrent les services d'un interprète anglais, du nom de George Brown, un commis officiel dans la traite avec les Indiens dont la femme et la famille étaient indiennes, et qui parlait les deux langues. [Les Algonquins] lui firent la requête de me demander par quelle autorité je coupais leurs forêts et prenais possession de leurs terres, ce à quoi je répondis que c'était en vertu de l'autorisation reçue à Québec et de leur Puissant Père le Roi, qui habite de l'autre côté de l'océan, ainsi que de sir John Johnson, lequel je sais être agent au Département des Indiens, car c'est par lui qu'il reçoivent leur montant d'argent annuel du gouvernement.
>
> Ils avaient peine à supposer que leur Père, le Roi, ou toute autre personne à Québec, m'aurait autorisé à couper leurs forêts et à ouvrir le pays au défrichement et à détruire leurs érablières et leurs territoires de chasse sans les en prévenir, puisqu'ils avaient paisiblement joui de ces terres depuis nombre de générations. Ils étaient d'avis que c'eût été beaucoup mieux si j'étais resté chez moi puisque la vie de leurs familles dépendait de ces terres de chasse, terres à sucre, endroits de pêche et autres biens, et qu'ils avaient crainte que d'autres difficultés allaient surgir, telles la prise de leurs castors, la destruction de leurs chevreuils, la coupe de leurs terres à sucre, ainsi que d'autres troubles. Ils ajoutèrent que je savais sans doute que la coupe des forêts signifiait la perte de leurs animaux et de tout ce dont ils dépendaient pour vivre.

Wright, bien sûr, ne fut pas cru par les Algonquins, qui savaient pertinemment que leurs titres fonciers sur tous leurs territoires étaient toujours intacts (et le sont d'ailleurs encore aujourd'hui) puisqu'il n'avaient pas fait l'objet d'extinction par la voie « légale » dictée dans la Proclamation royale de 1763.

L'invasion illégale de leurs territoires et la destruction de leurs ressources vitales fut pour le peuple anishnabe un processus long, cruel et d'une injustice consommée. Dans les années 1840, le chef algonquin Luc-Antoine Pakinawatik, arrière-arrière-grand-père du chef William Commanda, vit son peuple réduit à la famine et demanda au gouvernement de la colonie une réserve où sa nation pût reprendre vie. Un petit territoire, la réserve de Maniwaki (« Terre de Marie », en algonquin), leur fut accordé, où commença, pour ces Algonquins dépossédés et décimés par la faim, la pauvreté et les maladies, la période « moderne » du contrôle absolu exercé depuis sur eux par le ministère des Affaires indiennes et par les Églises de diverses dénominations.

L'esprit des Wampums demeure

Il est un fait connu que l'établissement du Canada s'est généralement réalisé en dépit de la justice due à ses peuples autochtones. Cela fut certainement le cas aussi en pays anishnabe. Les sources documentaires, de même que la tradition orale amérindienne, surabondent de preuves que les autorités coloniales et canadiennes n'ont réservé pour les Premiers Peuples qu'une seule option, celle d'une assimilation forcée. Et, paradoxalement, c'est peut-être cette intransigeance qui a été la plus forte raison de la survie spirituelle des autochtones. En effet, comment eût pu même exister la possibilité d'une foi autochtone en une quelconque valeur morale ou sociale de la proposition assimilatrice des autorités « blanches», au regard d'une exclusion aussi froide et inconditionnelle de toute la civilisation des Premières Nations?

Un grand et vrai miracle s'est produit au Canada et, peut-être particulièrement, en pays algonquin, territoire où est située notre merveilleuse capitale nationale, dont nous célébrons aujourd'hui un très important anniversaire. Ce miracle est qu'il existe toujours, inchangé dans le cœur des Sages anishnabek, un même désir de créer, avec leurs sœurs et frères canadiens et canadiennes, une société « où nous puissions tous vivre très bien ensemble». Voilà le sens de la vie d'un Sage tel que le chef et docteur William Commanda, que plusieurs d'entre nous avons eu l'occasion d'entendre nous direen anglais, en français et en algonquin: « Mes frères, mes sœurs, mes parents, nous sommes tous une famille. Vous êtes ma famille. Nous sommes tous les enfants de notre Créateur et de notre Mère, la Terre. Nous sommes capables de bien vivre, tous ensemble. Tous ensemble, nous sommes capables de soigner et d'honorer notre mère, la Terre, qui est malade et épuisée. Regardons-nous et traitons-nous comme les parents que nous sommes. Ensemble, nous arriverons à vivre bien, en sécurité et heureux. Moi, je vous aime, tous et qui que vous soyez. Je crois aux Wampums sacrées de mes ancêtres. Il n'y a que l'amour qui puisse nous guider. »

Écoutons, pour terminer, ce même profond message d'affection pour la Terre, dit par monsieur Frank Decontie, un autre Sage de cette nation:

> Il faut d'abord aimer la Terre et être attentif à ses sentiments. Il faut accorder toute sa valeur à la Terre. Ce que j'entends par ceci est qu'il faut prendre de la Terre seulement ce dont on a besoin. Cela veut dire prendre avec respect et honorabilité ce que nous offrent les animaux, les arbres, les oiseaux, les herbes, les médecines et les autres êtres de la Création …
> Il fut un temps où mes grands-pères et mes grands-mères marchaient sur cette Terre. Ils ont vécu sur cette Terre et leur vie a été de paix et d'harmonie. C'était cela la liberté. Les gens faisaient ce qu'ils devaient pour vivre et pour survivre; lorsque l'on vit avec reconnaissance, on a l'amour dans sa vie. Mes ancêtres vivaient de cette façon; ils ne causaient jamais de tort à quiconque. Ce sont là des enseignements spirituels. Ce sont des instructions spirituelles.

Je vous souhaite, au nom de mes frères et sœurs algonquins et autochtones de toutes les nations, une très belle et très joyeuse célébration et fais avec vous tous le vœu très spécial de voir notre très cher pays, le Canada, et sa belle et merveilleuse capitale, Ottawa, continuer de croître en beauté, sagesse, paix et harmonie pour toute la grande famille humaine et aussi, comme disent les Algonquins, non humaine!

16 octobre 2007

The Metaphor of the Accident: A New Historical Paradigm for the Inclusion of Canada's First Peoples[*]

Very few people know what is really happening to Canada's First Peoples. A new historical paradigm is needed if, as a society, we are to persuade ourselves of the importance of acknowledging the many social and moral wounds historically inflicted on the Aboriginal people and conscientiously addressing their myriad long-standing grievances, not merely to restore and effect long-overdue justice, but, principally, to afford the First Peoples of this country a new legal and philosophical basis on which to create for themselves a real capacity to survive as distinct human entities and thereby make their essential contributions to the positive evolution of the larger society. At the core of that new historical approach is the necessity to create and dispense, through public education, a new understanding of our country's history from the aspect of the First Peoples' view of their experience of contact with Europe, as well as

---

[*] A personal reflection dedicated to all First Peoples of America, or Abya Yala.

through the yet virtually non-existent study of the causes for the desertion of western Europe by vast numbers of its peoples from the end of the 15th century, and the ability of these newcomers to relatively quickly and easily dislodge, dispossess and supplant the original nations of the continent, which Europeans named their "New World". I wish to argue that the new historical paradigm that is here proposed is the first to possess the capability of fostering in all Canadians the mutual respect and empathy that alone can breed the genuine desire to create the best possible life and future for one another. It is also this author's judgement that, for obvious historical reasons, that desire exists, at present, far too little in our society.

The Collision between Europe and America

Around the year 1492, a monstrously large and potentially very destructive machine set out on a western course from western Europe. That machine had been constructed over a span of several centuries through the collaboration of many thinkers and engineers of various countries of that region, out of an ever more sharply felt need to go search outside Europe for new living possibilities. Great, devastating scourges, such as pandemics and frequent famine, had spelled the absolute necessity to see bold, skilled adventurers go out in search of a new life for old, tired Europe. Most critically also for Europe, the fall of Constantinople to the Arabs, in 1453, had meant the loss of its centuries-old route to the Orient—its gold, its silk and other riches, and its precious spices, indispensable for preserving meats and other victuals in Europe. Ancient travel accounts gathered in the Orient and, more recently, knowledge coming from Scandinavia had made known the existence of a 'new' continent beyond the Atlantic Ocean. Its natural richness and abundance had been revealed in the relations of the voyages of the Norse, who had frequented the northeastern shores of North America for almost three hundred years, beginning around 1000 AD.

The European travelling machine left from Spain in the summer of 1492 and landed in the Caribbean islands on October 12 of that year. That landing, that day, will forever represent the severest collision to occur in human history between two human civilizations. Over the span of these past 516 years, every single Native people and nation of what thenceforth became known as the continent of America was, in not only figurative terms, blown apart by the catastrophic shock of the European arrival. Many Aboriginal peoples and nations are still being shattered right at this moment in the aftermath of that arrival. As one example, one tribal entity of Central Brazil ceases to exist each passing year; and this continues. In very real fact, the vast majority of First Nations, right here in Canada, are at present barely surviving and losing strength as time goes by. I am well aware that many specialists refer to this state of our nations as 'cultural change', but such terminology only evinces an incapacity for empathy, which our new approach (or paradigm) means to address.

Wherever one looks in the colonial records, which are almost always little other than the glorified account of the establishment of Europeans and other immigrants here, one is bound to be impressed by the unfeeling tone often used in reference to the harsh conditions the First Peoples have been subjected to as a result of the massive arrival of new people to their lands. Since one needs to go beyond emotions in order to understand the reasons for those attitudes and behaviours, one has to have a grasp of the motives and needs of the adventurers who came here, in search of new lands, in their travelling machine. One has to know that there were on board the machine a great many powerful tools and weapons which would be needed in the task of taking over the space and the property of other peoples and also to rationalize and justify such appropriation. Some of the weapons that were to be the greatest determinants in the wars ahead were not even known to be in the machine's cargo. Those were the microbes, against which the 'Indians' (since it would be assumed that the landing had occurred in India) had no natural immunity. In the initial century after contact, between 80 and 95 percent of the individuals of any given 'Amerindian' people or nation were simply killed off by these new bacterial agents.

Knowing these facts is useful and liberating for us moderns in at least three ways: first, we learn that the people of the First Nations did not just unintelligently let themselves be run over, killed and dispossessed by the Europeans; secondly, we get to know for sure that the Europeans could never have eliminated so many millions of Aboriginal people without the presence of those pathogens that they were unwittingly carrying and obviously would not have wished to wreak such destruction on fellow humans; thirdly, we are brought to reflect on the healthier and better living conditions possessed by human societies when they strive to create for themselves and live under social and political systems based on closer observance of the laws of nature.

The total disappearance of the First Peoples of this land, so much expected and often hoped for until recently, did not materialize. Our challenge as modern thinkers and social actors is to assist in the task of repairing the extensive, often extreme damage left in the wake of the gigantic collision with the European machine. Much more than merely advocating for and applying principles of natural justice—a normal exercise in any evolved, free society—is to help foster in our country the awareness of a duty to re-create the living fabric of Aboriginal existence, using every precious shred of available documentation and living human memory. It is a task that requires not only technical and scholarly knowledge, but also and above all, a disposition of the heart and of the spirit to want to safeguard and nurture the deeper roots of our common connection with life itself. That task has everything to do with our will to protect life so that our children of the seventh generation can enjoy it in their time.

Canada needs to think in novel ways about its history of contact with its First Peoples. What has just preceded is a brief entreaty to Canadians to consider that there are two sides to our country's history, one of which, the Aboriginal one, is almost totally unknown.

In June of this year, our Prime Minister has, very commendably, expressed Canada's deep regrets for the harsh, often inhumane treatment received by tens of thousands of First Canadians in the Residential School system during as many as six generations. To me, some words still need to be said by our Prime Minister: I believe that a much more solid foundation will be established for Canada's unity with its First Peoples when our country says with heart, the words "Thank you": Thank you, our First Peoples for humanely undergoing the sacrifice of so many of the things you prized, including your very physical existence, so that Canadians can now have this country that they so much love.

The words "Thank you" have such a stronger spirit than the words "I'm sorry". They mean: "I'm grateful for what you have done for me. I wish to include you in my life. I wish us to live our lives together."

It has been my suggestion that a refreshed, two-sided vision of Canadian history is likely to be conducive to a renewed, more open and trusting commitment on both 'sides', if our country is to become the Circle of all its Peoples (human and non-human) that we all desire and need it to become. This will take our country far in the direction of our self-discovery as a nation, and thus of our success in the global community in future times.

Long live our dear, wonderful Kanatha, our country!

ÉDUCATION ET GOUVERNANCE AUTOCHTONE*

Nous, les Premières Nations, avons été placées sur la Terre par le Créateur. Nous avons été placées ici comme Gardiennes de notre Terre-mère pour vivre en harmonie avec Elle, avec les animaux et avec les autres êtres vivants. Pour nous, tous les êtres sont unis entre eux dans le Grand Cercle de la Vie.

Nos Anciens incarnent nos valeurs collectives de sagesse, de respect, d'humilité, de partage, d'harmonie, de beauté, de force et de spiritualité. Ils (et elles) ont préservé et transmis notre culture depuis d'innombrables générations. Le désir de nos Anciens d'une institution amérindienne d'études postsecondaires a conduit à l'établissement du Collège indien fédéré[1] de la Saskatchewan (Saskatchewan Indian Federated College – SIFC).

---

* Présentation à la conférence « Les sciences religieuses au Canada : passé, présent et avenir » tenue au Département d'études classiques et sciences des religions, Université d'Ottawa, 6 au 8 mai 2005. Cette présentation est basée sur un travail originellement fait à la demande de monsieur Ghislain Picard, Chef de l'Assemblée des Premières Nations du Québec et du Labrador (APNQL), en février 2003.

1 Le mot « fédéré » réfère à la fédération du SIFC à l'Université de Régina.

Le SIFC est un endroit spécial de savoir où la connaissance est reconnue, respectée et promue. Ici, les étudiants autochtones peuvent apprendre dans le contexte de leurs propres cultures, langues et valeurs. Ainsi enracinés dans leur culture traditionnelle, nos étudiants peuvent évoluer fièrement parmi la société majoritaire contemporaine. Notre collège universitaire, par ses programmes d'extension, atteint toutes nos communautés et leur offre la richesse de ses ressources.

Nos Anciens nous enseignent à respecter les croyances et les valeurs culturelles de toutes les nations. Notre collège fournit aux étudiants de toutes origines l'occasion d'apprendre dans un milieu éducatif culturel et philosophique autochtone.

L'attention aux enseignements reçus du Créateur confère aux Premiers Peuples une vision unique à contribuer à l'éducation supérieure en général. Grâce à la diversité et à l'étendue de ses programmes en études des Premières Nations, le collège occupe une position unique au sein des études supérieures canadiennes.

La structure physique du collège se doit de refléter le caractère unique, les valeurs culturelles, la dignité et le sens de la beauté possédé par les Premières Nations. Elle doit aussi refléter une reconnaissance appropriée du rôle des Anciens, des symboles de notre culture, ainsi que du lien unissant les Premières Nations à la Terre.

Le texte qui précède constitua, en octobre 1992, une réflexion collective extraordinaire de tous les membres du Saskatchewan Indian Federated College (Anciens, étudiants, professeurs, employés de soutien) ainsi que d'autres personnes d'autres milieux universitaires et gouvernementaux. Le but de cette réflexion était le lancement d'une campagne provinciale et nationale de financement et de sensibilisation au besoin du SIFC de se doter d'une structure physique propre et à la hauteur de sa mission. En effet, après seize ans d'existence et d'un succès éducatif phénoménal, le SIFC, la seule institution du genre au pays, était encore l'enfant pauvre et sans abri fixe de l'Université de Régina, mère de deux autres collèges à dénomination religieuse, confortablement logés sur son campus. La campagne lancée en 1992 a vu son aboutissement le 21 juin 2003, lorsque le SIFC changea son nom pour celui de First Nations University of Canada (Université canadienne des Premières Nations), et lorsque a été inauguré le splendide édifice de cette nouvelle université, une remarquable création de l'architecte métis pied-noir Douglas Cardinal, célèbre pour sa conception du Musée des Civilisations, à Ottawa, et pour plusieurs autres joyaux d'architecture.

Tout comme l'avait été l'établissement du SIFC en 1976, l'accomplissement de cette vision de l'édifice de l'Université canadienne des Premières Nations était une tâche monumentale, propre à décourager bien des esprits logiques et raisonnables. Mais nous disposions d'une inépuisable réserve de passion et de notre spiritualité amérindienne. Et nous avions à notre tête un capitaine d'une détermination d'acier, notre président Eber Hampton[2], docteur en éducation issu, comme il le dit à l'occasion d'un ton doux mais sérieux, de la nation « inconquise et inconquérable » des Chickasaws. J'ai eu, durant quatre ans, le privilège d'être le doyen aux études de cette institution unique.

La recherche universitaire sur les problématiques autochtones

Grâce à mon expérience de chercheur et de praticien en milieu éducatif autochtone, je suis familier avec les préoccupations, les angoisses et les espoirs des chercheurs. Je connais aussi intimement les attentes et les angoisses des responsables et des intéressés autochtones qui ont un rôle à jouer dans ces exercices de recherche, soit comme leaders politiques, soit comme professionnels de l'éducation, soit comme consultants et peut-être, surtout, comme citoyens des Premières Nations, lesquels sont, très communément, surpassés par la taille gigantesque et la nature du défi de l'éducation des Premières Nations.

Plutôt que de m'adresser à la nature particulière ou à la pertinence de travaux de recherches précis, je choisis de faire porter ma réflexion sur la question de la *pérennité*, c'est-à-dire comment, à long terme, allons-nous donner forme et existence au grand projet collectif des Premières Nations d'éduquer leurs citoyens de façon à assurer non seulement la survie, mais aussi la prospérité et la santé des peuples autochtones dans les temps à venir. L'importance de penser en termes de *pérennité* a surgi d'une rencontre avec un groupe de chercheurs québécois à laquelle j'assistai, en octobre 2002, à la demande de l'Assemblée des Premières Nations du Québec et du Labrador. Ce fut une idée que je soumis, et qui me vint surtout de diverses expériences professionnelles que je vécus comme administrateur de collèges universitaires amérindiens, notamment en

---

2 Le docteur Hampton, maître d'œuvre dans la concrétisation de l'Université des Premières Nations du Canada, est depuis retourné à sa carrière de professeur en sciences de l'éducation.

Saskatchewan et en Colombie-Britannique. Marqué par ces expériences, je suis toujours surpris de constater la faiblesse marquée de réflexion pratique dans ce sens dans d'autres provinces de l'Est du pays, dont le Québec.

Bien que l'on puisse facilement concéder que la nature particulière de l'histoire de la société québécoise, de même que l'évolution des relations de celle-ci avec les Premières Nations, ont été en plusieurs points différentes et souvent plus socialement positives que ce qu'elles ont été dans les provinces de l'Ouest, il reste que l'expérience éducative des autochtones dans les institutions non autochtones a été et continue d'être un échec dont la gravité s'exprime dans un énorme gaspillage de potentiel humain. Il faut, par conséquent, considérer la solution alternative la plus évidente à cet état de choses, c'est-à-dire identifier et prendre les moyens pour créer des institutions aptes à mettre un terme à la tragique histoire du contrôle de l'éducation des autochtones par les non-autochtones.

Cela dit, je me défends de penser que certains de nos étudiants autochtones ne trouvent pas dans les écoles, collèges et universités canadiennes des expériences éducatives très valables et valorisantes. J'ajouterai même d'emblée que certains des défis (surtout financiers, mais aussi politiques) particuliers aux institutions éducatives sous contrôle autochtone peuvent être si lourds que ces institutions autochtones sont parfois vues par certains étudiants, certaines communautés autochtones, comme portant un risque quant aux chances de succès scolaire à l'intérieur des contraintes qui leur sont propres, surtout dans leur phase initiale de développement. L'avantage très important de l'existence de telles institutions sous contrôle autochtone, cependant, est qu'elles permettent aux gens des Premières Nations de voir en elles, en relevant la tête, des flambeaux d'espoir dont la présence dit : « Nous sommes capables de penser par nous-mêmes et pour nous-mêmes. Notre savoir est important, voire précieux pour nous-mêmes et pour l'humanité. Oui, il y aura un avenir pour nos peuples, et ce sera l'avenir que *nous* aurons créé, avec notre esprit et notre génie propres, dans le respect de tous, tel que nous l'ont toujours enseigné nos Sages ». Aussi, ces institutions autochtones de haut savoir sont génératrices d'idées et de modèles dont ont besoin les institutions non autochtones afin de rendre leur action auprès de leurs étudiants autochtones plus signifiante. Dans la foulée de l'Université canadienne des Premières Nations et d'autres institutions similaires, de tels endroits deviennent les moteurs (autrement non existants) d'une transformation de la pensée conventionnelle au sujet de l'éducation des peuples autochtones. Graduellement, mais à coup sûr, on ne parle plus, au pays, du « problème des Indiens »: plutôt, on voit les Premières Nations comme une richesse qu'elles-mêmes possèdent et partagent, dans l'honneur et la fierté, avec ceux qui sont venus chez elles pour vivre mieux.

L'une des préoccupations majeures des organismes politiques autochtones au Canada est leur manque d'emprise sur les orientations, l'application et la coordination de la recherche faite par plusieurs organismes scientifiques de recherche. En règle générale, la nature même de toute recherche scientifique commande l'isolement de ceux qui la font. Les dirigeants politiques autochtones sont uniformément et constamment aux prises avec des problèmes beaucoup trop nombreux, graves et divers pour pouvoir procurer aux chercheurs l'orientation et, donc, la coordination qui donneraient à leurs travaux l'impact naturellement désiré. Lorsque, au hasard d'une évolution sociale toujours trop compliquée, des questions surgissent des communautés concernant le statut et la pertinence des recherches en cours, chercheurs et responsables politiques se retrouvent dans une situation inconfortable, voire professionnellement hasardeuse vu la volatilité typique des positionnements politiques dans nos sociétés amérindiennes et autochtones, chroniquement marquées au sceau de la fragilité. On voudrait pourtant faire mieux, on rêve de forums permanents sur l'éducation postsecondaire, on parle d'avoir ses propres institutions sous contrôle autochtone, mais comme personne ne possède ni le temps ni les ressources, on se contente d'une réalité à bien meilleur marché.

Construire la pérennité

Comment, me dis-je, avoir un effet positif même minime en l'absence de structures éducatives globales de facture autochtone propres à générer leurs propres théories pour un discours général sur l'éducation, donc sur l'avenir des gouvernements et des sociétés autochtones ? Pour moi, cela ne peut se faire sans l'existence d'une ou plusieurs institutions de haut savoir sous contrôle autochtone, œuvrant en complémentarité de celles de la société majoritaire non autochtone, peut-être selon des modèles similaires à celui de la fédération de l'une ou de plusieurs universités ou collèges universitaires canadiens, tels celui de l'Université Canadienne des Premières Nations et de l'Université de Régina.

L'image qui me vient à l'esprit lorsque l'on parle d'éducation autochtone sans concevoir la nécessité d'endroits propres à la générer est celle-ci : je vois une belle et bonne voiture, possiblement chargée de marchandises utiles, peut-être même précieuses (la recherche), mais n'ayant pas de moteur pour la propulser. La façon dont j'ai présenté mon idée de la pérennité en éducation postsecondaire autochtone est simple et de nature collaborative : les chercheurs des universités, québécoises et canadiennes, représentent un potentiel à la disposition des Premières Nations. Il faut que nous, Premières Nations, concevions la vision qui nous fera trouver la façon d'utiliser ce potentiel pour créer une suite à ces efforts de recherche. Nous avons ici la chance de faire constituer un fond de connaissances précieuses et indispensables pour créer notre éducation et notre enseignement futurs. C'est ici que je pense à la nécessité d'intégrer à la recherche une autre branche de savoir concernant les expériences d'autres Premières Nations avec leurs défis et leurs accomplissements éducatifs, nationalement et, aussi, internationalement. Qu'existe-t-il en termes de contrôle autochtone de l'éducation autochtone au pays, en Amérique, dans le monde ?

Mon credo en éducation

J'ai acquis, par profession et par vocation, une certaine expertise en éducation des peuples autochtones et je suis animé par une croyance inébranlable : je crois que notre peuple des Premières Nations a, à cause de sa philosophie et de notre histoire de contact avec les Euro-Canadiens et les Euro-Québécois, une responsabilité spéciale et incontournable de sensibiliser les nouveaux habitants de ses territoires aux plans de la philosophie et de la spiritualité, ce qui rejoint tous les domaines de la vie en société. Quatre ou cinq siècles de négation et d'assauts constants et de toutes sortes contre nos peuples n'ont pas réussi à leur faire perdre une foi fondamentale en leurs valeurs culturelles et spirituelles. Aujourd'hui, les gens des Premières Nations proclament haut et fort qu'elles ne veulent plus penser à leur éducation sans une connexion vitale avec la terre et avec les valeurs sociales et spirituelles héritées de leurs ancêtres.

Personnellement, je crois que l'éducation des Premières Nations doit se concevoir et s'enseigner d'abord sur la base des connaissances et des pratiques traditionnelles. Les porteurs reconnus de la connaissance et de la sagesse autochtones doivent jouer un rôle central dans l'éducation à tous les niveaux, même universitaire, ainsi que dans tous les domaines de la recherche sur nos sociétés autochtones. Je crois que tout le savoir moderne doit être regardé et évalué à la lumière de la compréhension spirituelle de la vie et de l'existence. Des sciences qui produisent beaucoup trop souvent l'insécurité et l'appauvrissement de l'humain peuvent être soumises aux lumières d'une très longue réflexion des peuples autochtones sur la nature profonde de la vie et des conditions de la santé, de la sécurité, en définitive, du bonheur de l'humain. Dans le même ordre d'idées, je n'admets pas que les peuples autochtones doivent, avant de pouvoir penser prendre les commandes de leur propre éducation, d'abord posséder une masse critique de chercheurs et d'enseignants agrégés par la communauté savante non autochtone. Je trouve inadmissible que l'on nous considère, ou que nous nous considérions, à ce point affaiblis et colonisés. Nous sommes une force positive bien vivante qui n'attend que la *vision* de son développement !

Dépasser l'objection du Collège Manitou

Il y eut naguère un Collège amérindien au Québec, le Collège Manitou, situé à La Macaza, à une centaine de kilomètres au nord de Montréal. Ce Collège exista quelques brèves années et fut fermé en 1975 par le ministère des Affaires indiennes. Manitou fut une merveilleuse tentative qui, même après toutes ces années, évoque un profond regret chez tous ceux qui y étudièrent, y enseignèrent, y travaillèrent ou simplement, comme moi, le connurent. La fermeture du Collège Manitou fut douloureuse, et, étrangement, la douleur dure encore. Usant du bénéfice de la rétrospection et de celui de mes expériences subséquentes en éducation autochtone, je puis aujourd'hui dire que Manitou était, dès son ouverture, voué à l'échec à brève échéance. Il manquait, dans la vision qui le sous-tendait, l'élément d'inclusion culturelle : Manitou n'était que pour les autochtones. Cette philosophie, en réalité, allait à l'encontre de la tradition autochtone, qui met un accent prépondérant sur le partage et l'inclusion. Voilà, selon moi, le défaut principal de la conception de Manitou, ainsi que la preuve que cette conception ne fut pas véritablement autochtone.

L'éducation, sous quelque bannière culturelle ou nationale qu'elle existe, doit être universaliste, afin d'éviter de tomber dans l'isolationnisme culturel. Mais cette universalisation est peut-être encore plus importante lorsqu'il s'agit d'éducation sous contrôle autochtone. En effet, l'expérience des autochtones dans les systèmes et programmes éducatifs étrangers convainc ceux-ci que les objectifs fondamentaux d'une telle éducation sont de nier, plutôt que de valoriser, l'unicité des individus et des collectivités qu'ils composent. Pour citer Eber Hampton :

> L'éducation indienne s'oriente autour d'un centre spirituel qui définit l'individu comme la vie du groupe. La liberté et la force de l'individu sont la force du groupe. L'individu ne forme pas une identité en opposition au groupe mais reconnaît ceux du groupe comme ses parents et inclut le groupe dans son identité [...]
>
> L'éducation [autochtone] est pour servir le peuple. Son but n'est pas la promotion individuelle ou le statut social [...] La société et l'éducation occidentales promeuvent et glorifient trop souvent la performance individuelle aux dépens des liens sociaux qui donnent un sens à cette performance. Il y a sur ce point un conflit inévitable entre l'éducation occidentale et l'éducation autochtone. Le succès de l'individu dans la compétition est une valeur implicite des écoles occidentales et, comme tel, est en conflit direct avec la valeur indienne de produire le succès du groupe par la performance individuelle.
>
> L'étudiant autochtone, dans une école [occidentale] qui non seulement exalte les valeurs occidentales mais place l'individu en opposition au groupe, sentira un conflit entre être autochtone et recevoir une éducation (*First Nations Education In Canada*, sous la direction de Marie Battiste et Jean Barman, Vancouver, UBC Press, 1995, p. 21 ; traduction libre).

Généralement, les autochtones ont une méfiance instinctive vis-à-vis de la vision occidentale de l'éducation, de même qu'ils ont une confiance tout aussi spontanée en une pratique éducative héritée de leurs traditions. De plus, la valeur culturelle et spirituelle de partage inspire chez la plupart des autochtones le sens d'une responsabilité d'enseigner au monde en général une autre vision de l'éducation, la leur, dans laquelle l'individu ainsi que sa collectivité sont respectés, renforcés et valorisés, sans égard à leur origine ethnique, leurs coutumes ou leurs croyances. Encore plus, dans la vision traditionnelle (circulaire) autochtone, la différence n'est pas seulement acceptée, elle est admirée et souvent intégrée. Tel qu'il ressort des quatrième et cinquième paragraphes du texte de la vision de l'édifice de l'UCPN, cité au début du présent document, une institution d'éducation autochtone tient l'inclusion pour un de ses principes moteurs. Un tel endroit de savoir croit aussi en sa mission éducatrice unique et nécessaire auprès de la société globale. Ces deux principes indispensables ont manqué au Collège Manitou. Je trouve donc irrecevable l'objection fréquemment faite que l'expérience d'un collège autochtone a déjà été faite au Québec et a échoué. Par ailleurs, de plusieurs façons notables, Manitou fut un succès : il permit à de nombreuses communautés amérindiennes de se rejoindre et de se connaître mutuellement et, de façon importante, Manitou aida à former des leaders dans plusieurs domaines pour les années qui suivirent. L'expérience doit être poursuivie… sur une base spirituelle autochtone. Au reste, l'expérience et le bon sens nous disent que la pratique de l'inclusion et l'ouverture d'esprit donnent accès aux forces de l'univers. Nos ancêtres des Premiers Peuples ont fait cela dès les premiers moments qu'ils virent des étrangers arriver chez eux. Si ceux-ci sont toujours des étrangers, et si notre besoin est de vivre ensemble et de vivre bien, l'éducation seule peut nous rendre capables de reconnaître notre parenté : une éducation pour l'humain et pour la vie, c'est-à-dire enrichie de la dimension spirituelle apprise et cultivée par les Premiers Peuples de ce continent depuis des centaines de générations.

Quelques statistiques

J'ai eu et j'entretiens constamment, comme Amérindien et comme professionnel de l'éducation, des contacts multiples et serrés avec nos étudiants, nos intellectuels autochtones et nos gens en général, et je n'hésite pas à dire tout haut que les citoyens de nos Premières Nations ressentent et expriment fréquemment une profonde insatisfaction vis-à-vis de l'éducation offerte dans les institutions de la société majoritaire. Au seul regard des statistiques sur l'éducation autochtone, on conçoit facilement que cette insatisfaction ait beaucoup à voir avec le désespoir social qui menace si sérieusement la survie même des Premiers Peuples canadiens.

Dans son livre *Quel Canada pour les Autochtones?*[3], l'avocate québécoise Renée Dupuis énonce de sombres chiffres concernant divers aspects de la vie des Premiers Peuples du Canada et du Québec. L'auteure parle de la « désintégration des sociétés autochtones », une « catastrophe » sociale qu'elle impute à l'indifférence injustifiable d'un pays aussi riche que le Canada. Offrant, à la fin de son livre, sa vision quant au redressement de cet échec, elle donne, au début de son ouvrage, des statistiques, dont quelques-unes sur le lamentable état de l'éducation autochtone :

> Les autochtones connaissent également un retard en matière de scolarisation. Les statistiques démontrent une légère augmentation de la fréquentation scolaire et du taux de diplômes obtenus, mais il n'en demeure pas moins que cela ne leur permet pas de rattraper la moyenne nationale. En 1996, deux fois plus de Canadiens (14 %) que de citoyens des Premières Nations (7 %) détenaient un diplôme d'études postsecondaires. Le nombre d'autochtones ayant fait des études postsecondaires (y compris des études universitaires) est environ deux fois moindre que dans le reste de la population. L'écart est encore plus élevé pour ce qui est des études universitaires : 4 fois moins d'Indiens (5,2 %) et 10 fois moins d'Inuits (2,3 %) que de Canadiens (21 %) on fait des études universitaires. Cela ne suppose pas nécessairement que ces études universitaires aient été achevées ; en 1996, seulement 3 % des Indiens avaient terminé leurs études et obtenu un diplôme, comparativement à 13 % pour l'ensemble de la population canadienne (p. 23).

Analysant la « grotesque synergie entre les écoles résidentielles de naguère et les prisons d'aujourd'hui », la sociologue Paula Mallea en décrit certaines choquantes

---

3 Ce livre a mérité à l'auteure le Prix du Lieutenant Gouverneur, catégorie Essai, en 2001.

conséquences dans le livre *Voice of the Drum* (Kingfisher Publications, Brandon, Manitoba, 2000, p. 23-24):

> Au Canada [...], le taux de chômage des autochtones est quatre fois supérieur à celui des non-autochtones. L'espérance de vie est beaucoup plus basse pour les autochtones – de sept à huit ans plus basse –; comparable, en fait, à celle des Nicaraguayens. Le taux de mortalité des autochtones de 25 à 44 ans est cinq fois plus élevé que chez les non-autochtones. Il y a plus de deux fois plus de suicides. La mortalité infantile est 1,7 fois plus élevée. Les problèmes reliés à la nutrition sont beaucoup plus communs. Enfin, alors que 8 % de la population canadienne dépend de quelque forme d'aide sociale, cela est le lot de 29 % d'autochtones.

La Commission royale sur les peuples autochtones, dont le Rapport fut déposé en 1996, comprend 44 recommandations touchant l'éducation. L'une de celles-ci est à l'effet des responsabilités vis-à-vis de la jeunesse autochtone. La Commission recommande :

> Que les écoles provinciales et territoriales contrôlées par les autochtones et servant la jeunesse autochtone développent et appliquent des stratégies globales d'appui à la jeunesse autochtone, incluant des éléments à élaborer en collaboration avec celle-ci, dont :

· une éducation culturelle en classe et dans des lieux informels ;
· une reconnaissance des dimensions spirituelle, éthique et intuitive de l'apprentissage ;
· une éducation incorporant l'analyse critique de l'expérience autochtone ;
· l'apprentissage comme moyen de guérison des effets des traumatismes, des abus et du racisme ;
· le développement et le soutien du potentiel intellectuel ;
· l'éducation sportive et à l'extérieur ;
· le développement du leadership ;
· les voyages – échanges de jeunes de nations autochtones de tout le Canada, de même qu'internationalement.

Les recommandations principales pour l'éducation des adultes ainsi qu'au postsecondaire mettent l'accent sur *l'allocation de fonds stables et adéquats, ainsi que sur l'accréditation des institutions autochtones postsecondaires qui se battent présentement pour leurs ressources, à la marge des collèges provinciaux et des systèmes universitaires.* Une université internationale des peuples autochtones est proposée, dont trois des fonctions seraient la connectivité entre les efforts régionaux, le développement des critères d'accréditation ainsi que la constitution d'un lieu de négociation des équivalences avec les réseaux universitaires existants.

Des recommandations concernant l'importance du rôle des Sages dans l'éducation reprennent celles de rapports antérieurs en définissant les façons d'intégrer le savoir traditionnel dans l'éducation des jeunes. Ces recommandations appuient également la proposition de l'échange de Sages de différentes régions et traditions, ainsi que leur mise en rapport en milieu scolaire avec les spécialistes non autochtones.

L'idée maîtresse des recommandations de la Commission Royale au sujet de l'éducation est que les gouvernements fédéral, provinciaux et territoriaux devraient reconnaître que l'éducation est centrale à l'exercice de la gouvernance et qu'ils devraient collaborer avec les gouvernements, les organisations et les autorités éducatives autochtones, lorsque cela convient, *pour appuyer le développement de systèmes d'éducation sous contrôle autochtone et fournir un financement à la mesure des responsabilités assumées* (Rapport de la Commission, volume 3, p. 444). Permettre l'espace pour des initiatives autochtones et stabiliser le financement des institutions autochtones aura un effet sur la qualité et l'efficacité de l'éducation qui continuera à être offerte par les institutions provinciales et territoriales, leur fournissant des modèles et des points de référence quant à la performance institutionnelle.

Conclusion : des lieux où s'entredécouvrir

La crise d'Oka, en 1990, a définitivement et finalement mis un terme à l'ère où la société non-autochtone se croyait en droit de penser que les autochtones n'étaient, en fait, que des vestiges d'anciennes sociétés tribales arriérées, c'est-à-dire que le problème autochtone était chose d'archives. Lorsqu'arriva l'impasse politique et militaire d'Oka, personne ne sut quoi faire, puisque « ces gens » n'étaient plus censés exister. On n'avait jamais pensé valable de les connaître, puisque, selon toute la science et la sagesse de l'histoire, les Indiens avaient tous disparu « à l'époque des Indiens ». Ce qui normalement aurait dû se régler en quelques heures autour d'une table commune dégénéra tout à fait mécaniquement en une crise qui fut majeure dans l'histoire politique et militaire du Canada, et causa une brèche sérieuse dans les relations entre Québécois et autochtones, que la plupart des gens croyaient très bonnes (puisque les Mohawks d'Oka n'étaient pas de « vrais » Indiens) et que l'on n'a pas réellement commencé à réparer (puisque la période de choc n'est même pas encore terminée).

Le grand dommage, et le grand danger, sont que, comme société, nous n'avons pas pensé à créer des lieux sociaux et des traditions sociales pour nous entredécouvrir, nous comprendre et nous apprécier. Pourtant, les autochtones, quant à eux, posèrent de tels gestes d'une façon très décisive dès leurs tout premiers contacts avec les Européens. Pour s'en convaincre, on n'a qu'à lire les écrits de Jacques Cartier, par exemple. Malheureusement, ce type d'attitude inclusive ne fait absolument pas partie du bagage idéologique qu'emmenaient avec eux les Européens.

On aura beau concevoir et plaquer sur les sociétés les ententes territoriales et sociales en apparence les plus justes, sophistiquées et même « braves », elles ne sauront produire l'harmonie, la paix, la justice et la santé pour les populations en cause si l'on ne permet pas d'abord à tous ces gens de se connaître, de se comprendre et, ainsi, de vouloir « faire corps ensemble », comme le visualisait le grand Kondiaronk, lors de son « Atsathaion » (discours avant son décès), en août 1701. Il faut permettre aux Premiers Peuples de ce pays de créer des lieux (les Ancêtres diraient des Feux) où tous les gens qui vivent maintenant ici et les autres qui viendront puissent apprendre à connaître et aimer leur nouvelle Terre-mère, s'y enracinent et la protègent et, ainsi, deviennent parents ensemble, plutôt que de demeurer des étrangers qui ne savent communiquer que par la législation, la force et l'intimidation. Oka nous a fait sortir de l'ère de l'ignorance innocente. Il est grand temps de créer l'ère de la connaissance et de la communication. Un jour, nous aussi, comme nos parents de l'Ouest, aurons le plaisir et l'honneur d'accueillir nos frères et nos sœurs de tous horizons dans nos écoles, nos collèges, nos universités. Ensemble, nous irons tellement plus loin dans nos potentialités.

Ho! Ho! Ho! Attouguet! (Merci beaucoup ! Niawen Kowa!)
He! He! Tsheneshkometnan! (Thank you very much!)

The Soul of Eeyou/Eenou Governance[*]

Meeyou-Pimat-tahseewin: An Eeyou Definition of Health

This Eeyou concept of health applies to the people or nation, as well as to the individual. To the Eeyou, as is the case for Aboriginal peoples generally, health is the result of consciously cultivating and maintaining balance between the four aspects, or components, of every person and therefore of the people, or nation. These components are the physical, the mental, the emotional and the spiritual.

---

[*] This text was prepared in April 2007 for the Cree Working Group on Cree Governance, under the authority of the Grand Council of the Crees of James Bay, Quebec. The words *Eeyou* and *Eenou* represent, respectively, the Cree autonym for Coastal and Inland Cree. For the purpose of simplicity, we will use the word *Eeyou*, except when it refers to an individual from an Inland community (such as Elder Philip Awashish of Lake Mistissini). On occasion, the plural forms, *Eeyouch* and *Eenouch*, may be used.

If there is illness in the individual, the curer will seek to treat the pain, or unease, at all four levels. Some sources of pain are only physical, such as an accidental bruise, cut or burn; however, the Indians of old have been recorded by early observers as explaining that most diseases originate in a suffering of the soul, often described as "unfulfilled desires". These same principles remain true about a nation and most specifically about kinship-based, traditionally egalitarian societies, such as the Eeyou, and virtually all small and medium-scale indigenous and peasant societies. It has taken all these centuries for Western medicine and social sciences to only begin to recognize these simple truths.

The Circle and the Sacred Number Four

For the traditional Eeyou, as for the traditional Amerindian, life is a sacred Circle of relations uniting all life in all its manifestations. The Circle is composed of four sacred elements: four sacred directions, all alive with a spirit; four ages in life, four parts of a day, of a lunar month, of a year; four sacred colours; four families of peoples, each with a special, sacred gift to share with the three others; four sacred elements: fire, earth, water, air; and so forth.

Since the person is made up of four sacred components, wellness will be restored only when the curer and the whole community have addressed the hurt, the want, the ailment located in every part of the sick individual. Those four parts have to be re-balanced and maintained in balance. The same holds true for the community, which is in reality an extension of the individual.

"The Sweetness of Life Has Been Lost"

These are the words used by an Eenou Elder (Elder Philip Awashish of Lake Mistissini) to explain why an unduly high number of Eenouch [plural form] are now suffering from diabetes and heart disease. These words speak to a grave *loss of feeling of togetherness* with the land and with all its peoples: animals, fish, birds, insects, and also with fellow humans united by a feeling of affection and respect towards the land and all life sustained by it. Such is the 'religion' of the Eeyou:

a feeling of closeness and love for Istchee—the Earth, our Mother. *That* is the sweetness that the Elder is speaking about. In order to heal, individually and collectively, the Eeyouch have to allow themselves (through their own system of governance) to move away from a fast, harsh, unfeeling, artificial world, back to their revered slower-paced, softer, sweeter, truer Eeyou ('Indian') world.

Animals, Rocks and Plants as People

Through the building of the hydroelectric dams, the Eeyouch began to be forced to turn away from their traditional circular world view. They were asked to understand and accept that their Land needed to be "developed economically". They were asked to see and treat their relatives, the animals, trees, rocks and plants, as "wildlife resources" that were waiting to be "harvested". Traditionally, each animal, each plant was a 'non-human person' who could be talked to, thanked, prayed to.

An animal is not simplistically a physical being, a certain number of pounds of meat; an animal is a 'someone'; a plant is not simply a physical 'thing' that has monetary value if you know how to package and market it.

Eeyou Medicine and Eeyou Intellectual Property

Upon first contact with incoming Europeans, Amerindians frequently and formally warned the latter that they were not to take even a sapling or a twig without the First Peoples' permission. Obviously, this was not meant to safeguard their own rights as proprietors, for the Native people do not claim to own fellow living beings; rather, it was to safeguard the dignity of these fellow living beings whom the Amerindians noticed the Europeans were taking and consuming without any sign of respect. That kind of behaviour greatly hurt the feelings of the First Peoples.

In their principles of governance, the Eeyouch would be well advised to first establish and affirm that they have lived and thrived on their Land for untold generations in good health because they have in fact had this relationship of interrelatedness and respectful fraternity, in the spirit of the sacred Circle of Life, with all the other living beings (this also includes the rocks) in their territories.

They should also explain to anyone bent on disrespectfully (and unlawfully) taking from their Land and commercializing plant-life, animal-life or rock-life, that the "products" derived thereof will not carry good or strong "medicine" because they have been taken and "processed" as objects; that is, without due respect. An emotional, spiritual, mental and physical communication has to take place between all beings if health and well-being are going to be produced and enhanced.

Research on Eenou Health and Eenou Concepts of Health

As can be felt in the words of the Eenou Elder cited above, the Eeyou are dismayed at having seen the quality of their people's life, and thus of its health, decline dangerously over just a few decades. There is a responsibility for scholars, in partnership with traditionalist Aboriginal people, to study and research the causes behind such loss of health in a population, especially an Aboriginal population that has been brought so rapidly and forcefully into the linear, anti-ecological Canadian mainstream and that, through this very process, has contributed so importantly to the further entrenching and enriching of this said Canadian (and Québécois) lifestyle.

As statistics show that the Eeyouch are more and more afflicted by more and more physical and other diseases, it is also the responsibility of professional researchers to help and enable the Eeyouch to recover their own philosophies and practices concerning health. The Eeyouch stand to benefit very importantly from such tangible demonstration of respect for their traditional world view and life ways, and also importantly, Canadians (and Québécois) themselves will, in the process, discover the real, unsuspected treasures of the civilization that the Eeyouch and the other First Peoples of the Land have elaborated in communion with Her (Mother Earth) long before Canada existed on it.

The Hunter's Democracy

According to conventional anthropological wisdom, hunting societies, such as the Eeyouch and northern peoples generally, have been seen and ranked in the lower scales of 'human evolution'. There is new scientific evidence that

Aboriginal peoples held and continue to hold a very different view on this question: the hunters are culturally and ideologically closer to an ideal human state of fine adjustment, therefore proximity to the supernatural world. In other words, hunters hold and practise the secrets of how and why humans must acknowledge and respect all forms and orders of life; *hunters practise the most elevated form of democracy*; they are the ultimate keepers of true democracy, which they and all Aboriginal peoples name *the Sacred Circle of Life*. In this light, re-creating Eenou governance appears as an effort that must be supported by the whole collectivity. As Eenou Elder Philip Awashish says: "The way things are (or are not) done, that is, *Eenou law*. It has to be put down on paper and given the status it deserves. The Eenou people have already put very much effort towards this goal; and time is of the essence."

Some Principles of an Eeyou-Centred Educational System

As suggested above, hunting societies, such as the Eeyou of James Bay and Northern Quebec, find it vitally important to transmit to successive generations a sense of intimate closeness to the land. Maybe even more than other Aboriginal peoples, the hunters feel that the land, *the Earth*, is their Mother and they apply their whole genius to knowing, understanding and foreseeing her every mood, feeling and message. This way of relating to their Land has allowed the Eeyou to live happily and successfully on it for untold generations. Their faith in their Land and in their ancestral wisdom is probably the most prized possession of every Eeyou. "We have lots of pride in being Indian, we have lots of pride in being able to live directly from the land and we want to continue this pride," said Chief Billy Diamond. Peter Hutchins, quoted in the same article, said: "The land is the center of their existence. It is peace, it is tranquility, it is harmony with nature.... And this is a communal concept. The land for them is a home and it is also a garden.... They are of the Garden."[1] Hutchins, explains the author of the article, was implying that Hydro-Québec was going to flood the Crees' garden and that this case was about cultural as well as natural destruction. Indeed, without this vibrant, flesh-and-soul connection

---

1 Hans M. Carlson. A Watershed of Words: Litigating and Negotiating Nature in Eastern James Bay, 1971-1975", The Canadian Historical Review (2004), Vol. 85, p. 61-84, p. 80.

to their Land, the reason and the right of the Eeyou to exist as a distinct people would likely wither and die.

This is why the way Eeyou education is conceived, designed and delivered is of such primary importance. It is the belief of many educators, and also my own, that there can be no genuine cultural survival without the transmission to new generations of a deep, ancestral sense of attachment to and respect for the Land and all of the elements that compose Her, that is, the 'Sacred Circle of Life'. The aim and the outcome of an Eeyou system of education have to be, first and foremost, the transmission of this strong feeling of respect and affection for the land.

In this regard, it is of very high importance that children, at their most tender age, be told the stories of their people in their own language, for like all Aboriginal languages, the Eeyou language is a code for the transmission of a timeless story of love for the land and of the land for the people. Stories infuse in a child's mind and heart the notions that, later in life, will enable that person to converse emotionally, spiritually, mentally and physically (Eenou/Eeyou *Meeyou-Pimaat-tahseewin*) with all other 'relatives' in the Circle, however seemingly insignificant they may appear to be.

The Eeyou/Eenou Concept of 'Wi-way-mag-nou'

Like many Aboriginal nations, the Eeyou have an educational concept, best told in their language and pronounced '*wi-way-mag-nou*'. It may loosely be translated into English as the *recognition* of the essential genius or innermost capacity of a child or person. This concept refers to the need for a family and a society to study, identify and recognize in a child the foremost ability, or talent, possessed by this new member of their society, for children are traditionally seen as gifts received from the world of spirits and are treated with the utmost care, love and respect.

A child, for instance, will be recognized as a natural healer; another, a civil leader; another, a keeper of stories; another, a future tradesperson; another, gifted for hunting, fishing or planting; and so forth. Then such children would be carefully placed under the guidance of men and women who possessed and had developed gifts similar to the ones possessed by those children.

One of the pitfalls of almost every approach to education successively tried on Aboriginal people, from the disastrous Residential Schools to so-called more modern educational systems, has been to try to force all children into pre-designed learning moulds, in total disregard for the way that the Eeyou (and Aboriginal) people think about children in general and about their own children in particular. I believe that the Eeyou concept of *'wi-way-mag-nou'*, and others, have to be brought back, studied and made to permeate the whole effort of creating an authentically Eeyou approach to Eeyou education. Some deep questions have to be asked if the Eenou are to create and put into effect systems of governance that are authentically Eeyou, instead of replicating what others have thought is best for the Eeyou. Should all Eeyou children be put through the same educational process? What about those children naturally gifted for becoming the keepers of nature's secrets, under the great hunters (*Indoh-hoh Ouje-Maooch*). The old language of the Eeyouch (the 'high Cree'), still possessed by the hunters, contains the knowledge about the interrelatedness of all the elements of nature. *Someone has to* preserve that language. If all the children are spending most of their time in *school*, who will be the keepers of the language, the art of conversing with the land, the Eeyou Land? And the same holds true for every child, including the ones naturally gifted to become excellent Eeyou businesspeople, Eeyou mechanics, Eeyou scientists and so forth. What I am proposing is that the Eeyou concepts about children, education, the place of the human in nature, put the Eeyou in a position where they can give the world very important new ideas about how to transform conventional, unproductive foreign concepts about these very things. Those Eeyou concepts also put the Eeyou in a position where they can create an educational system that they will be eager to embrace and apply to their collective life because it will be based on their own philosophical precepts and spiritual beliefs.

The Primacy of Elders in the Eeyou/Eenou Culture

In their language, the Eeyou do not have a way of referring to someone as "an old person". They say that someone is a "*Chisa-Eeyou*" (masculine form) or a "*Chisa-Eeyoushkwo*" (feminine form), which carries the idea of greatness; that is, of the respect due to a human being (relative) who has walked for a long time "on the human trail". As we have just seen, walking for a long time on the human trail in a spiritual way (with all the honest mistakes made along the way) implies having shown for all that time an example of love and respect for everyone and every different other being—the Earth, the animals, and especially the Creator and all the spirits that are in every thing.

In many cultures, Elders, or spiritual leaders, are called Holy Men, Holy Women. These people are holy because they have walked on the human path and have always endeavoured to be an example of a good, clean, generous heart. Eeyouch and Amerindian people generally hold such sages in the highest esteem, and the reason for this is not that these "*Chisa-Eeyouch*" have dutifully provided for their own during their active years. The true reason is that in the hearts and souls of these Elders are contained all the feelings, the thoughts, the stories that make the Eeyou proud to be what and who they are. I have lived with the Eeyouch in their bush camps and have been irreversibly marked by feeling and witnessing the tenderness and the reverence that is shown by everyone to these 'Great People' (the meaning of the name *Chisa-Eeyou* or *Chisa-Eeyoushkwo*).

For these and many other reasons, it is my feeling, as an Amerindian person, that the Eeyouch would be well advised, upon thinking about what is the soul of Eeyou governance, to take back from their people's memory the practice of establishing and using councils and the Senate of Elders as their first, foremost and most fundamental institution.

Eeyou/Eenou Civilization

The American continent, because it has been isolated from the other continents until recently, has at least as strong a claim as any other to having possessed and to still possess its true, its own global civilization. As a people that has evolved, lived and prospered in America for untold millennia, the Eeyou have every right to speak of themselves as a civilization. Furthermore, the word 'civilization' itself implies being competent to relate to other beings around oneself in a 'civil' way. On that score, it is impossible to doubt that a hunting people such as the Eeyou has for very long developed and practised very refined ways of understanding and honouring their relationships with every form of life in their known universe. (We have already elaborated on the idea of the Eeyou and other hunting peoples as practising the most elevated form of democracy and being the ultimate keepers of that so evasive and so cherished human concept.)

There is, nowadays (now that the dominant civilization feels less threatened by the Aboriginal civilization), much scientific and more mundane talk about "the Aboriginal cultures" and about the multi-faceted interest they represent for modern ('post-colonial') society. It is my belief, however, that the Eeyou and the First Peoples in general must not only speak to the non-Aboriginal world about their own civilizations (just as we have seen that they are doing), but also encourage the non-Aboriginal world to look to the circular civilizations as offering vitally important ideas and concepts concerning the global human and planetary survival. One more idea: it is a great thing to learn any non-Aboriginal language. However, if one wants to converse with Nature in a timeless, spiritual way, learn the Eeyou/Eenou *Ayimuwun* (language), or any Aboriginal/Indigenous language!

Watchiya!

A Reflection on Eeyou/Eenou Education[*]

I am not an Eeyou. My nation, the Wendat, and particularly my clan, the Tseawi, in which I am a customary chief, have close and long-standing ties with the Eeyou/Eenou. In fact, members of two branches of my clan are among the beneficiaries of the James Bay and Northern Quebec Agreement. I have lived in the Eeyou territory for extended periods of time and I am also a professional educator and a historian.

The topic of Eeyou education interests me in a very special way for among all the many Amerindian nations who compose my immediate social, cultural and spiritual world, I regard the Eeyou nation as the one that still maintains the liveliest ties with its ancestral Land and with all the beings that belong to that Land. I therefore approach this topic with two main interests at heart:

---

[*] This text was written in June 2007 for the Working Group on Cree Governance, under the authority of the Grand Council of the Crees of James Bay, Quebec. The words Eeyou and Eenou represent respectively the Cree autonym for Coastal and Inland Cree. For the purpose of simplicity, we will principally use the word Eeyou and occasionally alternate the two words.

first, I feel a strong urgency to assist the Eeyou in the exploration of the ways and means of devising a system conducive to cultural self-confidence and reaffirmation after the prolonged hiatus of colonial assault on and negation of the Eenou sense of self as an Aboriginal nation living and redefining its ways of contributing in a modern world. Second, my interest stems from my deep desire, as a Wendat and a Tseawi, to listen to and observe the Eeyou people with a view to helping other First Peoples, including my own, recover an ever surer sense of how to think and live in a traditional Aboriginal manner in a contemporary world.

This reflection will bear on the evolution of Eenou education through three periods: the pre-European, the post-contact and the rebirth periods.

The Pre-European Period

As is the case with all indigenous peoples before linear-thinking societies come to impose on them their own world view, the Eeyou once possessed a way of living that was perfectly adapted to the intimate nature of their physical and spiritual environment. That way of life was the result of the thought, and the physical and spiritual labour of thousands, even millions of intelligent, wise human beings, over hundreds of generations—that is, since the beginning of time, when the first Eeyou were created, on and from their very Land, or Mother Earth, Eeyou/Eenou Istchee.

The Eeyou had built a society where spirits were recognized, honoured and had their place, as relatives. As in many societies around the world, the spirits of ancestors were reborn and formed the new generations. In fact, the spirits, in their 'Land of Souls', had a perfect understanding of the human and earthly world. The souls of the departed heard about the wishes and needs of their human relatives through the latter's prayers, ceremonies and offerings, and acted according to a wisdom, unfathomable by humans, on behalf of their earth-bound relatives.

In such a society, children were seen as ancestors come back from the Land of Souls with ineffable desire to help re-create their people's ideal society. Beholding a newborn child stirred the most sacred emotions in all individuals:

here was an ancient soul of the people, cleansed of all past human interests and ambitions and coming back again fully charged with the pure, eternal power of the Great Spirit, *Chisa-mahn-dou*. Ayimuwun (the Eeyou language) holds concepts and words conveying the idea of the gifts contained in the soul of a child, which this individual must have the absolute freedom to explore and actualize for the benefit of her or his society. Besides, the excellence of the contribution of such individual, over a lifetime, will in large part depend on society's respect for that freedom to discover and develop those innate gifts.

This foregoing brief description of the Eenou's ancestral attitudes and views about children and their birth aims to introduce some of that society's concepts and ideas about education. First, there is a need to question whether conventional Western notions about education can adequately reflect Eeyou ideas about the meaning of education. For instance, the English word 'educate' itself implies the idea of leading someone 'out of' something negative or dangerous (*e*: out of + *ducere*: to lead). Thus, considering only the meaning of this essential word, we would already be very far away from the Eeyou view that the child (the new member of society freshly arrived from the world of spirits) has the power (which society will use) to bring society *back to* a state of balance, order and grace (instead of *away from* a state of disorder and possibly danger, as the word 'educate' implies). We thus see how the concept of 'education' itself may run directly against everything that the Eeyou believe should be the meaning and purpose of the training of children and/or young people in formal (especially non-Aboriginal) learning institutions.

In pre-European Eeyou society, Elders played a very central role in the training of children. Since the community was, and behaved as, one large, extended family, next of kin were not the only ones, or even were not always the ones who had the main role in determining and cultivating what a child's unique gifts were. Of course, mothers, grandmothers, aunts and other women had a primary role in identifying the core, innate qualities and traits of character in a child. Later on, upon reaching the age of puberty, boys (some girls also) went on a vision quest (it sometimes took more than one such quest) under the watchful eye of a specially appointed seer who alone, because they could base themselves on close and long observation of a specific child, could 'see' the essence of a child's soul, and thereby help him or her discover the sense of his or her life in relation to society.

A definite advantage for the positive development of an individual's inner qualities and gifts was the fact that knowledge was easily accessible, even for young people. Great orators spoke and no one was impeded from listening or attending, except perhaps at some war councils. Following proper protocol, anyone could seek counsel and obtain knowledge from the most prominent sages, curers, seers, artisans, artists, traders and other knowledge-bearers. Besides having the most solid mentors in given fields of knowledge, every child, especially if he or she showed respect, love and compassion to his or her Elders and community, had unlimited access to the most competent advisors in every domain and field of knowledge.

The Post-Contact Period

Since the appearance of humans on earth, there certainly did not occur an encounter of two more different civilizations as the one that took place between Europe and America on and after October 12, 1492. So violent was the shock that we can rightly speak of a terrible accident, rather than an 'encounter': on that day, the most linear-thinking societies in the world came unknowingly crashing against the most integrally circular societies on earth. So catastrophic was the clash that 515 years later, hardly anyone has yet been able to fully ascertain what truly happened and know how to talk or write about it. Indeed, if this were not the case, the world would be busy learning about life as a great Circle of relations and about how we should all live by the Circle, instead of continuing to force everyone to believe that life is a linear process, and that all living beings are merely matter to be transformed into the material and political power of leading elites.

Obsessively searching for gold and other riches, the first observers from Europe said about America's First Peoples that they were naturally mild, welcoming and generous, that they had virtually no interest in earthly possessions, and that they could probably easily be enslaved and even Christianized. These Europeans' linear world view, reinforced over centuries of monarchical oppression, unfortunately permitted them to instantly deny all worth in others. A valorous, commendable Christian and European in those times had to be a compulsive killer, robber and pillager who would never even pause to wonder whether the 'infidels' had any rights other than the one of serving the Christians and Europeans. Refusing to do this, they should not be left alive and God did not regard them as His children.

As time progressed, as Aboriginal numbers quickly thinned out and as 'civilization' claimed its 'due' place, methods of conquest (read: removal of the Indians, savages, pagans, infidels, etc.) became somewhat less drastic and violent. However, the very ingrained European views about the said infidels were not basically altered. Eventually, the most "civilized final solution" to the problem of the presence of 'Indians' was through *education*. Laws were enacted, so that by the end of the 19th century a gigantic, national program of assimilation of the Aboriginal peoples through 'Indian residential schools' was under way. Very few children escaped and if they did, it was by sheer chance. For generations on end, in many reserves, almost no children could be seen for ten months of the year. Despairing relatives took to alcoholism. The soul of communities had left. The gifts of the spirit world to its human relatives had been stolen and imprisoned in those so-called schools. Even worse, many of these sacred gifts were desecrated, abused, raped, sometimes made to die. Many victims escaped more mental torture by actually letting go of their lives. It was a horrible human tragedy, whose highly pernicious effects will be felt for a long time to come. Canada's Amerindian, Métis and Inuit peoples are very slowly and painfully recovering from efforts to 'educate' them.

The Eeyou people have not been spared from such sad attempts to deny and eliminate their soul. Even though the Eeyou have, over the last thirty years, worked strenuously and achieved partial success in devising and implementing culturally relevant programs and activities within their schooling systems, much more change needs to be brought about if the nation is to give itself a chance of re-creating a true Eenou way of learning that will give back to the people a sense of the worth of the civilization elaborated by its ancestors, as well as a sense of how this great legacy can contribute to solving a very serious social, spiritual, educational crisis that is a direct consequence of too much blind belief in linearity and that is now afflicting the whole global society.

The Period of Rebirth

The Eeyou (like all other Aboriginal nations) have a long and difficult road ahead in order to create for themselves the social and educational environment in which their future generations will once again be healthy in every sense. This said, it is also a fact that mainstream society now recognizes that the First Nations have not disappeared, as had long been predicted with absolute certainty, but that they are even gaining strength, politically and culturally, as months and years go by. Why this shocking discrepancy between expectations and reality, as it unfolds? Probably in good part for two reasons: first, the very injustice and violence of the treatment extended to First Peoples under colonial rule cancels virtually all possibility of belief in such (non-Aboriginal) thought system, and second, the obvious, alarming failure of that thought system to produce a culturally and environmentally balanced social environment, which means massive disinterest, even moral and emotional desertion, by the new generations from the vision proposed by the mainstream society. It has thus become common to speak about a new era of rebirth of the First People's ideology. This brings us directly to reflecting how we are to re-think Eeyou (and Aboriginal) education.

What primarily needs to be said is that the Eeyou/Eenou civilization has for untold generations found its balance, and its sense of beauty and order in an intimate obedience to the laws of the land that has given it birth and has sustained it. We can certainly say that even after the harsh period of colonial stranglehold, the heart of the Eeyou civilization is still strongly pulsating in exact unison with the heart of its Motherland, for such an ancient and powerful bond cannot be suppressed: it stays very much alive in the heart of every Eeyou. That affective bond *is all we need* to recreate an Eeyou educational environment. The Eeyou/Eenou people need to discover, treasure and enhance the deep belief that they have in themselves as a unique people richly endowed by the Creator.

Now, to think practically about their educational needs, the Eeyou/Eenou people need to reflect deeply about their present ways of dispensing an education to their young people. We have all heard success stories of how some young people have made it through the system, have achieved sometimes excellent standing in their secondary studies and, in some cases, undertaken and finished post-secondary studies, a very rare few at the MA and doctoral levels. However, we also have all heard very disquieting stories of how many pupils and older students, throughout the Eeyou territory, go through their formal schooling very painfully and often in acute despair. No conscious educator would disagree that we are seeing a great, tragic waste of human potential, most especially if we look at this situation of the youth through the eyes of the Elders. Let us ask ourselves why so many of these returning spirits decide to end their life and go back to the Land of Souls, and why so many others decide to go through their young life dulling their extreme pain by using alcohol, drugs and other substances. I personally believe we have to create, or rather re-create, a system of learning that accords with and respects the deep, wonderful belief in and love for the land that lies deep within the heart of every Eeyou, young and old.

I am not the first to say that it is entirely unacceptable and shameful to see the grossly high numbers of Eenou youth not finishing a secondary level of formal education. To me and to many others, it is absolutely unfair, even inhumane, to coldly expect these youth to succeed in an educational system that has no or very little regard for the cultural, intellectual and spiritual heritage of the children of a people possessing such an old and rich civilization as the Eeyou and to feel satisfied that two or three percent of these young people end up making it through.

Essentially, I am suggesting that in the quite momentous exercise of reflecting on and laying down the principles of their governance, the Eeyou people will be inspired to centre their thinking on the ancient, sacred belief in the unique worth of their civilization which, as I have intimated, is their most important possession. This is where every member of every community, especially the Elders, has to be invited to speak from his or her heart about the pain, the joy, the hope they have concerning their children and concerning the future of their people, the Eenou people. But the focus of the collective reflection has to be the (re)creation of the Eeyou way of forming, training, preparing their youth for a life sustained by Eeyou values.

The First Principle of Eeyou/Eenou Learning

Wise people everywhere have said that a human being gets formed, as a person, in the first seven to eight years of life, especially in the first three. This is when an Eenou child should be most consistently exposed to nature. At that stage, the Eeyou Ayimuwun (language) should be imprinted in the child's whole being, for true traditional learning is organically inscribed in the language. The use of Elders' knowledge must be systematic and pervasive at this stage, both at school and in the home. During this whole period of life, including upon the child's attaining conventional schooling age, an Eeyou child should be put in intense contact with the philosophy of his or her people, community, family. This can be effected by means of legends, stories, songs, dances, as well as by learning about family, community and national history. At this stage in their lives, children should also receive some knowledge about the non-Eeyou world, beginning with the world view and the life of other Aboriginal peoples. The goal of learning at this elementary stage is to give the children the critical capacity of perceiving and acknowledging the relationships that exist between and among all beings that make up the natural universe; in other words, children, upon attaining the second stage, have to be imbued with the reality of the Law of Universal Interdependence, the first and foremost natural law known to and observed by their Eenou ancestors from time immemorial. Also, very importantly, this stage in learning is the one during which families and communities can and do, through the observation of their new generations, begin to form an idea of the talents and potentialities of each individual child; and regardless of the types of life paths that these students will choose later, the contributions that they will make to their own society and to the larger world will be markedly and unmistakably an Eenou, an Eeyou contribution, thanks to their firm grounding in their own people's identity, which they will have acquired during the first stage of their life as learners.

The Principle of Mentorship

The great care that has been taken by parents, families, communities, as well as by the nation, throughout the first stage of the children's life as learners, must be built upon and continued at the next stage in the students' evolution. This is where we have to invent and institute a culture of mentorship. Rather than following conventional models of one teacher per class, communities and the Eeyou/Eenou nation itself have to design and adopt styles and ways of learning in small groups for youths who have similar interests and talents, and also provide one-to-one learning possibilities for individuals whose interests and talents are unique or particular enough to warrant such a teaching/learning style, as in the case of students interested in a curer's or in a medical doctor's or an artist's career.

In the case of the many children who will not specifically wish to pursue a traditionally oriented profession or trade, the ethnic or the cultural affiliation of the mentor would not necessarily matter. School (or Learning) Councils, however, would have to be very careful in the selection of would-be mentors to Eenou children/learners; the task of creating new models and systems for the facilitation of learning represents a great opportunity, but also a very delicate undertaking for any people, especially one for whom old models of education have been so devoid of cultural relevance and so problem-ridden as they have been for the Eeyou.

The Eeyou/Eenou as World Leaders

It has been my intention to conclude this presentation by expressing a personal hope, based on a deep belief, that the Eeyou envision themselves as possessors of a very important ideological and spiritual treasure which an ever-growing segment of the world's population is desirous to learn about. The Eenou have already experienced that the belief that many non-Eeyou people have in their traditional world view is one of the factors that determine whether important legal cases are won or lost and, therefore, whether the survival of Eeyou culture (indeed, civilization) is assured or not assured. It is all-important for the Eenou to fully appreciate the high place that their world view and civilization occupy in the eyes of the world.

Because they still maintain a functional hunters' culture and because they have (very rapidly) learned to integrate and utilize the political and legal thinking of a rich North American nation-state (Canada) to their advantage, the Eeyou people probably rates among the world's prominent cultures (I say civilizations) when it comes to choosing models for creating an ecological world for times to come. For this, I applaud the great resiliency of the Eenou, and for this I believe in the absolute importance of rediscovering and re-creating Eeyou educational models that proudly reflect the true thinking of the Eeyou/Eenou.

Watchiya!

Ottawa : une capitale immémoriale

Il y a très longtemps, si longtemps que seuls les esprits s'en souviennent, commença à battre le cœur d'un nouveau pays né de la Terre du nord. Celle-ci, au terme d'une longue gestation sous un épais manteau de neige et de glaces, s'enleva cette magnifique couverture et assista, heureuse, à cette naissance ineffable, tout ensoleillée.

Ce beau pays se remplit vite de peuples d'animaux, d'oiseaux, de poissons, d'arbres, de plantes, de pierres et de toutes sortes d'autres êtres et bientôt, le Créateur, Kitche Manito, y vint aussi créer un peuple d'humains, les Anishinabek. Kitche Manito, et plusieurs autres Esprits enseignèrent aux Anishinabek comment vivre dans leur pays et comment fabriquer toutes sortes de choses. L'une des plus merveilleuses d'entre elles fut le canot.

Les Anishinabek devinrent vite d'excellents voyageurs et apprirent à connaître chaque partie, chaque région de leur grand et beau territoire. Ils devinrent profondément épris de celui-ci. L'une des plus belles choses qu'ils connurent sur leur territoire, et qui les rendaient le plus heureux, était leur Kitche Sipi, leur Grande Rivière. L'eau la plus pure et abondante y coulait et la pêche et la chasse y étaient faciles et excellentes. Les Anishnabek aimaient tellement leur Grande Rivière que les familles et les clans qui vivaient le plus près d'elle se donnèrent le nom de Kitchesipirini : Les-Gens-de-la-Grande-Rivière. Kitche Manito avait réellement donné aux Anishnabek un paradis en héritage!

Au cours du temps, les différents peuples de tout ce grand pays anishinabe prirent l'habitude de se retrouver, durant les lunes sans neige, en certains endroits particulièrement riches et majestueux de leur territoire. L'un de ces « endroits de pouvoir », tel que les Premiers Peuples appellent ces lieux spéciaux, situé sur la Grande Rivière, reçut le nom anishnabe d'Ottawa, c'est-à-dire, endroit de rassemblement et d'échange. Ottawa est donc, depuis les temps immémoriaux, la capitale d'un très grand et beau pays qui était prédestiné à devenir le berceau du plus beau pays du monde actuel, le Canada!

Puis un jour, des peuples étrangers arrivèrent au pays des Anishinabek.* L'héritage culturel de ces gens les disposait à voir la réalité d'une manière très différente de celle des Premiers Peuples. Plutôt pratiques que contemplatifs, pour la plupart, ces hommes au teint plus pâle virent toute cette majesté et cette abondance naturelles comme une chance, encore inimaginée, de créer un pays d'une grande force et aussi, naturellement, d'une grande beauté. Très vite, tout fut mis à profit. D'abord, ce furent des arbres, les animaux et les poissons, puis l'eau, puis les pierres et les minerais, puis la terre elle-même. Très vite aussi, les Anishinabek perdirent tout ce qui les avait rendus forts, sains, libres et heureux.

Chose encore plus triste, ils virent sombrer leur rêve d'enseigner à leurs nouveaux frères et à leurs nouvelles sœurs, les très anciens et très vénérés secrets, hérités de temps très lointains, qui leur avaient permis de se faire une vie en parfaite harmonie avec la Nature et avec le Créateur de toutes choses.

Avec le temps, le site prédestiné et merveilleux d'Ottawa fut choisi pour être la capitale du pays incomparablement libre et beau que devint rapidement le Kanatha (Canada), un autre endroit sacré et prédestiné qui avait longtemps

---

* Le récent film de Richard Desjardins et Robert Monderie (Office national du film, 2007) «Le peuple invisible», est une très bonne illustration de cet aspect de l'histoire québécoise et canadienne.

existé dans le cœur et l'esprit du peuple de Stadaconé (ville et région de l'actuelle ville de Québec), un autre des Premiers Peuples d'ici. Ottawa fut la capitale de la Terre Mère des Anishinabek bien avant que ne commençât à germer l'idée qu'elle devienne la capitale de notre beau, grand et très cher pays, le Canada. Ottawa, notre capitale nationale, est une ville dont les racines puisent très profondément dans la terre toujours sacrée des Premiers Peuples. Les Anishinabek, quant à eux, sont toujours les possesseurs d'une civilisation d'une rare et grande richesse que le Canada, pour son mieux-être, commence maintenant à vouloir protéger et découvrir.

15 août 2007

Les premières civilisations des Amériques : retour sur l'histoire dans l'anthropologie[*]

Chers amies et amis, si je m'adressais à vous dans la langue de mes ancêtres hurons-wendats, je vous appellerais spontanément mes frères et mes sœurs. C'est donc comme mes parents que je vous regarde.

Il me fait plaisir de repasser par l'Université Laval, située en notre territoire ancestral huron-wendat, jamais cédé. J'ai étudié ici durant onze ans et je reviens aujourd'hui après une absence de seize ans. Il est doux de respirer l'air de mon pays et de me sentir bienvenu en cet endroit de haut savoir où j'ai naguère investi le meilleur de moi-même. Je dis merci pour cette invitation à Frédéric Laugrand et à Jean-Guy Goulet, de même qu'à Francine Saillant et aux autres organisateurs et organisatrices de cette très importante et très belle conférence.

---

[*] Présentation à la Conférence internationale d'anthropologie « Anthrolopogie des cultures globalisée. Terrains complexes et enjeux disciplinaires », tenue à Québec du 7 au 11 novembre 2007.

J'ai passé une bonne partie de ma carrière d'historien à réécrire, ou, si vous voulez, à désécrire l'histoire de mon peuple huron-wendat. La première fois que j'approchai l'académie pour parler de ce projet, on m'objecta que c'était là une tâche impossible, puisque tous les livres avaient déjà été écrits, par les religieux et les autres Européens qui avaient connu mon peuple au temps où il existait. Ces livres étaient d'ailleurs alignés sur les tablettes du bureau où je me trouvais. C'était, en réalité, le mot « réécrire » que j'avais énoncé qui était malvenu. L'intention irrespectueuse que ce mot trahissait était typique de certains Indiens, encore rebelles. Ainsi s'inaugura mon retour aux études universitaires, délaissées neuf ans plus tôt. J'avais maintenant 33 ans.

« Ta place est en anthropologie », me dirent les historiens de Laval de ce temps-là et, avec l'avantage de 25 ans de recul, je leur donne raison. Quand même, je m'obstinai à demeurer en histoire. Mon argument fut que « ce fut sur le champ de bataille de l'Histoire que mon peuple perdit, historiquement, et qu'étant très jeune, les miens m'avaient proposé la tâche d'écrire un jour d'autres livres d'histoire, pas d'anthropologie. Aussi, exprimai-je, j'avais laissé beaucoup pour revenir étudier en histoire et j'étais ici pour rester ».

Aujourd'hui, je dis avec une certaine fierté que j'ai aidé, avec les moyens dont je disposais, à faire changer la façon dont on écrit et enseigne l'histoire de mon peuple huron, autochtone et indigène. Discrètement et amicalement, mes professeurs et le directeur de mes deux thèses, mon ami Denys Delâge, me laissèrent suivre le chemin que j'avais choisi. Ils encouragèrent leurs collègues anthropologues à me prendre sous leur égide. C'est ainsi que je devins l'étudiant et souvent l'ami de grands anthropologues, tels que Bruce Graham Trigger, de McGill, ainsi que François Trudel et Pierre Maranda, de Laval. Ce fut Pierre Maranda qui porta mon travail à l'attention de Claude Lévi-Strauss, lequel m'encouragea de façon pressante et déterminante à développer ma vision de l'histoire. Je crois donc appartenir aussi à votre monde, celui des anthropologues.

Aujourd'hui, je veux faire avec vous un retour sur l'histoire dans l'anthropologie. Comme je le disais il y a un moment, j'ai une certaine fierté de m'être assez bien acquitté, devant mes parents et mon peuple, du devoir de commencer à asseoir sur de nouvelles bases conceptuelles l'étude et l'enseignement de l'histoire de mon peuple, et des autochtones en général. Bien sûr, d'autres gens, de toutes origines, iront plus loin sur ce chemin sans fin. Récemment, j'ai trouvé une nouvelle raison et une nouvelle façon d'expliquer pourquoi il est de toute importance d'continuer à expliquer l'histoire, ou de continuer à expliquer, l'histoire, encore très mal connue, de mon peuple huron-wendat. Pour moi, il ne s'agit plus simplement de revoir l'histoire dans le but d'aider à créer des outils conceptuels et jurisprudentiels devant faire avancer la cause de la justice due aux peuples autochtones ou, autrement dit, libérer mon peuple et tous les autres peuples violentés et niés par l'Histoire. Le désir qui fut toujours mien et qui n'a jamais cessé de croître en moi se résume dans une idée que m'a laissée ma mère, la docteure Éléonore Sioui Tecumseh, quelques années avant son départ pour le monde des âmes, lequel survint en mars 2006. Elle m'avait dit, au moins à deux reprises : « Personne n'a encore pensé à faire l'anthropologie de l'âme ». Je vous expose à présent ma nouvelle raison pour expliquer au monde l'histoire de mon peuple huron-wendat, puis terminerai ma présentation en vous parlant de l'idéologie d'Éléonore Sioui, ma mère, qui eut cette vision riche et régénérante pour l'anthropologie, pour l'histoire, pour nous tous qui vivons, rêvons et espérons.

Nadoueks et Algonquiens. La première civilisation du Canada

Le sentiment le plus commun définissant la perception qu'ont eue et qu'ont encore plusieurs générations, surtout mais pas exclusivement d'autochtones, est que l'histoire est un « ramassis de mensonges » ou, pour employer la vraie expression québécoise, « un paquet de menteries ». Le Canada n'est certes pas le seul pays où les gens, en général, vivent et meurent avec le sentiment impuissant que « quelqu'un » (c'est-à-dire le système, la société) n'a pas voulu qu'ils sachent « la vraie histoire ». Tout simplement, il y a dans l'air de notre pays, comme dans celui de bien d'autres, le sentiment qu'il faut croire, même si elle n'est pas vraie, en l'histoire qu'on nous conte sur nos origines nationales et aimer cette histoire, voire la vénérer, comme on devait le faire pour la religion, au temps peu lointain où il était socialement recommandé de maltraiter l'incroyant.

Pour point de départ de cette partie de mon propos, j'ai choisi d'exposer et de discuter un mythe très méconnu et que je juge tout à fait central à notre discours sur notre histoire canadienne et québécoise : *le mythe de l'Iroquois victorieux*. « Eh bien, diront certains, voilà un Huron qui, trois siècles et demi après les événements, n'a toujours pas reconnu la défaite de son peuple par les Iroquois ». Il y a dix-huit ans, toujours dans mon livre *Pour une autohistoire amérindienne*, j'avais déjà nommé la supposée destruction des Hurons par les Iroquois « la pierre angulaire de l'hétérohistoire amérindienne traditionnelle dans le Nord-Est ». Tout en ne désirant rien changer à ce que j'avais alors écrit sur ce sujet, je veux expliquer aujourd'hui pourquoi il m'apparaît vital, pour la saine évolution du pays par ailleurs si grandiose et prometteur qu'est le Canada, de soigneusement étudier ce concept, perçu par les miens comme un de ces mensonges de l'histoire. Je prédis aujourd'hui que, choisissant d'utiliser cette clé historiographique insoupçonnée, nous accéderons à une vision libératrice, unificatrice et fière de notre histoire commune.

D'abord, il faut remonter au début des années 1300 de notre ère et voir, au moyen de constats archéologiques et tout en nous aidant de la tradition orale, comment les ancêtres des Wendats, déjà riches de relations commerciales pluriséculaires avec un grand ensemble de peuples de quatre familles linguistiques distinctes (c'est-à-dire les familles nadouek ou « iroquoienne », algonquienne, siouienne et béothuk), entreprirent systématiquement de créer le Wendaké, un pays-cœur international, agricole et commercial, situé entre les lacs Simcoe et Huron actuels (à moins de deux heures au nord de l'actuelle ville de Toronto).

Le Wendaké, que les Français visitèrent durant les brèves années d'existence qui restaient à ce pays après leur arrivée, et qu'ils nommèrent Huronie, était un territoire de faible étendue, mais d'une importance stratégique unique, puisqu'il était situé à la croisée des routes commerciales majeures qui allaient à l'est, au sud, à l'ouest et au nord. À l'arrivée de Samuel de Champlain en leur milieu, en 1610, les Wendats, au nombre approximatif de 30 000 âmes, avaient environ 25 villes, villages et hameaux épars sur toute l'étendue de ce petit pays (de 56 kilomètres par 32) et non pas situés le long des cours d'eau et au bord des lacs, tel que c'était universellement le cas pour toutes les autres nations autochtones du reste du territoire aujourd'hui dit canadien. De plus, les Wendats avaient, depuis au moins deux siècles avant l'arrivée européenne, constitué une puissante confédération qui était elle-même le centre politique et commercial d'un *Commonwealth* autochtone unissant entre elles depuis encore plus longtemps des centaines de nations, grandes et petites, des Terres Boisées. Nous avons là, brossé à grands traits, le portrait de la civilisation autochtone qui constituait la force et la grandeur de la civilisation autochtone du Nord-Est et qui fut la base politique et commerciale que la France acquit par l'alliance judicieuse qu'elle fit avec ce très important ensemble de peuples au début du XVIIe siècle.

Cette grande et antique Société de Nations autochtones, dont le cœur wendat fut situé en territoire aujourd'hui canadien, fut détruite rapidement et radicalement 30 brèves années après la première visite de Champlain, non tant par le fait des épidémies européennes qui furent, comme on sait, absolument dévastatrices, ou des guerres intensifiées par la même venue européenne, mais en conséquence du retard qu'accusait la France au plan socioreligieux par rapport à son compétiteur colonial hollandais. En effet, alors que les Français imposaient à leurs alliés nadoueks et algonquiens des conditions religieuses strictes pour l'obtention d'armes à feu, les Hollandais vendaient librement des fusils aux Iroquois. À la veille de leur destruction finale, en 1649, les Wendats ne possédaient encore que très peu d'armes à feu avec lesquelles se défendre contre l'alliance hollandaise-iroquoise. « Le glas du grand système de traite des Wendats, écrit Francis Jennings dans son livre marquant, *The Ambiguous Iroquois Empire* (p. 325), fut sonné le 7 avril 1648, lorsque le gouverneur de la Nouvelle-Hollande, Peter Stuyvesant, autorisa la vente officielle de 400 fusils aux Agniers (Mohawks) à des prix outrageusement bas. En 1649, l'Hodenosaunee vint disperser le pays [wendat], déjà ruiné ».

Avant de parler de la situation politique et démographique des Hodenosaunee à l'époque de la destruction européenne du grand ordre géopolitique du Nord-Est, il est nécessaire d'établir que les Iroquois qui vécurent après ce grand et tragique affaissement amérindien du XVIIe siècle sont alors devenus, à cause du pouvoir de capture et d'adoption que leur conféra leur accès supérieur aux armes européennes, un amalgame fait d'un grand nombre d'entités amérindiennes survivantes, dont les composantes wendates, neutres, ériées, tinontatées et susquehannas (nations et confédérations aujourd'hui presque toutes disparues, à l'exception de quelques communautés huronnes-wendates et wyandottes) et algonquiennes de multiples origines. Aussi, pourquoi le nom « nadouek » et d'où vient-il ? Les Nadoueks sont simplement ceux qui ont reçu le nom d'« Iroquoiens » et qu'au regard de la nouvelle lecture autohistorique que nous sommes à faire, j'ai suggéré de démarquer historiographiquement de leurs congénères iroquois en les appelant du nom qu'avaient pour eux plusieurs Algonquiens. Les Nadoueks sont donc : les Hurons-Wendats, les Wyandots, les Ériés, les Neutres (Attiwandaronks), les Gens du Tabac (Tionontaté) et les Susquehannas (à strictement parler, les Iroquois et les Chérokis sont aussi des Nadoueks).

Au début du XVIIe siècle, les Hodenosaunee étaient une confédération relativement nouvelle. La tradition orale hodenosaunee rapporte que cette confédération fut le produit de la vision d'un prophète huron « que son propre peuple ne voulut pas écouter » et qui vint en territoire hodenosaunee, dans l'État actuel de New York, livrer son message d'entente et de paix, ce qui, selon la même tradition iroquoise, réussit à mettre fin à une période prolongée de cruelles guerres intestines. Malgré ce nouvel état de paix à l'interne, les Iroquois historiques n'étaient constitués que de cinq nations pas particulièrement populeuses, dépourvues de toute alliance extérieure politique et commerciale, ce qui équivaut à dire complètement entourées d'ennemis, la plupart nombreux et puissants. Les Cinq-Nations étaient bornées à elles-mêmes et méconnaissaient l'art du commerce extérieur. On pourrait affirmer que si les Européens n'étaient pas arrivés, la logique de l'évolution de leur société eût été de s'intégrer peu à peu à la civilisation d'ensemble qui fleurissait déjà depuis plusieurs siècles dans le Nord-Est. La venue chez elles du pacificateur huron Deganawidah peut être vue comme un signe annonçant une telle suite des choses.

Nos livres d'histoire du Canada nous ont enseigné et, très regrettablement, nous enseignent encore souvent que les bons et dociles Hurons ont été exterminés par les méchants et irrationnels Iroquois, que ces deux peuples n'avaient apparemment pas de rêve plus cher que de s'entre-détruire et que, pour cela surtout, ce rêve partagé se serait réalisé de toute façon pour l'un ou l'autre peuple ; par conséquent, les actions et la présence européennes n'y ont été pour rien, ou si peu, dans les gigantesques tragédies humaines que cette prétendue haine partagée entraîna. Il y a dans cette hideuse forgerie historiographique une charge de racisme anti-amérindien si puissante qu'en déterminer la portée à de multiples niveaux se présente comme une tâche immense dont l'histoire prendra encore beaucoup de temps à s'acquitter. Pourtant, il y va de notre fierté et de notre respectabilité en tant que nation, d'abord à nos propres yeux, puis aux yeux des autres nations. Notre pays, le Canada, ne trouve pas son origine dans le combat glorieux d'ancêtres européens contre des peuples sauvages brutaux et méprisables ; de tels peuples n'existent d'ailleurs tout simplement pas. Notre pays prend plutôt directement son origine dans la riche pensée circulaire d'une merveilleuse et antique civilisation autochtone que le Canada et le Québec ont encore à découvrir.

Comme l'a magistralement écrit l'ethno-historien Bruce Graham Trigger dans la deuxième édition de son important livre *Huron Farmers of the North*, parue en 1989, les Hurons n'avaient, même peu avant les événements qui aboutirent à leur dispersion finale, aucune raison d'agir par crainte des Iroquois. Au début de ce livre, Trigger réfute de façon concluante l'analyse de nombreux spécialistes sur le sujet de l'arrangement démographique du Wendaké, le pays des Wendats. Parlant de la logique culturelle pluriséculaire en force chez ce peuple, Trigger remarque que cette confédération travaille, même aux heures sombres de sa fin déjà imminente, en fonction de l'organisation du vaste monde commercial et diplomatique dont elle est le centre. Le Wendaké est un pays-cœur densément habité et intégralement organisé pour le commerce avec des centaines de peuples alliés comprenant des centaines de milliers d'individus, dont beaucoup apprennent et parlent le wendat ; l'Iroquoisie est un territoire fermé sur lui-même, peuplé peu densément de 20 000 à 30 000 mille personnes appartenant à cinq nations vivant loin les unes des autres, de l'autre côté du lac Ontario. Quels Iroquois pouvaient donc tant aspirer à aller exterminer les Wendats ? Et quels Wendats allaient donc négliger leur fonction centrale dans leur riche monde commercial pour aller assouvir leur propre soif irrépressible du sang de leurs parents hodenosaunee ?

En termes historiques très concrets, la France commit l'incommensurable faute de gaspiller l'énorme avantage politique et démographique que lui conféraient ses très nombreux alliés amérindiens en négligeant d'assister ceux-ci matériellement et militairement, au même moment où les Hollandais équipèrent librement et sans compter les cinq nations de l'Hodenosaunee et, contre toutes les probabilités, défirent pour toujours l'écrasant pouvoir français. Quant à eux, Hurons et Iroquois travaillèrent fréquemment à s'unir pour protéger leurs intérêts communs contre leurs instables et souvent perfides alliés européens, mais ceux-ci réussirent toujours, surtout grâce à leurs services d'espionnage opérés nommément par leurs missionnaires religieux, à frustrer les plans des Sauvages, quels qu'ils soient, et à avancer leur propre cause.

Voilà comment, pour arranger l'histoire à leur convenance, les religieux historiens français ont créé et forgé le mythe de la destruction des Hurons par les Iroquois. Mais comment ce mythe amoindrit-il les raisons de notre fierté d'être Canadiens, d'être Québécois ? J'ai créé la question et voici la meilleure réponse que je puisse offrir. D'abord, il est certain que tout processus d'appropriation coloniale doit s'accompagner d'une justification idéologique et religieuse. Le mythe de l'Iroquois victorieux n'est qu'une variante historiographique propre à notre contexte d'un tel besoin de justification. Mais il est également dans l'ordre de l'évolution d'une société qu'une telle mythologie soit un jour soumise à un examen à la lumière des faits et de la raison. Je crois que la période, dans l'évolution de notre société canadienne et québécoise, de la négation du fait et de la contribution des premiers peuples (amérindiens, inuit, métis) est maintenant révolue. Si je me fie aux jeunes gens avec lesquels j'interagis, surtout dans mes classes de philosophie et d'histoire des autochtones, les jeunes et les nouveaux Canadiens, de toutes les origines possibles, ne veulent simplement pas sentir passivement que l'histoire (surtout lorsqu'elle concerne les autochtones et les rapports avec eux) est « un ramassis de mensonges ».

Cette nouvelle génération de Canadiens, autochtones et non autochtones, est heureuse et édifiée d'apprendre que son pays, le Canada, ne s'est pas bâti grâce au glorieux et saint travail de colons qui, vaillamment et au risque de leur vie, vinrent répandre la lumière de la raison et de la foi malgré l'opposition bête de peuples sauvages qui, jusqu'à la venue de ces dignes civilisateurs, n'avaient eu cure que de courir les animaux dans les forêts pour s'alimenter, et de s'entre-tuer pour leur ultime plaisir. Les jeunes Canadiens auxquels j'ai le bonheur de parler et d'enseigner et desquels j'apprends aussi beaucoup sont, disais-je, heureux et édifiés d'apprendre que leur pays, le Canada, puise son essence spirituelle et philosophique dans une belle et antique civilisation, celle de ses Premiers Peuples. Même si cette civilisation fut rapidement et radicalement étouffée, elle n'en constitua pas moins le fondement sur lequel les élites coloniales des pays européens, tout en se disputant durement des biens mal acquis, établirent le pouvoir et la grandeur apparents qu'ils purent éventuellement exhiber. La civilisation nadouek-algonquienne fut et est le résultat de la pensée et du travail honnête et incessant de millions de gens sur de multiples générations. La France fut prompte à reconnaître l'immense et riche potentiel matériel que possédait la grande société autochtone héritière de cette civilisation et se greffa à celle-ci. C'est dans ce mouvement colonial original de la France que doit être vue la genèse de l'existence coloniale du Canada que l'on a connu. C'est dans l'étude et la compréhension de l'antique civilisation autochtone sur laquelle se fit cette greffe qu'il faut découvrir la vraie nature, le vrai potentiel, en un mot, enfin, l'âme de notre merveilleux pays, le Canada.

L'anthropologie de l'âme

« Personne n'a encore pensé à faire l'anthropologie de l'âme », m'a dit ma mère. Elle m'avait dit cela avec toute la passion qui la consommait lorsqu'elle désirait exprimer ce que le monde devait, pour sa survie, découvrir, reconnaître et étudier dans notre peuple. L'idée que l'on n'ait, jusqu'à présent, découvert que le corps matériel de l'Amérique a été exprimée par beaucoup de gens, illustres et non illustres, mais jamais, j'en suis sûr, personne ne l'a fait avec autant d'émotion et de conviction qu'elle. Ma mère, fille d'un chef traditionnel et grand chasseur et d'une femme-médecine réputée, ma mère, une conférencière internationale qui, à 68 ans, obtint son doctorat en philosophie et fut décorée par le Canada et par son propre peuple amérindien pour son œuvre de foi et de courage, ne put jamais parler de cette « chose », c'est-à-dire la nécessité de faire l'anthropologie de l'âme des Premiers Peuples, sans manifester une émotion si forte et si sincère que tous ceux et celles présents en restaient marqués pour toujours. Ce n'était plus elle qui parlait, c'était quelqu'un, c'étaient des ancêtres, des enfants à venir, c'était quelque chose de très grand, noble et ancien qui parlait par elle. Ma mère était dans une sorte de transe ; sa voix, ébranlée par des pleurs qu'elle réussissait à contrôler, disait des choses très belles et extrêmement importantes pour tous, pour toutes : *le monde ne pouvait, ne pourrait pas trouver l'équilibre, la santé ou le bonheur, le monde ne pourrait même pas survivre s'il ne découvrait pas l'âme des Premiers Peuples*. Il fallait faire l'anthropologie de l'âme, l'âme du *Premier Monde*, l'âme des Peuples qui sentent amour, foi et vénération pour notre Mère, la Terre.

Toute la science anthropologique a, jusqu'à présent, été basée sur la certitude qu'il fallait sauver de l'oubli le savoir et les façons de faire de peuples voués à disparaître et à se fondre dans une culture globale et globalisante plus avancée. Plusieurs penseurs autochtones et non autochtones disent, au contraire, que cette culture supercivilisée est devenue tellement étrangère aux sources et à la nature de la vie elle-même que son destin est de périr, ou de revenir à une conscience de l'interdépendance de tous les êtres qui composent ce que les peuples autochtones nomment le Grand Cercle Sacré de la Vie. Cette idée représente ce que fut la raison d'être et de vivre de ma mère. Ma mère est venue exister physiquement sur cette terre pour prier, agir et guérir le monde à partir de sa médecine spirituelle huronne et amérindienne. Voilà tout le sens profond des enseignements qu'elle a prodigués toute sa vie. J'ai choisi quatre poèmes d'elle, pour vous permettre d'être touchés par la médecine d'Éléonore Sioui.

OKIHOUEN WENDAT
LES HURONS SONT RICHES

En l'Amérindien
Sont contenus
Les larmes, les sourires
De l'Âme de la Terre Mère
Parce qu'enfanté par elle
Fécondée du Soleil
Dans un bruissement de l'Esprit
Encerclant ses Frères

Dans sa Re-naissance.

SATAQUEN
TON FRÈRE

Grand Esprit
Que nos frères
Reconnaissent en nous
Les dons
Dont tu nous as comblés
Pour que nous nous rencontrions
Dans un respect mutuel.

ONDENACAN
EXISTENTIALISME

Quel est cet Artiste qui dessine
Les courbes des cocotiers
Pour que l'homme puisse
En atteindre les fruits ?
Quel est celui qui fait
Le vent s'y prélasser doucement
Et, par sa douce brise
Filtrée à travers ses palmes,
Réconforter l'homme, son frère ?

Où est celui qui fait éclore
La mousseline multicolore
Et odoriférante des fleurs
Placées à la portée
De la main de l'homme
Afin de faire surgir
Son sourire ?

Qui fait pousser l'arbre à pain
Dont les fruits nourrissants
S'offrent à la faim de l'homme ?

Où est celui qui,
De la Terre Mère
Fait naître le bananier,
Pain quotidien des Caraïbes ?
Qui donne à la mer
Sa fécondité et sa force
Lorsqu'elle est en travail ?

Qui construit les matins et les nuits
Imbriquant les heures, les unes aux autres,
Dans leurs formes différentes
Et qui se fondent en un Tout ?

Je Te sens
Lorsque je mange
Le silence du Soleil
Et bois les chocs de la mer.
J'entends Ta présence
Où se mire mon esprit
Dans le reflet du Tien,
Y dessinant le cœur de l'homme.
Où Te caches-Tu ?
Où dois-je Te trouver ?
Car je Te cherche sans cesse
Dans le vent, murmurant Ton nom,
Au cœur des rochers.

ACHARO
COLLIER DE PARTAGE

Le Grand Esprit
A donné à l'Homme Rouge
La vertu de connaître
Les racines, les plantes
Qui protègent nos santés, nos vies
Ainsi que celles de nos frères
Blancs, Jaunes et Noirs.

Chers sœurs, chers frères, je vous remercie de m'avoir écouté. Ho! Ho! Ho! Attouguet!

Bibliography

Adams, Howard. *A Tortured People. The Politics of Colonization.* Penticton (BC): Theytus Books, 1995.

Adams, Howard. *Prison of Grass. Canada from the Native Point of View.* Toronto: New Press, 1975.

Alfred, Taiaiake. *Heeding the Voices of our Ancestors. Kahnawake Mohawk Politics and the Rise of Native Nationalism.* New York: Oxford University Press, 1995.

Alfred, Taiaiake. *Peace, Power, Rightousness. An Indigenous Manifesto.* Oxford: Oxford University Press, 1999.

Alfred, Taiaiake. *Wasàse. Indigenous Pathways of Action and Freedom.* Vancouver: Broadview Press, 2005.

Anderson, Emma. *The Betrayal of Faith: The Tragic Journey of a Colonial Native Convert.* Harvard University Press, 2007.

Anderson, Karen Lee. "Huron Men and Huron Women: The Effects of Demography, Kinship and the Social Division of Labour on Male/Female

Relationships among the 17th Century Huron." Ph. D. Dissertation, University of Toronto, 1982.

Barbeau, C. Marius. *Huron and Wyandot Mythology.* Memoir 80. Ottawa: Department of Mines, Government Printing Bureau, 1915.

Battiste, Marie and Jean Barman (editors). *The Circle Unfolds First Nations Education in Canada.* UBC Press, 1995.

Beck, Horace P. "Algonquin Folklore from Maniwaki". *The Journal of American Folklore*, Vol. 60, No. 237. Jul. – Sep., 1947.

Blouin-Sioui, Anne-Marie. "Histoire et iconographie des Hurons de Lorette du XVII au XIX siècle." Thèse de doctorat, Université de Montréal, 1987.

Brody, Hugh. *The Other Side of Eden. Hunters, Farmers and the Shaping of the World.* Vancouver: Douglas & McIntyre, 2000

Burkhart, B.Y. «What Coyote and Thales can Teach us: an Outline of American Indian Epistemology» in A. Waters (editor). *American Indian Thought.* Malden: Blackwell, 2004.

Campeau, Lucien, s.j. *La Mission des jésuites chez les Hurons, 1634–1650.* Montréal: Bellarmin 1987.

Canada. Indian and Northern Affairs Canada. *The Canadian Indian – Ontario.* Ottawa: Indian and Northern Affairs Canada, 1982.

Chamberlain, J.E. «From Hand to Mouth: The Postcolonial Politics of Oral and Written Traditions» in M. Battiste (editors). *Reclaiming Indigenous Voice and Vision.* Vancouver: UBC Press, 2000.

Dickason, Olive P. *Canada's First Nations. A History of Founding Peoples from Earliest Times.* Oxford and New York: Oxford University Press, 2002.

Dickason, Olive P. *The Myth of the Savage.* Edmonton: University of Alberta Press, 1984.

Dickason, Olive Patricia. *A Concise History of Canada's First Nations.* Toronto: Oxford University Press, 2008.

Divison of Labour on Male/Female Relationships among the 17th Century Huron." Ph.D. dissertation, University of Toronto, 1982.

Dobyns, Henry F. *Their Number Become Thinned. Native American Population Dynamics in Eastern North America.* Knoxville: University of Tennessee Press, 1983.

Dooyentate, Peter Clarke. *Origin and Traditional History of the Wyandots.* Toronto: Hunter, Rose, 1870.

DuFour, John. "Ethics and Understanding" in A. Waters (editors.). *American Indian Thought.* Malden: Blackwell, 2004.

Elliot, Charles. *Indian Missionary Reminiscences, Principally of the Wyandot Nation.* New York: Lane and Scott, 1850.

Engelbrecht, William E. *Iroquoia: the development of a Native world.* New York: Syracuse University Press, 2003.

Frideres, James S. *Aboriginal peoples in Canada.* Toronto: Prentice Hall, c2005.

Giroux, Dalie. "Dieu est-il mort en étude des idées politiques. Sur l'aporie de l'opposition entre les idées et les monde" dans *Revue canadienne de science politique*, Vol. 37, No. 2, 2004.

Giroux, Dalie. "Éléments de pensée politique autochtone." *Politique et Sociétés*, Vol. 27, No 1, 2008, à paraitre.

Gordon M. Day. "The Name 'Algonquin'." *International Journal of American Linguistics*, Vol. 38, No. 4., Oct., 1972.

Green, Leslie C. and Olive P. Dickason. *The Law of Nations and the New World.* Edmonton: University of Alberta Press, 1989.

Guédon, Marie-Françoise. *Le rêve et la forêt. Histoires de chamanes nabesna.* Québec: Les Presses de l'Université Laval, 2005.

Hamilton, James Cleland. "The Algonquin Nanabozho and Hiawatha". *The Journal of American Folklore*, Vol. 16, No. 63, Oct. – Dec., 1903.

Havard, Gilles. *La Grande Paix de Montréal de 1701.* Montréal : Recherches amérindiennes au Québec, 1992.

Heidenreich, Conrad E. *Huronia. A History and Geography of the Huron Indians, 1600–1650.* Toronto: Kichesippi Books, 1993.

Hessel, Peter D.K. *The Algonquin Nation: the Algonkins of the Ottawa Valley: an Historical Outline.* Arnprior: McClelland and Stewart, 1971.

Hultkranz, Ake. *Conceptions of the Soul Among the North American Indians.* Ethnographic Museum of Sweden, Monograph Series 1. Stockholm: Caslon Press, 1953.

Jacob, Annie. *Le Travail, reflet des cultures : du Sauvage indolent au travailleur productif.* Presses Universitaires de France, 1994.

Jaenen, Cornelius J. *Friend and Foe: Aspects of French-Amerindian Culture*

Contact in the Sixteenth and Seventeenth Centuries. Toronto, McLelland and Stewart, 1976.

Jennings, Francis. *The Ambiguous Iroquois Empire.* New York, W. W. Norton: 1984.

Jennings, Francis. *The Creation of America. Through Revolution to Empire.* Cambridge University Press: 2000.

Jennings, Francis. *The Empire of Fortune.* New York, W. W. Norton: 1988.

Jennings, Francis. *The Invasion of America: Indians, Colonialism and the Cant of Conquest.* Chapel Hill: University of North Carolina Press, New York, W. W. Norton: 1976.

Jones, Arthur E. *"Wendake Ehen," or Old Huronia.* Toronto: 5th Report of the Bureau of Archives of the Province of Ontario, 1908.

Knopf, Kerstin (editor). *Aboriginal Canada Revisited.* Ottawa University Press, 2008.

McGregor, Stephen. *Since Time Immemorial: "Our Story": the Story of Kitigan Zibi Anishinabeg.* Maniwaki: Kitigan Zibi Education Council: Anishinabe Printing, 2004.

Merrell, James H. and Daniel K. Richter. Eds. *Beyond the Covenant Chain: The Iroquois and their Neighbors in Indian North America. 1600–1800.* University Park: Pennsylvania State University Press, 2003.

Nabigon, Herb. *The Hollow Tree. Fighting Addiction with Traditional Native Healing.* McGill-Queen's University Press, 2006.

National Museum of Canada. *The Algonkians.* Ottawa: National Museum of Canada, 1938.

Neil, Roger (editor). *Voice of the Drum.* Kingfisher Publications, Brandon, Manitoba, 2000.

Newhouse, David R., Cora J. Voyageur, and Dan Beavon (editors). *Hidden in Plain Sight: Contributions of Aboriginal Peoples to Canadian Identity and Culture.* Toronto: University of Toronto Press, 2005.

Ouellet, Réal. *Sur Lahontan.* Québec : L'Hêtrière, 1983.

Paul, Daniel N. *We were not the Savages. A Micmac Perspective on the Collision of European and Aboriginal Civilisation.* Halifax: Nimbus, 1993.

Pritchard, Evan T. *No Word for Time. The Way of the Algonquin People.* San Francisco / Tulsa: Council Oak Books, 1997.

Ralston, Saul. *A Fair Country: Telling Truths about Canada*. Penguin, 2008.

Ramsden, Peter G. "An Hypothesis Concerning the Effects of Early European Trade among Some Ontario Iroquois." *Canadian Journal of Archeology*, no.2, 1978.

Sioui, Miguel Paul Sastaretsi. "The Amerindianization of Western Thought". (Personal papers, 12 pages. 2008).

Sioui, Georges E. *For an Amerindian Autohistory: an Essay on the Foundations of a Social Ethic*. Montreal: McGill-Queen's University Press, 1992. (Publication originale en français : Pour une autohistoire amerindienne : essai sur les fondements d'une morale sociale.)

Sioui, Georges E. *Huron-Wendat: the Heritage of the Circle*. Vancouver: UBC Press and Michigan State University Press, 1999. (Publication originale en français : Les Wendats : une civilisation meconnue.)

Sioui, Georges E. *La vie, la poésie et la pensée d' Éléonore Sioui Tecumseh*. En préparation aux Presses de l'Université d'Ottawa.

Smith, Linda T. *Decolonizing Methodologies. Research and Indigenous Peoples*. Dunedin: University of Otago Press, 2003.

Snow, Dean R. *The Iroquois*. Oxford: Blackwell, 1994.

Sowter, T.W.E. "Algonquin and Huron Occupation of the Ottawa Valley". *The Ottawa Naturalist* 23(4): 118–126.

Stonechild, Blair. *The New Buffalo. The Struggle for Aboriginal Post-Secondary Education in Canada*. University of Manitoba Press, 2006.

Tanner, Helen Hornbeck (editor). *Atlas of Great Lakes Indian History*. Norman: Oklahoma University Press, 1987.

Thomas, Jacob Chief. *Teachings of the Longhouse*. Toronto: Stoddart, 1994.

Tooker, Elizabeth. *An Ethnography of the Huron Indians, 1615–1649*. United States of America: Syracuse University Press, 1991

Trigger, Bruce G. *Natives and Newcomers: Canada's Heroic Age Reconsidered*. Montreal and Kingston: McGill-Queen's University Press, 1985.

Trigger, Bruce G. *Sociocultural Evolution: Calculation and Contingency*. Oxford: Basil Blackwell Publishers, 1998.

Trigger, Bruce G. *The Children of Aataentsic: A History of the Huron People to 1660*. Montreal and London: McGill-Queen's University Press, 1987

Trigger, Bruce G. *The Huron: Farmers of the North*. 2nd Ed. New York: Holt, Rinehart and Winston 1990. Reference: 1990a

Tully, J. 2002 «Political Philosophy as a Critical Activity» in *Political Theory* 30(4).

Turgeon, Laurier. "Basque-Amerindian Trade in the Saint Lawrence during the Sixteenth Century: New Documents, New Perspectives." *Man in the Northeast*, no. 40 (1990b):81–7

Turner, Dale. *This is not a Peace Pipe. Towards a Critical Indigenous Philosophy*. Toronto: University of Toronto Press, 2006

Valaskakis, Gail. *Indian Country. Essays on Contemporary Native Culture*. Waterloo: Wilfrid Laurier University Press, 2005

Vizenor, Gerald. *Manifest Manners. Narratives on Postindian Survivance*. Lincoln and London: Nebraska University Press, 1994

Warrick, Gary A. *A Population History of the Huron-Petun, A.D. 900–1650*. Cambridge, 2008.

Watherford, Jack. *Indian Givers: How the Indians Transformed the World*. New York: Crown Publishers, 1988.

Williamson, Ronald F. and Michael S. Bisson. *The Archaeology of Bruce Trigger*. McGill-Queen's University Press, 2006.

Wright, James V. *The Ontario Iroquois Tradition*. Anthropological series 75, National Museums of Canada, Bulletin 210, Ottawa, 1966.

Composed by Sandra Friesen in Adobe Caslon Pro, a typeface originally designed by William Caslon in the early 18th Century. Adobe's revival was designed by Carol Twombly using specimen pages printed by Caslon between 1734 and 1770.